BANKING IN THE AMERICAN SOUTH
from the Age of Jackson to Reconstruction

Banking in the American South
from the Age of Jackson to Reconstruction

LARRY SCHWEIKART

LOUISIANA STATE UNIVERSITY PRESS

BATON ROUGE AND LONDON

To the four most important men in my life:

Earl Albert Schweikart, 1906–1961
Virgil W. Chandler, my stepfather since 1966
Robert J. Loewenberg, a virtuous and trusted friend
W. Elliot Brownlee, my mentor and adviser

Copyright © 1987 by Louisiana State University Press
All rights reserved
Manufactured in the United States of America

Designer: Diane B. Didier
Typeface: Linotron Caledonia
Typesetter: G & S Typesetters, Inc.
Printer: Thomson-Shore, Inc.
Binder: John H. Dekker & Sons

10 9 8 7 6 5 4 3 2 1

LIBRARY OF CONGRESS CATALOGING-IN-PUBLICATION DATA
Schweikart, Larry.
    Banking in the American South from the age of
Jackson to Reconstruction.

    Bibliography: p.
    Includes index.
    1. Banks and banking—Southern States—History.
2. Monetary policy—Southern States—History.
3. Southern States—History—1775–1865. 4. United States
—History—Civil War, 1861–1865—Finance. I. Title.
HG2604.S39 1987   332.1'0975   87-12784
ISBN 0-8071-1403-0

CONTENTS

TABLES

ACKNOWLEDGMENTS

In writing the present book I incurred several debts. I especially thank Curtis Mosso, computer support adviser at the University of California, Santa Barbara, and Ed Greenberg, computer support adviser at Arizona State University, who devoted considerable time and effort to locating and constructing programs that would process the data on banking indicators and other statistics.

Four major grants supported my research. The F. Leroy Hill Fellowship from the Institute for Humane Studies, Menlo Park, California, and a travel grant from the University of California, Santa Barbara, made possible travel and research in the South in 1983. An Arthur H. Cole grant from the Economic History Association supported research in 1984, and computer expenses and other associated costs of preparing the manuscript for publication were significantly reduced by a grant from the Earhart Foundation in cooperation and conjunction with the Institute for Humane Studies. I am deeply grateful for this aid, without which completion of the manuscript would have been delayed. I also thank the University of California, Santa Barbara, for the Regents Fellowship that provided me with research time. The University of Wisconsin Center at Richland gave me time from my teaching duties there so that I could present papers at several historical conventions and at Northwestern University during 1984–1985. My thanks to the steering committee at the Center. The University of Dayton and the University of Dayton Research Institute extended considerable support.

As important as the financial support given me were the scholarly comments and criticism offered by several colleagues. Richard Sylla increased and expanded my understanding of money in the antebellum period and made several helpful suggestions about North Carolina in particular. Hugh Rockoff directed and focused my prose, especially as it related to free banking. Morton Rothstein was consistently supportive and encouraging and provided a host of well-considered comments on political-cultural interactions in the South. James Roger Sharp gave me greater insight into the Jacksonians and their views on banking. These individuals, and John McFaul, George Green, Eugene White, Mansel Blackford, Roger Lotchin, Walter Grinder, Lance Davis, and John Kunkel, read and offered suggestions on the book in its entirety, sacrificing time and energy that they might otherwise have devoted to their own projects. Peter Temin provided comments on part of the book, as did Robert Loewenberg. These professionals saved me from innumerable errors of fact and interpretation, but the final decision to heed or ignore their advice was of course my own. I bear sole responsibility for any errors of fact or interpretation yet remaining.

I am particularly grateful to J. Mills Thornton III, who generously allowed me to use his home during my 1984 research trip. Even more important, however, was Thornton's donation of his research time to check my data on Alabama banks. For this contribution, and for his most helpful conversations with me on southern banking and politics, I am deeply in his debt.

My thinking on the problems discussed on these pages benefited considerably from the all-University of California conference on economic history held in the spring of 1983. Roger Ransom, Richard Sutch, and other colleagues offered valuable suggestions, as did participants on a panel at the 1984 Southern Historical Association meeting, a panel at the Economic History Association meeting, and participants in a Northwestern University seminar in economic history in 1985. My thanks go to Thomas West, Jeffry Wallin, Harold Woodman, Charles Calomiris, and Joel Mokyr, as well as to Morton Rothstein, for thoughts and comments voiced at these meetings.

Certainly no research work is possible without the generous assistance of an army of librarians, research assistants, curators, and archivists. I can mention only a few of them here, but all are worthy of praise. I am particularly indebted to Lee Shepard and Howson Cole of the Virginia Historical Society for giving me access to the unprocessed Thomas Branch collection. The entire staff at the Southern Historical Collection at the University of North Carolina facilitated my research and tried to furnish me with all of the copies and obscure material I requested. Although it would be impossible to name all individuals, a word of appreciation must be said for the library staffs of the following institutions: the Arkansas History Commission, Duke University, the University of Georgia, the University of Florida, the Tennessee Library and Archives (thanks to Marylin Bell Hughes in particular), David Ferro at the Division of Archives of the State of Florida in Tallahassee, the Virginia State Library in Richmond, the South Caroliniana Library at the University of South Carolina, the Mississippi Department of Archives and History, Tulane University, Samford University, the Alabama State Archives, and the University of California (Santa Barbara) Library. The interlibrary loan service of Arizona State University ordered and processed more than three hundred microfilm items; special thanks to Jewel Hayden.

I am grateful to Mark Buse for his work with the monetary statistics and computers. I also thank Michael Konz, Rajan Nair, James O'Neill, John Walters, Kenn Rapp, and Roger Riviere for their research assistance. Steven Paroni accompanied me on several research trips and provided important help. Michael Konig always offered support and encouragement. Jack Steinhoff labored heroically as my typist and editor. Thanks also to Margaret Fisher Dalrymple and Elizabeth L. Carpelan at LSU Press and to my copy editor, Marcia Brubeck. Brophy College Preparatory in Phoenix allowed me to schedule my duties in such a way as to leave time for research and writing. Shari Schweikart was supportive and understanding during the writing process. I will always owe my parents more than gratitude.

At the University of California, Santa Barbara, Carl Harris worked into the wee hours of the night training me to run the computer programs. Stephen DeCanio made himself available at a moment's notice many times to answer questions and to offer assistance. I owe my greatest single debt, however, to W. Elliot Brownlee.

Finally, to Jesus Christ I owe everything of lasting value. In this age when many strive to separate themselves from faith, I pray that I might be more fulfilled in it.

ABBREVIATIONS AND SHORT FORMS

Acts, Ga.	*Acts of the General Assembly of the State of Georgia*
Acts, La.	*Louisiana Laws, Statutes, etc. Acts Passed by the Legislature of the State of Louisiana*
Acts, Va.	*Acts of the Assembly of the Commonwealth of Virginia*
ADAH	Alabama Department of Archives and History
AHC	Arkansas History Commission
BMC	Bank of the Mississippi Collection
CBC	Canal Bank Collection
Directors' Minutebook	Minutebooks of the Board of Directors of the Georgia Railroad and Banking Company, central office, Augusta, Georgia
DU	Duke University
Governors' Letterbook	Letterbooks of the Governors of Georgia, University of Georgia
Laws, Ga.	*Laws of Georgia*
Laws, N.C.	*Laws of North Carolina*
LC	Library of Congress
Louisiana Documents	*Documents &c, Relative to the Investigation on Banks by the Joint Committee of the Senate and House of Representatives of the State of Louisiana,* 14th Legis., 2d Sess., 1840
LSU	Louisiana State University
MDAH	Mississippi Department of Archives and History
SBA	State Bank of Alabama
SCL	South Caroliniana Library
SHC	Southern Historical Collection

Statutes at Large, S.C.	*Statutes at Large of South Carolina*, XI (reprint 1873)
Stockholders' Minutebook	Minutes of the Stockholders of the Georgia Railroad and Banking Company
TLA	Tennessee Library and Archives
UG	University of Georgia
UNC	University of North Carolina
VHS	Virginia Historical Society

BANKING IN THE AMERICAN SOUTH
from the Age of Jackson to Reconstruction

INTRODUCTION

Efforts to reconcile Jacksonian democracy with the aristocratic character of the slave South—apparently contradictory themes—abound in
the writings of American history. Democrats, supposedly representing
the "common man," eventually championed slavery via states' rights,
whereas many Whigs moved into unionist circles, thus indirectly supporting abolition. The contradiction became even more glaring when
historians extended their studies beyond slavery to the entire spectrum
of issues dividing the antebellum parties. Nationalist-minded Whigs advocated federal support of a variety of projects designed to promote economic growth and the improvement of the condition of the "common
man." Democrats, powered by a strong distrust of corporate power and
"moneyed interests," seemingly favored less government involvement
and, perhaps concomitantly, a less dynamic economy, with less chance
for the common man to advance economically and socially.[1]

Banking and money policy in antebellum America have frequently

---

1. See Glyndon Van Deusen, *The Jacksonian Era, 1828–1848* (New York, 1959),
264–65; Edwin Miles, *Jacksonian Democracy in Mississippi* (Chapel Hill, 1960), 168–71;
John McFaul, *The Politics of Jacksonian Finance* (Ithaca, N.Y., 1972), xiii; and James Sharp,
The Jacksonians versus the Banks: Politics in the States After the Panic of 1837 (New York,
1970), x, 3–24. That most Democrats *thought* they opposed a growing centralized government although they did not actually do so remains an inconsistency in political theory that
has been almost universally overlooked by historians. I discuss this point at length in my
Ph.D. dissertation, "Banking in the American South, 1836–65" (University of California,
Santa Barbara, 1983).

been viewed as a key with which to unlock such political mysteries of the period, a process that would in turn lead to a better understanding of Jacksonian politics and the secession movement. Several historians have therefore addressed the theme in a national context and have produced some of the most highly praised works on Jacksonianism, economics, and antebellum banking of the last forty years. Still, the South has provided the most prominent subject for inspection; the existence of slavery seems to have contradicted the Jacksonian concept of freedom openly. J. Mills Thornton and Edmund Morgan have argued that southerners' underlying assumptions about the nature of freedom made slavery necessary in order to allow all whites to live equally as free men. Southern attitudes toward banks often reflected this ethic as it applied in another economic arena: *freedom* also meant being free from government interference in one's daily life or from control by a large, impersonal corporation, such as a bank or a railroad company. The result, however, was yet another contradiction in that, aside from the rhetoric, the policies of the two major political parties seemed to move inevitably toward greater centralization of government power—for the Whigs a growing federal government. The Jacksonians centralized power at the state level, but Jacksonian national leaders gradually found themselves pursuing policies that reduced the power of the states and, more clearly, that of individuals over their own lives. Southerners' efforts to reconcile these paradoxes eventually provided the themes for several historical works. The unresolved paradoxes reflect the need, identified by Harry Scheiber, for "a new typology of the antebellum Southern states as to their socioeconomic structure and the way in which diverse interests related to the policy process."[2]

The present book attempts to supply such a "new typology." It is my aim to show that the banking structure of the antebellum South reflected the political paradoxes involved in trying to meet egalitarian ends within the context of freedom as much as did the slavery issue. Although these paradoxes can be explained, we may well ask whether southerners resolved them and, indeed, whether they can be resolved at all.

Banking regulatory policy provided one setting wherein southerners

2. Harry Scheiber, "Government and the Economy: Studies of the 'Commonwealth' Policy in Nineteenth-Century America," *Journal of Interdisciplinary History*, Summer, 1972, p. 150.

of different ideologies and political views labored to resolve the contradictions they faced. Political attitudes toward banking regulation at the state level fell into two very broad and general categories—one that favored competition and one that ascribed the central role of economic activity to the state or federal government. These attitudes varied, not according to strict political affiliation or even to geographic sectional divisions, but according to historical experience with, and development of, commercial centers. Insofar as the parties formulated policies on the national level, they both leaned toward centralization, a tendency again well illustrated by banking.

Banking has provided a testing ground for aspects of southern antinomies unrelated to regulatory policy and especially for explanations of southern economic behavior that rely on class analysis. When we deal with bankers' entry into banking and with their mobility within the profession, it is difficult to conclude that any narrowly defined banking "class" existed. Bankers were influenced by a variety of factors that affected each individual differently, including market forces, ethnicity, kinship ties, political ideology, and local social status. Thus bankers grappled with paradoxes on many different levels within a broader framework of commercial and capitalistic attitudes that nevertheless separated them from the planter groups in southern society. Interpretations of southern bankers' social status usually reflect certain assumptions about their investment tendencies, which without question mirrored their response to the confusions of the age. Despite some generally unsupported assertions to the contrary, the South did not suffer from a lack of capital growth. Bankers' investments thus responded to a market that competed for their credit.[3]

I decided to study these problems primarily during the years 1836 to 1865, albeit with several important qualifications. First, because much of the current literature relies on the banking statistics compiled by J. Van Fenstermaker, I wanted to avoid merely reproducing his pathbreaking work or those studies that relied on it, although many of the authors in question, including Van Fenstermaker, may have had different objectives than I. Because his statistics, which ended with the year

---

3. The "lack of capital" thesis is presented in works published as recently as 1985. See William Pease and Jane Pease, *The Web of Progress: Private Values and Public Styles in Boston and Charleston, 1828–1843* (New York, 1985), 46–48, 177–81.

1837, necessarily overlapped with mine, I tried to develop a broad por-
trait by combining the data into a single series dating from 1819 to the
Civil War. Second, although the choice of a starting date was somewhat
flexible, I tried to provide historical background for individual states
whose banking development preceded 1836. My intention was to en-
compass as much as possible any specific ramifications in the southern
states of Jackson's war on the Bank of the United States and yet to avoid
another detailed study of the Bank War per se. The collapse of most
chartered banks in the South by 1865 effectively separated the antebellum period of southern banking from the postbellum period.

Critics of southern banking in general have blamed the financial structures in the South for encouraging and perpetuating the slave-based
plantation system; one historian has viewed banking as primarily responsible for the continuation of southern slavery. Economic historians,
who took as themes either growth and development, on the one hand, or
soundness of banking, on the other, have implied that the failure of the
banking system caused an absence of capital and thereby contributed to
the South's failure to industrialize.

Traditional historians and economists who have elaborated economic
theories by which to test the charge have generally relied on the "soundness" interpretations of Bray Hammond and Fritz Redlich (wherein a
banking system was judged according to its ability to pay its liabilities) or
on the growth interpretations of Richard Sylla, Milton Friedman, and a
host of "new" economic historians, which evaluated banking's contribution to regional or national growth. George Green, in his study of Louisiana banking, perceptively described a good system as a mixture of
both and as sensitive to a myriad of other factors, not the least of which
is politics.[4]

I address these arguments on a state-by-state basis and on the regional

---

4. Susan Feiner, "The Financial Structures and Banking Institutions of the Ante-
bellum South, 1811–1832" (Ph.D. dissertation, University of Massachusetts, 1981); Fred
Bateman and Thomas Weiss, "Manufacturing in the Antebellum South," in Paul Uselding
(ed.), *Research in Economic History* (Greenwich, Mass., 1976), I, 1–45; George Green,
Finance and Economic Development in the Old South: Louisiana Banking, 1804–1861
(Stanford, Calif., 1972); and Jeffrey Hummel, "The Jacksonians, Banking, and Economic
Theory: A Reinterpretation," *Journal of Libertarian Studies*, Summer, 1978, pp. 151–65.
Hummel's essay, despite its deep theoretical flaws, is probably the best essay on banking
historiography of the Jacksonian period yet to see print.

level, in the process identifying as a central element in the discussion of banking's contribution to state economic growth the degree to which states regulated their banks and, more important, what states expected from them. For economic, cultural, ideological, and political reasons, southern states followed one of two broad patterns of development, one based for the most part on free-market concepts and the other based on concepts of state planning and control. Again, these were related more to business heritage than to political labels. The former approach tended to advance both soundness and growth the most.

Any explanation of how these views developed goes to the very heart of the problems facing the Jacksonians, the South, and, eventually, the nation. Economically, the states having commercial and business centers, where the operations of the market were clearly visible every day, developed regulations designed to restrict the market as little as possible. Businessmen influenced banking legislation, which discouraged inflation, and state ownership and/or control of banks was limited. State competition through a state-owned bank received little support, and state banks were clearly restricted in their ability to alter or disrupt the market. States in which these general statements applied I shall call "Old South" states; and I use the term to describe attitudes and patterns of entrepreneurial development rather than a period in the South's history. States with Old South attitudes include the Carolinas, Virginia, Georgia, and to some extent Louisiana. In the Old South, such views of business practices were solidly in place when the "Age of the Common Man" arrived and thus served as a brake on economic egalitarianism.

States more inclined toward tight state control or state initiative were those lacking vigorous commercial histories. Because they were also areas more recently developed, certain immigrant groups, families, or cliques dominated their finances early. Arkansas, with its Seviers, exemplified the trend. Reaction to one group's control ("special privilege" as seen by the Jacksonians) often led to strict laws, to state monopoly, or to a state-dominated system, although state control did not necessarily mean monopoly in banking. In Mississippi and Florida, state governments used the credit of the state to back private banks with bonds. The dominant power or initiating force was therefore that of government rather than that of the market. The five-state group (Alabama, Arkansas, Florida, Mississippi, and Tennessee) that viewed the government's role in the economy in this way can be labeled the "New South." The term designates an attitudinal approach and not the postbellum period.

States that leaned toward market control developed stronger banking systems, which made a *relatively* larger contribution to state economic development than did those adopting the opposite approach. The presence of strong banking systems, then, tended to moderate the attacks on banks that were later seen in the states in which the financial systems had collapsed. Where the state was viewed as the primary mechanism of economic activity, economic disruptions almost universally ensued. The common man of Jacksonian rhetoric paid the price for distrust of banks and fear of corporations.

Although the Jacksonians frequently succeeded first in spreading their antibank apprehensions among the public at large and then in exaggerating them, the Democrats' banking theories actually differed little from those of their opponents. Clearly Whigs favored a government lead in the arena of business and economics. Many times Jacksonians arrived in office on a wave of electoral enthusiasm to repair damage done by Whig policies (such as the state-backed bank bond scheme in Louisiana) only to be thrown out themselves in the next election because they offered nothing different. The political economy of both parties, deliberately on occasion but more often unintentionally, drifted toward greater concentration of power in the hands of the state, and ultimately the federal, government. This tendency later became apparent to many former southern Whigs, who found that their concepts of legislative power at the federal level were gradually giving way to a view that accepted and even favored a more powerful chief executive. States'-rights rhetoric notwithstanding, the Jacksonian Democrats so concentrated power in the executive branch that in 1860 Abraham Lincoln's election virtually guaranteed secession. A close look at banking policies can therefore shed considerable light on the tendencies of both parties toward a powerful centralized government. Alexis de Tocqueville, the perceptive French visitor, concluded that statism was the promise of American life and noted that the government "picks out every individual singly from the mass." He further predicted that the "concentration of power and the subjection of individuals will increase." Tocqueville's fears about centralization before the war became a reality after it. The Jacksonians had led the attack on banks of issue, but the central government of the Republicans finally closed them permanently.[5]

Banking in the antebellum South provides a crucible for the testing of various social and class interpretations that place bankers at the center of the slavery controversy. Eugene Genovese, for example, has argued that "southern banking . . . tied the bankers to the plantations," creating a relationship in which "the bankers could not emerge as a middle-class counterweight to the planters but could merely serve as their auxiliaries." Another student of southern banking has maintained that southern bankers represented a "subsumed class of money-merchants . . . who provided finance and credit [and] often had interests which were different from the interests of the masters." Both interpretations view bankers as a class and necessarily reach a conclusion about economic development—that class struggle among different levels of banker-planters led to ever higher levels of investment in agriculture, stifling economic growth—that does not square with evidence presented here or elsewhere. Because I deal with development issues separately, I will examine these class arguments in light of evidence available regarding a variety of bankers—public, private, commercial, and state and their intermediaries. Regardless of the criteria used (entry into the business, wealth, mobility within the profession, mobility within a particular job, or even class consciousness on the part of participants), I suggest that no banking class per se may be said to have existed in the South. Southern bankers did foster attitudes about commerce and the integrated capitalistic economy as a whole that the planters did not share. Yet evidence of planter domination is also absent. Indeed, the planters were usually those who complained about the lack of agricultural capital. That bankers may have been indistinguishable as a separate class does not mean

5. Alexis de Tocqueville, *Democracy in America* (New York, 1945), I, 3, II, 109, 204, 317. Harry Jaffa concluded that Lincoln resolved the conflict created by the Declaration of Independence, which included both Lincoln's concept of equality before the law and Stephen Douglas's principle of consent of the governed. See his *Liberty and Equality* (New York, 1965), 18, and *Crisis of the House Divided: An Interpretation of the Issues in the Lincoln-Douglas Debates* (New York, 1959). But even Lincoln's Aristotelian leanings could not rescue the principle of egalitarianism from Thomas Hobbes, John Locke, and Jean-Jacques Rousseau, with their "state-of-nature" philosophy (Larry Schweikart, "The Mormon Connection: Lincoln, the Saints, and the Crisis of Equality," *Western Humanities Review*, Winter, 1980, pp. 1–22).

that they were weak links in the economy, however, and on occasion banks were capable of cooperative efforts.[6]

Limitations of space forced me to omit border southern states that did not join the Confederacy. I hoped that, by defining the South as the Confederacy, I could establish the presence (or absence) of direct links between prewar politics and wartime effects. A student of Mississippi's wartime finances, for example, has traced the state's inability to obtain foreign credit during the Civil War to its failure to pay off bank-related bonds issued by the state prior to the Panic of 1837.[7]

I limited this book to the Confederate states with two exceptions. I omitted Texas because of its late entry into the Union. Its economy did not develop to the point where it could significantly affect the data or interpretations presented here. I also omitted West Virginia and for the same reasons. Neither omission, nor even the decision not to include Kentucky or Missouri, should affect the evidence presented here. Any effect that such states might have had upon interpretation of the data, I believe, although from admittedly fragmented results, could almost without exception reinforce my conclusions. The inclusion of these states, moreover, would not greatly change the more important non-empirical issues that I raise here.[8]

Banking in the American South provided a testing ground for parties and their ideology, opportunities for immigrants and ethnic groups to advance economically, and a chance for individuals to match their investment and entrepreneurial skills against the forces of the marketplace. Banking generated capital for a growing region, and the banking system had just begun to bloom when it was shaken by war. As much as the physical destruction of banks set back southerners, and as much as the inflationary binges destroyed southern finances, the Republicans' National Bank Act effectively buried southern banking. The tax placed on bank notes proved a substantial disadvantage that more than offset

6. Eugene Genovese, *The Political Economy of Slavery* (New York, 1961), 22; Feiner, "Financial Structures," 144.

7. William Coker, "Cotton and Faith: A Social and Political View of Mississippi Wartime Finance, 1861–1865" (Ph.D. dissertation, University of Oklahoma, 1973).

8. For material on Texas, see Joseph Grant and Lawrence Crum, *The Development of State-Chartered Banking in Texas* (Austin, 1978), who suggest that, prior to the Civil War, only one chartered bank existed, although several private bankers did business (pp. 17–20).

the creation of a few national banks in the South. Whigs, who moved into Bourbon, or Conservative, circles after the war, never voiced dissatisfaction with the Republican banking legislation in theory but only attacked its practical operations, which left the South with a disproportionately low circulation. Indeed, the success of a Republican administration in making the Jacksonians' dream a reality suggests that the goals of the two parties were not far apart.[9]

9. Robert Loewenberg, *Equality on the Oregon Frontier: Jason Lee and the Methodist Mission, 1834–1843* (Seattle, 1976), 3, 40, 42–43. The present study has proceeded from a nondeterministic, nonhistoricist approach, which also rejects the separation between the "value-free" and "value-laden" schools of historiography. The most concise exposition of the two appears in Robert Loewenberg, "'Value-Free' Versus 'Value-Laden' History: A Distinction Without a Difference," *Historian*, May, 1976, pp. 439–54. All historicism and most modern political philosophy, especially that which plagued the Jacksonians and the Whigs, stems from the widespread and continuing acceptance of the state-of-nature theories, the evolution of which is described in Leo Strauss, *Natural Right and History* (Chicago, 1953), and Eric Voegelin, *The New Science of Politics* (Chicago, 1952).

1

THE POLITICAL ECONOMY OF BANKING IN THE JACKSONIAN SOUTH

In the histories of Jacksonian political battles, the discussions of banks have prompted most observers to pit Bray Hammond's entrepreneurial thesis against the "liberal-reformer" interpretation offered by Arthur Schlesinger, Jr. Hammond, in a brilliant seminal work, described the Jacksonians' war on the Bank of the United States (BUS) as a struggle in which small, aspiring businessmen sought to free themselves from a restrictive banking system. He interpreted the conflict as "a sophisticated one of enterpriser against capitalist . . . and of Wall Street against Chestnut [Street]." Schlesinger's no less ambitious work, which predated Hammond's, depicted popular democratic efforts to rein in a dominant business class. Echoing William Graham Sumner's assertion that the Bank War marked a "premonition of the conflict between democracy and plutocracy," Schlesinger called it "the irrepressible conflict of capitalism" in which business interests maneuvered to dominate the mechanisms of government while the common man, using only his franchise, fought to keep government under popular control. Until quite recently, historians have, with slight deviations, tended to categorize banking politics of the period in one of the ways that I have mentioned even if they basically disagreed with the economic interpretations offered by Hammond or Schlesinger.[1]

1. Bray Hammond, *Banks and Politics in America from the Revolution to the Civil War* (Princeton, 1957), 328–29; Arthur Schlesinger, Jr., *The Age of Jackson* (Boston, 1945), 514; William Graham Sumner, *Andrew Jackson*, rev. ed. (Boston, 1899), 265; Charles Sell-

Jacksonian policy toward banks was never monolithic. It was often a hasty, slapdash concoction, stirred by several political cooks reading different recipes, but it had a character that both the entrepreneurial approach and Schlesinger's interpretation failed to recognize. The central fact of the period was that Jacksonian banking policy "moved unswervingly from a vague belief in the desirability of hard money to the advocacy of regulatory powers over banking by public monitors." More significant, the Jacksonians as a party organization did not have to plan such increased regulation by government (even though they did so at times), nor did they have to enact such a policy approach with unanimity before it could be of consequence. Rather, the Democrats' view of politics reflected certain fundamental assumptions about human nature that entailed a hostility toward banks and other corporations and, of far deeper consequence, inexorably impelled power to be gradually centralized in the federal government, especially in the chief executive.[2]

Any evaluation of the Jacksonians' banking policies must take into account the goals of Jacksonian democracy and their implications. A central linchpin of Democratic programs, "the view of equality that made men 'interchangeable' for all practical political purposes," meant that intermediate institutions of any sort impeded interchangeability. The Jacksonians first turned their attention to large, easily identifiable institutions, especially King Caucus and corporate power. The Jacksonian viewpoint defined itself in terms of a thoroughgoing egalitarianism. If adherents disagreed on other matters, they could unite within the theoretical parameters of this goal. Equality and interchangeability required that the common man be freed from control by special interests, the worst of which were symbolized by the Bank of the United States.[3]

Banking and economic issues offered the opportunity to embody in real policy terms the ideal of equality, but the complexity of these issues also meant that they topped the list of questions on which the Democratic party was divided. The Democrats inherited a mixed and ofttimes contradictory heritage from the Jeffersonians, one tradition stemming

ers, Jr., "Andrew Jackson versus the Historians," *Mississippi Valley Historical Review*, March, 1958, pp. 615–34; Edward Pessen, *Jacksonian America: Society, Personality, and Politics* (Homewood, Ill., 1969), 352–93.

2. McFaul, *Politics of Jacksonian Finance*, 1.

3. Carl Russell Fish, *The Rise of the Common Man* (New York, 1969 [1927]); Lynn Marshall, "The Strange Stillbirth of the Whig Party," *American Historical Review*, 1967, pp. 445–68; Loewenberg, *Equality on the Oregon Frontier*, 46 (n. 18), 231.

from James Madison, whose views on banking approached those of the Federalists, and another from John Taylor of Caroline, who abhorred the idea of a centralized national bank. Economic growth in the 1830s, and the new economic outlook that accompanied it, placed more strain on the remaining fragile sources of agreement. Because much of the growth that engulfed the country could rightly be credited to banks, the party spoke softly even in registering its criticism of financial institutions. Still, any division or disunity within the Jacksonians' ranks threatened to erode the concepts upon which the party rested—states' rights, rotation in office, and so on. This was a party designed to soothe any chafing differences, such as those over slavery and banking, with the cool salve of patronage. Could not the rewards of federal and state appointments induce Jacksonians to cease opposing banks if the party so desired? After all, a fundamental factor motivating the founding of the party was the desire to prevent the slavery question from shattering the country, and the unifying mechanism was the promise of party and government jobs. The party that had apparently succeeded in muffling the slavery debate as of 1832 could surely bring into harmony the dissident views on banking.[4]

Antibank groups prepared for accommodation purely from a resigned acknowledgment that the economy was doing well. Prior to the Panic of 1837, few political moderates in the party chose to risk their seats over banking issues. After 1837, the political climate changed, and opposition to banks became a litmus test for loyal Democrats as "hard-money" men suddenly and surprisingly began to dominate the party in a number of states. Diverse views within the party did not prevent so-called hards from controlling important policy votes.

Anyone looking for consistency in Jacksonian thought would be disappointed, but the Democratic tendencies frayed the party's ideological fabric throughout the nineteenth century nowhere more than over questions involving the composition of the nation's currency. As a result there was even greater disarray in the preferred banking system, with each rival group invoking its own heritage of political thought. "Hards" cited the teaching of William Gouge and, earlier, John Taylor, who had viewed paper notes as evidence of poor or even corrupt business practices. Taylor went so far as to attack banks for oppressing society. No one

4. Sharp, *Jacksonians vs. the Banks*, 4.

really indicated explicitly whether paper money or the banks themselves were the agents of oppression. Generally, in the period before
the Panic of 1837, groups differed most regarding the usefulness of a
central bank. Several Jacksonians opposed a national bank less than has
generally been assumed, especially if the national bank in question was
their own. This fact became clearer only after the Civil War, when several members of the hard-money faction of the Democratic party supported greenbacks. Francis P. Blair, Jr., a Jacksonian stalwart, in 1869
blamed a "stupendous national debt" for the passing of the "golden age"
of Jacksonianism's hard money. Blair identified the various nationally
chartered banks, holders of the debt, as the main burden saddling the
people. "Why may not the Government bank on its own credit?" he
asked. In a suggestion that revealed the similarities between the old
Jacksonians and the postwar Republicans, Blair supported the abolition
of private banks and instead sought to establish a single government
agency that would issue greenbacks. Eventually Jacksonian tendencies
also surfaced in the antibank sentiment of the Populists, who urged a
substitution of greenbacks for national bank notes and similarly demanded an abolition of banks. Populists and Greenbackers hardly represented aberrant elements of Jacksonianism but rather were its essence;
their unwavering goal was control of the money supply, regardless of its
composition, and they were aided in their quest by the central-bank
Republicans.[5]

    5. *Ibid.*, 6–7; McFaul, *Politics of Jacksonian Finance*, xi. Robert Sharkey, questioning
the same apparent contradiction between the Jacksonians' deflationary position and the
Populists' inflationary tendencies, also saw an "important thread of continuity" between
George Pendleton, William Allen, Francis P. Blair, Jr., and other hard-money Jacksonians,
and the soft-money western Democrats. Both groups distrusted "banks, bankers, and particular bank notes," and since a deflation would have been necessary to resume a gold
standard, the western Democrats—and later the Populists—preferred greenbacks, "the
money of the people," in Sharkey's words. See *Money, Class and Party: An Economic
Study of Civil War and Reconstruction* (Baltimore, 1959), 104–107. Among the more
recent authorities on Jacksonianism to perceive the complexity of trying to establish any
consistent political theory on banking and money issues extending from the early "re-
formers"—the Jacksonians—to their successors, the Populists (and, according to this theory, the Progressives) is Edward Pessen. Pessen, a self-admitted liberal and admirer of
Schlesinger, had to explain why, if Jackson was a reformer, he made war on the entire banking system, especially the paper money system that "enabled the economy to undertake
projects which otherwise might not have been attempted" (*Jacksonian America*, 145).
Aside from trying to justify the Democrats' actions on the money question, Pessen had to
logically meld their hard-money position and the tendency of twentieth-century Keynesian
liberals to favor inflationary policies. Worse, Pessen admitted, "working men paid in paper

Neither the Populists after the war nor the Jacksonians before it really intended to eliminate all banks. As David Martin has shown, some type of new national banking system was the proposed final beam in a gold-based Jacksonian financial structure. The first plank, the Gold Bill, which passed in August, 1834, hiked Alexander Hamilton's 15:1 mint ratio to 16:1, a price more in line with world specie rates. By enacting this crucial legislation, the Jacksonians were able to keep gold from pouring out of the country. Next the nation needed more gold supplies, and so branch mints were established at New Orleans, Charlotte, and Dahlonega, Georgia. By placing all of these mints in the South, the Jacksonians showed that they had not lost their flair for patronage. On June 25, 1835, Congress enacted the third law in the structure by extending legal-tender status to foreign coins, further enhancing the gold and silver supply. Prohibition of small notes was the fourth step, and establishing a new central bank was the final action in the plan, although the Jacksonian definition of a bank varied greatly, and Martin maintained that it developed "during and after the struggle with the B.U.S.," meaning that it was not an early phase of Jacksonian thought only discarded at a later date.[6]

Destruction of the BUS forced Jackson to rely on the deposit banks, or the "pet banks," for control of the monetary system, a measure that Jackson viewed with horror as chaotic. Once in place, the deposit-bank framework caused Jackson to contemplate any further changes toward a public-owned national bank only reluctantly. Ultimately Jackson faced the choice of centralizing the pet system further or scrapping it and installing a different central bank.[7]

Generally, three major bank policy options were available to the federal government in this period (although each obviously entailed a spectrum of options within itself). One was to create and maintain a central

money whose value fluctuated wildly—seemingly always downward—understandably took a dim view of the stuff, some of them even responding to theorists like Gouge" (145). Yet he implied that the federal government's divorce from central banking had much to do with the economic stagnation of the post-Panic period (152–53).

6. Both Richard Timberlake and David Martin have noted the necessity of increasing Hamilton's 15:1 mint ratio to bring it in line with world specie prices at 16:1 was crucial to the Jacksonians' attempt to control the monetary system (David Martin, "Metallism, Small Notes, and Jackson's War with the B.U.S.," *Explorations in Economic History*, Spring, 1974, pp. 227–47 [quotation on p. 235]; Richard Timberlake, Jr., *The Origins of Central Banking in the United States* [Cambridge, Mass., 1978], 45).

7. McFaul, *Politics of Jacksonian Finance*, 41.

bank with the authority to control, or greatly to influence, the note-issuing activities of state-chartered banks, free banks, or private banks. Such an institution would have note-issuing powers of its own and could maintain control by constantly presenting other banks' notes for collection in its notes or specie. Another option was to establish a national bank that had no note-issue capability but merely served as an ancillary institution to the Treasury to act as the fiscal agent for the government, something along the lines of the independent treasury system proposed by Martin Van Buren. A third option was to allow complete laissez-faire banking, wherein bank currencies compete in the absence of a national currency. As for the composition of the currency under these systems, it is widely believed that Van Buren and others favored hard money because it was a self-regulating device that monitored banking. Indeed, one recent student of Jacksonian banking has argued that the "attack on the Bank [of the United States] was a fully rational and highly enlightened step toward the achievement of a laissez-faire metallic monetary system." The evidence of the Jacksonians' *political* intention suggests otherwise, as does their activity in supporting state banks rather than private banks.[8]

Nowhere were the centralizing tendencies of the Democratic program perceived more astutely than in the South, which was always vigilant with respect to states' rights. In the South, hard money never properly meshed with the overall Jackson program, but metallists found their niche in the Democratic party. Opposition to banks and corporations had often been interpreted as a battle against privilege, and so the banking question and states' rights gradually fused together, but Van Buren and others promoted hard money only for its usefulness in destroying state banks. Thus factions within the party clashed, leaving party ideology twisted in the wreckage. To understand specific political battles in the South in terms of this Jacksonian dilemma, we must examine the party's theoretical conflicts on the banking issue in more detail.

Andrew Jackson in 1829 suggested to Amos Kendall his own plan for a national bank to substitute for the BUS, which would "afford an [*sic*] uniform circulating medium" and would "transmit the money of the United States from one section of the union to another and to foreign parts." Basic Jacksonian policies on banking and money issues evolved

---

8. Hummel, "Jacksonians, Banking, and Economic Theory," 161.

from the banking theories of William Gouge, who viewed banking as a warehouse service wherein banks were expected to keep high levels of specie in their vaults at all times. Gouge saw fractional reserve banking as a type of fraud. Ultimately, the independent treasury idea would contain similar precepts about banking and would seek to enforce the specie convertibility of the nation's monetary system, with the Democrats ultimately hoping to achieve a metallic currency. Jackson's letter clearly shows that he intended to have the nation on a single gold *or paper* standard as long as it was uniform. The strong implication is that Jackson was not at all opposed to centralization when he considered it in the interest of his party. Because Democrats' views found little support in the mainline financial community with "de facto authority over the money supply," the Democrats moved to gain public control of the monetary system through their five-point plan. Jackson's previously uncited plan nevertheless remains a significant document because, when viewed in the context of Democratic legislation *and* the political theories of Isaac Bronson, Charles Duncombe, "Gallatin," and other Jacksonians, it explains the tendencies of southern states to rely on the state governments, rather than on the market, to control banking.[9]

Certainly neither Jacksonians in general nor the party as a whole clearly defined their positions on many issues (including banking), but Jackson and other party leaders often responded to most problems by expanding the role of the federal government. Most of Jackson's maneuvers with the banking system ultimately brought greater control by the central government, even if it was unintentional. Still, the shrewd Van Buren and perhaps even Jackson well knew that official control in a legalistic sense was often unnecessary if political appointments could achieve the same ends. When Jackson told his cabinet on March 19, 1833, that a new bank should be considered if, after a "full and fair experiment," the pet banks proved unsuccessful, he specifically underscored the government's right to appoint the president and directors and to maintain a "thorough knowledge" of the bank's transactions.[10]

9. Martin, "Metallism, Small Notes, and Jackson's War with the B.U.S.," 236, 243–44; "Plan for a National Bank," in Amos Kendall to Andrew Jackson, November 20, 1829, Box 1, File 6, TLA.

10. James Richardson (ed.), *A Compilation of the Messages and Papers of the Presidents* (Washington, D.C., 1907), II, 462, 529, annual addresses of December 8, 1829, and December 6, 1830; William Gouge, *A Short History of Paper Money and Banking in the United States* (Philadelphia, 1833), 233–34; Martin, "Metallism, Small Notes, and Jackson's

On these points, Jackson had received considerable secondhand prodding from noted banker Isaac Bronson of New York. Bronson, a hard-money financial genius who had twice brought legal suits to force banks into specie resumption, wielded considerable political influence with Churchill Cambreleng, chairman of the House Ways and Means Committee. Bronson's affinity for centralized banking dated as far back as 1814, when he had drawn up a plan for a national bank only to watch it crumble when Congress chartered the second Bank of the United States. In 1832, Cambreleng urged Bronson to write a pamphlet stating the case for a new national banking system. By February 1833 Bronson had responded with *Outline for a Plan for a National Bank with Incidental Remarks on the Bank of the United States,* of which he was co-author, although his backing of such a bank was directly tied to attempts to charter a bank of his own.[11]

Unlike many dreamers of the day and harmless political hacks, Bronson had a plan with which to implement his national bank scheme. In a detailed letter to Elisha Whittlesey, a Whig representative from Ohio, Bronson suggested commissioning his own bank as the fiscal agent of the government, which would "then like the custom house become a part of the fiscal machinery of the treasury." The beauty of the plan lay in the fact that it would "render unnecessary any specification of powers except such as will be contained in the articles of association; and thus *remove that bugbear—constitutional scruples* [emphasis added]." Bronson then made a startlingly canny request of Whittlesey: "Can you without *appearing yourself* cause this proposition to be stated *Hypothetically,* by some one of the right *caste;* to Mr. Woodbury, Mr. Taney, Mr. Kendall, Mr. Benton of the Senate; whichever you should suppose most likely to think favorably of the plan?" Although the letter was marked "not sent," Whittlesey apparently received a similar draft, for he soon replied that the timing was wrong for such a proposition. Jackson was happy with the

---

War with the B.U.S.," 236, 243–44; Frank Gatell, "Spoils of the Bank War: Political Bias in the Selection of Pet Banks," *American Historical Review,* October, 1964, p. 36; Memorandum from Andrew Jackson to Members of the Cabinet, March 19, 1833, cited in Robert Remini, *Andrew Jackson and the Bank War* (New York, 1967), 113. Also see *ibid.,* 125, 131–35, 155, 172.

11. Abraham Venit, "Isaac Bronson: His Banking Theory and the Financial Controversies of the Jacksonian Period," *Journal of Economic History* (1944), 201–14. See the letter from Bronson to G. Tomlinson, January 24, 1834, cited in *ibid.,* p. 208, n. 21.

pet bank system. Bronson in writing to a Whig, however, showed how closely related the two parties really were in their thought.[12]

Death ended Bronson's role in 1838, but other theorists filled the void, most notably Charles Duncombe. As late as 1841 this Jacksonian argued, in *Duncombe's Free Banking*, for "centraliz[ing] the government of the currency; thereby furnishing us with the advantages of a United States bank." Duncombe wished only to remove the "influence *of private interest, of credit, and of politics.*" He clearly opposed a hard-money standard and advocated instead limiting paper issues to "three times the amount of specie actually in [the bank's] vaults." Duncombe also proposed establishing "Banks of Discount" controlled by the states on a regional basis, a scheme that in intent remarkably resembled the Federal Reserve Board plan. Similar suggestions appeared in a pamphlet by a Virginia Jacksonian essayist who signed himself "Gallatin."[13]

Even as Bronson and Duncombe wrote, the Jacksonians had already embarked upon a different path toward a centralized system through the pet banks. Jackson himself had told James Hamilton in 1834 that the use of state banks would allow the administration to "introduce a metallic currency throughout the union." The Washington *Globe* bragged that public deposits would lead to "the gradual suppression of the issues of small bank notes." Cambreleng crowed that the pets would prove "instrumental in the great work which has been so successfully commenced, of reform in our currency." Moreover, the deposit banking system gave Jackson almost "complete executive control" over fiscal policies of the nation, and accordingly, it "represented an enormous extension of executive power." More important, as Tocqueville and others observed, the mechanisms built into the party system inexorably—if subtly—tended

---

12. Bronson to Elisha Whittlesey, February 26, 1836, cited in Venit, "Isaac Bronson," 210. Also see pp. 208–209, letters cited in notes 22–23, and the response to the pamphlet by Condy Raquet, the editor of the *Free Trade Advocate and Journal of Political Economy* (Philadelphia, 1829).

13. Charles Duncombe, *Duncombe's Free Banking: An Essay on Banking, Currency, Finance Exchanges, and Political Economy* (New York, 1969 [1841]), 2–4; "Gallatin," *Thoughts on Banking with Reference to the Trade and Currency of the United States* (Richmond, 1841), pamphlet in VHS. The attitude that is generally associated with the Jacksonians is described in William Leggett's "Monopolies," in Lawrence White (ed.), *Democratick Editorials: Essays in Jacksonian Political Economy by William Leggett* (Indianapolis, 1984), 277–83. Also see pp. 74–83, 261–63, 284–89. Leggett opposed "all monopolies" (p. 278) but not a monopoly by the state.

toward centralization. Whig bankers who shared the goal of a privately owned central bank would have been shocked to see that in many ways they were compatible with Jacksonians predisposed toward centralization. Again, although centralization was the ultimate destination, most of the party faithful saw only the first leg of the journey.[14]

Standard as well as revisionist interpretations of the Bank War have missed this point because historians have overlooked the regulatory capacity of gold convertibility. Thus the Jacksonians pursued contradictory political ends by destroying the BUS: if one takes the Jacksonian goals at face value, then a party that wished to make all men "autonomous" and to remove all distinctions between individuals must realistically be assumed to have wished to control fiscal and monetary policy as well. In fact, if men were to be "autonomous," no man could be allowed to gain financial control of another. The Whigs also viewed freedom in economic terms, but whereas the Jacksonians viewed man as free only if he was not subject to outside control, the Whigs saw freedom from external control as a situation to be realized only by having the state encourage economic growth so that each individual could fulfill his potential. For the Whiggery, exploitation of this potential in antebellum times called for a national bank. To the Jacksonians, the liberation of men from the control of corporations also indicated the need for public control of financial institutions. This interpretation explains the natural tendencies of each party to support central banks under various guises. Recent writers addressing the Democrats' actions from a hard-money perspective have tended to view the Jacksonians in a positive light, arguing that the Jacksonians' policies were "antistate." Evidence suggests that the Democrats moved in the opposite direction by establishing, nurturing, and encouraging a system in which government grew in size and authority with each election.[15]

14. Andrew Jackson to James Hamilton, February 2, 1834, in James Hamilton, *Reminiscences of James A. Hamilton* (New York, 1869), 269–70; Washington *Globe*, March 28, 1834; Churchill Cambreleng, quoted in McFaul, *Politics of Jacksonian Finance*, 73; Gatell, "Spoils of the Bank War," 36.

15. Richard Timberlake, Jr., "The Specie Standard and Central Banking in the United States Before 1860," *Journal of Economic History*, September, 1961, pp. 318–41 (quotation on p. 319); Hummel, "Jacksonians, Banking, and Economic Theory," 161–62, 162 n. 12. An elaboration on and critique of the Libertarian view appears in Schweikart, "Banking in the American South," 307–308. For the inherent tendency of the parties toward a centralized government, see Robert Remini, *The Election of Andrew Jackson*

Many Jacksonians, and indeed many Americans, accepted without question the Jeffersonian premise that more democracy meant less government. The shortcomings of this view became especially clear in the case of the hard-money standard and the war on the BUS. What good would it have done the Democrats if they had indeed thrown out the "moneyed interests" only to see them replaced with similar groups under free-banking laws or under individual state regulation? Benton himself expressed the sentiment: "I did not join in putting down the Bank of the United States to put up a wilderness of local banks." Indeed, many Jacksonians viewed the state government as the regulator of last resort. The point here is that, both in practice and in the extension of their logic, the Jacksonians in fact identified the central government as the final arbiter.[16]

Several approaches were taken to the creation of banks in this period. The most common involved a bank that remained a private institution and consisted of an individual or, more likely, a group of individuals who received a corporate charter from the state legislature. Banks represented a leading area in the movement to extend charters with limited liability to corporations in the United States, and this nation led most others in granting such charters. Charters also represented "special privilege." A second form of banking that became popular in the South was the state bank, in which the state sold bonds to obtain money to capitalize the bank. The degree of control exercised over these banks varied with the state. Some states also established real estate banks, which had as their goal the extension of credit to agricultural borrowers. These institutions often allowed property to be pledged in return for stock in the bank as well as for loans. These banks were seen at first as the agents of democracy and as the antithesis of "special privilege." Finally, private, unincorporated bankers throughout the South engaged in financial operations as a minor part of their other major business concerns.

Regulation of Jackson's pet banks generated considerable concern that the state-chartered banks might also have special privileges and, as a

---

(Philadelphia, 1963), 51–71 and passim; Robert Remini, *Martin Van Buren and the Making of the Democratic Party* (New York, 1959), 84–146; Richard Brown, "The Missouri Crisis, Slavery, and the Politics of Jacksonianism," *South Atlantic Quarterly*, Winter, 1966, pp. 55–72.

16. Thomas Hart Benton, *Thirty Years' View* (2 vols.; New York, 1859), II, 10.

remedy, that the government benefits would be dispersed more widely. This possibility was of course exactly what Benton and various hard-money men feared. "Hard money," usually invoked as a rallying cry, was the sincere goal of many Jacksonians, but for some it heralded only a means toward an egalitarian end. The latter group wanted private note issue ended so that the government could control the currency and regulate any corporations or business elites that might pose a threat to the concept of equality.[17]

Following the suspension of specie payments by banks during the Panic of 1837, political pressures superseded strictly economic considerations in the circles of both parties' leaders. A major policy separation occurred along two separate and distinct lines: banking and money. Democratic plans for centralizing the banking system under a new national bank were temporarily abandoned, although considerable support still existed for a centralized deposit-bank system. Nevertheless, the strongest national Democratic support came for a complete divorce of the government from the banks. The party split on the question of whether to destroy all banks or to allow local banks to continue operations. Some party spokesmen, like Benton, thought that a return to state banking would pull the nation toward a specie standard. Benton therefore favored the independent treasury. Others, like William Rives, opposed Van Buren's plan but felt deep concern about protecting states' rights. With the advent of the independent treasury, the states'-rights voices seemed to have won a victory.[18]

Democrats divided on another issue as well, that of hard money versus soft money, with brokers in the middle. Rives, one "soft" leader, characterized a group that could ally itself with Whigs on banking matters. Fellow Virginian and editor Thomas Ritchie of the Richmond *Enquirer* played the role of mediator, attempting to act as a broker for the sake of John Claiborne and William Gwin. Although such brokers settled party disputes regularly, they demonstrated a great inclination to do so for personal gain. The last group, the "hards," reflected varying degrees of persuasion. More radical hards viewed banks as inherently imbued with special privilege and wished to abolish all of them. Less dogmatic hards

17. Hummel, "Jacksonians, Banking, and Economic Theory," 162n.
18. Sharp, *Jacksonians vs. the Banks*, 10–14; Hummel, "Jacksonians, Banking, and Economic Theory," 161.

were prepared to settle for major bank reforms. Egalitarianism ce-
mented these groups together.[19]

It makes sense to distinguish between hard-money supporters and
soft-money supporters, but to understand exactly what different groups
wanted or expected from specific policies, we should further differentiate between those who wanted hard money because it was economically
the most stable currency and those who favored hard money or any
other restrictions on banks for primarily egalitarian motives. I shall call
the former group economic stabilists and the second group egalitarian
metallists. Apart from the fact that any of the hard-money men could fall
into either category, various political considerations, such as individual
state interests, local issues, or ideological quirks, could further modify
any single Jacksonian's approach to the banking question. Economic stabilists included William Gouge and probably J. F. H. Claiborne of Mississippi. Alexander McNutt, also of Mississippi, and J. H. Hammond
of South Carolina typified the egalitarian metallists. Archibald Yell of
Arkansas was representative of those whose reasoning on the issue
changed over time.

In summary, the Jacksonians, pursuing their goal of a metallic currency, did so in the name of equality, which they defined as autonomy.
Many Jacksonians realized that control of the money supply was the ultimate goal, whether it was attained through metallism or through a national banking system, because only such control could assure autonomy. By actions deliberate and inadvertent, the Democrats moved
toward centralization. Whigs, who advocated greater participation by
government in the economy, also lumbered toward centralization, although they wished power to remain in the legislative branch rather
than in the executive. Both parties moved in essentially the same direction, impelled to a great degree by the question of banks and money.

POLITICS AND STATE BANKING DEVELOPMENT

Given the parties' many disparate characteristics, it might seem difficult
to answer the questions "Who was a Southern Democrat?" and "Who

19. Sharp, *Jacksonians vs. the Banks*, 14–15. There was also a hard-money/Copper-
head connection. See Frank Klement, *The Copperheads in the Middle West* (Chicago,
1960), pp. 251–53, and Ronald Formasino and William Shade, "The Concept of Agrarian
Radicalism," *Mid-America*, January, 1970, pp. 3–30.

was a Southern Whig?"—especially on the bank issue. Individual case studies of the more representative and important southerners may be helpful, but fully to appreciate the complexity and variety of hard-money antibank Democrats, we must take a broader view of the clashes within.

We might choose John F. H. Claiborne as a representative Jacksonian in developing Mississippi. Although Claiborne retired from politics in 1838 to publish newspapers and to write history, he had nevertheless had a long career of public service by that time. At his retirement, he bragged to Levi Woodbury that he was the strongest man in Mississippi. He had written the vast majority of political editorials for the Jacksonians. Mississippi's loose party development made it necessary to take no firm stance on the banking issue, and Claiborne claimed at different times to favor and to oppose a national bank.[20]

Claiborne's interest in banking issues quickly transcended ideology. Claiborne was engaged in land speculation and procured mortgage lists from local banks in an attempt to predict foreclosures. He once borrowed ten thousand dollars for a single speculation. He frequently profited from information given him by W. W. Corcoran of Washington, whose connections included William Lewis, a Jackson acquaintance. Using information obtained from Corcoran, Claiborne engaged in a variety of pursuits and even acted as the agent of the Rodney Bank in Mississippi. His political career effectively ended before he had to choose between economic stabilism and egalitarian metallism, but his overall self-concern and lack of ideological commitment seem to place him in the former group.[21]

By the late 1830s, Claiborne's party influence had diminished relative to that of another rising star, Alexander G. McNutt. A hard-money governor from 1838 to 1842, McNutt received praise as "one of the few men who endeavored . . . to prevent the evils of our present corrupt system of banking." McNutt personally underwent a metamorphosis

20. Sharp, *Jacksonians vs. the Banks*, 56–59; J. F. H. Claiborne to Levi Woodbury, November 11, 1838, Levi Woodbury Papers, Series 2, LC.

21. Robert Walker to J. F. H. Claiborne, October 7, 1839, J. F. H. Claiborne Papers, LC; William Gwin to Claiborne, October 9, 1839, *ibid.*; William Gwin to Dwight Freeman, October 26, 1839, *ibid.*; Henry Cohen, *Business and Politics in America from the Age of Jackson to the Civil War: The Career Biography of W. W. Corcoran* (Westport, Conn., 1971), 9–10.

that closely paralleled the overall evolution of the party on bank matters, moving from a position of reform to advocacy of prohibition. His original hope for conciliation with the banks rested more on pragmatic considerations than on philosophical grounds. Upon assuming the governorship, McNutt found the state's banking system "so interwoven with our habits, business and contracts [that it] has become a necessary evil, and cannot speedily be eradicated, without involving the whole State in utter ruin." Suggestions to give the legislature the power to repeal charters at its whim never found adequate support.[22]

Overriding all other problems was the predicament of the Union Bank of Mississippi. Capitalized at $15.5 million, it stood as a major political liability to whichever party was unlucky or unskillful enough to be blamed for its demise. Panic conditions had slowed bond sales, and the state had backed the bank with an issue of bonds and with its "full faith and credit." McNutt had maneuvered in such a way that he could later disclaim the bank.[23]

McNutt makes an interesting case study, for he drifted toward the egalitarian metallist position as the bank issue grew more volatile. Vetoing some of the other bank-chartering bills, he maintained that "circulation and value of paper money depends mainly on its convertibility into specie—not entirely on the ultimate solvency of the corporation issuing it." During the campaign for governor in 1839 and 1840, McNutt's appeal shifted markedly to the "ultras" in the party—those hard-money men who would readily have backed a bank-prohibition law—but to soften his image for the electorate, supporters made it known that he preferred specie-paying banks only when they were strictly regulated. This stand in its turn aroused the indignation of some ultras. During the same campaign, the ultra editor of the Jackson *Mississippian* perceived that local Democratic support for the independent treasury put the

22. For information on McNutt, see Sharp, *Jacksonians vs. the Banks*, 61–66. Quotations appear in the Jackson *Mississippian*, June 23, 1837, January 19, 1838. Also see *ibid.*, May 5, 19, June 9, 13, July 14, August 18, 1837, September 20, 1839, and Dudley Jennings, *Nine Years of Democratic Rule in Mississippi: Being Notes upon the Political History of the States, from the Beginning of the Year 1838, to the Present Time* (Jackson, Miss., 1847), 23–24.

23. Sharp, *Jacksonians vs. the Banks*, 63–64. Many other Mississippi banking companies were chartered with the support of both parties. See the Jackson *Mississippian*, February 9, 16, 23, 1838, July 19, 1839.

Democrats and the Whigs in the same nest, "advocating a National Bank, as well as the whole legion of pet banks." McNutt's gradual shift toward an ultra-hard-money position represented a temporary general party trend. Senator Robert Walker, "who earlier never could, by any stretch of the imagination, have been called a hard-money man, now decried 'the whole paper system . . . as destructive to the morals, dangerous to the liberties, and ruinous to the true interests of the American people.'" Democrats succeeded in dissociating themselves from their earlier partial support of banks, and from the independent treasury, thereby winning the legislature and returning McNutt to the governorship.[24]

Upon meeting with the legislature in 1840, McNutt stated bluntly that bank reform was useless, that the Union Bank in particular should be liquidated, and that $5 million in state bonds backing it should be repudiated. Planters had been the prime beneficiaries of the bank, but when it floundered, they shifted their stance easily; the ranks of the bondholders were composed largely of foreigners and northerners. Repudiation replaced reform as the focus of political controversy, with McNutt arguing on increasingly egalitarian grounds that the state should abandon bondholders. The major bank stockholders and bondholders were wealthy, he argued, and had used their positions to increase their riches. They therefore represented the enemy of all Jacksonians, "special interests," and not the majority of the voting populace. McNutt's impassioned orations drove some Democrats into the arms of the Whigs. On one occasion he so infuriated former Democratic governor Hiram Runnels—"the prince of Bank thieves"—by toasting Runnels' prospective dueling opponent Volney Howard that Runnels was reported to have tracked down McNutt on a Jackson street and beat him with his cane.[25]

24. Jackson *Mississippian*, February 23, August 10, 1838, June 28, 1839; John Stewart to Duncan McLaurin, December 25, 1838, Duncan McLaurin Papers, DU; Robert Walker to constituents, *Niles Register*, August 24, 1834. Walker's position greatly resembled that of Claiborne. See James Shenton, *Robert John Walker: A Politician from Jackson to Lincoln* (New York, 1961), Chap. 2; J. F. H. Claiborne, *Mississippi, as a Province, Territory and State, with Biographical Notices of Eminent Citizens* (Hattiesburg, Miss., 1880), 409, 415–20; J. F. H. Claiborne to William C. Rives, May 31, 1840, William C. Rives Papers, LC.

25. The paper carrying the story suggested that the event was a fabrication. See Sharp, *Jacksonians vs. the Banks*, 69–76; Jackson (Miss.) *Southron*, January 30, 1841; Miles, *Jackson Democracy in Mississippi*, 39; John Stewart to Duncan McLaurin, July 30, 1840, Duncan McLaurin Papers, DU; Jackson *Mississippian*, July 31 and August 7, 1840; *Niles Register*, August 15, 1840.

By 1842, the repudiators had conquered the last strongholds of bond payers, leaving one Whig to remark that only the taxpayers remained among those favoring the bond payoff. The final bond skirmish occurred in 1853, when the state supreme court ruled in favor of payment, but a public referendum effectively upheld repudiation.[26]

The ultras next set their sights on repudiation of the Planters Bank bonds, cloaking their redistributionist plans in egalitarian rhetoric. Why, asked the ultrahard editor of the Vicksburg *Sentinel*, "should a few rich men be allowed the privilege of drawing interest on three dollars for every one they possess?" Still the state's "rich men"—the planters—had already obtained the fruits of the bank, and others would absorb the losses. Numerous Democrats did not share the repudiation attitude only because it threatened to aid Whig election hopes by splitting the Democrats. Repudiationists triumphed, but no sooner had the antibond group won the election of 1843 than another controversy arose, this time over the Briscoe Bill, designed to effect a final disposition of banks. Under this proposed law, banks could not collect debts due them. As might be expected in the controversy, a newspaper published information about the bill's author, Parmenas Briscoe, showing that he owed the banks nearly thirty thousand dollars. Whigs attached an amendment negating the key collection clause, and so support of the *real* Briscoe Bill separated the bank Democrats from the ultras. Again the radical factions of the party carried the day, and the original bill went on the books. Mississippi would feel the effects of its repudiation when it approached many of the same sources of credit during the Civil War and found itself sharply rejected. As of 1847, the Mississippi public supported repudiation, although an attempt in that year to prohibit the legislature from chartering any banks failed. Many banks had failed in the depression, and it was generally conceded that there was no longer a need for such a law.[27]

26. John Stewart to Duncan McLaurin, March 24, 1842, Duncan McLaurin Papers, DU; Joseph Baldwin, *Flush Times of Alabama and Mississippi: A Series of Sketches* (New York, 1957 [1853]), 55.

27. Dunbar Rowland (ed.), *Mississippi: Comprising Sketches of Counties, Towns, Events, Institutions, and Persons, Arranged in Cyclopedic Form* (Atlanta, 1907), 1:200; Volney Howard to John Quitman, March 1, 1843, and Samuel Gholson to John Quitman, March 7, 1843, J. F. H. Claiborne Papers, MDAH, Jackson, Mississippi; Jackson *Statesman*, July 22, August 5, 13, 19, October 21, 1843; Sharp, *Jacksonians vs. the Banks*, 84–85; Jackson *Southron*, August 23, 1843.

Democrats had much freer rein in Arkansas, where for sixteen years a Democrat carried the state's seat in the U.S. Senate. Siding eagerly with minority Whigs in chartering both banks in the state, the Democrats succeeded in turning the banks again into predominantly agricultural institutions. One was an outright real estate bank. In the early stages of the panic, both failed, and Democrats eventually grew so hostile toward banks that they passed a prohibition law. The Democratic governor, Archibald Yell, who had once enthusiastically engaged in speculative activities of his own, quickly turned against banks after the panic. Yell, characterized as a typical Jacksonian, was torn between the speculative spirit of the times and a sincere desire for a national hard-money currency. He exaggerated the power of the state's banks, asking whether the legislature was "ready to see the price of all our staple products raised and depressed at the will and caprice of these organizations." [28]

Yell was fortunately not involved in the most sordid incident in Arkansas's banking history. When the affairs of the Real Estate Bank were concluded, sectional politics devolved to an even lower plane, pitting local cliques against one another. The contest between the probank and antibank groups reached a violent climax. Joseph Anthony, a House leader of the antibank forces, introduced a resolution on November 25, 1837, indicting the Real Estate Bank for being detrimental to equal rights. John Wilson, head of the probank group and speaker of the House, responded with a report denying all of the charges and, in a routine matter a week later, announced the recent passage of a bill in the Senate encouraging the killing of wolves, to which a House spokesman later added an amendment to make scalps "good currency throughout the State." A proviso was thereupon added, requiring that a statement by the official accepting the scalps accompany them. Anthony offered an amendment requiring the president of the Real Estate Bank to sign all of the certificates, an attempt at humor that proved fatal. Wilson, who happened to be president of the bank at the time, sensed an insult and charged down from the Speaker's chair, bowie knife in hand. In the short exchange that ensued, the infuriated Wilson stabbed Anthony. [29]

28. See Melinda Meek, "The Life of Archibald Yell: Chapter I, Early Life," *Arkansas Historical Quarterly*, Spring, 1967, pp. 174–75, 178, 181–83; Blocher, *History of Arkansas Finances* (Little Rock, Ark., 1876), 22.

29. For specifics of the controversy, see *Arkansas Gazette*, November 21, 1837, May 30, June 20, 1838; "Report of the President of the Real Estate Bank of the State of Arkan-

Wilson had a brief and, by all accounts, pleasurable stay in jail until he was tried and acquitted. Meanwhile control of the Real Estate Bank remained in the hands of a group of Jacksonians known as the "Bourbons," the "family," or the "Seviers," a wealthy family active in local politics. Family members had appointed the first bank officials, had controlled subsequent appointments, and were the heaviest borrowers. Whig planters, although also heavily indebted to the bank, played heavily upon the inability of the Democrats to wrest official control of the bank from the "family" even after control had passed into the hands of trustees. Democrats retaliated by trying to fix the blame on Albert Pike, the Whig attorney for the bank, and on the cashier, Thomas Newton, also a Whig.

Pike had indeed engaged in chicanery. Exploiting the authority of his position, he gave himself a permanent position in the bank's affairs. He performed his duties as attorney over a thirteen-year period, receiving more than $28,600 in fees. Pike's actions might have been less than professional, but his intimate knowledge of the bank's records left officers and trustees alike over a barrel, regardless of their political affiliation.

Whigs, meanwhile, dusted off the Jacksonians' speeches to inveigh against the Real Estate Bank. The people, one Whig paper blared, would gladly pay direct taxes for a legitimate purpose, "but that we should be taxed to pay the debts [incurred by bonds] of the most *aristocratic* monopoly of land holders in the United States is unbearable." Trustees empowered to liquidate the bank continued selecting members of the Bourbons whenever a vacancy arose, as it did only infrequently, for no one left a trusteeship except involuntarily, by death. Even the judge who ruled that the assignment of the Real Estate Bank's assets to the trustees was legal was himself a debtor. Not until 1855 did the legislature muster the votes needed to snatch the bank from the trustees' clutches. The issue continued to trouble politicians considerably until that time. Governor John Roane, writing to his friend General Henry Wilcox in 1850, asked for the general's opinion: "What should be done [regarding] the Banks and the state indebtedness? . . . pay the bonds or repudiate the debt"? He concluded, "The one we cannot do, and the other would disgrace us." The governor and the legislature waited five

---

sas," *ibid.*, December 12, 1837; *Journals of the Special Session of the General Assembly of the State of Arkansas, 1838*, 23, 298–99; William Pope, *Early Days in Arkansas* (Little Rock, Ark., 1895), 224–25; Alfred Arrington, *The Lives and Adventures of the Desperadoes of the South-West* (New York, 1849), 65–66.

more years before they gained control of the banks. Arkansas showed that, in a conflict between antinomic ideology and misguided policy, neither party could claim a victory.[30]

The traumatic escapades of the Arkansas and Mississippi banks had paved the way for virtual prohibition in both states. In both, the attempt to make the state the primary instrument of financial control for the benefit of agricultural groups, especially planters, had failed. In neither case had any party adopted a basically laissez-faire approach. Jacksonians constantly waffled between hard money and strict regulation, whereas the Whigs drifted from advocating state control of local institutions to supporting the concept of a privately owned federal bank. At no point did either party try to remove banking from the politicians' control.

In Louisiana, where the reform bank act of 1842 provided what is often viewed as a major hard-money victory for the Democrats, Solomon Weathersby Downs, of northern Louisiana, was a somewhat typical Democratic leader. Heir to a fortune in slaves and land, Downs nevertheless found the Jacksonian egalitarian message attractive. Serving as a senator in the state legislature, and later as a member of the state constitutional convention, Downs eventually moved into national circles by joining the Louisiana delegation to the national Democratic convention in 1844. From 1847 to 1853 he was a U.S. senator. Democratic governor Alexander Mouton made Downs his speech writer. In his acceptance address, Mouton spoke of war on the state's banks, a line taken from General Downs. Despite his wealth, Downs tended toward egalitarian metallism.[31]

Downs's personal successes were not mirrored in the state's Democratic party in general. Whigs had, in fact, passed the 1842 law, albeit only with great reluctance and Democratic prodding. By 1845, when a constitutional convention was summoned, Democrats could direct policy themselves; they enjoyed a two-to-one margin over Whigs at the convention. Even so, the majority failed to prohibit banks but succeeded instead in prohibiting new banks and in allowing existing banks to survive only through their charter periods. Jacksonians eventually

30. Little Rock *Arkansas State Gazette*, February 17, 1841; John Roane to Henry Wilcox, August 26, 1850, Eno Collection, AHC, Little Rock, Arkansas; Blocher, *History of Arkansas Finances*, p. 8.

31. Minnie Ruffin and Lilla McLure, "General Solomon Weathersby Downs (1801–1854)," *Louisiana Historical Quarterly*, January, 1934, pp. 5–47; Charles Sellers, Jr., "Who Were the Southern Whigs?" *American Historical Review*, January, 1974, pp. 335–46.

called a state constitutional convention in 1845, which prohibited state aid to banks. The constitution was overwhelmingly approved, and the banking issue appeared to have been settled. Democrats essentially controlled the state from 1843 to 1846 and even forced passage of a temporary repudiation of state bonds issued or guaranteed for the banks. The end of the 1840s witnessed a recovery of the state's economy, mixed with a general contraction of banking services due to the new constitution. Pressure from commercial groups allowed Louisiana to avoid the long-term hardships of Mississippi by arranging payment of its bonds.[32]

Both parties had helped create the Bank Act of 1842. At the time the Whigs were credited with or blamed for its impact. A general deflation and temporary recession were due anyway, but the Bank Act exacerbated the difficulties. As a consequence, Democrats pinned the depression on the Whigs and took over the governor's mansion and the statehouse with an antibank majority. It is somewhat ironic that such a strong reform act, credited to the Whigs, removed them from power. Carrying their momentum into the constitutional convention, the Democrats took the opportunity to institute their quasi-prohibitive planks on finance. Hard money dominated the convention, but faced with the state's deficit and large debts owed to the banks, neither Whig nor Democrat suggested that Louisiana absorb the eighteen million dollars' worth of state bond issues. In 1843, the legislature allowed banks to accept state bonds for debts owed them. These bonds had dropped in value by 70 percent, so that bank stockholders and foreign bondholders suffered substantial losses.

New demands for credit rose with economic expansion. The burden of satisfying this demand ultimately fell on the Democrats and their constitutional restrictions. When the state sold its bank stocks, thereby causing a specie drain at the banks, they often responded by tightening bank credit. In a thirty-year cycle, bank stockholders and borrowers paid for initial debt outlays by the state on their behalf. Louisiana's productive economy, its commercial groups, and its competitive banking policies, unlike those in Arkansas, fortunately tempered the banking system so that banks could survive. Indeed, many observers felt that the 1845 constitution had given monopoly privileges to the existing banks, whose 15

32. See, for example, William Adams, "The Louisiana Whigs," *Louisiana History,* Summer, 1974, pp. 213–28.

to 25 percent profit rates should have sent Democrats into a frenzied tirade against special interests and hard money. Reality had asserted itself, however, and Louisiana's economy, and particularly that of New Orleans, needed more banks, not fewer.

If the Democratic "triumph over the banks in Louisiana was . . . the most dramatic and most publicized of the hard-money men's victories in the Southwest," it was also the most short-lived. In 1852, another constitutional convention reconsidered banking issues. The Whigs clung desperately to special privileges and state-chartered banking. Democratic appeals for a free-banking law met with only partial success. Legislators were empowered by the constitution to create banks under either method as a compromise measure. Freed to embark upon a new path, the 1853 Louisiana legislature passed a free-banking law, albeit one insisting on market—not par—valuation of bonds. By 1857, four free banks, holding more than two million dollars worth of railroad and internal-improvement bonds, led the way for banks to play a role in the growing economy.[33]

Alabama's recovery was somewhat slower. A series of Democratic administrations, ultimately directed by Benjamin Fitzpatrick, liquidated the state banks after bitter political clashes, but whereas Alabama's antibank fervor is sometimes likened to that in other southern states, there were important differences. All states of the New South had relied on state banks designed to aid planters, but only in Alabama and Arkansas did the state institutions face such limited competition; elsewhere in the New South government authority had been used to swamp the state with banks, as in Mississippi and Florida. Tennessee remained somewhat an exception, because the Memphis commercial interests were too strong to be effectively subjected to monopoly, and the state took a cautious attitude toward chartering private banks that stressed solvency. Accordingly, having the run of the state's finances in their control, the Alabama and Arkansas institutions not surprisingly generated some of the most bitter controversies regarding their control. Both systems collapsed from financial ineptitude; from questionable, if not scandalous, business practices; and from monopolistic tendencies, ills that were

---

33. Sharp, *Jacksonians vs. the Banks*, 115–16; George Green, *Finance and Economic Development in the Old South: Louisiana Banking, 1804–1861* (Stanford, Calif., 1972), 133–35; Arthur Rolnick and Warren Weber, "Free Banking, Wildcat Banking, and Shinplasters," *Federal Reserve Bank of Minneapolis Quarterly Review*, Fall, 1982, pp. 10–19.

magnified by the panic. (It is important to note that private bankers with limited resources could exist in great numbers without threatening the monopoly as long as they had relatively little capital and did not apply for a charter. Barriers to entry restricted big competitors.)

By 1839, Whigs had made a substantial political recovery in Alabama because of the continued recession. Many Jacksonians had rethought their positions on private banks. Although Democrats still hoped to convert the banks into institutions that would be subject to public control, many hill-country Democrats came to attack the state bank as a corrupt congregation of capital. Democrats and Whigs often united to keep control of the banks' directorships in the hands of the legislature. Individuals in both parties owed money to the state bank and its branches, with Whigs outborrowing Democrats. Documents listing the borrowers and their debts, which had supposedly been turned over to Governor Benjamin Fitzpatrick, allegedly disappeared.[34]

In April and May 1841, several members of the legislature participated in a scheme to pass "fictitious bills of exchange" on the state bank, which was "for a time *the sensation.*" As a result the image of banking in the state deteriorated further. By 1842 the antibank Democrats had joined the Whigs in forcing the dissoluton of the Bank of Alabama. With the demise of the Planters and Merchants Bank in late 1841, only one private bank remained in Alabama. The ensuing contraction by 1849 had persuaded the Democrats of their error in preventing the chartering of any banks.[35]

Taxation to repay the bank-induced debt became the major topic of political conversation. The bank slowly moved out of the cotton business. The Bank of Mobile stepped in to supply a sound, if quite inadequate, currency in the South; Tennessee and Georgia notes circulated elsewhere. Small notes and shinplasters also circulated. By the end of the decade, Whigs and banks seemed to be gaining in popularity because

34. On the Alabama Whigs, see William Hallett to Arthur Bagby, November 9, 1839, Governor's Correspondence, Bagby, ADAH, Montgomery, Alabama; Adam Hollinger to James Dellet, December 23, 1840, James Dellet Papers, ADAH; Thomas Alexander et al., "Who Were the Alabama Whigs?" *Alabama Review*, 1966, pp. 5–19, and their "The Basics of Alabama's Ante-bellum Two-Party System," *Alabama Review*, 1966, pp. 243–76; William Brantley, *Banking in Alabama, 1816–1860* (Birmingham, Ala., 1961, 1967), II, 154–55.

35. *Flag of the Union*, November 9, 1842; Brantley, *Banking in Alabama*, II, 188–94; Mobile *Register*, January 7, 1843; William Garrett, *Reminiscences of Public Men in Alabama for Thirty Years* (Atlanta, 1872), 212.

of an increasing demand for capital and the concurrent dissatisfaction
with the lending policies of the state bank, which had directed money
away from the most rapidly growing areas. Businessmen in Montgomery
and Mobile joined with proponents of industrialization throughout the
state to advocate new bank charters or even free-banking laws. By 1849,
private bank advocates, led by Henry Collier, had triumphed in the
elections.[36]

As in other states, the Jacksonians' antibank fervor in Alabama had
created results exactly the opposite of those desired, for control of the
state's finances had shifted from a public institution to a private one controlled by special interests. Jacksonians had offered strong market incentives for "foreign" intervention from other states and Europe, and they
had strongly, if accidentally, encouraged small-note issues and the circulation of shinplasters. The Democrats helped the Whigs saddle the
state with massive debts and resorted to taxation for repayment. Unfortunately, the burden fell on the backbone of the party, the common
man. Alabama's example, like that of Arkansas, is stark exactly *because*
the Democrats were so effective in pursuing their programs. Seldom
had the Jacksonians' policies generated such a chasm between intention
and result; their policies imposed hardship most often on those already
most afflicted.

Political struggles of a different sort characterized the middle period
in Virginia, where in the crucial years 1837 to 1842 the Whigs controlled
the legislature. Throughout much of the turmoil editor Thomas Ritchie
and William Rives played lead roles, occasionally in agreement and often
in opposition. After the specie suspension, the legislature came into session under governor David Campbell, whom Whigs found neither a
strict hard-money man nor a "shin plaster patriot." To Campbell, a west-
erner with the common touch, the aristocratic tidewater groups were
"arrogant" and disgusting: "They think the world does not produce their
equals." Campbell had nonetheless succumbed to the political sophis-
tries of editor Ritchie, whose *Enquirer* favored only reform, not radical
reaction against the banks. Ritchie's paper ran mostly antibank columns,

36. *Monitor*, August 13, May 28, June 18, 1845; Thornton, *Politics and Power*, 47. See
Alabama Senate Journal, 1839–40, pp. 6–20, 1841–42, pp. 13–15, 1847, p. 17, 1849–50,
pp. 315–16, 348–53; *House Journal*, 1839–40, pp. 154–60, 1849–50, pp. 25–26, 200–
217. Industrialist David Pratt also advocated the creation of new banks in a public letter to
the *Flag and Advertiser*, June 24, 1847.

although the attacks on banks were mild compared with those in the New South states, largely because of the influence of commercial groups. Ritchie determined the parameters of the debate, then relayed his readership's conclusions to Campbell.[37]

Occasionally a writer came remarkably close to recognizing the logical extension of the Jacksonians' arguments only to allow the moment to pass, obscured by ideological clouds. A correspondent who called himself "Jefferson" suspected that Whig policy sought to destroy local banks with the Democrats' help in order to establish a new national bank. Although his opinion was remarkably similar to the insight offered by the ultra editor of the *Mississippian*, "Jefferson" nevertheless failed to realize that his own party had moved in exactly the same direction many times.[38]

Ritchie meanwhile lobbied Campbell endlessly, "red hot for hard money." He feared free banking, denouncing it as a "northern fad." Rives, working to carve his own conservative niche in the party, labored to persuade Campbell of a more moderate view, denouncing as "visionary and impractical" Democrats who wanted to eliminate all banks and institute a metallic currency. Campbell agreed with Rives. In the special session of the legislature, Campbell enjoined the lawmakers to allow the specie suspension to pass without penalties. Democrats splintered on a bill to relieve the banks and utterly disintegrated when a resolution to allow small-note issues passed. Small notes were a necessity in a commercial economy and represented a highly charged issue to the Democrats. More of them voted for the small-note bill than for the relief bill, and as a body they were more unified, but in terms of the legislation's importance in the Democratic program, they had voted a rear-guard action. In Virginia, the five-point plan was marching backward. Respected Jacksonian hard-money men even preferred reforms that could make banks "what they ought to be—commercial institutions, confined to mercantile operations and placed under the closest restrictions" as a means to destroy all banks.[39]

37. Richmond *Whig*, August 1, 1837; David Campbell to William Campbell, February 21, 1837, David Campbell Papers, DU; Richmond *Enquirer*, June 2, 9, 1837.

38. Richmond *Enquirer*, June 2, 1837.

39. David Campbell to Maria Campbell, June 3, 1837, David Campbell Papers, DU; William Rives to David Campbell, May 22, 1837, *ibid.*; Richmond *Enquirer*, June 13, 20, 27, 1837, November 30, 1838, January 12, 1839; *Niles Register*, June 17, 1837. Also see Charles Ambler, *Thomas Ritchie: A Study in Virginia Politics* (Richmond, Va., 1913).

Radical voices remained. One writer chastised the state for knuckling under to bank power, "shamefully sacrific[ing] the rights and interests of the *many* to the selfish and unjust demands of the *few.*" Enough advocates of "radical reform or extermination of our present paper system" still skulked about the legislative halls to mobilize a majority vote at an advantageous moment. By the estimates of Virginia conservatives in 1838, fewer than thirty hard-money men held seats, however. Rives, together with other moderates, hoped to convince Van Buren that he had to abandon a hard-money position. Van Buren's announcement of his independent treasury policy during the special session of Congress effectively squelched Rives's hopes.[40]

Virginians perceived a nascent national bank (though one lacking lending powers that could easily be added later through charter amendment) and recognized that groundwork had been laid for a major assault on states' rights. Ritchie sensed that the independent treasury "would increase the already too large power of the Executive," complete with "a new batch of Federal agents." John Brockenbrough, president of the Bank of Virginia and a Democrat, favored the independent treasury; he feared that another private national bank of greater power would be the alternative. Dismissing the idea of a metallic currency as "too silly . . . to dwell on," Brockenbrough took a stance far short of the radicals' position. In general, Virginia bankers had been "cautiously hostile to BUS operations," feeling that their own well-regulated state system already provided what the BUS only promised to provide. In their minds, the independent treasury could certainly operate no better.[41]

Numerous resolutions in the Virginia legislature never saw a vote. Proposals to instruct the state's U.S. senators to vote against the independent treasury also fell by the wayside largely because most Democrats in the state supported Van Buren's plan. Stung by their lack of success in swaying the main body of Democrats, Rives and his supporters considered a third-party movement. They met with early successes, convincing Whigs that they had much in common with the deposit-bank Democrats. Throughout the posturing, Ritchie supported Rives, and hard-

---

40. Richmond *Enquirer*, July 11, 1837; Sharp, *Jacksonians vs. the Banks*, 228–29.
41. Thomas Ritchie to Martin Van Buren, August 20, 1837, Martin Van Buren Papers, LC; John Brockenbrough to William Rives, May 20, 1837, William C. Rives Papers, LC; McFaul, *The Politics of Jacksonian Finance*, 27.

money Democrats almost set up an alternative newspaper to the *Enquirer.* Conservatives under Rives and the Whigs eventually united.[42]

Virginia's 1837 general banking law, enacted just before the panic, made some concessions to concerns that would soon be the Democrats' greatest, especially in the prohibition of notes under ten dollars. Eradication of these small-note issues represented the first in the Jacksonians' five-point plan to control the currency and formed a critical part of the program. If small notes could be controlled, then larger issues might also be regulated, but any movement in the direction of a gold standard hinged on a favorable resolution of the small-note question. After the initial panic, the legislature declined to impose penalties against the suspended banks. A resolution designed to give the legislature the power to amend or repeal the charters of any banks taking advantage of the relief act narrowly lost. Suspending again in 1839, banks once more gained a relief bill from the Whig-controlled legislature. The *Enquirer* immediately demanded "THE SPECIE STANDARD—*a radical reform, or total extermination of our present paper system.*"[43]

Democrats who railed against the relief given the banks in the form of waivers failed to recall that the state, as a stockholder in the banks, would only lose if they closed. Virginia banks had been some of the best regarded in the country, and they paid dividends regularly. Efforts to force resumption before the banks had stabilized their ratios failed. Banks resumed on September 15, 1842, well ahead of their scheduled deadline. The hards in the party had lost all the major votes, despite the fact that, on most bank votes, the majority of the Democrats joined the ranks of the radicals. The strong record of the state's banks, the power of Ritchie and other brokers, the state's partial ownership of the banks, and the lack of hard-money leadership no doubt in part explain the Jacksonians' ineffectiveness. Many hards took the party at its word, however, and believed that it opposed central banking of all sorts. Unable to choose between two groups, and sometimes three, that offered different central-bank programs, the befuddled Virginia Democrats never pursued any single plan as their contemporaries did in other southern areas.

42. Thomas Ritchie to James McDowell, January 1838, Folder 27, James McDowell Papers, SHC, UNC.
43. Richmond *Enquirer,* March 10, 1838, December 21, 1839.

North Carolinians did not lack their share of egalitarian rhetoric about banking. Congressman Lauchlin Bethune, replying to a constituent's inquiry as to whether he would vote for the recharter of the BUS, answered with a very politicianlike response. He was entirely convinced that some such institution was important but commented, "The one in existence has done much to undo the stable [monetary situation]." He also feared that the bank's powers could "add to the opulence and influence of the wealthy—oppress and grind the poor—Create a privileged order, and finally overturn the happiest form of Government ever devised." Bethune followed many of his Jacksonian contemporaries into the quagmire of constituency demands and party direction. He did not wish to see the BUS rechartered, and yet he promised to vote for rechartering the BUS if the voters so desired. At one point, Bethune criticized banks, corporations, and similar institutions of "associated wealth" that represented "main pillars and key stones of monarchies and aristocracies," but he had earlier acknowledged the bank's constitutionality and "had actually proposed to charter two or three similar banks." It would be unwise to generalize about all of North Carolina on the basis of Bethune's record, but it seems safe to say that the Jacksonians there were less interested in banking than in other egalitarian themes.[44]

Georgia presented what should have been the typical Whig-Democratic alignments over the banking issue. In Georgia the Central Bank, which was entirely state owned, at first came under fire from both hard-money men and Whigs. Further realignment forced the hard-money Democrats into a league defending the Central Bank with their soft-money partisans against the Whigs. In 1839, Democratic governor Charles McDonald heaped praise on the Central Bank and blame on the private banks for the ongoing currency problems. Extracting pay-

44. Lauchlin Bethune, "To My Fellow Citizens, The Freemen and Voters of Moore, Montgomery, Anson, Richmond, Robeson, and Cumberland," June 20, 1831, Deberry Papers (microfilm), cited in Harry Watson, *Jacksonian Politics and Community Conflict* (Baton Rouge, 1981), 165; Lauchlin Bethune to Duncan McLaurin, April 22, 1832, in Duncan McLaurin Papers, DU; Fayetteville *Carolina Observer,* July 26, 1837. James McDowell, another North Carolina banker, was active in bank-related political issues. See, for example, John Letchery to James McDowell, March 18, 22, 1838, Thomas Hart Benton to James McDowell, April 22, 1838, James McDowell Papers, SHC, UNC. Also see the Fayetteville *North Carolina Journal,* November 3, 1836, which charged that "the banks, the brokers, stockholders, the rich and the arrogant [are] all opposed to Van Buren and the People," and Watson, *Jacksonian Politics,* 207.

ment for their support, the Democrats soon had the bank increasing the volume of its issues, again along the lines dictated by a strict adherence to avowed party goals. Economic reality struck the bank in 1843, and its failure left only the private banks to provide capital for Georgia's economy. Georgia, one of the few places in which the Jacksonians followed the model Democratic program faithfully and without modification by opposing private banks and supporting the state bank, had nevertheless increased the economy's dependence on special interests and had reduced state control over the market, with the private banks alive and in most cases healthy and the state bank bloated and beached. Georgia's Jacksonians suggest a political party that, like the bar patrons of Lautrec's paintings, saw its ideals exaggerated only to logical ends. Election of a Whig governor in 1843 marked the final public verdict on the subject of banking in Georgia.[45]

South Carolina, economically far more stable than Georgia, nevertheless demonstrated that ideological flaws can turn the stream of reason into unchanneled quicksilver. With South Carolina's record of solid financial institutions, even the Democrats who advocated abolishing the banks were few, but they found themselves attacking the Bank of the State and at the same time refraining from substantial criticism of the private banking houses. Controversy had surrounded the bank's favorable treatment of the Nesbitt Manufacturing Company. Two powerful individuals with antibank tendencies, Christopher Memminger and Governor J. H. Hammond, leaned toward the position of the egalitarian metallists. Memminger, at the time chairman of the House Ways and Means Committee in the state, felt his own bank interests threatened. Their attacks started in 1841 but merely smoldered until the mid-1840s, when a pamphlet war broke out between supporters and opponents. Of all the state banks, the Bank of the State of South Carolina stayed closest to its intended purpose and kept the cleanest record. Attempts to restrict its powers failed, although as late as 1849 Democratic governor W. B. Seabrook assailed the bank as "a dangerous institution, anti-Republican in its character and tendency, . . . the evils inevitably arising from the connection of a monied corporation and the State." Thus

45. Niles Register, January 18, 1840; Paul Murray, The Whig Party in Georgia, 1825–1853 (Chapel Hill, N.C., 1948).

throughout the South, Jacksonians' policy responses to banking had run the gamut, from opposition to the national bank (but not private and state banks), to opposition to private banks but not state banks, to opposition to all banks, and finally to the acceptance of private banks but not state banks. With slavery exerting increasing pressures on Jacksonian thought, the Democrats by the 1850s had dropped banking as an issue.[46]

Florida was the only seaboard state not to share in the conservatism of Virginia, the Carolinas, and Georgia. Politics that had centered on individual personalities in the early years soon gave way to a primitive alignment structure based on continued territorial status versus statehood, with advocates of the latter winning a solid, if unspectacular, victory in the popular referendum of 1837. Florida Whigs had felt the sting of the panic; they were in the majority of the territorial councils that had given a territorial guarantee to the bonds of the two large banks, and they had often been officers or stockholders in these institutions. Whiggery traditionally endorsed such banks with the intent of bringing about a commercial boom. Florida Whigs proved no exception. Democrats, including a number of nonresidents, had their own interests in Florida's banks. Lot Clark, a New Yorker, and "Duff" Green, of Jackson's Kitchen Cabinet, were both involved in establishing and promoting the Southern Life Insurance and Trust Company, one of the "big three" Florida financial institutions of the 1830s. It did not become involved in the question of territorial bonds, but it suffered during the depression and was generally treated as a bank in all political discussions. Specie suspension by some institutions had placed all banks squarely in the middle of the debates over the proposed state constitution. Democrats fanned the fires by constantly mentioning the "Whig bankocracy." In their editorials Democrats tried to pit against the small farmers the wealthy planters who rode in their "coaches and four" and wore "purple linen." Indeed, the important Florida banks conspicuously resided in Leon and Jefferson counties, where the planters had influence. Special parties, such as the Mechanic's and People's Ticket Against the Bank, sprang up, trying to link bank supporters with the North. There even circulated the ludicrous charge that the banks and abolitionists were in league together,

---

46. South Carolina *House Executive Document* No. 226, p. 633; William Sumner, *A History of Banking in the United States* (New York, 1896), 432; John Jay Knox, *A History of Banking in the United States* (New York, 1900), 565; J. Mauldin Lesesne, *The Bank of the State of South Carolina: A General and Political History* (Columbia, S.C., 1970), 52–58.

despite the fact that the banks had almost one-third of their stock in mortgages on slaves. Banking dominated the convention.[47]

Delegates selected to write the constitution divided into committees. The six-man committee on banking and incorporations evenly split into pro- and antibank groups. When the committee's report reached the convention floor, it included recommendations to restrict future legislatures in their powers to issue corporate charters. One section requested that the state create a state bank based on the property bank model. Voting to adopt the committee's bank article, the convention satisfied neither group and produced a document featuring contradictory views. To the majority of members, who were antibank, the single most important aspect of the banking question was the liability of the state for the bonds already issued. If the panic forced the three major banks into collapse, the delegates did not want the infant state presented with a monstrous bill. Most bonds were sold in the North or to foreigners, and so repudiators easily argued that Floridians would not suffer from nonpayment. Slipping through the committee, the convention, and then the ratification process by the narrowest of margins, the constitution became law with an article prohibiting the state from pledging its faith and credit to any corporation.

Democrats won significant victories from 1839 to 1845. They forced Florida banks out of business or discouraged entrepreneurs from starting new banks, but they could not keep out foreign corporations. Between ten and fourteen agencies of New York, Charleston, and Savannah banks opened between 1845 and 1853, joined by at least fourteen private banks: Floridians paid the higher costs of obtaining credit from distant places. Repudiation of Florida's bank-related territorial bonds also passed in 1842 after a long fight, so that Florida appeared on the defaulter's list with Mississippi. Foreign holders of the Florida bonds presented their claims for international arbitration without success. Democratic victories in Florida were not wholly due to antibank sentiment: banking laws had to be considered in light of other political, economic, sectional, and social variables (for example, by the 1850s even the

47. Dorothy Dodd, *Florida Becomes a State* (Tallahassee, 1945), 44–45; Caroline Brevard, *A History of Florida* (De Land, Fla., 1924), I, 217; Fred Marckhoff, "The Development of Currency and Banking in Florida," *Coin Collector's Journal*, September–October, 1947, pp. 118–23 (quotation on p. 121); David Y. Thomas, "A History of Banking in Florida," manuscript in University of Florida, P. K. Yonge Library of Florida History.

Know-Nothings had worked their way into the money controversy, a development that further obscured any traditional divisions). By failing to support its own chartered banks, Florida encouraged an invasion of agencies from other states and nonchartered banks over which the state had little control.[48]

Overall, states of the New South showed that Whig and Democrat differed less than has generally been thought. On the national level, both were originally committed to a national bank of one sort or another but for different reasons. Although the Democrats wanted to place the means of controlling the monetary system in the hands of the executive for regulatory purposes, the Whigs wanted a centralized bank for growth purposes. Where the former approach ensured increased centralization of political authority, the latter guaranteed more economic centralization. Either path could easily lead at a later date to a debauching of the money supply, either through outright inflation (the Whigs) or through patronage, political favors, and, eventually, federal giveaways (the Democrats).

Traditional interpretations of the Jacksonian period have sometimes found the southern Whigs' support of economic nationalism as puzzling as the hard-money/greenback connection of the Democrats. States'-rights southerners seemed to have little in common with the proponents of the American system, whose policies portended a consolidation of power in the hands of the national government, so that one historian felt prompted to call southern Whiggery the "Great Aberration." Yet southern Whiggery was no more antinomic than hard-money egalitarianism. Neither the southern Whigs nor the egalitarian metallists realized that they were merely approaching the same goal from different angles.[49]

On some issues, southern Whigs appeared to be more concerned with states'-rights issues than the Democrats. Southern Whigs, for example, urged that surplus federal revenues be returned to the states and opposed federal assumption of state debts. Their distinctive feature, how-

48. Edwin McCrady L'Engle to Edward [?], April 8, 1855, Edwin L'Engle Papers, SHC, UNC.

49. William Cooper, *The South and the Politics of Slavery, 1828–1856* (Baton Rouge, 1978), Chap. 5; Thomas Brown, "The Southern Whigs and Economic Development," *Southern Studies*, Spring, 1981, pp. 20–38; Arthur Cole, *The Whig Party in the South* (Washington, D.C., 1913), Chaps. 1, 2; Sellers, "Who Were the Southern Whigs?" 335–46; Thomas Abernethy, "The Origins of the Whig Party in Tennessee," *Mississippi Valley Historical Review*, 1927, pp. 504–22.

ever, which was proudly acknowledged by most, was their emphasis on a national scope—the goal of uniting the country by making regions economically interdependent. Representative Alexander Stuart of Virginia implored his fellow congressmen to "look at it as a *whole*, and not confine our views to mere local or sectional interests. . . . We should look at the grand system, intimately connected together, wisely fitted to each other." Southern Whigs constantly contended that the economic interdependence created by their policies would unify the country so tightly that "all attempts, whether of abolitionists or of abstractionists, to destroy our beloved Union, will be laughed to scorn for centuries to come."[50]

In short, southern Whigs generated little regional enthusiasm for the party's large-scale national schemes. Yet a difference in attitude began to separate Whigs from Democrats even if the break did not come exactly along party lines. On the one side stood those who saw the South in the context of a growing national and international capitalist economy. These individuals interpreted freedom in terms of participation and competition. On the other side were the planters and the yeoman Democrats, who withdrew from the commercialized, industrialized world with horror. They saw that world as the antithesis of freedom.

States' rights per se were thus not the issue in the eyes of southerners. Freedom, banking, and, in the context of the economy, the right to vote on economic issues were. Banking questions tended to align several groups behind the Whigs, most notably merchants, individuals with extensive commercial interests, lawyers, and newspaper editors. Although such issues also tended to attract some planters to these groups, most southern Whigs did not adopt the states'-rights views of the planters. Therefore, although planters were an important group in the Whig coalition, they tended to be subordinate to the other elements, and their role must often be seen in the context of their other activities. Henry Marston, for example, a planter from East Feliciana Parish, Louisiana, was also active in the merchant loan business, in urban real estate devel-

50. Speech on the tariff quoted in Alexander Robertson, *Alexander Hugh Holmes Stuart: A Biography* (Richmond, Va., 1925), pp. 37–39; "Manifesto of Seventy-nine Cotton Planters of Adams County, Mississippi, in Favor of Protection to American Manufactures," *Plough, the Loom, and the Anvil* (*American Farmers Magazine*), November, 1848, pp. 288–89 (dated Oct. 24, 1844). The *Augusta Chronicle* took this reasoning one step further: "Every man retained in the factories of Lowell, or the furnaces of Pennsylvania, is a customer of the farmer and planter, and every man driven from them to seek the west must of necessity become a rival" (March 9, 1849).

opment, and, of course, in banking. He often acted as a lawyer and agent and held to old-line Whig policies. Jackson, he believed, stood for "demon democracy." In the 1850s, Marston supported a unionist position. As in Marston's case, the real leadership in local Whig organizations often came from businessmen in the larger urban areas and frequently included important bankers such as Hugh L. White in Tennessee. A study of Alabama, one of the states most analyzed for its political tendencies, revealed that from 1836 to 1856 a greater number of congressmen and legislators who were planters were also Democrats (forty-seven to thirty-four). By 1840 in North Carolina twenty of twenty-one directors in the two leading banks were Whigs. Quite often the banking issue itself contributed to the formation of the Whig party, as it symbolized the national vision that Whigs came to share.[51]

Thomas Branch and his family, who played an important role in Richmond politics, represented typical leaders of the Virginia Whigs. By making themselves conspicuous as directors of banks and mercantile houses and as promoters of transportation projects, they attempted to influence urban Virginians to adopt a national view of economic relationships. It eventually forced most Whigs to try to reconcile slavery as an institution and capitalism as an economic reality. After the war the Branches continued to advocate large-scale projects, backing railroads, cement companies, and even public baths in Richmond.[52]

One student of the southern Whigs, analyzing the composition of the party, emphasized their national connection in the ideological sense. That is, the southern Whigs were certainly drifting toward Clay's nationalistic policies by the early 1840s, with a new national bank as the focal point. They saw the dangers inherent in such a shift of power, however, especially in the 1850s as the North began to outdistance the South greatly in population. A substantial doctrinal reassessment thus became necessary, and southern Whigs abandoned their stress on intersectional dependence. Whereas the Democratic party had been formed to es-

---

51. Sellers, "Who Were the Southern Whigs?" 340–42; Jacob Pulwers, "Henry Marston, Ante-bellum Planter and Businessman of East Feliciana" (M.A. thesis, Louisiana State University, 1955), 162–99; Grady McWhiney, "Were the Whigs a Class Party in Alabama?" *Journal of Southern History*, November, 1957, pp. 510–22; U. B. Phillips, "The Southern Whigs, 1834–1854," in *Essays in American History Dedicated to Frederick Jackson Turner* (New York, 1910), 215.

52. Jack Maddex, Jr., *The Virginia Conservatives, 1867–1879* (Chapel Hill, 1970), pp. 8–9.

tablish a revolutionary process in which state sovereignty would be maintained by the subordination of the national government to party discipline, the Whigs had hoped to subordinate states' rights to a national program of economic interrelationships. The Democratic strategy crumpled when personalities were factored into the equation: no chief executive was willing to make his office responsible to the party. Increasingly the party depended on a personality to lead it. Whigs failed just as thoroughly. Individual states ultimately depended on the system of economic relationships to pursue sectional interests and abandoned party doctrine when those interests were threatened. Nor was it just a matter of personal incentives versus group incentives. After all, the Democrats offered patronage to individuals, whereas the Whigs aimed their benefits at sections, yet neither group succeeded in holding together its national party.

Banking at an early date provided the standard against which the logic of each party was to be judged. The Democrats, through their pursuit of a centralized banking system, originally hoped to organize it around hard money. Before there could be equality of opportunity, money must be available whether the market would normally supply it or not. The government would have been required to fill the void if the market could not do so. This trick was not easily turned with a gold standard. Heralding a "new war" in Congress, the Washington *Globe* predicted "*Gold* and *paper* will become badges of parties, like the red and white roses were formerly in England. A man will soon be known as belonging to the *Gold party* or the *Paper party*." Blair, the author, then seemingly anticipated his future move into greenbackism by adding that the new war would pit "the *bank* of the US against the *mint* of the US." The true battle concerned government control of the money supply. Even at the state level observers feared state influence on party-selected directors, "a set of Jacobins . . . under the malignant influence of whore democracy."[53]

Political necessity had forced Van Buren to seek a substitute for the pet bank system in 1837, a "period of transition," as the *Democratic Review* called it. Van Buren's independent treasury "actually would have increased the federal responsibility for state banking operations," but it could not have made loans. Antibank forces, and many hard-money ad-

---

53. Washington *Globe*, July 15, 1834; L. Tazewell to Thomas Ambler, February 10, 1844, VHS.

vocates such as Calhoun, supported the independent treasury on the assumption that it would require only specie payments to the government and would therefore regulate banks. Another plan, to have the Treasury accept state notes, "promised even more forceful regulation of state banks than did specie payments." Any system using the independent treasury, then, guaranteed greater federal involvement in banking affairs. More significantly, the ease with which the Democrats shifted from the specie-requirement proposal to the state-note proposal revealed that their real intentions had little to do with hard money and much to do with centralized power. They were making no crude grab for power, as they understood the essence of greater centralized control in this area to mean greater fredom and equality for everyone. Again, the Jacksonians were driven by the inexorable logic of positions whose final destinations they had not yet perceived.[54]

Two southerners—the former Whig and genuine states'-rights advocate Calhoun and the Virginian Rives—finally sensed the direction of the Democratic strategy, especially after Levi Woodbury's 1837 report, which contained significant revelations that economic stabilists within and outside the party found horrifying. Woodbury conceded that on the basis of the government's specie reserves the government could issue its own notes and that these should go into circulation to constitute a new national currency. He advocated establishing "some *paper medium* of higher character and other than what now exists in private bills of exchange *or notes of state banks*" (emphasis added). Rives, shocked, warned Virginia Governor David Campbell that the "real design of some . . . is to make war upon, and finally destroy state institutions." Government "paper money, which is to supersede and displace the state currencies" was the true goal, he realized. Calhoun, whether or not he understood the subtleties as well as Rives, submitted an amendment to the independent treasury bill that was in guile worthy of Machiavelli. He introduced an amendment that disrupted the Van Buren supporters enough to make the Senate table the bill.[55]

Whigs, meanwhile, who walked a tightrope between supporting their national bank and opposing Van Buren's schemes, offered a strategy that mystified Democrats. Silas Wright of New York wanted to know how

54. McFaul, *Politics of Jacksonian Finance*, 200–201.
55. *Ibid.*, 196, 199; Timberlake, *Origins of Central Banking*, 65.

"those who saw such benign influences to the local institutions from the wholesome restraints of a national bank, should see such baneful effects to follow the same influences, when flowing from the public Treasury?" Yet Wright had also unwittingly commented on a contradiction within his own party. As for the Whigs, they merely wanted *their* bank, but they preferred to see any bank owned by individuals, not by the government. Whig opposition held off the independent treasury until 1840, when it passed. Tippicanoe's victory in November, however, put Whigs in power, and they repealed the independent treasury, substituting their own bill to incorporate a "fiscal bank," which would include a clear admission that it was a policy-making national bank. Whig hopes were shattered by Harrison's death. Harrison's successor, the Virginian John Tyler, vetoed the new bank bill and a second one submitted thereafter.[56]

By the 1850s, both parties had changed their stance on banking issues. Before the Panic of 1857, banking simply took a back seat to sectional issues. The parties did not decline because banking became less important, of course, although in some ways the banking issue did lose its edge because the parties were being eroded. Following the panic, there came a gradual acceptance of banks, without heavy state involvement in state banks. In essence, the Democrats and Whigs had agreed on a general principle of local laissez-faire despite the Democrats' general distrust of the market and the Whigs' feeling that it was inadequate. True state and local regulation now had to control banks; gone was the golden hand of Jacksonian policies or a Whig-backed BUS. Inasmuch as neither side could claim a victory, however, neither had to absorb the loss. The solution was convenient. Each party could attend to other matters, convinced that it had "established" banking policy for the nation.[57]

56. Timberlake, *Origins of Central Banking*, 66–67.
57. W. McWhetten to William Johnson, October 10, 1851, William Johnson Papers, SCL. For the general dissolution of the antebellum parties, see Mark Stegmaier, "The U.S. Senate in the Sectional Crisis, 1846–1861: A Roll-Call Voting Analysis" (Ph.D. dissertation, University of California, Santa Barbara, 1975), and Schweikart, "Banking in the American South," table 4.1.

2

THE PANIC OF 1837 AND ITS AFTERMATH

Seldom in its past had the nation as a whole enjoyed such prosperity as in the early 1830s. No major war had troubled the country for fifteen years. Blessed with peace, Americans turned their energies to their economy. Foreign markets grew uninterruptedly, and trade bloomed. Productivity surged dramatically with the rise of northern manufacturing, although agricultural productivity, bolstered by the addition of new lands in Alabama, Mississippi, Florida, and Arkansas, also improved. Liberalized land policies encouraged settlement even when it served speculators. Enthusiastic immigrants exploited trends in both land usage and technology, adding to efficiency gains. Canal building swept the North, initiating a transportation revolution and sparking demand for capital, which in turn generated calls for more banks. All the elements for a continued boom seemed to be in place.[1]

Cotton, more than any other single product, seemed to act as a bellwether of success. Home consumption exceeded ninety million pounds in 1831. The export of cotton proved even more lucrative. The export crop was valued at fifty million dollars in 1834. Sales to Britain, with its surging textile industry, had increased rapidly, with little prospect of a pause, so that the price was further encouraged to rise. Southerners relied more and more on cotton as a source of income, as a basis for credit, and as a foundation of their banking system. Louisiana, Arkansas, Mississippi, and Florida chartered property banks (banks that were capi-

1. W. Elliot Brownlee, *Dynamics of Ascent: A History of the American Economy,* 2d ed. (New York, 1979), 147.

talized by the state, with property designated as collateral for the issuing of stock) specifically designed to make cotton land the linchpin of banking enterprises. In other agricultural states, the demand for credit forced state governments to charter their own banks, with capital raised by state bond sales, or to allow the incorporation of banks capitalized by private investors. As long as cotton continued its upward spiral in both price and volume, it would continue to determine many banking and business habits. Indeed, during the panic, specie became so valuable that cotton replaced it as a reserve on which banks could issue notes.[2]

To be sure, agriculture had not prompted the banking boom in all parts of the nation or even in all parts of the South. Industrialization, after all, marked the post-1830 years. The contributions to the economy made by advances in technology and the early formation of factories in many areas of the country led the Jacksonian age to be regarded as a critical period in the nation's economic development. Some southern states, especially those along the Atlantic coast, had already depleted the soil or had found their opportunities for broadened trade with interior sections curbed by poor transportation. Younger states along the Gulf coast still had vast rich lands awaiting eager settlers and talented farmers. River systems that connected with the major port cities of New Orleans and Mobile, together with the winding river areas in the northern Alabama region, provided a natural transportation network that was denied the older regions. Often in the public mind all that was needed to develop the land in these areas was capital. It was thought that a bank alone was necessary for capital. Across the nation the creation of banks responded to diverse calls for capital to finance industry, transportation, and agriculture. Nearly four hundred banks by 1835 had joined the more than three hundred already in business, and another two hundred would appear by 1840, when their total capital exceeded $358 million. Although the forthcoming depression would decimate large segments of the banking community, completely eliminating chartered banks in many states, its effects were uneven. Individual southern states had reached different levels of maturity in their banking systems by 1836.[3]

2. Reginald C. McGrane, *The Panic of 1837* (New York, 1965), 18–19; *Senate Documents*, 24th Cong., 1st Sess., Secretary of the Treasury Reports, 1835–36; Lewis Gray, *History of Agriculture in the Southern United States to 1860* (Washington, D.C., 1933), II, 890–91, 894–901.

3. Douglass North, *The Economic Growth of the United States, 1790–1860* (Englewood Cliffs, N.J., 1961), 189.

Certainly all southern states shared some financial characteristics—virtually all of the states exhibited growth in their major monetary indicators following the Panic of 1819—but between panics, states pursued vastly different paths to growth. Their chief differences reflected varying access to trading centers, political developments unique to each state, and differing degrees of reliance on the agricultural sector. Although broad categorization runs the risk of deemphasizing or ignoring idiosyncratic features, the patterns of southern regulatory development generally tended to encourage either competition and little state activity on the one hand or heavy state involvement and control on the other. The BUS also operated branches in Charleston, Fayetteville, New Orleans, Norfolk, Richmond, Savannah, Natchez, Mobile, and Nashville at different times, but these existed outside the framework of state regulations.

Alabama and Arkansas would encounter great difficulty with their banking facilities, although Alabama's began auspiciously enough. At Huntsville, nine educated and experienced Alabamians formed the Planters and Merchants Bank in 1816 (the bank had actually received a charter as the Planters and Mechanics Bank, but it always went by the former name and officially changed its name in 1818). The demand for money was far greater than the bank's capacity to meet it. LeRoy Pope, "the Father of Huntsville," and his directors completely controlled the bank and with it northern Alabama's money supply, creating a fear among some Alabama yeomen of oppression by wealthy elites. Opposition to Pope's dominance of the finances of the state prompted the creation of a state bank, but the law, passed in 1823, could not take effect until the state found the capital needed for the bank, which became a reality only in 1825. It had branches, but these had their own presidents, operated independently of each other, and were linked only by their responsibility to the directors of the system, who were elected by the legislature. Its reason for being was to provide agricultural credit to the small farmers in the northern part of the state.[4]

4. Brantley, *Banking in Alabama, 1816–1860*, 1:3, 7, 12; J. Mills Thornton III, *Politics and Power in a Slave Society: Alabama, 1800–1860* (Baton Rouge, 1978), 35–36, 40–51; Larry Schweikart, "Alabama's Antebellum Banks: New Evidence, New Interpretations," *Alabama Review*, July, 1985, pp. 202–21; David Abrams, "The State Bank of Alabama, 1841–45" (M.A. thesis, Auburn University, 1965). The primary sources on Alabama banking are found in the SBA Papers in ADAH. The ledger books of all of the branches, letterbooks of the Mobile branch, and directors' minute books of the branches are included in

The ensuing struggle to put the Huntsville bank out of business ended successfully for those who tried to give the state bank a near-monopoly. Other competitors still in business included the Tombeckbe Bank in St. Stephens and the Bank of Mobile, both established in 1818. The Bank of Mobile demonstrated consistent growth, but the Huntsville bank's charter was revoked in 1825 when it did not resume specie payments dating from the Panic of 1819, as it had agreed to do.

Arkansas, on the other hand, lacked chartered banks until 1836, when the legislature created the infamous Real Estate Bank, a property bank based on the concept established by the Consolidated Association of the Planters of Louisiana, although no evidence exists to indicate that the Arkansas legislators ever looked outside their own borders for a model. Lands given as collateral were in fact highly overvalued or even worthless. The bank's directors loaned liberally to friends and virtually without limit to themselves. The Real Estate Bank, like its sister institution, the Bank of the State of Arkansas, was utterly futile from its inception. The latter encountered little success in obtaining the specie it needed to open, partly because of the timing of its creation and the concurrent panic. Both would have struggled greatly even without the panic; with it, they suffered early death.[5]

Florida, Mississippi, and Tennessee pursued a slightly different approach to the creation of credit. During its territorial period, Florida's plantation owners succeeded in chartering the Bank of Florida at Tallahassee, opening in 1829. By 1832, however, it had become so unpopular with the territorial council, which found it too insensitive to public needs, that the territory chartered the Central Bank with the express purpose of putting the Bank of Florida out of business. The Central Bank accomplished its mission and bought out its competitor in 1833 only to find itself absorbed by the Union Bank shortly after the panic.[6]

---

the collection as well as the correspondence of the Mobile branch and the minute books of the Northern Bank of Alabama (chartered in 1852). For developments in this early period, see *Senate Journal*, 1839–40, pp. 10–11, 1841–42, p. 13; Andrew Armstrong to James Penn, October 17, 1835, January 7, 1837, Armstrong to Levi Woodbury, August 19, 1837, George Gaines to W. D. Stone, October 1, 21, 1836, all in Cashier's Letterbook, Mobile branch; Charles LeBaron to Andrew Armstrong, August 3, 1837, Correspondence, Mobile branch, all in SBA, ADAH. Also see William Scroggs, "The Financial History of Alabama, 1819–1860" (Ph.D. dissertation, Harvard University, 1907).

5. W. B. Worthen, *Early Banking in Arkansas* (Little Rock, Ark., 1906).

6. Marckhoff, "Development of Currency and Banking in Florida," pp. 118–23; J. E. Dovell, *History of Banking in Florida, 1828–1954* (Gainesville, Fla., 1955), 1–40.

Other Florida banks operating before the depression included the Bank of Pensacola, chartered in 1831, which had a substantial stake in the Alabama, Georgia, and Florida Railroad Company. More important was John Gamble's Union Bank, created in 1833 largely as a result of the tremendous political backing of the planters that Gamble commanded. Much of its popularity stemmed from the ease with which planters could obtain loans by mortgaging their lands. Florida soon relied on the territory's "full faith and credit" to support the banks. The legislature created a third financial giant in the 1830s—the Southern Life Insurance and Trust Company, which was also dominated by planters and received similar state support. Falling land prices brought the downfall of the Union Bank, whereas the Southern Life Insurance Company concentrated specifically on cotton speculation.

In Mississippi, the Bank of the Mississippi, chartered in 1809, "was the chrysalis of [the] demand for the promotion of Mississippi's virgin agricultural and commercial interests." Located at Natchez, the bank practiced conservative lending policies and established a record of financial integrity. In 1818, it became a state bank, in essence giving additional control to the state in exchange for its monopoly, but it maintained moderate lending levels and eventually triggered backlash by the growing population in areas other than Natchez as different segments demanded equal access to the bank's favors.[7]

Pressure for greater credit peaked with the incorporation of the Planters Bank in 1830 in direct violation of the legislature's covenant with the Bank of the Mississippi, whose directors decided to close rather than acquiesce in what they believed to be an inflationary flood. As this bank gradually liquidated and ceased its operations, finally closing in 1844, the Planters Bank commenced operations. Mississippi backed the bank's bond sales, as Florida supported its local banks' start-up operations. The Planters Bank received heavy criticism for its practices, with opposition cresting during the panic. Banking privileges were granted freely in the 1830s, and railroad banks spread like pollen across the state. None of these banks exceeded the giant Mississippi Union Bank in size or scope, with its huge capital stock of $15.5 million raised by the sales of bonds,

7. Charles Brough, "The History of Banking in Mississippi," *Mississippi Historical Society Publications*, 1960, pp. 317–40 (quotation on p. 318). For primary sources on Mississippi banking, see Journal of the Stockholders of the Bank of the Mississippi and Charter of the Bank of the Mississippi, Box 1, Folder 6, in BMC, MDAH.

for which the state pledged its credit. The bank had been designed to serve the agricultural sector and found its debt piling up when panic conditions slowed bond sales, a problem for which the state devised the less than honorable solution of repudiation of its bonds. Other banks had failed in droves, but the collapse of the Union Bank had particularly long-lasting effects for Mississippi, for it placed the state on the international defaulters' list. Mississippi would not obtain foreign credit until after the Civil War.[8]

Frontier trade led to the development of informal means of commercial credit and exchange in Tennessee. By 1807 the Nashville Bank had received a charter. Four years later, Hugh Lawson White founded the Bank of the State of Tennessee, in Knoxville. By 1816 the ever-increasing commerce had stirred a demand for more credit. Felix Grundy and Nashville merchants exerted pressure on the legislature to secure a branch of the BUS in Nashville.[9]

Those who already owned stock in the state bank opposed competition, so that the legislature levied an annual tax of fifty thousand dollars against any "foreign" bank or branch, although other Tennessee banks opened with the lawmakers' blessings. Rural areas tended to support the state bank, but White and his supporters had earned the enmity of commercial centers, which feared that a hodgepodge of notes would flood the cities. State bank supporters defused the antagonism by suggesting that the smaller rural banks join the state system as branches, thereby creating a more unified structure.

Recovering from the Panic of 1819, the state extended relief to debtors through the creation of a loan office, which became the second Bank of the State of Tennessee. Chartered in 1820, this state bank expected to be capitalized with the proceeds from sales of state land. Its loans

8. *Mississippi Senate Journal*, 1835, p. 21. Also see Robert Weems, "The Bank of the Mississippi: A Pioneer Bank of the Old Southwest, 1809–1844" (Ph.D. dissertation, Columbia University, 1952).

9. Thomas Abernethy, "The Early Development of Commerce and Banking in Tennessee," *Mississippi Valley Historical Review*, December, 1927, pp. 311–25; Claude Campbell, *The Development of Banking in Tennessee* (Nashville, Tenn., 1932); St. George Sioussat, "Some Phases of Tennessee Politics in the Jackson Period," *American Historical Review*, October, 1908, pp. 51–69; Claude Campbell, "Branch Banking in Tennessee Prior to the Civil War," *East Tennessee Historical Society Publications*, 1939, pp. 34–46; Larry Schweikart, "Tennessee's Antebellum Banks: Part I," *Tennessee Historical Quarterly*, Summer, 1986, and "Tennessee's Antebellum Banks: Part II," *ibid.*, Fall, 1986. Primary sources on the Bank of Tennessee are located in the Bank of Tennessee Collection, TLA.

quickly fell short of demand, however, and it became the target of political opposition from all sides.

By 1828 the original state bank had folded because White had taken a seat in the U.S. Senate and could not run the bank's affairs. Tennessee was thus left with one state bank and four major private banks: Yeatman, Woods and Company, the Bank of Nashville, the Farmers and Mechanics Bank in Nashville, and the Fayetteville Bank. Failure of the Bank of Nashville in 1826 signaled the beginning of hard times for Tennessee banking. Corruption surfaced in the state bank in 1830, and a series of investigations revealed substantial losses. The revelations concerning the state bank occurred at roughly the same time as Jackson's war on the BUS. Tennesseans thus faced a rapid contraction in banking services in the early 1830s. They reacted by calling a bank convention in 1832 that produced the new Union Bank of the State of Tennessee. The legislature had also moved in 1832 to force all banks in the state to be state chartered. Accordingly, competition diminished prior to the Panic of 1837.

A somewhat different view of the role of state government developed in the Atlantic coast states and Louisiana. Early Georgia credit needs were filled by the second Bank of the United States and private South Carolina banks until 1807, when the Planters Bank of the State of Georgia at Savannah received a charter. Using a surplus derived from property sales dating to the Revolution, public land sales, and payments collected by the state for the 1802 cession of its western lands to the United States, the Georgia state government sought to invest this money in a state bank and established the Bank of the State of Georgia in 1815. Georgia also chartered the Bank of Darien with a similar goal. In the case of each bank, the state owned stock and appointed some directors. Besides private bank operations, Georgia obtained a branch of the BUS in Savannah.[10]

Banks survived the Panic of 1819. No Georgia bank failed until 1832, but a shift to a hard-money policy became apparent after 1819. Still, the period between panics marked tremendous economic growth and expansion of agricultural production.

Banking developed in North Carolina largely from an attempt to retire the state's currency, which had been displaced by U.S. currency. Indeed,

10. Thomas Govan, "The Banking and Credit System in Georgia" (Ph.D. dissertation, Vanderbilt University, 1936), pp. 2–6. Also see Milton Heath, *Constructive Liberalism* (Cambridge, Mass., 1954), 205 and *passim*.

by 1809 "the currency of the United States was recognized as the lawful currency of the state." Two banks were chartered in 1804, the Bank of Cape Fear and the Bank of Newbern, with a combined capital of $450,000, to assist in purging state currency, but the attempt backfired because the banks realized by 1807 that they could use the state notes to pay their own debts, keeping the dearer bank notes and specie. North Carolina responded in 1809 by placing a tax on bank stock and limiting excessive note issues. A more significant development involved the creation of the State Bank of North Carolina with the expressed purpose of absorbing the existing banks. Charter provisions stipulated that no other banks could be chartered until the state bank charter expired in 1830.[11]

Existing banks, however, were reluctant to find themselves driven out of business. They managed to compromise with the legislature during 1814, when North Carolina sorely needed additional banking capital. Under the conditions of the compromise, the banks received charter extensions to 1830 in return for increases in their capitalization. Fears also arose over the effects posed by a state bank monopoly. Together, the three banks increased circulation, contributing to the inflation that accompanied the Panic of 1819. All banks survived the panic and were joined by a BUS branch at Fayetteville in 1825, but the panic's effects on debtors and the concurrent antibank sentiments ironically gave the banks new leverage. The banks contended that they had structured their loans to comply with their charter expirations and that charter extension would allow significant debtor relief.[12]

Disappointment with the State Bank of North Carolina provoked efforts to charter a new state institution. Initial attempts failed, but in 1833 the assembly finally created the Bank of the State of North Carolina. By the mid-1830s, North Carolina had a well-capitalized banking system with solid competition, but worry both about the effectiveness of the state bank and about its power lingered after the panic.

South Carolina established the Bank of South Carolina in 1801 as the state's first chartered financial institution, although the BUS had operated a branch in Charleston since 1792. Soon thereafter the State Bank

11. William Boyd, "Currency and Banking in North Carolina, 1790–1836," *Historical Papers, Trinity College Historical Society*, Series 10 (Durham, N.C., 1914), 68–71; William Blair, *A Historical Sketch of Banking in North Carolina* (New York, 1980 [1899]); Brantson Holder, "The Three Banks of the State of North Carolina, 1810–1872" (Ph.D. dissertation, University of North Carolina, 1937).

12. Blair, *Sketch of Banking in North Carolina*, 6.

of South Carolina began operation. For almost a decade these banks handled all of the state's credit allocation. In 1810, two more banks were added. Then, in 1812, the legislature chartered the powerful Bank of the State of South Carolina. Nine more banks received charters before the panic. Despite its highly solvent position, the Bank of the State proved as controversial as most state banks and faced charges of favoritism in lending and occasional corruption by the officers and administrators.[13]

Charleston held the state's banking monopoly until 1820, when cotton spread into the interior and took with it a demand for credit. The legislature feared that it would be unable to maintain control of any new banks created in the interior, and it hesitated to issue charters. As a result, interior areas often went begging for banking services until the 1830s, when growth in the inland populations and dissipation of the ill effects of the Panic of 1819 led to a change in the legislators' attitude. Prior to 1837, then, South Carolina had not experienced the rapid banking growth of other states, and its existing banks had been quite sound.

Virginia's banking history began with the charter of the Bank of Virginia in 1804. Operating from Richmond, the bank opened branches in several cities, a practice followed by the Farmers Bank of Virginia in 1812. By 1836, three more banks had opened for business, but Virginia sustained a policy of gradual development. Still, demand for loans had increased so much by 1836 that the state had to either grant more charters or increase the capitalization of existing charters. The legislature responded with a general banking law in 1837, then chartered the Exchange Bank of Norfolk and simultaneously provided for an increased capitalization of the banks in operation.[14]

Virginia subscribed to stock in every bank chartered in the state, thereby giving the state a greater ability to regulate financial activities, but it never outright dominated its banks. Whereas Mississippi and other southwestern states gained population, Virginia actually lost, and the pent-up demand for credit that struck booming plantation states never took root in Virginia after the 1830s. Railroads and other internal improvement schemes, which often led to the creation and expansion of

13. Alfred Smith, *Economic Readjustment of an Old Cotton State: South Carolina, 1820–1860* (Columbia, S.C. 1958), 193–202.

14. George Starnes, *Sixty Years of Branch Banking in Virginia* (New York, 1931), 30–31; Allen Gruchy, *Supervision and Control of Virginia State Banks* (New York, 1937); William Royall, *A History of Virginia Banks and Banking Prior to the Civil War* (New York, 1907).

banks in other states, were pursued seemingly without conviction in Virginia.[15]

The history of Louisiana banking began in 1804, when W. C. C. Claiborne established the Louisiana Bank, capitalized at $300,000 and allowed to increase its capital to two million dollars at a later date. Congress approved a New Orleans branch of the BUS soon after the Louisiana Bank appeared, and when its charter expired, the territorial legislature created two new banks to replace it, the Bank of New Orleans and the Planters Bank. The first survived the panic; the Planters Bank suspended operations in 1820.[16]

Plans to resolve a series of nagging state deficits, resulting from the depressed economy and traceable to the War of 1812, involved a proposal to charter a state bank called the Louisiana State Bank. Like other state banks, it would have had as one of its duties the lending of funds to the state. Existing private banks had ameliorated debts from the War of 1812 with loans, provoking complaints that interest rates were usurious and increasing support for a state institution. The proposal did not materialize until 1818, when the legislature chartered the Louisiana State Bank, capitalized at $2 million. Its five branches outside New Orleans plus its home office were compelled to let the state purchase $500,000 worth of stock and select six directors.

Louisiana came through the Panic of 1819 unscathed and entered a period of substantial growth in the 1820s. Dips in the economy were often accompanied by natural disasters, such as the yellow fever epidemic that struck New Orleans in 1819 and 1822, the floods that destroyed crops in 1823, and the drought that struck agriculture in 1827. Debtors' relief movements led to passage of a bill to create the Bank of Louisiana in 1824, including five rural branches. When the officers failed to lend at levels deemed adequate by the legislature, the senate, which was rural in orientation, tried to replace all the bank's officers and to enforce more favorable banking policies.

Perhaps the most significant pre-panic development was the charter-

15. Avery Craven, *Soil Exhaustion as a Factor in the Agricultural History of Virginia and Maryland, 1606–1860* (Gloucester, Mass., 1965), 130–34.

16. Green, *Finance and Economic Development*, 18; Edwin Davis, *Louisiana: The Pelican State* (Baton Rouge, 1959), pp. 672–67, 110–15; Joseph Menn, *The Large Slaveholders of Louisiana, 1860* (New Orleans, 1964), Chap. 1, *passim*; Henry Rightor (ed.), *Standard History of New Orleans* (Chicago, 1900), 579–83; Stephen Caldwell, *A Banking History of Louisiana* (Baton Rouge, 1935), 26–29, 32, and *passim*.

ing of the Consolidated Association of the Planters of Louisiana, a property bank capitalized at $2 million and backed by $2.5 million in mortgages. The capitalization depended on bond sales to attract specie, but slow and inadequate sales required the association to seek state support. Even then, the bank had trouble selling state bonds.[17]

Good cotton harvests and rapidly growing trade through New Orleans in the 1830s made the creation of still more banks necessary. The City Bank of New Orleans and the Canal Bank and their branches were created in 1831; the massive Union Bank was chartered in 1832. Capitalized at two million dollars, the Union Bank again used the technique of obtaining state bonds to sell for its capital base. Three more banks received charters in 1833, including another property bank, the Citizens Bank, and were also underwritten by state bond sales. By 1836 the state had chartered six more banks, all of which had failed or gone out of business by 1847.

Overall, then, southern states pursued a policy of large-scale state involvement, as in Alabama, Arkansas, Florida, Mississippi, and Tennessee, with either direct state participation in banking or state underwriting of bank bonds, or took a more laissez-faire attitude that featured a balancing of the market and regulation and provided for the chartering of banks without regard to their competitive impact on the state bank, as in the Carolinas, Georgia, Louisiana, and Virginia. Although the state participated to some extent in each case, the overall attitude toward state initiative suggests a simpler picture. The categories that differentiate one state from another were often less rigid than I have indicated here. Still, attitudes toward economic growth explain a great deal about policy results. Older commercial areas, with thriving businesses and established, more diversified economies, viewed it as dangerous to place economic control in the state's hands without any local market mechanisms to check and balance state authority. Newer areas, relying more heavily on agriculture, tended to see the state as the guardian of equality through its power to create banks and its regulatory authority. There can be no doubt that such state involvement occasionally stemmed from the tight money policies of existing banks, as in Mississippi, but a desire to take control away from one elite often meant that power was merely

17. See Emile Grenier, "The Early Financing of the Consolidated Association of the Planters of Louisiana" (M.A. thesis, Louisiana State University, 1938).

redistributed to a different elite, often on the pretext of compensating for a "lack of credit" or for some perceived market failure.

PRELUDE TO PANIC

The South, upon the eve of the Panic, had ninety-nine chartered banks, numerous railroad companies issuing money in their corporate names, and dozens of private bankers, factors, or other financial intermediaries performing a variety of banking services. Chartered banks held a total capital of $188 million, although capitalization statistics could be misleading, as we have seen in the cases of Arkansas and Florida. Although the view that specific unsound banking principles caused the financial disruption in 1837 was long ago rejected, it is true that the questionable practices of some southern banks did contribute. Local entrepreneurs followed many unsound banking practices, with some regularity in some cases. Loans to planters often involved fraudulent or unsubstantiated security: Florida bankers accepted slaves "simply enumerated as 'Tom,' 'Dick,' 'Sally,' or 'Mary,' with no further description," and the temporary transfer of slaves from one plantation to another characterized plantation borrowings. Specie requirements were sometimes fulfilled when the stockholders borrowed the proper amount of specie to commence operations and satisfy the law, then returned it after the bank's opening.[18]

Especially in the case of the states dominated by one or two agricultural crops, it was difficult to separate land speculation, agricultural production, and credit. Any planter hoped his land values would increase, and many were not averse to selling at a profit and moving on. Often the planter possessed no collateral other than land, slaves, or cotton. Planters "on the make" frequently lacked even slaves. Speculative spirits and wild optimism seemed especially evident in Alabama and Mississippi, where the "flush times" peaked in 1836, with land sales in the latter state alone totaling 3,267,299.33 acres. Climbing prices carried cotton from ten to twenty-one cents a pound in three years. Banks multiplied rapidly, trying to keep pace with the thirst for credit. Land companies sprang up all over the South. Some, like the New York and Mississippi Land Company, involved northerners. Bankers did not hesitate to join

18. McGrane, *Panic of 1837*, 26–27; Andrew Armstrong to Robert White, April 16, 1836, to E. L. Fourniquet, November 3, 1835, to Daniel Riggs, August 18, 1835, Cashier's Letterbook, SBA, ADAH.

in the speculation. The treasurer and an important financial backer of the Chickasaw Land Company, formed in 1834, was John Tindal, president of the Tuscaloosa branch of the State Bank of Alabama.[19]

Andrew Jackson's Specie Circular of July, 1836, which stipulated that only gold or silver would be accepted in payment for public lands, caused many of the speculating companies to request specie from their eastern financial backers. For decades historians routinely pointed to the Specie Circular as a major contributor to the panic, if not its cause. By and large, historians accepted the general assessments of the panic offered by contemporary observers. Peter Temin presented the first serious challenge to these earlier interpretations.[20]

Virtually all accounts of banking in the South during the Panic of 1837 followed the general framework offered by Bray Hammond, who contended that Andrew Jackson's political maneuvers from 1832 to 1836 had a significant, if not dominant, effect on the economy of the United States. Jackson, upset with the actions of the Bank of the United States and its president, Nicholas Biddle, set out to destroy the bank. He vetoed its recharter and successfully extracted the federal deposits from the bank in 1832, depositing them in state banks, known as the pets. Jackson also executed the distribution of the federal surplus to the various states in 1836 and, according to the theory, fueled an inflationary boom, especially in the West. There land prices rose because of speculators. In the absence of the restraining powers of the BUS, state and "wildcat" banks happily filled the craving for credit by issuing their own notes. Jackson brought the boom to a screeching halt by issuing the Specie Circular in 1836. The circular was designed to squeeze out inflation and restore solvency to the banking system. Just as Jackson had supposedly started an inflationary boom with the distribution of the surplus, he plunged the country into recession with the circular. In tandem

19. James Oakes, *The Ruling Race: A History of American Slaveholders* (New York, 1983), 37–68; Baldwin, *Flush Times of Alabama and Mississippi*, 60, 63; Dennis East, "New York and Mississippi Company and the Panic of 1837," *Journal of Mississippi History*, 1971, pp. 299–331; John Moore, *Agriculture in Ante-bellum Mississippi* (New York, 1958), 69–71; Andrew Armstrong to [?], October 27, 1836, to Levi Woodbury, April 19, 1837, George Gaines to F. S. Lyon, October 3, 1837, Cashier's Letterbook, SBA, ADAH.

20. East, "New York and Mississippi Company," 308–309; Mary Young, *Redskins, Ruffleshirts, and Rednecks* (Norman, Okla., 1961), 167. In Alabama there was great competition among the branches of the state bank for the funds from the surplus. See Andrew Armstrong to K. M. Whitney, November 28, 1835, SBA, ADAH.

with the boom inflation, the circular shocked the banking system by draining specie from the East to the outlying areas, but worse, the combination of the distribution and the circular produced disorder because the banks receiving the surplus were not those that held gold and silver.[21]

Peter Temin, on the other hand, has argued that Jackson's policies had little impact. No significant decrease in the ratio of bank reserves to liabilities occurred, although inflation occurred as a result of increased Mexican silver production. The silver went in turn to China for U.S. imports of Chinese goods and to Britain to pay for Chinese opium consumption. British investors buying American securities transferred specie to the United States, which the British scarcely missed because of their inward flow of Mexican specie. In 1836 the British government raised interest rates to stem the outward flow, increasing interest rates in the United States as well, causing the panic. In view of other nuances, Temin viewed Jackson's distribution of the surplus and the Specie Circular as relatively unimportant in the fluctuations of the Jacksonian economy.[22]

To understand fully the specific effects of the panic on southern banking, we must examine certain elements of Temin's hypothesis more closely. Although Temin admitted that a "boom psychology" existed in the 1830s, he rejected the idea that federal land sales caused higher cotton prices to be anticipated. Admittedly it took time to put new lands into production, but new lands meant that the volume produced by plantation owners could increase, and thus returns should increase rela-

21. See Lucius Polk to William Polk, December 22, 1833, TLA. For historians who accept the thesis that the Specie Circular caused or contributed to the panic, see Brough, "History of Banking in Mississippi," 317–40; Starnes, *Sixty Years of Branch Banking,* 86–90; and Claude Campbell, "Banking and Finance in Tennessee During the Depression of 1837," *East Tennessee Historical Society Publications,* 1937.

22. Peter Temin, *The Jacksonian Economy* (New York, 1969), 18–21; Andrew Armstrong to E. F. Conreggs, August 5, 6, 1836, to James Durro, September 28, 1836, Cashier's Letterbook, SBA, ADAH. For others in agreement with the "Soundness School," see Van Deusen, *The Jacksonian Era,* 105–106; Richard Hofstadter, *The American Political Tradition* (New York, 1948); Marvin Meyers, *The Jacksonian Persuasion* (Stanford, Calif., 1960); Walter Hugins, *Jacksonian Democracy and the Working Class* (Stanford, Calif., 1960), 45, 178–79; Sumner, *History of Banking,* 230–32; Oscar Handlin and Mary Handlin, *Commonwealth: A Study of the Role of Government in the American Economy: Massachusetts, 1774–1861* (New York, 1947), 179; George Taylor, *The Transportation Revolution* (New York, 1951), 340–42. Numerous American history texts, cited by Temin (pp. 21–22, n. 14), also accept this interpretation.

tively. New lands were not as subject to soil depletion as the older lands. Plantation owners, then, should have expected greater returns from federal land sales, whether or not the price of cotton went up absolutely.[23]

Temin also suggested that the Specie Circular arrested inflation because it "reduced the supply of land available to future purchasers." On the contrary, however, it only increased the price: it did not change the supply. Although "the diminution of land sales may have added to inflation," because a reduction in land purchases "freed money for other uses," one can be even more specific as to the actual expectations of the participants. If the marginal costs of paying specie in 1836 were passed on to farmers and plantation owners, their anticipations about opening new lands would have become bleak. Federal lands, in reality, would have been unavailable to any except the very wealthy, the most specie-hoarding speculators, or private bankers.[24]

THE SOUTH AND THE PANIC OF 1837: A NEW INTERPRETATION

Arkansas provides an interesting case study for testing the various hypotheses because it has several unique characteristics. First, the records of the Fayetteville branch of the State Bank of Arkansas included the decisions of the board of directors as well as the minutes, and so a thorough record for the years 1840–1846 (the dates of the only remaining letterbook) exists. Second, Arkansas had little specie initially and received virtually none from the distribution of the surplus revenue. As a result its specie is clearly identifiable, and so the ratios are easy to follow. Third, Arkansas was the state most likely to have available land in the late 1830s.[25]

23. Temin, *Jacksonian Economy*, 106–107. In addition it is possible, if one takes the evidence presented by Robert Fogel and Stanley Engerman (*Time on the Cross* [Boston, 1974]) regarding the efficiency gains associated with gang labor, that some economies of scale would also contribute to increased returns. William Parker, however, has expressed doubt that such economies existed. See William Parker (ed.), *The Structure of the Cotton Economy of the Antebellum South* (Berkeley, Calif., 1970).

24. Temin, *Jacksonian Economy*, 125. East, "New York and Mississippi Company," 327; Julia Smith, *Slavery and Plantation Growth in Antebellum Florida, 1821–1860* (Gainesville, Fla., 1914), 132–33.

25. Letterbook, Fayetteville Branch of the State Bank of Arkansas, AHC. Also see Ted Worley's articles: "The Arkansas State Bank: Ante-bellum Period," *Arkansas Historical Quarterly*, Spring, 1964, pp. 65–73; "Arkansas and the Money Crisis of 1836–1837," *Journal of Southern History*, May, 1949, pp. 178–91; and "The Control of the Real Estate Bank

Like the Real Estate Bank, the State Bank fell into difficulties almost from its inception. The board of directors had hoped to start operations soon after the bank was chartered in 1836, but Arkansas' portion of the federal surplus arrived late, and even then drafts on other banks representing this specie could be exchanged only for other notes. Bond sales slumped, and the bank's discounts soared. During these difficulties, there was a clear recognition that British investments—not presidential activities—caused the lack of increased specie circulation.

Arkansas papers viewed eastern speculators as supplementing the inflation, purchasing large lots at low prices and then selling at higher prices. When word of the revenue distribution reached Arkansas, the legislature anxiously attempted to qualify for the reception. The state had already pledged its share, $382,335, for the State Bank's capitalization, but little of the money circulated, and specie was almost impossible to obtain. Arkansas treasurer William Woodruff received, in Feburary 1837, two drafts totaling $95,583.83 from the U.S. treasurer, both drawn on Mississippi banks. He soon received a third draft of $50,000 and in April tried to cash all three in Mississippi. Although the Mississippi banks' cashiers claimed they could remit in specie, they instead offered to borrow the money from Arkansas and pay interest. Woodruff extracted only a promise from the Agricultural Bank of Mississippi to pay $100,000 in specie in July 1837.[26]

After Woodruff had returned to Little Rock, he learned that the Agricultural Bank had suspended specie payment. Shocked and surprised, he charged back to Natchez to demand the state's specie, without success. Meanwhile, as if the federal government were playing a cruel joke on Arkansas, another $95,583.83 in two drafts, drawn on the Planters Bank and the Agricultural Bank, arrived in Little Rock.[27]

By November 1837, frustrated directors of the Bank of the State of Arkansas had $90,000 in specie and $186,000 in other notes and drafts. Woodruff had come up empty in his search for gold and silver, and critics even accused him of siphoning off specie for his own purposes. Woodruff's

---

of the State of Arkansas, 1836–1855," *Mississippi Valley Historical Review*, December, 1950, pp. 403–26.

26. Little Rock *Arkansas Gazette*, August 2, May 1, 1836. See also Andrew Armstrong to Robert White, April 16, 1836, to Levi Woodbury, July 29, 1836, to James Durro, September 28, 1836, all in Cashier's Letterbook, SBA, ADAH.

27. *Arkansas Gazette*, November 14, 1837; *Report of the Treasurer of the State of Arkansas* (Little Rock, 1837).

tale, although the evidence is only impressionistic, suggests that, even if specie ratios did not increase in every bank, no bank willingly parted with any of its specie in vault.[28]

One crucial argument in Temin's thesis is that the public's willingness to hold bank notes in place of specie did not increase; as a result Temin concludes that the stock of specie must have increased. Once British interest rates rose, the specie flow ended. It should be noted that increased specie by itself does not adequately explain new note issues. Although it may account for the pre-panic inflation, there was a change in the character of reserve ratios for the period after that analyzed by Temin. The Arkansas Real Estate Bank began operations with $111,967 in specie and a circulation of $156,910, for an apparently solid R^1 reserve ratio (specie to notes) of 0.73 (see Table 1). By the beginning of 1838, its issues doubled, without any corresponding increase in specie, dropping the ratio to roughly half the previous level. Note issues grew at such a tremendous rate that May 1840 circulation had jumped to $759,000, with no noticeable increase in specie. By 1842, liabilities, although reduced, totaled $514,398 and specie only $47,602, for a ratio of 0.07! Such a drastic drop in the absolute amount of specie, the amount of notes and liabilities, and the relative reserve ratio in 50 percent of Arkansas's existing banks suggests that some banks were unwilling to curtail their note issues. A better clarification of the revisionist thesis is thus afforded by extending the analysis beyond 1838–1839.[29]

In short, Temin's basic foundation remains convincing and sturdy, but many specifics should be revised when dealing with the South. Federal land sales in the South did not retard inflation and may have spurred greater exchange in private and state lands as well as higher prices. Bankers tended to try to retain specie whenever possible, and some banks issued new notes despite falling specie levels, a phenomenon in contradiction to Temin's assertion that the specie level increased.

28. *Arkansas Gazette*, June 6, July 11, July 18, 1837. Also see Andrew Armstrong to [?], June 7, 1836, to Levi Woodbury, July 29, 1836, SBA, ADAH.
29. Temin, *Jacksonian Economy*, 22, 24; *Report of the Accountants Appointed to Investigate the . . . Real Estate Bank of Arkansas* (Little Rock, Ark., 1856), 4–5, 15. Of course, specie ratios were strong elsewhere before the panic. See Andrew Armstrong to Daniel Riggs, August 18, 1835, SBA, ADAH. Special thanks to Peter Temin for his suggestions regarding the Arkansas data (Temin to Schweikart, March 7, 1984).

Table 1. Reserve Ratio Statistics of Southern Banks, 1834–1838 ($ millions)

No. of Banks	Year	Loans and Discounts	Notes in Circulation	Deposits	Due Other Banks	Specie	Specie Notes (R¹)	Specie N÷D (R²)	R³	National Reserve Ratio
					Alabama					
1	1834	7.1	2.3	1.1	0.02	0.77	0.33	0.22	0.22	0.27
1	1835	10.9	5.4	2.2	0.55	1.2	0.22	0.14	0.13	0.13
3	1836	18.1	7.0	3.0	1.83	1.5	0.21	0.15	0.13	0.16
3	1837	26.0	7.5	5.6	2.39	0.79	0.10	0.06	0.06	0.20
2	1838	25.4	9.3	4.3	1.62	0.73	0.08	0.05	0.05	—
					Arkansas[a]					
1	1837	0.32	0.008	0.07	0.00	0.19	8.77	0.08		0.20
2	1837	—	0.165	0.18			0.88			
	1838[b]						0.80			0.23
					Florida					
2	1834	0.23	0.13	0.06	0.00	0.01	0.07	0.05	0.05	0.27
3	1835	1.82	0.50	0.22	0.18	0.24	0.48	0.33	0.26	0.18
5	1836	2.57	0.76	0.48	0.15	0.53	0.69	0.42	0.38	0.16
7	1837	3.44	0.70	0.43	0.20	0.17	0.61	0.53	0.26	0.20
6	1838	3.27	0.62	0.41	0.17	0.16	0.25	0.15	0.13	—
					Mississippi					
2	1834	9.89	2.13	1.87	0.68	0.35	0.16	0.08	0.07	0.24
2	1835	11.14	2.46	2.46	0.31	0.46	0.18	0.03	0.08	0.14

Table 1 (continued)

No. of Banks	Year	Loans and Discounts	Notes in Circulation	Deposits	Due Other Banks	Specie	Specie Notes (R^1)	Specie N&D (R^2)	R^3	National Reserve Ratio
9	1836	24.35	5.07	5.34	2.22	1.36	0.26	0.02	0.10	0.16
12	1837	29.32	7.48	4.71	3.04	0.96	0.12	0.07	0.06	0.20
11	1838	29.00	—	—	—	0.76	—	—	—	—
					Tennessee					
1	1834	3.39	2.53	0.11	0.18	0.06	0.02	0.02	0.02	0.27
3	1835	6.04	3.27	0.66	0.11	0.29	0.08	0.07	0.07	0.18
3	1836	9.86	5.20	1.51	0.39	0.25	0.04	0.03	0.03	0.16
3	1837	10.50	3.06	2.49	0.62	0.52	0.16	0.09	0.08	0.20
3	1838	11.20	2.62	1.50	0.66	0.59	0.22	0.14	0.12	—
					Georgia					
13	1834	7.89	3.69	1.00	0.49	1.8	0.49	0.36	0.34	0.27
13	1835	8.49	4.70	1.45	1.05	2.18	0.46	0.35	0.30	0.18
14	1836	15.45	7.94	3.29	1.07	2.60	0.32	0.23	0.21	0.16
20	1837	15.93	5.00	2.12	1.95	2.47	0.49	0.30	0.27	0.20
20	1838	15.70	7.46	2.79	2.41	2.66	0.35	0.26	0.21	—
					Louisiana					
5	1834	16.10	2.04	4.31	0.93	1.98	0.97	0.31	0.27	0.27
9	1835	34.50	4.72	6.79	3.35	2.53	0.53	0.21	0.17	0.18
16	1836	59.10	7.90	11.48	11.81	3.10	0.39	0.03	0.09	0.16
16	1837	55.59	7.55	7.42	9.13	2.72	0.36	0.18	0.11	0.20
16	1838	56.86	6.28	7.66	8.12	3.99	0.63	0.28	0.18	—

		North Carolina								
4	1834	2.33	0.95	0.32	0.26	0.25	0.26	0.19	0.16	0.27
3	1835	3.44	2.05	0.65	0.19	0.45	0.21	0.16	0.15	0.18
3	1836	5.76	3.31	1.38	0.26	0.88	0.26	0.19	0.17	0.16
3	1837	5.29	2.49	1.21	0.17	0.68	0.27	0.18	0.17	0.20
3	1838	4.57	2.27	0.75	0.18	0.70	0.31	0.23	0.21	—
		South Carolina								
1	1834	2.79	1.20	1.02	0.01	0.26	0.21	0.11	0.11	0.27
3	1835	5.22	3.39	1.71	0.08	0.91	0.26	0.17	0.17	0.18
7	1836	16.14	6.52	4.16	1.92	2.43	0.37	0.22	0.19	0.16
9	1837	15.10	4.45	3.49	0.69	1.32	0.29	0.16	0.15	0.20
11	1838	16.40	5.08	3.31	1.40	1.61	0.31	0.19	0.16	—
		Virginia								
4	1834	11.21	5.72	3.02	0.08	1.18	0.20	0.13	0.13	0.27
5	1835	14.60	9.18	4.23	0.45	1.55	0.16	0.11	0.11	0.18
5	1836	18.02	9.10	5.27	0.55	1.60	0.17	0.11	0.10	0.16
5	1837	15.90	7.18	2.90	0.54	1.36	0.18	0.13	0.12	0.20
5	1838	15.90	—	—	—	1.37	—	—	—	—

[a] Accounts refer to only one bank; data were too early to include circulation.

[b] Data are included for the Real Estate Bank.

Sources: (a) J. Van Fenstermaker, The Development of American Commercial Banking, 1782–1837 (Kent, Ohio, 1965), Tables B-1, B-2, B-7, B-6, B-16, B-21, B-25, B-26, B-28; (b) Individual bank reports made at varying dates in the year; House Executive Document 30, 25th Cong., 1st Sess.; House Executive Document 79, 25th Cong., 2d Sess.; House Executive Document 156, 25th Cong., 3d Sess.; House Executive Document 172, 26th Cong., 1st Sess.; House Executive Document 111, 26th Cong., 2d Sess.; House Executive Document 226, 29th Cong., 1st Sess.; House Executive Document 68, 31st Cong., 1st Sess.; House Executive Document 66, 32d Cong., 2d Sess.; House Executive Document 102, 33rd Cong., 1st Sess.; House Executive Document 82, 33rd Cong., 2d Sess.; House Executive Document 102, 34th Cong., 1st Sess.; House Executive Document 87, 34th Cong., 3d Sess.; House Executive Document 107, 35th Cong., 1st Sess.; House Executive Document 112, 35th Cong., 2d Sess.; House Executive Document 49, 36th Cong., 2d Sess.; House Executive Document 77, 36th Cong., 2d Sess.; House Executive Document 25, 37th Cong., 3d Sess.; House Executive Document 20, 38th Cong., 1st Sess.; Senate Executive Document 2, 37th Cong., 2d Sess.

PANIC CONDITIONS AND BANKERS' REACTIONS

Other evidence testifies to a long-term absence of specie over much of the South after the panic. Arkansas state bank directors who met to discuss possible further accommodations concluded, "It was inexpedient at the present time to make any further discounts." Two weeks later, the cashier, William M. Ball, summarized the opinion of the board of directors: "Much difficulty has signaled from the present disarrangement of the currency of the country on account of the recent dispersion of payments of the Banks [branches of the BUS], in addition to widespread reports prejudicial, not only to this institution but to the integrity, discretion and judgment of those whose duty it is to direct the same." The directors, indifferent to the special pleadings of friends and the "virulent reproaches of enemies," nevertheless deemed it "unwise, inexpedient and unsafe" to resume specie payments. They devised a compromise to alleviate some of the pressure by allowing people in Fayetteville (the location of the branch) to buy land with bank notes. Because the state had to pay the federal government in specie, the letterbook referred to state lands.[30]

Mobile and New Orleans were particularly low on specie. The cashier at the Mobile branch of the Bank of Alabama reported, "Prospects in New Orleans for procuring specie are . . . gloomy but a supply must be had on some terms, as our stock . . . is diminishing from 2 to 4000 dollars daily." Even before receiving word on the shortage in New Orleans, cashier Andrew Armstrong of the Mobile branch suggested to the president of the Commercial and Rail Road Bank in Mississippi that the monetary problems required "much caution and a curtailment instead of enlargment of operations." Specie was low everywhere, and one Charleston correspondent suggested trying to obtain gold from Havana.[31]

The continuing depression led bankers to try a variety of temporary measures, including delaying specie resumption, obtaining loans, issuing post notes, and dealing in cotton. The State Bank of Arkansas had fallen into such desperate straits by August of 1841 that it authorized cotton speculation to pay the interest on its capital stock, a solution that

30. Letterbook of the State Bank of Arkansas, January 3, 15, 1840, AHC.
31. George Gaines to [?], January 7, 1837, Andrew Armstrong to George Gaines, April 19, 1837, and to John Taylor, March 1, 1837, Cashier's Letterbook, SBA, ADAH; L. M. Niley to Farish Carter, May 29, 1837, Farish Carter Papers, SHC, UNC.

Alabama and Mississippi banks had already tried. Tennessee, Mississippi, and Alabama bonds suffered in New York markets. Cashiers extended themselves to keep the customers' paper from being rejected, and many banks allowed notes under protest or due for collection to be renewed. Mobile bankers even dispatched an agent to procure specie in Cuba. Everywhere the pressure revealed itself in the increasingly sharp exchanges between correspondents.[32]

Falling cotton prices and land values ruined a number of banks in several states that relied on mortgages for security. At least five major real estate banks conducted business before the panic: three in Louisiana, one in Florida, and the one in Arkansas. Only the Arkansas bank failed immediately, but the property bank concept was severely damaged, and many smaller property banks folded. After 1842, two of the Louisiana property banks had failed, Florida's Central Bank was absorbed by the Union Bank, and the Union Bank of Mississippi collapsed amid a flurry of repudiationist sentiment. No bankers had abandoned the idea of agricultural credit, but plantation loans secured by property or slaves, each with a value subject to substantial speculation, had to be balanced with short-term commercial loans and better specie reserves.[33]

During the boom period, many banks, whether the property or the

32. Letterbook of the State Bank of Arkansas, September 4, 1840, February 22, August 27, 1841, September 3, 1842, AHC; Andrew Armstrong to George Gaines, April 19, 21, to Levi Woodbury, June 8, 1837, George Gaines to Commodore Dallas, April 26, 1837, to Jonathan Emmanuel, April 26, 1837, to Levi Woodbury, April 30, 1837, to Robert Palfrey, April 22, May 6, 1837, to F. S. Lyon, October 3, 1837, all in Cashier's Letterbook; W. Pool to J. Hull, May 29, 1837, Correspondence, Mobile Branch, Minutes of the Montgomery Branch of the Board of Directors, February 19, 20, 26, 1839, March 1, 1840, Minutebook, Montgomery Branch, all in SBA, ADAH; Henry Ewing to S. R. Richards, July 14, 1839, to William Holmes, July 2, 1839, to Jacob Little, August 10, 1839, to H. Hogg, September 26, 1839, to [?] Bean, October 10, 1839, to A. O. Keyes, October 17, 1839, to P. Wallace, October 30, 1839, to W. W. Frazier, November 23, 1839, all in Bank of Tennessee Letterbooks, Record Group 47, Box 8, Vol. 16, TLA; Thomas Erskine to Samuel McCorkle, September 25, 1837, McCorkle Papers, Real Estate Banking Company of Hinds County Record Books, all in MDAH. Tennessee, it will be noted, did not lose specie, but the reason was apparently largely the management of the state bank by cashier Henry Ewing, who doggedly strove for increased efficiency. See, for example, Ewing to S. R. Richards, July 30, 1839, Bank of Tennessee Letterbook, Record Group 47, Box 8, Vol. 16, TLA. Also see depositions regarding collections in Record Group 47, Box 20, Folder 19, *ibid.*

33. George Green, "The Louisiana Bank Act of 1842," *Explorations in Economic History,* Summer, 1970, pp. 399–412. For the problems of property banks, see *Edward Boisgerard and John Delafield v. Samuel Neill,* Case 2650, 1842, and *Edward Boisgerard and John Delafield v. Abram McWillie,* Case 2654, 1844, both in Drawer 90, MDAH.

commercial variety, had sold their bonds in Europe. In cases where the state had issued its own bonds on behalf of banks, the state bonds found their way to Europe. The combined effects of the rising British interest rate, the sinking price of cotton, and domestic crop shortages forced New York banks to press their debtors and compelled Europeans to pressure the banks. Suspension of specie payments by New York banks initiated a chain of suspensions throughout the country. Businesses suddenly closed, companies failed, and farmers found it more difficult to market their crops. Southern financiers watched the New York market closely. Specie had been withdrawn from New York banks in substantial amounts prior to suspension—more than $650,000—but southern banks stood up well to the panic effects until the New York banks suspended. Once some southern banks had suspended, however, knowledgeable investors expected similar action by other banks. Richard Bolton, a land speculator involved in the New York and Mississippi Land Company, warned that most of the southwestern banks would follow the Agricultural Bank and Planters Bank of Mississippi in suspending specie payments. Others foresaw similar developments.[34]

Exceptional soundness had characterized most of the state and private commercial banks of the southern states on the Atlantic seaboard. Virginia's banks, for example, faced no danger of insolvency by themselves, but the threat posed by a specie drain to the North made southern suspension necessary. Not all types of banks were affected to the same degree. Property banks, which depended on land values to guarantee ultimate solvency, were extremely subject to fluctuations in land prices. Many state banks, especially in Alabama, Arkansas, and Mississippi, suffered critical wounds; the worst losses occurred in areas where the state either monopolized or dominated the banking field, and usually these losses resulted specifically from the tendency to issue too many notes. Except in Arkansas, where note issues soon swamped the state's banks, and in Florida, where there was a huge unexplained specie increase, the states of the New South had an R^3 ratio (notes, deposits, and notes due) of 0.06 in 1837. (Tennessee actually gained specie; see Table 1.) Without the competitive balance of the market in these states, "bank bills were

---

34. The Mobile branch of the Bank of Alabama, for example, had a correspondent relationship with John Delafield's Phenix Bank in New York. See Andrew Armstrong to E. L. Fourniquet, November 3, 1835, Cashier's Letterbook, William Wright to Armstrong, June 26, 1837, Correspondence, Mobile Branch, all in SBA, ADAH.

'as thick as Autumn leaves in Vallambrosa,' and credit was a franchise."
Likewise, banks closely tied to railroad or other internal improvement
companies found their securities too illiquid for conversion into cash and
suffered consequent distress. Where banking policies had been sound,
the panic was less disruptive. One South Carolina bank, the Bank of
Georgetown, avoided specie suspension entirely in 1837. In 1839 all
but five Charleston banks continued to redeem notes at par in specie.
Georgia banks suspended in 1837, but all except one had returned to
regular exchange by 1838.[35]

Even in some of the areas that suffered from large-scale banking disruptions, the liquidation of some banks had little impact on the economy
as a whole. Louisiana's value of trade and earnings from its cotton crop
reached new levels in 1839 and 1840, whereas private bankers took over
in states that had reacted by prohibiting banks. The 1846 state ban
against banking in Arkansas, which sought to eliminate all banks, actually ended the chief source of financial and monetary instability there—
the state-sponsored banks—and allowed private entrepreneurs to move
in. There were virtually no complaints about banking after the state institutions closed, and many of the private bankers saw their businesses

35. For primary sources on North Carolina during the panic, see the Raleigh *Register*,
March 28, April 11, 18, May 16, August 7, 28, September 25, 1837, January 29, 1838;
Fayetteville *North Carolina Journal*, April 20, 27, 1837; Henry Potter to Willie P. Mangum,
December 31, 1834, Charles L. Hinton to Willie P. Mangum, June 10, 1837, in Henry
Shank (ed.), *The Papers of Willie P. Mangum* (5 vols.; Raleigh, 1950–56), II, 265, 503–504;
P. Stewart to Duncan McLaurin, May 17, 1837, Duncan McLaurin to John McLaurin,
April 8, 20, 1837, D. McKenzie to Duncan McLaurin, February 19, April 26, 1840, all in
Duncan McLaurin Papers, DU; Thomas Ruffin to J. B. G. Roulhac, May 13, 1837, in J. G.
de Roulac Hamilton (ed.), *The Papers of Thomas Ruffin* (4 vols.; Raleigh, 1918–20), II, 69;
George Mordecai to Duncan Cameron, July 20, 1837, Andrew Kevin and Brothers to
Duncan Cameron, October 16, 23, December 18, 1839, Thomas Bennehan to Duncan
Cameron, February 13, 1840, J. W. Pegram to Duncan Cameron, October 28, 1839, all in
Duncan Cameron Papers, SHC, UNC; George Mordecai to Thomas Jones, April 11, 1840,
Joseph Jones Papers, DU; William A. Graham to William Gaston, August 17, 1841,
William Gaston Papers, SHC, UNC; William Haygood to Martin Van Buren, August 15,
1840, in Elizabeth McPherson, "Unpublished Letters from North Carolinians to Van
Buren," *North Carolina Historical Review*, April, 1938, p. 134; Baldwin, *Flush Times*, 1.
The second suspension of 1839 and the subsequent depression struck Georgia banks more
severely; only thirteen of twenty-four survived to 1844. One Tennessee banker was irate
over a report that his healthy bank had failed (Henry Ewing to [?] Sylvester, September
20, 1839, Bank of Tennessee Letterbook, Record Group 47, Box 8, Vol. 16, TLA). One
North Carolina bank had no trouble because it was located next to a mine. Observers
urged bankers to take advantage of their proximity to mines. See L. M. Niley to Farish
Carter, May 29, 1837, Farish Carter Papers, SHC, UNC.

survive even the war. Similarly, in Florida the failure of the "big three banks" (the Bank of Pensacola, the Union Bank, and the Southern Life Insurance and Trust Company) elicited a legislative response of repudiation and exceedingly strict regulation. Only one failure of the three actually related to the panic, and none went out of business before 1843, but the result was the same as in Arkansas. Private bankers or agencies of banks from nearby states filled the vacuum.[36]

REINTERPRETING THE MONETARY DATA

The South's experience of the panic requires further explanation. Traditional groupings of monetary data by region, which place Louisiana in the southwestern region with Arkansas, Alabama, Mississippi, Tennessee, and Kentucky and group Virginia, North Carolina, South Carolina, Georgia, and Florida in the southeastern region, have been a source of chronic confusion. Although Louisiana had a great deal in common with the New South in its available land, settlement, growth rates, and percentage of kind in export crops, several characteristics nevertheless made it unique. The most pertinent were its commerce, business structure, and experience factors (and later, its active Whig party). In other words, Louisiana should more properly be grouped with the Atlantic coast states—Virginia, the Carolinas, and Georgia—to illuminate the commercial influences there. Again, I term this category the Old South. Florida, on the other hand, had more in common with the Gulf coast and Southwest, and so it deserves to be placed in the New South with Alabama, Mississippi, Arkansas, and Tennessee. Reserve ratios for these groupings, adjusted for the omission of Kentucky and Texas, appear in Tables 1 and 2.[37]

Mississippi, although experiencing specie increases until the Specie Circular, lost a substantial amount—$400,000—of specie from 1836 to 1837. Its banks continued to issue notes freely, however, plunging its R^1

36. Green, *Finance and Economic Development*, 26; Worthen, *Early Banking in Arkansas*, 114–23; Marckhoff, "Development of Currency and Banking in Florida," 109–23.

37. Temin, *Jacksonian Economy*, 75; J. Van Fenstermaker, *Development of American Commercial Banking* (Kent, Ohio, 1965), 186–247. This grouping calls into question Jay Mandle's analysis of the postbellum South, in which the plantation states were viewed as a subregion of the South. See "The Plantation States as a Sub-region of the Post-bellum South," *Journal of Economic History*, September, 1974, pp. 736–38.

Table 2. Reserve Ratio Averages, 1834–1837 ($ millions)

Year	R^1 Specie: Notes	R^2 Specie: Notes & Deposits	R^3 Notes, Deposits, and Deposits Due	National Reserve Ratio
		Old South		
1834	0.42	0.22	0.20	0.27
1835	0.32	0.20	0.18	0.18
1836	0.29	0.15	0.15	0.16
1837	0.31	0.19	0.16	0.20
		New South		
1834	0.14	0.16	0.09[a]	0.27
1835	0.19	0.13	0.13	0.18
1836	0.30	0.15	0.16	0.20
1837	0.24[a]	0.16	0.24	0.20[b]

[a] Excludes Arkansas.
[b] Adjusted for Arkansas.
Sources: Van Fenstermaker, *Development of American Commercial Banking*, appendixes; Brantley, *Banking in Alabama*, Appendix; (Arkansas) *Report of the Accountants.*

reserve ratio to less than half its 1836 level. Although its deposits shrank only marginally, both its R^2 (notes, deposits, and specie) and R^3 ratios also remained low, and R^3 declined by 40 percent. Tennessee's reserve ratio increased, and its specie nearly doubled: the state's banks cut their note circulation to the extent that the R^1 increased four times and the R^2 threefold. These calculations reveal that there were several ways for banks to increase their reserve ratios. Banks could gain specie, as happened in Tennessee and Florida, or they could reduce circulation, as was more often the case. Aggregate data such as those used by Temin do not address the dynamics of banks' operations, nor do they readily reveal the procedures that a state's banks followed. The paths followed by states' banks fit the Old South–New South dichotomy well, however: the New South used the increase in specie to create more loans and notes (and to increase its reserve ratios), whereas Old South states contracted emissions to match dropping specie levels.

Although no Old South bank improved its actual specie reserves, Virginia, Georgia, and North Carolina achieved more soundness in their reserve ratios, and Georgia improved in all three categories. In the New South, however, each state increased its loans. Arkansas, Alabama, and Mississippi, the three areas in which new lands were most available, did so in defiance of a specie drain. These three states, in fact, saw their R^1 ratios halved, and the latter two had almost a 50 percent decline in their R^3 ratios as well. As a result, whereas Old South banks scrambled to improve their ratios, reducing their circulation to keep up with their specie reductions, the New South took advantage of the specie obtained through the circular to issue new loans. Thus the inflation, which Temin attributed to purchases redirected after the shutoff of federal land sales, appears to have been caused by the note issue based on new specie obtained because of the circular.

If we apply the investment data presented in Table 14, and assume that most loans went for land, it becomes clear that a significant modification of both the traditional and revisionist approaches is needed, because, with some important qualifications, there was a specie flow to only certain parts of the West, that is, to the states with available land. Florida and Tennessee both improved their specie reserves. If, as Temin argued, specie levels in the United States increased between 1831 and 1838, then clearly money was leaving the South, especially Alabama, Mississippi, and the Old South.[38]

Not all bankers recognized this trend immediately. Some, such as the usually shrewd officers of the Bank of Charleston, ascribed the difficulties directly to the cotton fluctuations rather than to changing specie levels. The reaction was the same, however. When the first depression ended, banks immediately sought to restore their reserve ratios. During the subsequent depression these banks attempted to issue more notes to offset specie increases, but when a decline in the importation of silver occurred in the late 1830s, the banks should have been able to reduce note issues and still maintain their reserve ratios. Not all southern banks did so, but as might be expected, the major banks in areas where the specie drop would first be felt reduced their issues.

PUBLIC CONFIDENCE: ALABAMA AND TENNESSEE AS CASE STUDIES

Apparently the shrinking reserve ratios in Arkansas, Alabama, and Mississippi after 1837 were to be explained by more than just new note

38. Temin, *Jacksonian Economy*, 71.

issues. Much stemmed from a change in public confidence. The public, less willing to hold money in the form of bank notes, exhibited an overall loss of confidence in the entire banking system.[39]

Alabama, for example, turned its legislative efforts to restoring normalcy after the 1837 runs. Lawmakers, most of them planters, crowded into Tuscaloosa boardinghouses and inns to seek solutions, which understandably contained numerous quick fixes, some of which had merit. Some observers suggested that the state should aid individuals and enable them to retire their embarrassing debts. Governor Clement Clay argued that bank money had become "*too abundant* and *too cheap*," but inasmuch as banks were hopelessly interrelated, he urged leniency, even to the point of altering the law that required banks that suspended to forfeit their charters. The state's banks had contracted their money supply by more than one million dollars and redeemed it in specie. Consequently, the public held a substantial amount of specie in Alabama. A report to the Alabama senate in 1837 showed the total capital of the banks in the state to be $10,141,846, with the state banks' R^1 ratio to be 9:1 (0.11), whereas the private banks had a ratio of 3.5:1 (0.28).[40]

Eliminating the specie drain in Alabama involved following the course chosen by other states: simply legalizing the suspensions and extending the time for payment of debts owed the banks. The assembly also passed a bond issue of five million dollars, however, with the state largesse to be deposited in the five state banks. There the bonds would be sold to bolster the capital of the banks. Success depended on the scheme's critical assumption that the specie drained from the banks would be returned as payment for the bonds, yet there existed no reason why local citizens should have given up good money (specie) for bad (bonds) when,

39. Hugh Rockhoff, "Money, Prices, and Banks in the Jacksonian Era," in Robert Fogel and Stanley Engerman (eds.), *The Reinterpretation of American Economic History* (New York, 1972), 448–58, esp. 452, 454; Susan Lee and Peter Passell, *A New Economic View of American History* (New York, 1979), 122. For the activities of the Bank of Charleston, see the annual *Proceedings of the Stockholders* (Charleston, 1841–48).

40. *Alabama House Journal*, 1837, p. 5; "Consolidated Statement of the Bank Reports, June 13, 1837," in Brantley, *Banking in Alabama*, appendix, I, 293. Rumors of corruption among the directors and official swindling filled the air. See *Alabama Senate Journal*, 1837 (Annual), pp. 17, 44; *Alabama House Journal*, 1837 (Annual), pp. 30, 75, 78, 105, 106, 130, 155, 170; Harrison to Andrew Armstrong, June 26, 1837, John Campbell to Arthur Bagby, January 1, 1837, C. S. Aces to Bagby, January 1, 1837, Thomas Mays to Bagby, January 6, 1837, Correspondence, Mobile branch, SBA, ADAH; *Abstract of the Journal of the Joint Investigation Committee*, reprinted in Brantley, *Banking in Alabama*, II, 13–14.

had they actually wanted to purchase bonds, they could have used state bank currency.

Using the new bond issue, Alabama bankers issued more notes but remained intractable when it came to parting with specie. Consequently some reserves grew, and the Tuscaloosa branch reported a specie-to-circulation ratio of almost 50 percent as of November 7, 1837. Other branches were not nearly as sound. The Decatur branch had only $9,800 in specie to cover four million dollars' worth of assets. Its R^3 ratio dropped from 0.08 on November 1, 1836, to 0.006 on June 1, 1837. A similar nose dive in the general ratios of the rest of the state system occurred. Even with the solid Tuscaloosa branch, altogether the state bank and its branches saw their collective reserve ratios drop from an unimpressive 0.09 in 1836 to 0.05 by mid-1837. Private Alabama banks held one-third of all the specie in the state. There was, in essence, a specie drain from the weaker branches of the state bank to the stronger ones and from the stronger branches of the state bank to the strongest private bank, the Bank of Mobile. The only solution to the specie drain, as the Alabama commissioners saw it, was to "purchase exchange based on shipments of cotton."[41]

Private Alabama banks, especially the Bank of Mobile, had also allowed certain directors or friends to have access to large loans, but when an investigating commission inspected the Bank of Mobile, its members found the bank in favorable condition overall. A private competitor in Mobile, the Planters and Merchants Bank, had started the panic in a strong position (0.63 ratio) but had lost two-thirds of its specie while more than doubling its note issue. Rapid and dramatic specie losses were common in commercial Mobile, as seen in the case of the state bank's branch there, which saw its specie reserves decline by more than $200,000.[42]

By January, 1839, Mobile banks had resumed specie payments, much to the relief of farmers who had suffered under the high discount rates and state competition. Alleged corruption in the state system rapidly surpassed the depression as a major source of concern for Alabama citi-

41. Brantley, *Banking in Alabama*, II, 21; *ibid.*, Appendix, "Exhibit of the State and Condition of the Banks of the State of Alabama," November 1, 1836, June 1, 1837, p. 294. The figures given by the commissioners vary somewhat from those given by Fenstermaker. The data in R^3 for 1836 and 1837 are from these reports.

42. *Ibid.*, appendix.

zens until a second suspension buffeted them in Feburary, 1839. Not all banks suffered during the suspension: the Huntsville branch had almost twice as much specie as it had notes, and its bills circulated at a premium; in addition, the Tuscaloosa branch continued its strong showing. Legislators lost patience with the banks and passed a law setting July 1, 1841, as a deadline for banks' resumption of specie payments. Yet prospects for resumption were not bright. Elections of new bank officers in 1840 led to the release of reports that the Tuscaloosa branch had only $7,000 in specie, and public confidence plummeted. Attempts to borrow $100,000 from the Mobile branch failed. Soon other branches that had attempted partial resumption abandoned such efforts.

The Alabama papers reflected public awareness of these developments. David Hubbard, an astute Alabama congressman, pinned the blame for the panic directly on the Bank of England and its need to stem the specie flow from that country. Hubbard also cited conditions in England as responsible for the drop in the price of cotton in May 1840. He was not alone. The influential *Flag of the Union* likewise asserted that the price of cotton was "fixed" in England. Its editorial asked, "PLANTERS HOW DO YOU LIKE IT?" Such observations tend to support the public-confidence thesis.[43]

Cotton speculations, meanwhile, proved ruinous to the state bank system. The weaknesses of Alabama's system had been exposed by the panic; they were not caused by it. Bad banking policies had cracked under the pressure of the panic, but the state did not repudiate its foreign debts. Moreover, many of the uncollected loans could be repaid when general prosperity returned.

Whereas Alabamians began to regard their state bank as a source of disruption, Tennesseans blamed the inflation on wildcat banks and began to call for a state bank to regulate the currency. Tennessee banks had curtailed note issues. The Union Bank of Nashville cut its circulation by more than one million dollars in less than four months. To offer relief the bank accepted notes from banks in both Mississippi and Alabama.

Although the two major Tennessee banks remained solvent, they faced charges that they had given a few select commission merchants their business, to the detriment of local planters and farmers. A legislative in-

43. *Flag of the Union*, March 25, May 13, 1940. Also see Schweikart, "Alabama's Antebellum Banks."

vestigation found only that public mistrust of many bills required banks
to do business only with known agents of high credit standing. The legislature also heard from bankers, however, who claimed to be laboring
under a heavy debt to eastern banks. Flows to the East became unbal-
anced; in 1839 the Bank of Tennessee informed a customer that it had
ceased checking "on any Eastern point" and held notes "until something
can be procured from some other source." Given Tennessee's increase in
specie and its banks' reserve ratios, either the bankers did not understand their situation or, more likely, they delayed payment in specie until the last possible moment. Henry Ewing, cashier of the Bank of Tennessee, stated flatly in a letter to a customer that no bank officer "could
become y[our] agent in gaining specie from any Bk. in this state." Moreover, the bank "cannot engage in buying and selling any Bk. notes."
Tennessee chartered a new state bank to smooth the disruptions by in-
jecting money into the economy through investments in internal improvements, but Tennessee gave its bank the diametrically opposed
goals of maintaining a sound currency and of furnishing financial relief to
the citizenry. This approach to reform was hasty and ironic, because
Tennessee had specie reserves and reserve ratios that were growing and
improving proportionally faster than in any other southern state except
Florida.[44]

Specie resumption in January, 1839, brought a return of confidence
and an end to hoarding. Another flood of gold and silver into the state
ensued. October's resuspension temporarily halted this flow, and a general resumption lagged until 1843. Since the outset of the panic, Tennessee had followed the path chosen by Alabama and had resorted to
state action. Tennessee had gone this route once before, and in both
cases the quality of the notes was extremely low. Public confidence had
resulted in greater reliance on banks of known quality. Reaction by the
state legislatures did little to change public perceptions.

States of the Old South responded to the panic with considerably less
alarm. Private banks in states of the Old South received their share of
criticism, but their reductions in circulation quickly stabilized their
positions. North Carolina and Virginia actually improved their ratios

44. Henry Ewing to Jacob Little, August 10, 1839, to H. Hogg, September 26, 1839,
to [?] Bean, October 10, 1839, to W. W. Frazier, November 23, 1839, all in Bank of Tennessee Letterbook, Record Group 47, Vol. 16, TLA. Also see Schweikart, "Tennessee's Antebellum Banks" (parts 1 and 2).

from 1837 to 1838 (only North Carolina's R^2 ratio suffered a 0.01 decline). Georgia and South Carolina contracted their notes in circulation
by almost two million dollars each. Only Louisiana did not drastically
reduce its circulation over the same period, although it did decrease its
deposits by $4 million (see Tables 1 and 2).

The depression itself dragged on until 1843, by which time legislatures had tried a variety of remedies to prevent another such panic
from occurring, or to punish banks for suspending in the first place, or
both. Many of the states had antisuspension laws on the books at the
time of the panic or had enacted stay laws suspending debt collection
until conditions returned to normal. In some cases, these laws relieved
debtors of paying in specie until the banks themselves resumed specie
payments or until the usual rules of debtor-creditor relationships again
were in force. In the Old South the panic generated political controversy. Hard-money men of all political persuasions called for sound
banking laws. Responses varied in degree and diversity of style, and
regulation sparked heated battles in the state legislatures. Public confidence in banks of the Old South never dipped to levels as low as those in
Alabama and Tennessee, where the state bank offered a clear target.
Still, the public seemed less confident in the systems backed by the
state than in the smaller private institutions.[45]

SMALL-NOTE ISSUES AS A RESULT OF THE PANIC

One of the most immediate and noticeable results of the panic was the
severe shortage of small coin. The most mundane daily transactions became an exercise in credit and discounting. Virginia, Tennessee, Louisiana, and Mississippi had laws against the issue of notes under five dollars
as of 1832. Although Georgia permitted such issues, it tried to force
them out of existence with incremental taxes. When taxation failed,
Georgia also passed a prohibition law in 1832. The problem of small note
issues among individuals as well as businesses, companies, or towns not
only persisted since the state's inception but spread during the panic.
Increasingly tough penalties on such issues evidently inspired neither
fear nor concern in practitioners. From 1837 to 1841, small notes so

45. Schweikart, "Banking in the American South," chaps. 2 and 3, presents a more
detailed treatment of the regulatory results of the panic. For the effects of stay laws, see
Peter Coleman, *Debtors and Creditors in America: Insolvency, Imprisonment for Debt,
and Bankruptcy, 1607–1900* (Madison, 1974).

swamped the state that merchants refused to receive them. Business threatened to come to a halt generally. Individual city authorities took over by issuing their own bills based on city credit and made them receivable for taxes. Such temporary solutions kept the gears of commerce lubricated until 1842, when the legislature permitted some banks to issue notes in denominations up to four dollars.[46]

Generally, where no merchants, cities, or state governments offered a solution that suited local citizens, the people merely ignored the law. Shinplasters became a way of life. In Virginia, local small bills grew so scarce that the Cohens of Baltimore filled the void with their own notes.

Unaccounted currencies, especially small-note issues, played an extremely important role in the antebellum southern economy but have defied attempts at measurement or quantification. It was a crime to issue such bills in many southern states, and they were driven out of existence by the National Bank Act. They differ from state bank notes, however, in that only fragmentary evidence about them remains, in the collections of numismatists. Transportation companies of all sorts—bridges, toll roads, ferry companies, and municipal enterprises—issued token currency, which is some of the most easily traced. Roland Faulkner estimated that more than fifty million pieces were issued. He found a single private collection with four thousand separate types of coins in it. Georgia chartered 150 "potential currency-issuing organizations" between 1810 and 1866, and more than fifteen hundred varieties of currency of this type circulated in the state. In addition to the private corporate issues, both cities and counties issued scrip in Mississippi, North Carolina, and Tennessee. Companies, too, printed notes that entitled the holder to payment in merchandise. Such currency proved quite popular in southern railroad companies, where it could be exchanged for transportation. Florida, without chartered banks of its own, relied heavily on unaccounted currencies for its circulating medium.[47]

46. Govan, "Banking and Credit in Georgia," 30–32. The Milledgeville city council authorized printing $4,000 in change bills but did not announce terms of payment. See James Bonner, *Milledgeville: Georgia's Antebellum Capital* (Athens, Ga., 1978), 132.

47. Richard Timberlake, Jr., "The Significance of Unaccounted Currencies," *Journal of Economic History,* December, 1981, pp. 853–66; Robert Cornely and Claude Murphy, *Georgia Obsolete Currency: A Checklist* (N.p., 1962), 14, foreword; Neil Carothers, *Fractional Money* (New York, 1967 [1930]), 95–97, 193, 343; Roland Faulkner, "The Private Issue of Token Coins," *Political Science Quarterly,* 1901, pp. 320–24. Timberlake concluded that the unaccounted moneys were the "monetary equivalent of astronomical

Small notes moved to the center of the political stage during the 1830s. Related to the debate over small notes, and in some cases at the heart of it, was the urge among some Jacksonian metallists "to purge the currency of small bank [and, of course, nonbank] notes and replace them with gold and silver coins." At the root of this movement lay an even more fundamental disagreement regarding the nature and purposes of a nationalized banking system itself. It is well known that many antebellum money theorists regarded only gold and silver as representing true money. Not all Jacksonians accepted this premise, but those who did—Thomas Hart Benton being one of the best known—were outspoken and influential. According to this theory, banks, if they were permitted to do so, would substitute paper money for specie, driving specie out of circulation and replacing it with paper until marginal banks collapsed under a burden of worthless notes. Banks therefore sought to prohibit small-denomination notes to lure specie into circulation, supplemented by the advantage of "nationalizing" the monetary system through the minting of U.S. coin. Large transactions might still be carried out through the use of bills, but the general circulating currency would be specie.[48]

Democrats controlling state legislatures tried to eradicate small-note issues, as in Georgia's case. In other states, Whig-Democrat coalitions attained the goal of prohibition, Whig votes being secured with promises to stabilize the money supply. Arkansas prohibited notes under five dollars, and Alabama forbade the circulation of foreign currency under five dollars. Individual charters in other states contained similar provi-

---

'black holes,'" and as a result, "the apparent decline in the velocity of money during the nineteenth century is seen simply as a mistake in accounting" ("Unaccounted Currencies," 17). For an interpretation of the specie standard that differs from Timberlake's, see Richard Sylla, "Monetary Innovation in America," *Journal of Economic History*, March 1982, pp. 21–30.

48. Martin, "Metallism, Small Notes, and Jackson's War with the B.U.S.," 227–47 (quotation on p. 228). Richard Rimberlake argued that "a consciously directed central bank policy was incompatible with adherence to metallic standards" ("The Specie Standard and Central Banking," 319). For views of money by Jackson's contemporaries, see Daniel Raymond, in Ernest Teilhac, *Pioneers of American Economic Thought in the Nineteenth Century* (New York, 1936), 22; John Taylor, Albert Gallatin, Tench Coxe, in Virgil Wilhite, *Founders of American Economic Thought and Policy* (New York, 1958), 212–13, 336–37, 354–64; John McVickar, Jacob Cardozo, Willard Phillips, and Francis Walker, in Joseph Dorfman, *The Economic Mind in American Civilization* (New York, 1946), II, 516–52, 554, 585–91, 749–51; Jacob Hollander (ed.), *Minor Papers on the Currency Question, 1809–1823, by David Ricardo* (Baltimore, 1932), 146; Benton, *Thirty Years' View*, I, 187.

sions. Yet these Democrat-sponsored successes never went past the state level. More grandiose national attempts to limit or eliminate bank paper failed. Both movements, however, represented a deeper, more important goal of national monetary control. Destruction of the BUS was only half the battle; the real aim was to gain control over the state's power to charter banks that could issue notes. It was a small step from the elimination of small notes to the elimination of all state bank notes.[49]

JACKSONIAN POLICY IMPLEMENTATION
AND BANKERS' RESPONSES

Some specific reactions to the panic manifested themselves in public policy. Care must be taken, however, not to ascribe to the panic effects traceable to other causes. In view of the widespread allegations of corruption in the Arkansas and Alabama banking systems, for example, the regulatory systems may have been so poorly designed that large-scale disasters were likely even without the disruptions of the panic. The same can possibly be said of banking in Mississippi and Florida. Moreover, prohibition, invoked in Arkansas and virtually in effect in Florida until 1853, was *not* a type of regulation but rather the admission of regulation's failure. There would in any case have been efforts to control officers whose fast fingers or flitting quill pens relieved their employers of vault cash or subsequently to punish the culprits when the sheriff apprehended them in a blaze of civic glory. Such illegal activities were no fault of policy responses to the panic. Bank statutes had been continuously redefined and loopholes had been progressively eliminated since the birth of each state's system; the panic merely instilled in some people a greater willingness to take risks because the incentives changed. Reginald McGrane reported, in his work on the depression, a number of criminal escapades involving hundreds of thousands of dollars. In 1839, $23,000 in notes were stolen from the Bank of Darien, Georgia, for which president Anson Kimberly ordered new notes issued, and the Columbia branch of the Bank of Tennessee was robbed of $28,000. Other instances of fraud or theft occurred, so that the list could be amended or extended, but perhaps the most unusual of the escapades was the hoax

49. The Jacksonians' views on banking policy *before* the panic are seen in Amos Kendall to Andrew Jackson, November 20, 1829, II-L-1, Box 1, File 6, TLA; Jennings, *Nine Years of Democratic Rule*, 47. For small-note laws, see Sumner, *History of Banking*, 248–52, 333.

perpetrated by Joseph "Shocco" Jones. This North Carolinian swept into Mississippi in 1839 masquerading as a Treasury Department agent empowered to collect deposits of the federal government that had been placed in pet banks. He also posed as an agent of the Bank of Cape Fear, North Carolina, who had packages of money to deposit. On the basis of the reputation he generated with his "money," Jones extracted a loan from the Real Estate Bank of Columbus, Mississippi. Within a few months it became clear to everyone that Shocco Jones was a swindler whose relish of a practical joke exceeded his interest in profits. Jones's antics contributed to the collapse of the Real Estate Bank.[50]

DAILY BANKING OPERATIONS IN
THE ANTEBELLUM PERIOD

Shocco Jones and his ilk were exceptions, not the rule. Most bankers plied their trade honestly and conscientiously. It is helpful to understand their activities and responsibilities. Henry Ewing of the Bank of Tennessee epitomized the efficient cashier. He checked the bookkeeping techniques of his branch cashiers, notifying them of errors and suggesting improvements. In a letter to A. G. Hayes, Ewing instructed Hayes that the "practice at his [bank] has been uniformly to charge in [credit] int[erest] to int[erest] a/c [account]." The result was that the balance "is as often on the de[bit] as the [credit] side of our bank statement." Charging credit interest to the interest accounts, Ewing explained, was done in order "to show the true state of that a/c." To another cashier, Ewing delivered a somewhat pointed criticism. He found "upon examination of your statement that you have omitted entirely one side of the form proscribed by the Constitution." Ewing reminded the cashier that "the information required by that side of the statement is frequently very important, particularly the list of [bank] notes on hand." Sending the proper form, Ewing advised, "You will in the future pursue it."[51]

50. McGrane, *Panic of 1837,* 137; Bonner, *Milledgeville,* p. 51; Henry Ewing to H. Hogg, September 26, 1839, Bank of Tennessee Letterbook, Record Group 47, Vol. 16, TLA; Edwin Miles, ed., "Francis Leech's 'The Mammoth Humbug'; or, The Adventures of Shocco Jones in Mississippi, in the Summer of 1839," *Journal of Mississippi History,* January, 1959, pp. 1–39.

51. Henry Ewing to A. G. Hayes, n.d. (1839), Bank of Tennessee Letterbook, Record Group 47, Series 5, Vols. 15 and 16, TLA; Ewing to S. D. Mitchell, August 10, 1839, *ibid.*

In this case, although the cashier's faulty bookkeeping was not costly, it had led to confusion, as fifty dollars was not accounted for. Ewing was "at a loss to ascertain the amount of your circulation." Although the sum was not in itself very important, the statement "does not exhibit the true situation of [your branch]." Ewing carefully avoided extreme criticism, however, noting that he was "aware of your correct habits in general" and was "satisfied that any error is from mere inadvertance," to which Ewing was "as liable as others."[52]

As cashier, Ewing kept close watch over the specie reserves. It was dangerous to run low on gold or silver, but it was also unprofitable to keep too much on hand. Ewing recommended to one cashier who wanted to send twenty-five dollars in specie to the Bank of Tennessee followed by twenty-five dollars more that he invest half of it in a Philadelphia check instead. "In consequence of the small demand for specie now [June 1839] and the early fall of the Rivers, this [bank] will not require more than the first lot," he advised. In another instance, when discussing the settlement of balances concerning the "Memphis [Bank]" (perhaps the Bank of Memphis) with S. R. Richards, Ewing insisted that it "is not the wish or . . . function of this [bank] to [claim] specie from that [exchange], & if a check on the above terms cannot be had, extend the time by adding interest." If they could not accomplish the exchange under these terms, Ewing admonished Richards to "write me on what terms [the bank] proposes to settle balances" and to "attend to this matter at your earliest convenience." Other cashiers performed with equal competence. William Compton, a cashier at the Decatur branch of the Alabama state bank, personally directed the legislative policy that resulted in the chartering of the Southern Bank of Alabama.[53]

Not all cashiers, however, even in the Bank of Tennessee system, were as capable and honest as Ewing. Cashier E. W. Dale of the Tennessee State Bank had apparently embezzled more than $20,000, because the president of the bank, Felix Robertson, in a report to the House of Representatives, claimed that the bank had won a suit against the cashier for $22,396. In Arkansas, the escapades of William Ball, Abner Thornton, and other cashiers of the State Bank and the Real Estate Bank damaged

52. Ewing to Mitchell, August 10, 1839, *ibid.*

53. Ewing to W. W. Frazier, June 21, 1839, *ibid.*; Ewing to S. R. Richards, June 14, 1839, *ibid.* It is also interesting to note that Ewing's bank, even in the still stormy economic climate, did not want specie or at least did not want an abundance of it.

those already weak institutions. Even when no wrongdoing had occurred, a cashier was constantly under the threat of investigation and was exposed to accusation. Prominent cashiers, such as D. A. Davis and Charles Mills, were subjected to personal examination or criticism, but these annoyances came with the job. Most cashiers remained loyal and honest. In one case, L. S. Webb, cashier of the Windsor Branch of the Bank of North Carolina, complied with the request of Reverend C. B. Cassell that he be sent cash in return for a direct draft made out to Webb. The cashier appealed to the reverend, "Please don't make anymore light bills in my favor, as it is against the Bye Laws of the Bank." Future circumstances might require that "it would be necessary to make a witness of me," Webb warned. In another case, Webb merely returned a draft made out to himself.[54]

Apart from the great responsibility and temptation to engage in illegal activity, a cashier's job was tedious. John Ehringhaus, cashier at the Elizabeth City branch of the Bank of North Carolina, reported working until nine o'clock many evenings, even though business was slower than had been hoped. During "court week," Ehringhaus had to stay open on Sunday because of the crush of work. In addition to keeping the regular hours, the cashier had to attend board meetings, which were usually one night a week. John Cheesborough, cashier of the Bank of Charleston, reported his business routines to his wife. "This is Wednesday evening," he wrote, "when you know I am always called to the Bank."[55]

When it came to balancing the books, the cashier had to cope with a problem unfamiliar to any modern banker. Besides dealing with a variety of notes and coin (and the common problems of illegibility, erasures, and failure to endorse notes), cashiers often received notes torn in half to

54. *Report of the President of Bank of Tennessee to the House of Representatives, October 5, 1843* (Nashville, 1843), p. 7; letter (unintelligible) to Farish Carter, April 10, 1836[?], Folder 14, Farish Carter Papers, SHC, UNC; Thomas Wright to G. W. Fisher, March 9, 1848, *ibid.*; L. S. Webb to Rev. C. B. Cassell, October 31, 1860, Bank of North Carolina (Windsor Branch) Account and Letter Book, vol. 14, *ibid.* Also see letter of December 21, 1860, *ibid.*

55. John Ehringhaus to Duncan Cameron, February 2, March 9, 1837, Letterbook, Elizabeth City branch of the Bank of North Carolina, 1826–41, quoted in William Griffen, *Ante-bellum Elizabeth City: The History of a Canal Town* (Elizabeth City, N.C., 1970), 75–76; Govan, "Banking and Credit in Georgia," 225; John Cheesborough to wife, Lou, December 21, 1859, John Cheesborough Papers, SHC, UNC; letter of December 21, 1860, and *passim*, Bank of North Carolina (Windsor Branch) Account and Letter Book, vol. 14, *ibid.*

prevent theft when money was sent through the rather unreliable mail, particularly when private individuals were employed as couriers. When the first half of a note was received, the banker sent word to the party to forward the remaining half.

Presidents and directors were less involved in daily activities, but their responsibilities weighed on them just as heavily. Most banks relied on the cashiers to double-check the work of the bookkeepers and to attend to daily administration. Cashiers, in most cases, reported either to the president or to the board of directors. If the president represented an officer independent of the board, then the cashier reported to him, and he made the regularly scheduled reports to the board. Board meetings usually occurred once a week or once a month, depending on the system. Occasionally, the president made a report to state authorities or to the legislature, although the chairman of the board usually performed such tasks. Salaries for presidents, although good and much better than those of cashiers and other employees, offered no obvious promise of wealth. Jacob Walker of Arkansas, in a letter to a relative, reported that he had been appointed president of the State Bank "and that my salary is $1200 [a year]." He also cautioned, "We have almost perpetual struggle for office here. The confirmation of my appointment is doubtful."[56]

The directors appointed the presidents in most banks, and at twelve hundred dollars the position's pay about equaled the years of effort at other, lower positions. In some cases, of course, the presidents and directors alike profited monetarily well beyond the constraints of their salaries. A principal advantage associated with directorship or presidency was access to loans. Alabama's state bank directors and officers used their positions to extract huge loans and benefits. Baldwin's recollections of the period compared the road "through the bank operations [to] the road through Hounslow Heath, every step a robbery."[57]

Directors at the State Bank of Arkansas were notoriously corrupt. They "resolved to lend themselves permanently the sum of $90,000," although the bank's operating capital was only $110,000. W. D. Blocher, who attacked the bank with vigor in his *History of Arkansas Finances*, contended that the "officers and stockholders . . . were the principal beneficiaries." Reports of the trustees and receivers showed Blocher's appraisal to be somewhat understated, but although loans to officers and

56. Jacob Walker to [Judge] David [Walker?], May 21, 1837, AHC.
57. Baldwin, *Flush Times*, 262; Garrett, *Reminiscences of Public Men*, 42–44, 608.

directors consistently proved a problem throughout the South they were not generally considered illegal or even unethical in most cases.[58]

Scandals involving directors and officers broke the routine nature of banking, as did occasional violent episodes that evoke visions of the early frontier. One of the worst episodes of bank-related violence took place in Memphis, where the Farmers and Merchants Bank had been forced to suspend operations in May 1847. The suspension received considerable attention because the bank had generally been regarded as stable.

Jephtha Fowlkes, a physician turned financier, was elected a director together with Seth Wheatley, Joseph Watkins (also president of the Mutual Assurance and Trust Company), and General Levin Coe on January 6, 1847, and immediately began an intrigue against the other directors, especially Wheatley. In so doing, Fowlkes made an enemy of the editor of the Memphis *Eagle*, calling him a "creature" guilty of "pilfering, swindling, and perjury." On January 26, 1848, two eastern stockholders instituted legal action, and three days later the sheriff served an injunction against the officers of the bank, an action that attracted a crowd. The mob sought to take possession of the bank and its papers, and so forth, and "axes were freely used." Finally, the opposing groups agreed that only the officers would enter the bank, and the sheriff received the keys.[59]

After two years of legal wranglings, the court appeared ready to turn the bank back over to Fowlkes and the directors. Opponents and creditors of the bank persuaded former director General Levin Coe, a prominent lawyer, to oppose returning the bank to Fowlkes. Coe, some felt, was the only man who could rescue the bank, but others, including E. W. M. King and Alanon Trigg, regarded Coe as an enemy of Fowlkes. After making a court appearance, Coe and two friends ran into Trigg and one of his friends. In the ensuing gun battle, Trigg was killed and Coe suffered a fatal pistol shot in the back. The deaths of Coe and Trigg and the turmoil surrounding the bank took its toll on popular support. Although the bank remained convincingly solvent, its notes dropped to 25 percent discounts. After six years the bank was dead.[60]

58. Blocher, *History of Arkansas Finances*, 18, 36.
59. Jesse the "Scribe," *Chronicles of the Farmers' and Merchants' Bank of Memphis (1832–1847)*, ed. James Roper (Memphis, 1960), introduction.
60. *Memphis Daily Appeal*, October 10, 12, 1847, January 26, 30, February 3, 1848; *Chronicles*, introduction; John Keating, *History of the City of Memphis and Shelby County* (Syracuse, N.Y., 1888), I, 271–72, 297–98, II, 244–47.

Fortunately for most bankers, such incidents were the exception, not the rule. Boredom and tedium marked the teller's life; eyestrain and worry, the cashier's; and tough decisions on loans and never-ending public relations, the director's and officer's. Letterbooks from dozens of southern banks testify to the constant record keeping necessary in all bank work. Manuscripts from employees bring alive the pride they felt in their work.

Nevertheless, the details of everyday banking, and the attitude with which most bankers approached them, explain much about bankers in the South. First, they were busy people. Even if the so-called planter-bankers existed in great numbers, the supervision of banking operations by its nature soon required a commitment to agriculture or to business. Both William Godfrey and William Johnson chose banking. Cashiers and presidents were quite engrossed in their banks' daily activities, although they could, and often did, participate in community and civic affairs, social events, and politics. Sometimes participation in outside activities was healthy or even necessary to the reputation of the bank. There is no evidence, however, that bankers in general regarded these activites as any sort of public display of "class consumption." When cashier Charles Kinney wrote to Reverend Harvey Stanley, "Great embarrassment prevails in our place," he was probably sincerely concerned about his bank's reputation. Kinney and his conscientious contemporaries typified the majority of antebellum southern bankers, whose exploits hardly aroused the same public interest as those of Ball or Evans.[61]

Second, southerners knew as well as easterners that they stood to gain more by letting debtors remain in business and pay off their debts than by foreclosing, although they required a sign of faith on the part of the borrower. One North Carolinian lamented that he had been "overrun with New York collections [and] . . . compelled to pay them some to keep them quiet." More typically, however, as Henry Ewing of the Bank of Tennessee noted, directors were "anxious to avoid commencing suit

61. Charles Kinney to Richard Creecy, January 5, 1841, Letterbook of the Elizabeth City Branch of the Bank of the State of North Carolina, State Archives, and Kinney to Rev. Harvey Stanley, August 23, 1841, Edmund Ruffin Beckwith Papers, SHC, UNC, both quoted in Wayne Payne, "The Commercial Development of Ante-bellum Elizabeth City" (M.A. thesis, Old Dominion University, 1971), pp. 55–59. For other reactions to the panic among North Carolina bankers, see Joseph Letchery to James McDowell, January 31, Thomas Hart Benton to James McDowell, February 3, 1838, James McDowell Papers, SHC, UNC.

against any citizen." Options for farmers in Tennessee included drafts on
New Orleans banks at a terrific total fee (approximately 10 percent total
charges), or they could turn to private bankers and Tennessee chartered
banks. The latter institutions had to deal with their own discounted
paper, and so they often issued "postnotes," which paid 10 percent interest but were not collectible for a year from the date of issue. Like other
state banks, the Bank of Tennessee had to apportion its credit "demo-
cratically," but banks in general tried to help other competitors for the
good of the economy. Robert Dickens of Greensboro assured North
Carolinian banker James Webb that he would "lend . . . funds as fast as
we can receive them." Tennessee banks also sought ways to distribute
the costs of procuring specie among the branches. A handsome profit or
consequential loss could be had in speculating on a variety of bank bills
and drafts. Likewise, businessmen had to endure inconvenient and costly
trips from Mississippi to Mobile and New Orleans in order to obtain exchanges on northern banks.[62]

Third, collection and processing of paper during the inflation and depression years led to an effort by many bankers to refine and improve
their operations. Henry Ewing at the Bank of Tennessee constantly
worked at smoothing transactions with the branches and with other
banks. In 1839 he admonished his fellow cashiers to settle all of their
balances, then instructed them on proper note marking for due bills. He
told businessmen that in order "to facilitate our exchanges" he would
"seal up y[our] circulation & advise you of the [amount] & state upon
the receipt of such advice." Ewing asked the merchant to do the same
"& the owed party would receive a post note." When Britain failed to
pay costs associated with shipping specie to any one branch, Ewing ad-

62. Gary Browne, "Eastern Merchants and Their Southwestern Collections During
the Panic and Deflation, 1837–1843," *Southern Studies*, Winter, 1980, pp. 315–30 (quotations on pp. 322, 322 n. 15); M. H. Wells to George H. Wells, February 10, 1845, Collection No. 3034, SHC, UNC; Henry Ewing to O. N. Callom, June 14, 1839, to William
Holmes, July 2, 1839, to S. R. Richards, July 30, 1839, all in Bank of Tennessee Letterbook, Record Group 47, Vol. 16, TLA; Robert Dickens to James Webb, February 6, 1838,
James Webb Papers, SHC, UNC. On collections in general, see Samuel Child to James
Webb, February [?], 1838, *ibid.* Also see Robert Dickens to James Webb, February 6,
1838, Samuel Child to James Webb, June 4, July 23, 1839, Samuel Mitchell to James
Webb, May 15, 1839, in James Webb Papers, [?] to Roger Gregory, May 16, 1836, Virginia
State Archives; Hardee and Zacharie to Moses Taylor, January 11, 1839, to Travers and
Alexander, January 15, 1839, in Hardee and Zacharie Papers, J. C. Claiborne to R. B.
Robinson, June 26, 1839, in Dromgoole Papers, all in SHC, UNC.

justed the accounts of all branches for their share of the cost. More than once he criticized cashiers for being late in forwarding their monthly statements and exhorted them to furnish complete information. These relatively minor but inescapable changes in business resulting from the panic enhanced efficiency in banking.[63]

Changes in business organization during and after the panic period generally occurred less drastically in the South than in the North. Agriculture was still not viewed as a business, nor had the southern advocates of "scientific farming" pressed their case yet. Banks in the immediate post-panic South reflected this overall absence of evolving management techniques. The management structure of southern banking remained relatively unchanged.

Whereas business organization changed little in the wake of the panic, states investigated ways of strengthening their own banking systems. Considerable regulatory activity followed. For the most part, new regulations reinforced or modified existing laws, although the passion with which legislative reforms were argued in the legislative halls gave the debates an air of freshness. The egalitarian tendencies of Jacksonianism combined with banking rhetoric to create diverse banking regulations and crystallized important presuppositions that made the policies of the Old South different from those of the New South.

63. Henry Ewing to O. N. Callom, June 14, 1839, to S. R. Richards, July 14, July 30, November 14, 1839, to Charles Loflin and Sons, September 6, 1839, to S. Mitchell, November 14, 1839, all in Bank of Tennessee Letterbook, Record Group 47, Vol. 16, TLA. For other difficulties in collecting or processing money, see the letter from [?, Marion, Perry County] to James Webb, February 6, 1838, James Webb Papers, SHC, UNC. Other organizational redefinition is described in Mary Cumming, *Georgia Railroad and Banking Company, 1833–1945* (Augusta, Ga., 1957 [1945]), 31, 35, 50, 58. Still, the theory of organization and structure offered by Alfred Chandler, Jr. (*The Visible Hand: The Managerial Revolution in American Business* [Cambridge, Mass., 1977]) does not apply to southern banking at this point in its development.

3

PUBLIC POLICY AND BANKING REGULATION IN THE OLD SOUTH

The panic of 1837 left in its wake a host of failed and suspended banks and exposed various legislative structures that had proved inadequate to withstand the financial storm. Southern banks operated under a variety of different corporate charter provisions—in this respect they differed little from their counterparts in the North—and varying degrees of effort were needed to restore them.

In most of the Old South, the unusual soundness of the banks had given lawmakers a false sense of security and had made them reluctant to tinker with apparently adequate public financial policy. When the panic struck, they did not overreact. States of the Old South kept competition as an essential feature of their regulatory structure and in general sought to modify their banking laws only slightly. By the 1850s, most had developed policies that provided a framework for competition, with the state serving as an arbiter (and sometimes competitor) but not as an agent of total economic planning. Policy development after the panic tended to reinforce the division in southern society between those who favored further commercialization and industrialization and those committed to plantation agriculture. Those unafraid of burgeoning capitalism worked to establish laws directed toward capital formation and monetary stability.

A substantial foundation of public policy toward corporate regulation already existed by 1837, with southern states producing a patchwork of laws that resembled one of the three general types of policies that Bray Hammond described for the states of the upper Mississippi valley during the same period: absolute prohibition of bank credit, state monopoly, or laissez-faire. Banking in both the Old and the New South, however, also often included a fourth option, whereby a state-operated bank competed in varying degrees with state-chartered, privately owned and operated banks. This arrangement proved to be more popular in the South than in Hammond's "early West," where policy tended toward extremes. In these Old South states, where sudden reaction occurred, as in South Carolina, it was mostly from the shock associated with a disturbance in what had been an otherwise stellar financial history. The moderation with which Old South states approached banking policy after the panic suggests that they began with more solid foundations. Even in South Carolina, which reacted with perhaps the greatest shock, policy modifications were tempered with an understanding of commercial necessities.[1]

SOUTH CAROLINA VERSUS THE BANKS

South Carolina's brush with panic conditions proved traumatic. South Carolina struggled longer with the problem of ensuring solvency through legal methods than most other states. The state's banks had operated with such marked success that they were well known in the North and abroad. Their bills passed current in every state and "were regarded with such confidence that they were hoarded." As a result, the suspension of specie payment by these bastions of finance shocked popular confidence. The General Assembly's response—a tax—altered the charters of the banks in 1840 by making them liable to pay the state 5 percent interest per year on all of their issued notes. The act also imposed penalties on the officers for noncompliance, mandated monthly audits and statements by the officers on the banks' conditions, and required the banks to notify the governor of their intent to comply. Failure to do so could, under the provisions of the act, cost them their charters.[2]

Pressure on the legislature for tighter regulation had mounted since 1837 but subsided when good times temporarily returned in 1838. Criticism again increased after five Charleston banks suspended specie pay-

1. Bray Hammond, "Banking in the Early West: Monopoly, Prohibition, and Laissez Faire," *Journal of Economic History*, May, 1948, pp. 1–25.
2. W. A. Clark, *The History of Banking Institutions Organized in South Carolina Prior to 1860* (Columbia, S.C., 1922), pp. 149–51; *Statutes at Large, S.C.*, XI (reprint 1873), 100–12.

ments with the downturn in business in 1839. Business interests criticized the banks but acquiesced in the suspension, realizing that the alternative drain of all specie reserves would cripple the banking concerns beyond recovery. Farmers, fearing a sharp reduction of credit, had joined businessmen. Rumors of a "bankers' conspiracy" were heard in the rural areas. Many small farmers and merchants in South Carolina suspected that monetary contractions resulted from deliberate manipulation by bankers for their own interests. Planters such as George McDuffie, R. F. W. Allston, and J. H. Hammond also expressed their concern, although they opposed changing the lending policy of the Bank of the State of South Carolina, which, unlike most state banks, was "relatively liquid . . . due to its policy of investing mainly in short term paper." This liquidity would decrease, some observers suggested, if policy were changed to favor a higher proportion of agricultural loans or even to make the bank a strictly agricultural bank. Gradually the legislature seemed to bend under the pressure until the antisuspension bill passed. The subsequent response of the banks, which has been almost universally overlooked, provides an insight into the antebellum understanding of banking and corporate law.[3]

Committees of the major South Carolina banks met, on February 3, 1841, calling for a general convention of banks three days later. Before convening, the members had asked each bank to provide legal assessments from its solicitors. Seven solicitors or law firms submitted their written opinions, of which the convention printed 1,000 copies in pamphlet form for distribution. Disagreement marked the opinions. James Walker, the lawyer for the powerful Bank of South Carolina, in December 1840 had rendered a preliminary opinion indicating that the bankers were considering their options and were preparing a defense before the act even became law. Walker's early opinion expressed his belief that the clause requiring the banks to add the act's provisions into their charters represented an alteration of the charters, previously considered to be a violation of a contract with the stockholders and there-

3. See *The Proceedings of the Agricultural Convention and of the State Agricultural Society of South Carolina from 1839 to 1845* . . . (Columbia, S.C., 1846), 197; *Charleston Patriot*, May 17, 1837; *Charleston Courier*, May 18, 1837. For Allston's views, see R. F. W. Allston, *Memoir on the Introduction and Planting of Rice in South Carolina* (Charleston, S.C., 1843), p. 14. Hammond expressed his sentiments while he was governor (Message of Governor J. H. Hammond, *Senate Journal*, 1843, pp. 9–10, 23).

fore illegal. Citing "innumerable cases" as having decided that the state legislature could not "repeal, impair, or alter" a charter, Walker maintained that this provision impaired contractual obligation and was therefore also unconstitutional. He suggested that penalties for nonperformance of the audits would be so injurious as to "terminate" the life of the bank. They were, he inserted, "the offspring of party heat, rather than of wise legislation." Yet the final provisions raised the most serious question: could banks suspend specie payments without forfeiting their charters? Although Indiana courts had upheld such a provision, Walker concluded in the negative, without offering a detailed review, which he continued to formulate. A month later, however, he supplied a more comprehensive discussion of the forfeiture clause, arguing that the refusal by a bank to pay "only creates a right in the holder of the note to sue." Furthermore, in the charters' provisions penalties were "always to be expressed, and can never be implied." Thus Walker reaffirmed his earlier conclusion that the forfeiture of a bank's charter as penalty for suspension was unconstitutional.[4]

H. A. DeSaussure, of the State Bank of South Carolina, concurred with Walker's view, contending that the essential question involved not whether corporations could forfeit their charters for abuse but whether suspension constituted an abuse. "I do not find," he wrote, "a single provision requiring the redemption of [the State Bank's] notes in gold and silver coin as a fundamental condition of its corporate existence." Consequently suspension of payment "would no more vacate the charter . . . than a refusal or omission to comply with his contracts would disfranchise an individual citizen." J. L. Petigru, of the Bank of Charleston, agreed.[5]

Three other representatives found suspension of specie payments adequate for revocation of charters. C. G. Memminger, the legal agent for the Planters and Mechanics Bank (and later to be the secretary of the treasury for the Confederacy), in a lengthy opinion concluded that the only escape clause available to the banks was a specific exemption provi-

---

4. *Minutes of the Convention of Banks* (Charleston, S.C., 1841), 3–6. Walker's first opinion is dated December 29, 1840, and his second opinion is dated January 26, 1841. The Indiana ruling to which he referred is *The President, Directors, and Company of the Bank of Vincennes: The State Bank of Indiana* v. *The State of Indiana*, 1 Blackford's Reports, 267.

5. *Minutes*, 6–9, 17–18.

sion in the charter. Lacking specific provisions or exemptions, Memminger thought, "a Court would be warranted in pronouncing judgment of forfeiture against them." Concurring with Memminger, A. G. Magrath of the Charleston Insurance and Trust Company warned that suspension of specie payments violated "one of the most positively implied conditions" of charters, and his opinion was seconded by the firm of Peronneau, Mazyck, and Finley, representing the Union Bank. That trio regarded refusal to pay specie as "a serious abuse of one of the most important powers of the corporation by which forfeiture . . . may be incurred."[6]

The apparent division within the banking community reflected less disagreement over banking policy than might be supposed. All that was rendered was the legal opinion of each bank's solicitor, and the discrepancies more accurately reflected the complexity of the law in dispute. Still, this complexity made the disagreements no less serious and the disputants no less intransigent. Lawyers clearly illustrated this point by appearing on opposite sides of the case in court in 1841, with Memminger opposing Legaré, Petigru, and Walker.[7]

Convention minutes show no actual delegate vote on these opinions or any other discussion of them. Certainly no corporation loyal to its own stockholders could allow itself to be drawn into a nominally illegal action from solidarity with its competitors. The legal counsel for half the banks involved had concluded that failure to add the required section to the charters would put the banks in danger of vacating their charters. Within three months the state instituted legal proceedings against the violators, making proposals for a united response from the financial community largely academic. Of the five Charleston banks that had suspended specie in 1839, three accepted the modification to their charters, leaving only two in violation of the act. It was significant that the Bank of the State had not suspended; the legislature was free to attack private banks without harming the state's own financial house. Technically the attorney general had instituted proceedings against all offending banks, but the Bank of South Carolina, the oldest and most prominent bank at that time, was selected as the target for the state's test

6. *Ibid.*, 9–17, 21–25.
7. The solicitor for the Southwestern Rail Road Bank submitted an opinion quite different from the other six, but that bank had a charter that was subject to the laws of other states as well as to the laws of South Carolina. See *ibid.*, 18–21.

case. By May of 1841, the case was being heard by Judge A. P. Butler at Charleston. Henry Bailey, the attorney general, and Armistead Burt joined C. G. Memminger, of the Planters and Mechanics Bank, in arguing the state's case; equally famous lawyers Hugh Legaré, James L. Petigru, and James Walker represented the Bank of South Carolina. Judge Butler considered three preliminary questions first (a) Are South Carolina corporations franchises? (b) Is the Bank of South Carolina a corporation? (c) Can a private corporation be dissolved by a forfeiture judgment? He decided each proposition in the affirmative and then moved to the critical point: did suspension incur the liability of forfeiture? Proceeding from the assumption that war and acts of God could justify suspension, he noted that a suspension of specie payments by banks was hardly novel. Nor could the judge find precedent for charter forfeiture under similar circumstances in other states. In fact, he asserted, by suspending, the bank had reacted responsibly to protect itself and to serve the interests of the community. He therefore ruled in favor of the bank.[8]

In a reargument hearing in May 1843, Justice John S. Richardson, delivering the court's opinion, ruled that gold and silver constituted the "only legal tender in payment of debts" and that bank bills merely served as substitutes "only while they are secured in their payment of such coin." Although he conceded that payment in specie was "a consequence of reason and law," not by "the expression of its charter," he nevertheless found violation of the promise to pay by suspension. The violation constituted "an explicit abuse . . . of the bank charter." (He had just stated the *opposite*.) Nevertheless, he subjected the bank to forfeiture.[9]

Time proved a great ally to the banks. Even before the cases had been decided, banks had returned to paying specie. They therefore petitioned the legislature to allow them to accept the provisions of the 1840 act. Consequently, on December 19, 1843, the legislature offered amnesty to any bank announcing its intention to accept the provisions of the forfeiture clause. The state's remaining option for noncompliance

8. *The State vs. The Bank of Charleston*, 2 McMullin 439; *The State vs. The Bank of South Carolina*, 1 Speer 433. Also see *The Bank Case: A Report of the Proceedings in the Cases of the Bank of South Carolina and the Bank of Charleston. . . .* (Charleston, S.C., 1844), and Lesesne, *Bank of the State*, 43–44.

9. Clark, *History of Banking*, 154–56.

was revocation of the offending institution's charter. Banks and other corporations could no longer presume that their charters rendered them immune from further legislative tampering, even if only in "the public interest."[10]

A serious blow had been struck at the flexible discount method by which early banks remained solvent in times of crisis. There were only two ways for a bank to break a run without closing: either prevent people from asking for their money or find a way to give it to them. In line with the first method, antebellum banking relied on the discounting of notes to break runs. Under this practice, a customer who wanted to exchange notes for specie (of which the bank was short) could get the specie but not as much as the notes were nominally worth. A hundred-dollar note, for example, might be discounted 10 percent, whereupon the customer could receive only ninety dollars in specie at that time. The banker promised, however, that if the customer waited—for example, two weeks or a month—the bank would redeem the note at 100 percent par in specie. Customers then faced the choice of receiving some specie immediately or retaining the notes for full payment later. To break a run, a bank increased the discounts as much as necessary, perhaps as much as 40 or 50 percent, but it remained in business until conditions eased and it could again redeem in specie. Some lawmakers viewed the practice as a violation of the conditions to which banks had agreed in their charters.

Perhaps most important, however, the concept of a charter as a contract obligating a corporation to fulfill certain responsibilities was altered so that compliance with the original charter provisions established by the legislature (the offer) no longer constituted acceptance. None of the courts considered this issue, although a similar ruling had been decided in Alabama in 1820 in favor of immunity from contractual and charter alteration by the legislature. The Supreme Court had ruled in the Alabama case *Logwood* v. *The Planters and Merchants Bank* that a bank charter was a contract between the state and the stockholders of the bank and that this obligation could not be impaired by the legislature in subsequent acts. Nullification of this contract concept represented a reversal of the *Logwood* decision, apparently without consideration for precedent in other states. Ultimately the banks had only reflected the

10. *Statutes at Large*, S.C., XI (reprint of 1873), 234, 259–62, 281–82.

state's economic problems, not caused them, and the attempt to force banks onto a specie standard displayed the lawmakers' lack of understanding of the discount process, whereby banks maintained their solvency. Removal of the discount power actually made banks more susceptible to future failure, not less, because the only option facing a bank with no specie and no ability to suspend was bankruptcy. Bankers may have yielded to political reality, but their tactics in court were, at best, curious. Apart from Walker, none of the probank voices had even argued the *Logwood* contract concept in the South Carolina cases.[11]

South Carolina's legislature, like those of other southern states, could tinker with the banks' discount practices because there was a state bank with vast public funds subject to mobilization at the hands of the legislature. The constitutionality of the state bank concept had been upheld in 1837 in *Briscoe* v. *The Bank of the Commonwealth of Kentucky*, which ruled that state bank notes did not fall under the constitutional ban on bills of credit because they were designed to circulate as money. This opinion implied that state banks existed on equal footing with state-chartered banks founded on private capital.[12]

Yet in a narrow sense and over a carefully defined issue, the court had delivered a judgment on the equality of a state financial institution to its private contemporaries and competitors. Thus the private banks chose not to pursue an interesting legal course that was open to them: they might legally have forced the lawmakers to put the Bank of the State of South Carolina on the same specie standard that it had invoked for the private banks. No one seemed to realize the significance of the legislation's timing, coming as it did after the second crisis when fewer banks actually suspended. Because the Bank of the State had not suspended, any punitive measures would not apply to it. President Colcock of the Bank of the State had in fact recommended that his bank not suspend in 1837, and he hoped to take advantage of the situation to liquidate weaker private banks. More simply, Colcock may have wished to eliminate some of the competition. Still, the South Carolina solicitors failed to grasp the subtleties of the case. Just as the banking community's lawyers had not invoked *Logwood*, so they seemed to pass up *Briscoe*. Again, a precedent existed: Arkansas had challenged the legality of the

11. *Thomas Logwood vs. President, Directors and Company of the Planters and Merchants Bank of Huntsville,* 1 Minor Reports 23.
12. *Briscoe* v. *Bank of Kentucky,* 11 Peters 326.

State Bank of Arkansas by appealing a previous ruling that contradicted *Briscoe*.[13]

Agricultural interests had supported the state bank, and the legal developments provided a mild victory over the commercial interests. The court rulings, which were potentially devastating, were not pursued at great length because of the recovery. The private South Carolina banks had been stable, and for many of them the panic was an inconvenience.

REGULATORY POLICY IN THE OLD SOUTH: SOUTH CAROLINA

Even with the inadequacies demonstrated by the banks' lawyers, South Carolina developed into a model for other states of the Old South when banking policies were discussed. South Carolina developed a system of exceptional soundness—only one bank failed in the state. All banks withstood the financial storms of 1837, 1839, and 1857 with relatively minor damage (see Table 3). One bank, the Bank of Georgetown, was the only bank in South Carolina and in all of the South that did not even suspend specie payment during the Panic of 1837.

A loan company and a private bank, the Bank of South Carolina had operated for more than ten years when the state chartered the Bank of the State of South Carolina in 1812. By that time two other private banks had commenced operations. One striking aspect of the private banks was their high capitalization—$1 million for two, $800,000 for one, and $0.5 million for one—and by 1860 each of them had reached $1 million in capitalization. Despite the presence of several private institutions, the legislature was excessively reluctant to grant charters to private banks in South Carolina, an attitude that contributed to the system's stability but led to occasional shortages of money. Private banks, restricted to short-term loans (sixty days), left a void to be filled by the longer-term lending of the Bank of the State of South Carolina, and yet most of its business, at least in Charleston, was commercial. Eventually, branches at Columbia and Camden handled the agricultural loans. Competition from private banks left little room for the state to engage in financial shenanigans with its own institution.[14]

Whether the Bank of the State of South Carolina provided sufficient agricultural credit became the subject of great controversy. Early re-

13. *McFarland et al.* v. *The State Bank* (of Arkansas), 4 Arkansas Reports 44.
14. Smith, *Economic Readjustment*, 195–96, and table 18, p. 194. For creation of these banks and branches, see *Statutes at Large*, S.C., VIII, 24, 33–37.

Table 3.   The Commercial Banks in South Carolina Prior to 1865

Bank	Date(s) Chartered	Capital ($ millions)	Location	Remarks
Bank of South Carolina	1792	1.00	Charleston	Closed 1865
Bank of the United States (branch)	1792 1792	— —	 Charleston	Discontinued 1811
State Bank of South Carolina	1810	1.00	Charleston	Closed 1865
Planters and Mechanics Bank	1810	1.00	Charleston	Closed 1865
Bank of the State of South Carolina	1813	Varying amounts	Charleston	Closed 1865
Second Bank of the United States, Branch	1817	—	Charleston	Discontinued 1835
Bank of Hamburg	1824	0.50	Hamburg	Failed 1826
Bank of Cheraw	1825	0.20	Cheraw	Failed 1826
Commercial Bank	1831	0.80	Columbia	Closed 1865
Merchants Bank	1833	0.40	Cheraw	Closed 1865
Bank of Charleston	1833	3.16	Charleston	Closed 1865
Bank of Camden	1835	0.45	Camden	Closed 1865
Bank of Hamburg	1835	0.50	Hamburg	Closed 1865
Bank of Georgetown	1836	0.20	Georgetown	Closed 1865
Southwestern Railroad Bank	1836	0.87	Charleston	Closed 1865
Louisville, Cincinnati, and Charleston Railroad	1836	6.00	Charleston	
Union Bank	1842	1.00	Charleston	Closed 1865
Planters Bank of Fairfield	1852	0.30	Winnsboro	Closed 1865
Exchange Bank	1852	0.50	Columbia	Closed 1865
Bank of Chester	1852	0.30	Chester	Closed 1865
Bank of Newberry	1852	0.39	Newberry	Closed 1865

Table 3.   (continued)

Bank	Date(s) Char- tered	Capital ($ mil- lions)	Location	Remarks
Peoples Bank	1852	1.00	Charleston	Closed 1865
Farmers and Exchange Bank	1852	1.00	Charleston	
Bank of Sumter	1852/56[a]	—	—	
Western Bank of South Carolina	1852/53[b]	—	—	

[a]Chartered 1852, but failed to get necessary capital; rechartered 1856, but failed to reorganize.
[b]Chartered 1852, but failed to get necessary capital; privilege extended to 1853, but failed to reorganize.
Source: Lesesne, Bank of the State, p. 141.

ports by the president made plain the bank's heavy involvement in agriculture. When the bank came under attack in the 1840s, it tried to emphasize its heavy investments in farming and plantations. Charleston's influence ran contrary to the emphasis on agriculture, and the bank's policies often reflected the dichotomy.[15]

The legislature felt an added pressure from existing banks to refrain from chartering any competitors, but this statement raises several questions. Concern about corporate power is directed not at newly created, small, or barely profitable businesses but rather at strong and existing companies that turn substantial profits. South Carolina lawmakers likely never quaked in their shoes, thinking about a "corporate giant" such as the Bank of Hamburg. Regulators viewed corrupt banking practices as the target and sought to make charters as strong as possible. Even in South Carolina, the creation of new banks was not so very slow. Nine banks were chartered from the founding of the Bank of the State of South Carolina to 1836 and were joined by the four existing private banks. Private banks had considerable powers in their charters for the creation of branches. It is therefore surprising that the legislature did

15. See Governor James Hammond's message, *Senate Journal*, 1843, pp. 9–10, and *A Compilation of All the Acts, Resolutions, Reports, and Other Documents in Relation to the Bank of the State of South Carolina* (Columbia, S.C., 1848), 392, 397, 411, 454, 471–72.

not promote the creation of branches instead of chartering as many banks as it did.

Other "vested interests" in the assembly wished to protect the Bank of the State of South Carolina. Groups petitioned the legislature several times to charter a bank in Columbia and met with disappointment each time, specifically because the assembly feared that such a bank would compete against the Bank of the State of South Carolina. No doubt many Charleston merchants wanted to avoid competition from the interior. Clearly, new banks would compete *not* in the cities, where the existing banks had the credit business locked up, but in the rural areas served, at least in theory, by the state bank. The conflict over bank and/or branch charters merely highlighted the rural-urban, planter-coastal rivalries. In South Carolina, the business groups clearly recognized that rural credit was fraught with dangers, in terms of both inflationary potential and illiquid security.

Businesses and commercial groups that influenced banking legislation sought to avoid monetary fluctuations and to ensure solvency. High capitalization indicated the concern for stability and solvency. The Bank of Charleston, chartered in 1834 with $2 million in capitalization, was the extreme case. The bank could increase its capital to $4 million after paying a 2.5 percent bonus at any time during its twenty-one-year charter existence. It met with considerable opposition from proponents of the Bank of the State of South Carolina. Judge Henry Colcock, president of that institution, recommended increasing the capital of the state's bank rather than chartering a new bank. Opposition gradually subsided. The new bank succeeded. Stockholders in an 1837 meeting were able to authorize the increase in capital. Depressed economic conditions dampened the optimism somewhat, even though the stock subscriptions exceeded $1.1 million.[16]

The strength of this bank and others in South Carolina revealed itself in the Panic of 1857, when the Bank of Charleston and nine other banks in the state maintained specie payments. Its notes were exchanged at

16. J. N. Cardozo, *Reminiscences of Charleston* (Charleston, S.C., 1886), 46–47; *The Charter of the Bank of Charleston, December 17, 1834, and Renewal of Charter, December 20, 1853* (Charleston, S.C., 1871). Also see *The Story of the South Carolina National Bank* (N.p., n.d.); John Van Deusen, *Economic Bases of Disunion in South Carolina* (New York, 1970 [1928]); W. J. Montgomery, *Historical Outline of Banking in South Carolina from Colonial Days to the Present Time* (N.p., 1907); George Williams, *History of Banking in South Carolina* (Charleston, S.C., 1900).

par throughout the United States, England, and Europe. It delivered dividends of 10 percent a year to its stockholders. The bank had developed an important business with Charleston's commercial houses. Its solvency allowed it alone to plead good behavior when the legislature passed the bill amending bank charters in the event of suspension.[17]

South Carolina's incorporation process involved a certain amount of egalitarianism in that stock subscriptions for new banks had to be open to anyone with money. To guard against local monopoly control over stock, commissioners were appointed by the legislature and were ordered to the far reaches of the state. Anyone seeking to control a bank by buying a majority of its first issue of stock shares had a tough row to hoe. In the act incorporating the small bank at Winnsborough, for example, thirty commissioners were appointed at a total of ten sites, usually a courthouse. Each site had a trio of commissioners, so that bribery would have been expensive and difficult. Moreover, the commissioners were often directors of other banks or otherwise prominent citizens who considered their job a public service. It certainly did not hurt their position in society, either. Their duty was to open subscriptions for two days in April, following a one-month notice in the newspapers. Upon expiration of the specified deadline, the commissioners forwarded their subscription lists to the main office of the bank; if all the stock was not sold, the main branch commissioners could reopen sales from April to August. Winnsborough's charter provisions were typical.[18]

Use of the commissioner system for stock subscription served purposes apart from making monopolies difficult to obtain. First, it stimulated interest throughout the state, allowing a bank to do business in all parts. Second, it reflected democratic impulses that surfaced from time to time among legislators and kept pace with the rising appeal of Jacksonian egalitarianism. Finally, the publicity performed the legitimate and important function of disseminating information. No bank could spring up in secret in South Carolina, and openness itself contributed to the banks' solvency and strength.

A special charter applied to the South Western Railroad Bank, originally formed as the Louisville, Cincinnati, and Charleston Rail Road Company, whose banking powers were granted by the South Carolina legislature in December 1836. All those holding stock at the time of the

17. *Charter, Bank of Charleston*, 10.
18. *Statutes at Large, S.C.*, XII, 121–28.

change would continue to hold their stock. New stock purchasers could take one bank share of fifty dollars for every hundred-dollar railroad stock share purchased, so that each bank share was linked to a railroad share and could not be transferred without it. This provision kept the bank from acquiring a life of its own and abandoning the railroad. Opening stock subscriptions for a year in four states—the Carolinas, Tennessee, and Kentucky—the bank corporation also underwent a name change, becoming the South Western Railroad Bank. Directors of the two institutions remained "distinct and separate" bodies; capital remained separated as well. With the home office in Charleston, the bank had branch banking powers, yet these, and indeed its corporate existence, depended upon consent and ratification of the charter in two of the three other participating states.

By closely allying itself with Charleston, the railroad bank hoped to provide some of the services for which the Bank of the State of South Carolina had been created and thereby to gain support from the coast city. Because the bank and its branches were to spread banking services throughout the state, however, it would eventually be able to muster interior support as well. Although its opening was delayed by the Panic of 1837, the South Western Railroad Bank commenced operations in 1840 and until the Civil War remained an effective house of finance in Charleston.

THE BANK OF THE STATE OF SOUTH CAROLINA: A SPECIAL CHARTER

Most other South Carolina banks seem to have fallen under these general charter provisions, but the single significant and controversial exception was the Bank of the State of South Carolina. Henry Colcock presided over the bank during the tumultuous panic period, and had guided the investment of the surplus revenue, using some of the money to purchase Louisville, Cincinnati, and Charleston Rail Road Company stock.

Specie suspension, invoked by the Bank of the State and by all other banks in the state, led to lawsuits against the Bank of South Carolina and the Bank of Charleston. In the second suspension, which had caused the lawsuits, however, the Bank of the State and the Bank of Charleston had continued gold and silver payments. Yet it was never clear that the state intended to put its *own* institution on the same legal grounds by requiring specie payments if it suspended. Indeed, the comptroller general, William Hayne, had conveniently excused the first suspension (in which the Bank of the State participated) but found the second unreasonable. Earlier, in 1838, the legislature had made the bank a "big policeman" by ordering it to reserve at par currencies issued by private banks, a measure that "excited the wrath of the offending banks." Sufficient funds never arrived from the legislature to enforce this dictum, nor was it entirely feasible for the Bank of the State of South Carolina to do so.[19]

When disaster struck on April 27, 1838, in the Charleston fire, the legislature passed a fire loan bill in a special session. Funds from the state totaling $2 million were borrowed by the state and placed in the Bank of the State, to be lent to those who needed to rebuild burnt businesses. Private bankers feared that the bank's president had devised the loan scheme in order to increase the bank's capitalization. The controversy served to remind South Carolinians that any aid or assistance provided by the state's agencies carried a price tag. Two years later the fire loan issue arose over the subject of capitalization. Efforts to "reduce the public debt" by taking $1.5 million from the bank's capital failed to pass committee. Bank opponents revived the fire loan by trying to cancel all fire-loan stock not in use in Charleston. This measure was defeated. Both James Hammond and C. G. Memminger continued to fight the bank. When one of the directors cost the institution a great deal of money in 1846, a move was made to require publication of the names of bank's debtors. Senator J. M. Felder, who allied himself with Hammond and Memminger, summarized the antibank feeling in speaking to William Simms: "One of the greatest curses in our state is the vile concubinage of bank and state." When the two "cohabited," he observed, the bank "runs into politics and politicians run into the bank," and "foul disease and corruption ensue. . . . Bank first, state second, Bank master, state slave, Bank head, state tail."[20]

Ironically, the fire loans may have saved the bank. Supporters presented evidence to a special legislative committee appointed to investigate the bank, showing that Europeans would look unfavorably upon the destruction of the Bank of the State of South Carolina because it would

19. Greenville *Mountaineer*, October 18, 1839; *Reports and Resolutions, 1838,* 116–17; *Reports and Resolutions, 1839,* 3–4, 14.
20. Charleston *Courier*, May 30, June 1, 1838, February 15, 1849; F. H. Elmore, *Defense of the Bank of the State of South Carolina* (Columbia, S.C., n.d.), 19–20, 87; *Legislative Proceedings, 1841,* 85, 149, 151, 158, 162.

involve repudiation of the fire bonds held by Baring Brothers, C. J. Hambro and Son of London, and other overseas investors.[21]

Opponents of the state bank, led by Ker Boyce and J. H. Hammond, moved to a flank attack. Responding to Memminger's pamphlet calling for a state-backed bond issue of $1 million to fund railroad construction, Boyce, former president of the Bank of Charleston, contacted Hammond, asking him to write a response. Hammond's retorts, published under the name "Anti-Debt" and entitled "Railroad Mania," soon moved from attacks on state funding of railroads to criticism of the bank. Hammond argued that the bank had assumed larger funds of borrowed capital than it paid in public debt. Moreover, no agency had ever effectively audited the bank. The only way to initiate such an audit, he contended, was to liquidate the bank. President Franklin Elmore, responding to Hammond's pamphlets with his own under the name "Fair Play," cited the investigations of the legislative committees and observed that the bank had given the state profits equal to its capital as well as 7 percent interest. Skirmishing in the newspapers kept the bank alive as a political issue; however, Elmore's appointment by the governor to fill the Senate seat of John C. Calhoun, who died in 1850, removed one of the primary personalities from public attention.[22]

Selection of the directors also brought the bank constant criticism. In 1859 an examining committee reported that more than half of the bank's losses during a twenty-year period had come from defaulted loans made to directors, but the committee could recommend only greater care in choosing the board members.[23]

With charter expiration looming ahead in 1856, supporters sought early rechartering of the state bank in 1851 along with a number of private banks. All were rejected by the private bank forces, which remained steadfast in their opposition to the state bank and were still strong enough to muster a majority for an occasional crucial vote. With five years remaining on its charter, the bank was in no immediate danger. Private banks and the Bank of the State, put in the same boat by the legislature, thus accepted a set of measures, introduced by Governor

21. *Reports and Resolutions*, 1846, 41–65, 69–71; *Senate Journal*, 1846, 148–50; *Senate Journal*, 1847, 34, 62, 85, 92, 105.

22. "Anti-Debt," *The Railroad Mania and Review of the Bank of the State of South Carolina: A Series of Essays by "Anti-Debt"* (Charleston, S.C., 1848); "Fair Play," *Reply to "Anti-Debt" on the Bank of the State of South Carolina* (Columbia, S.C., 1848).

23. See, for example, Lesesne, *Bank of the State*, 114.

John Means, that featured compromise: the state bank was rechartered (with some charter changes); three private bank charters were renewed; eight private banks were incorporated; and under the new charter the state bank could not subscribe for railroad or internal improvement stocks without the legislature's consent.[24]

Banking drifted away from public debate until the Panic of 1857. Lawmakers, thinking that they had prevented specie suspension with the 1840 laws, were shocked to see ten banks suspend specie payments. Meeting in November 1857, the assembly offered a plethora of bills and resolutions aimed to institute sound currency. Confused as to whether they should hold the suspended banks to the laws of 1840, some members advocated amnesty from the existing law but enforcement of tougher new provisions. Finally a bill emerged providing for postponement of the 5 percent penalty inflicted by the 1840 law and delaying the penalty until January 1, 1859.[25]

Branch banking regulations had never caused as much controversy as the laws dealing with small-note issue and other regulatory provisions. Since 1813, the Bank of the State had engaged in branch banking activities. Its first branch, located at Columbia, served that city as its only bank until the establishment of the Commercial Bank in 1832. Like the other branches and agencies scattered throughout the state, the Columbia branch of the state institution remained under the control of the Charleston directors. Each kept independent books and paid its own operating expenses. Branch policies soon resembled those of the main bank and overall were considered successful within their capital limitations and organizational roles. Private banks in South Carolina were also permitted to have branches. Branch banking, although occasionally discouraging independent competitors, usually moved banking services into areas where they were needed, and branches could be operated quite economically. Branch banking represented another distinguishing

24. *House Journal,* 1851, 31, 39, 48, 153, 161–62, 233–34; *House Journal,* 1852, 18–20; Charleston *Courier,* October 14, 1852, November 24, 1852; *Statutes at Large, S.C.,* XII, 149–51, 212–14.

25. "XYZ," *The Bank Question* (1858), 10–11, 32; *Reports and Resolutions,* 1857, 14, 76–77; *Reports and Resolutions,* 1858, 130–31; *Senate Journal,* 1857, 19–20; *Statutes at Large, S.C.,* XII, 630–32, 699, 783, 860; *Statutes at Large, S.C.,* XIII (reprint, 1875), 164. Also see *Russells Magazine,* August, 1858, pp. 385–95; *Letter of William Gregg to Thornton Coleman, June 8, 1858* (Charleston, S.C., 1858); *Speech of William Gregg, Member from Edgefield District, in the Legislature of South Carolina, December, 1857, on the Bank Question* (Columbia, S.C., 1857).

feature of states that allowed or encouraged private banking competition. Branching provided a point of agreement between planters and farmers, who benefited from rural branches, and commercial groups, which viewed it as a source of diversification and risk sharing that provided economic stability. Ultimately, branching helped extend commercial attitudes into the interiors of states in the Old South and thereby contributed to the further evolution of capitalist attitudes within them.[26]

Regulatory Policy in Georgia

Georgia had looked closely at the South Carolina model when establishing its banking policies. Like South Carolina, Georgia had a state bank that did not monopolize the state's finances. The Bank of the State of Georgia had been the third major bank to be chartered in the state, preceded by two private banks (the Planters Bank and the Bank of Augusta; see Table 4). The state had also received credit from the branch of the BUS of Charleston. Georgia's legislature reserved subscriptions of capital stock for the state in each of the private banks. Continuing this practice when it chartered a fourth bank, the Bank of Darien, in 1818, the state was also careful in each case to use its stock ownership to appoint directors to the private banks, thus ensuring that the interests of the state were represented on the bank boards. Bank stock was seen as an important source of state revenue, but although public investment in private enterprise was fairly common in the state, Georgia did not reserve enough directorships to give the state control of the banks, apart from its control of exactly half of the Bank of Darien's directorships. Except for the expressed regulatory conditions of the charters, no general banking regulations controlled the actions of the banks until 1820, when the general assembly required the banks to submit annual statements of condition to the governor.[27]

26. John Chapman and Ray Westerfield, *Branch Banking* (New York, 1942), 38–41. Eugene White has argued that the failure to implement national branch banking after the Civil War was a major flaw in the Federal Reserve System, which suggests that the Old South was again in the forefront of regulatory policy for banks. See *The Regulation and Reform of the American Banking System, 1900–1929* (Princeton, 1983), 6–7.

27. Lorimer Freeman, "The Central Bank of Georgia" (M.A. thesis, University of Georgia, 1919), 4–5; Oliver Prince, *A Digest of the Laws of the State of Georgia, etc.*, 2d ed. (Athens, Ga., 1837), 50–55; *Laws, Ga.*, 1821, pp. 74–102; *Laws, Ga.*, 183, p. 1; *Ga. Senate Journal*, 1822, pp. 56–57, 148–49. Also see Govan, "Banking and Credit in Georgia."

Table 4. The Commercial Banks in Georgia Prior to 1865

Bank	Date(s) Chartered	Capital ($ millions)	Location	Remarks
Bank of Augusta	December, 1810	0.30; 1834: 0.90	Augusta	$0.05 of capital reserved for the state
Planters Bank of the State of Georgia	December, 1810	1.00	Savannah	$0.0001 of stock reserved for the state
Bank of the State of Georgia	December, 1815	1.50	Savannah	$0.60 of stock reserved for the state
Bank of Darien	December, 1818	1.00	Darien	$0.50 of stock reserved for the state
Marine and Fire Insurance Bank Company	December, 1825	Specie in vault	Savannah	
Bank of Macon	December, 1825	0.30	Macon	
Augusta Insurance and Banking Company	December, 1827	0.50	Augusta	Charter repealed in December 1832
Merchants and Planters Bank	December, 1827	0.30	Augusta	Granted any religions, charitable, or literary institution incorporated by the state the right to subscribe to bank stock
Central Bank of Georgia	December, 1828	General funds of state	Milledgeville	Loans to be apportioned by county population
Bank of Columbus	December, 1828	0.30	Columbus	
Mechanics Bank	December, 1830	0.20 can raise to 0.40; 1836: can raise to 1.00	Augusta	
Commercial Bank of Macon	December, 1831	0.40	Macon	

Table 4. *(continued)*

Bank	Date(s) Chartered	Capital ($ millions)	Location	Remarks
Bank of Hawkinsville	December, 1831	0.20–0.40	Hawkinsville	
Insurance Bank of Columbus	December, 1831	0.30	Columbus	
Central Railroad and Banking Company	December, 1835	1.50 for banking	Savannah	
Georgia Railroad and Banking Company	December, 1835	0.50 for banking	Atlanta	
Bank of Milledgeville	December, 1835	0.50	Milledgeville	
Ocmulgee Bank of the State of Georgia	1836	0.50	Macon	Opened in 1837
Western Bank of Georgia	December, 1836	0.40	Rome	
Monroe Railroad and Banking Company	December, 1836	0.30 for banking	Macon	
Bank of Brunswick	December, 1836	2.00; 1837: allowed to increase to 3.00	Brunswick	No report made prior to 1837
Chattahoochie Railroad and Banking Company	December, 1836	0.10 for banking	Columbus	
Bank of St. Mary's	December, 1836	0.25	St. Mary's	
Planters and Mechanics Bank of Columbus	December, 1836	1.00	Columbus	Did not report until 1838

Ruckersville Bank Company	1841	1.38	Ruckersville
Bank of Brunswick	1841	0.20	Brunswick
Monroe Railroad and Banking Company	January, 1842	0.951	Monroe
Phenix Bank	January, 1843	0.296	Phenix
Atlanta Bank	1854	0.80	Atlanta
Bank of Savannah	1854	0.500	Savannah
Interior Bank	1854	0.100	Griffin
Cherokee Insurance and Banking Company	1857	0.125	Dalton
Exchange Bank	1857	0.050	Griffin
La Grange Bank	1857	0.150	La Grange
Bank of Commerce	1857	0.498	Savannah
Mechanics Savings Bank	1857	0.250	Savannah
Bank of Fulton	1857	0.104	Fulton
Southern Bank of Georgia	1857	0.500	Rainbridge
Bank of Middle Georgia	1857	0.125	Macon
Bank of the Empire State	1857	0.154	Rome
City Bank	1857	0.375	Augusta
Union Bank	1857	0.300	Augusta
North Western Bank	1857	0.050	Ringgold
Bank of Athens	1857	0.100	Athens
Timber Cutters Bank	December, 1858	0.050	Savannah

Sources: Van Fenstermaker, *Development of American Commercial Banking,* Table A-8; *House Executive Document 172,* 26th Cong., 1st Sess.; *House Executive Document 102,* 33d Cong., 1st & 2d Sess.; *House Executive Document 77,* 36th Cong., 2d Sess.

These provisions seemed adequate until Georgia experienced a bank failure in 1832. Subsequently, the legislature passed a stricter reporting act requiring banks to make semiannual reports that were to include the names of stockholders, the amount of stock owned by each stockholder, and a complete accounting of the bank's assets. After the panic, the general assembly again tightened reporting requirements so that banks had to report the amounts loaned to directors as well as the name of any stockholder owing more than $10,000. Banks resisted the 1839 law. Many refused to comply with it or otherwise ignored it. Directors of the Georgia Railroad and Banking Company reported only the aggregate amount owed by the directors and, following the governor's demand that the bank comply fully, rescinded the aggregate report altogether. Instead, the directors authorized the president "to make a report in conformity with such laws as were in existence at the time the charter of the company was passed."[28]

Failure to enforce the law followed; indeed, the state authorities displayed no enthusiasm for its enforcement. Stockholders supported efforts to avoid the law, and banks modified their business to present favorable reports. The steps taken often included curtailing business and tidying up stray accounts one to two months prior to the report's due dates. Georgia had strict regulatory provisions in its banks' charters and deliberately sought to prevent any group from gaining monopoly control over each bank by maintaining an open stock subscription system. Stock subscription books, under the watchful eyes of "commissioners"—that is, well-known and respected citizens in each county—were kept open for a period of thirty days, during which time no person could subscribe more than one hundred shares. After thirty days, anyone could purchase unsold stock. Proportional voting provided another safeguard against monopolistic control.[29]

Georgia banks, like those of other states, might forfeit their charters for violations. The state also established an indebtedness limit of three times a bank's capital stock. Specie redemption requirements differed

28. *Acts, Ga.*, 1832, 29–31; *ibid.*, 1839, pp. 28–29; Directors' Minutebook, Augusta, Georgia, I, 364; Annual Message of Governor Charles McDonald, *Senate Journal*, 1840, pp. 10–11; Stockholders' Minutebook, I, 139–40. Comments on the 1832 act are found in *Georgia Messenger*, May 2, 1833, and in Wilson Lumpkin to W. J. Hunter, April 8, 1833, and Lumpkin to Thomas Cumming, April 19, 1833, Governors' Letterbook, 1833–35, pp. 37, 46–47.

29. *Georgia Messenger*, April 9, 1846.

from those of South Carolina. Failing to redeem might lead to a judicial action against the bank for charter forfeiture, and holders of notes could protest for nonpayment, with potential recovery of legal interest against the defaulted notes (in South Carolina, banks were forced to affix an amendment to their charters promising as much). Georgia's law remained a tool to be used selectively in particular situations rather than against all banks across the board in that it required proof of a loss due to nonpayment of specie. This situation contrasted with that in South Carolina, where all non-specie-paying banks were *already* in violation of the statutes.[30]

Georgia's banks had suspended specie payments in 1837, but only after suspension in large commercial centers in the North. Governor William Schley declined to use the forfeiture power against the banks, recommending instead that the legislature set a specific resumption date. Georgia legislators rejected this idea until other banks in the country began to pay specie again. When the bankers agreed at a general convention held in Charleston in June 1838 to resume on January 1, 1839, a number of them wanted earlier resumption. By October most state banks had resumed specie payments. Weaker banks were protected by an 1838 act that forced each bank and its branches to receive its own notes for debts owed it. Thus patrons of stronger institutions could not drain the specie from those banks with smaller reserves using notes of the larger banks.[31]

A second wave of suspensions in late 1839 brought severe criticism from lawmakers. Almost none of the twenty-one commercial banks and their sixteen branches had failed, the reasons being the practice of persuading note bearers to accept interest-paying checks on New York banks instead of specie, their exceptionally strong ratios of specie to demand liability, and the "home redemption" law. Only two states had higher ratios of specie to demand liability than Georgia, and those ratios had risen in the two years prior to the panic. Even so, the legislature viewed

---

30. Lucius Q. C. Lamar, *A Compilation of the Laws of the State of Georgia Passed by the Legislature from the Year 1810 to the Year 1819, Inclusive* (Augusta, Ga., 1821), 105, 115; William Dawson, *A Compilation of the Laws of the State of Georgia, Passed by the General Assembly, Since the Year 1819 to the Year 1829, Inclusive* (Milledgeville, Ga., 1831), 70. Compare the charter provisions in Georgia banks with South Carolina's act of 1840.

31. *Georgia Senate Journal*, 1837, 10–13; *Senate Journal*, 1838, 20–21; *Georgia Messenger*, December 7, April 12, 1837, June 7, 1838, August 23, 1838; *Acts, Ga.*, 1838, 44.

the second suspension as an indication of insecurity and an undue hardship on debtors. Governor George Gilmer urged the legislature to review the banks' latest reports and to mandate immediate resumption, but the assembly hesitated. Legislators passed instead a law authorizing brokers and banks to recover damages of 10 percent on notes not redeemed by the bank in specie.

Favorable conditions returned after the initial Panic of 1837, encouraging the state to adopt a free banking law. New banks had to follow all the rules of the chartered banks with the major exception that they were allowed to come into existence by filing certificates of intent with the state comptroller and the clerk of the district's superior court. Two banks joined the state's financial community under the law: one failed in the latter parts of the depression, and the other closed officially, legally, and voluntarily in 1854. Serious opposition to free banking from planters in established Cotton Belt counties, who often had interests in chartered banks, and from businessmen in commercial areas, who were concerned with stability in the money supply, combined with the strength and success of the many commercial banks and especially their branching power, effectively kept free banking from catching on.

Panic conditions reappeared after a short respite, and by 1840 the legislature's patience had ended. The legislature authorized the governor to institute judicial proceedings against banks not complying with resumption and simultaneously extended a year of grace to the banks. Eleven banks and eight branches resumed, accounting for more than 75 percent of Georgia's banking capital (exclusive of the Central Bank). Judicial action in 1841 resulted in the forfeiture of four banks' charters, although six remaining private banks, which neither forfeited nor immediately resumed, stayed in business. No other banks lost their charters or failed until the depression of 1857. Democratic Governor Charles McDonald, who had eagerly ordered judicial actions against the noncomplying banks, at different times advocated that a single bank in Savannah, with branches, regulate and unify the monetary system. Nevertheless, he concluded in 1842 that "banks of all descriptions [were] injurious to the people."[32]

32. *Acts, Ga.*, 1840, 26–27; *Acts, Ga.*, 1843, 21–22; Augusta *Chronicle and Sentinel*, March 30, 1841; Governors' Letterbook, 1841–43, pp. 143–44, 148; *Georgia Senate Journal*, 1843, 28; *Georgia Senate Journal*, 1842, Governor McDonald's message; Augusta *Chronicle and Sentinel*, September 26, 1840.

Two thorny and continuing problems hindered attempts to pass logical and comprehensive banking laws. First, small note issues, known as "shinplasters" and common to all states, proved difficult to regulate. The theoretical problem of balancing a state bank property in the market context was more serious. Because any state bank violated basic principles of laissez-faire, any state with such a bank had to make a pragmatic evaluation of the costs of such an institution in the market context.

Georgia's first concern—shinplasters—afflicted virtually all states in the antebellum period. Change bills, or small notes of twenty-five to seventy-five cents in value, remedied a typical deficiency in the money supply, namely the lack of small-change coins. Early efforts in Georgia to stop small issues included taxation at 8 to 20 percent, followed by laws allowing holders of such notes to recover three times the amount from the signer. If a bank refused to redeem, holders could by law recover 25 percent in damages. Ignoring the law in droves, people continued to use small notes until, in 1818, the General Assembly passed a law making each dollar note issued subject to a penalty of one hundred dollars, half of which would go to anyone willing to be an informer.[33]

By 1832, Georgia had outlawed the issue of these shinplasters by banks. Individuals continued their own issue of shinplasters well into the Panic of 1837 until merchants began to refuse them. Cities, most notably Macon, Augusta, and Savannah, all attempted to assist by issuing city notes. These survived as long as the municipalities accepted them for taxes. Their circulation grew until they began to be discounted, sometimes as much as 70 percent. Macon, the hardest hit of the "cityplaster" towns, ultimately cut the circulation by requiring each citizen to pay half his taxes in small notes. Whigs gained control of the legislature in 1842 and returned to the policy of allowing specie-paying banks to issue small bills, a policy that continued through 1860. Whig policy allowed enough small bills to remain in circulation to facilitate small trade, which benefited smaller merchants and farmers.[34]

33. *Acts, Ga.*, 1860, 21–23; Lamar, *Laws, Ga.*, 103–11, 884, 891–92, 1106–107, 1192–94; *Darien Gazette*, September 7, 1824; *Southern Recorder*, August 8, September 26, 1829; Dewey, *State Banking Before the Civil War*, 630–73; Govan, "Banking and Credit in Georgia," 26–29.

34. *Georgia Senate Journal*, 1831, 22–23; *Georgia Senate Journal*, 1832, 21–22; *Acts, Ga.*, 1832, 26–27; *Acts, Ga.*, 1840, 28–29; *Acts, Ga.*, 1841, 21–22; *Acts, Ga.*, 1842, 31–32; *Acts, Ga.*, 1851–52, 21; *Georgia Messenger*, August 8, 1833, December 10, 1840, November 25, 1841, September 4, 1845, March 26, 1846.

Georgia's Central Bank, unlike the Bank of Darien, which was owned by the state but operated like any other commercial bank, was both owned by the state and operated as an agent of the state government. Chartered in 1828, the bank had the egalitarian purpose of giving credit to those persons not already served by existing banks. John Jay Knox suggested that the purpose behind the bank's creation was to evade the provision in the Constitution that prevented states from issuing bills of credit. In this statement he was partly correct. Public officials, however, could not resist the thought of using a state bank's profits "to relieve the citizens from taxation, enable the state to progress advantageously in internal improvements, and perfect its system of public education." Early in the Central Bank's history, it encountered little opposition: it was conservatively managed, and its directors, James Camak and Samuel Boykin, carefully avoided antagonizing the private commercial bankers. The bank experienced early success by directing its operations only to areas that other banks chose to ignore, making longer-term loans than the private institutions. It therefore avoided the seasonal credit flows that characterized other banks.[35]

Operating successfully in its first years, the Central Bank brought the state roughly fifty thousand dollars a year from its profits. Opposition developed when the Central Bank received state deposits of Georgia's surplus revenue in the bank. By placing the surplus in the Central Bank rather than dispersing it evenly among all banks, the state entered into direct competition with private lenders: it had specie available when no other banks did. With the federal government's interruption of the distribution, the central bank suddenly found itself in the unenviable position of asking for loans from banks with which it had just recently competed. Assuming that the federal government would complete the distribution, the legislature authorized the Central Bank to discount loans to the full amount of the forthcoming portion. Despite these errors in public relations, the governor fully supported the bank.[36]

35. *Georgia Senate Journal*, 1823, 15–18, Governor John Clark's message; *Georgia Messenger*, July 25, 1833, August 4, 1842; Circular letter to the Banks of Georgia, February 8, 1829, *Georgia Senate Journal*, 1829, 235–38; *Georgia Senate Journal*, 1832, 13–14, Governor Wilson Lumpkin's message; Annual Report of the President of the Central Bank, *Appendix to the Senate Journal*, 1834, 50; *Acts, Ga.*, 1832, 23–24, 257–61; John Jay Knox, *A History of Banking in the United States* (New York, 1900), 575.

36. *Georgia House Journal*, 1829, 14–17; *Georgia Senate Journal*, 1830, 198–99; *Georgia Senate Journal*, 1833, 353–56; *Georgia Senate Journal*, 1837, 10–13; *Georgia*

Proponents of the state institution favored extending full note-issue powers to the bank and over strong opposition passed an act permitting the bank to make a loan distribution of $750,000. Opponents, led by such notable Georgians as George Crawford, Robert Toombs, and Alexander Stephens, feared such an abuse of state power. They signed a protest against the "perversion and debauchery of public powers." Even James Camak, one of the original directors, had warned against converting the bank into a note-issuing competitor: "*Such a change in its fundamental principles would be very hazardous* independent of the constitutional objections that might be raised against it." Undaunted by the din of opposition, the bank added to its distribution by accepting $100,000 worth of Western and Atlantic Railroad scrip to support the railroad's construction. Thus the bank injected notes into the economy almost solely through state agencies (the railroad was owned by the state, and the employees worked for the state).[37]

Yearly the debt grew, and the legislature continued to skim off any profits the bank had. Consequently the Central Bank defaulted on its New York loan in 1840. Its reputation and credit suffered greatly, and the bank's statements revealed its declining position. By November 1840, the bank's bills in circulation exceeded its assets by $500,000. During 1841 the legislature directed the bank to pay more than half a million dollars to meet the appropriations of the General Assembly. It also urged the directors to pay the debt to the New York banks by selling bank stock. As the Central Bank's notes flooded into the Georgia economy, local merchants and private bankers registered their opposition. Beginning with Macon merchants, then spreading to Augusta and Savannah, the notes of non-specie-paying banks were gradually discredited, but notes of the Central Bank were still receivable for taxes, and up-country banks continued to receive them. Under these circumstances, the notes of the Central Bank still circulated freely.[38]

Messenger, November 10, 1836, December 19, 1839, December 9, 1841; Directors' Minutebook, I:170–71; *Report of the Commissioners Appointed to Investigate the State Finances* (Milledgeville, Ga., 1839), 11–19.

37. *Georgia Senate Journal,* 1839, 410–12; *Georgia Messenger,* August 11, 1842 (Camak quoted "by Lowndes").

38. Report of the Committee on the Central Bank, *Georgia Messenger,* December 9, 1841; Directors' Minutebook, Branch IA, pp. 110–11; Governor Charles McDonald to T. T. Teleston, May 12, 1840, Governors' Letterbook, 1835–40, p. 459, and March 13, 1841; Governors' Letterbook, 1841–43, p. 63; *Georgia Senate Journal,* 1840, 10, 12–13.

Efforts by merchants to force the Central Bank into fiscal responsibility boomeranged when, in 1842, a superior court judge warned sheriffs against receiving the depreciated bank bills. All judgments had thus become payable in the notes of specie-paying banks and restricted Central Bank notes' circulation. County grand juries called for the repeal of the bank's charter. Worse, from the state's point of view, Central Bank notes were accepted in payment of taxes, even at their discount, and the depreciated currency that flooded into the treasury put Georgia on the road to bankruptcy. Reluctantly, the governor informed the general assembly in 1842 that taxation was necessary. He also urged the legislature to relieve the bank of the burden it incurred by the acts ordering it to pay interest on the debt and its payment to the state's Western Atlantic Railroad. Saving the bank thus meant ending its career; the restrictions limited it to renewals of existing loans and collections. George Crawford assumed the governorship in 1844, determined to administer the last rites to the Central Bank. The bank, by his order, ended its renewals on existing loans.[39]

Red ink still engulfed the bank. Its estimated deficit of 1845 exceeded $300,000, leading Crawford to the inevitable conclusion that the state would somehow have to complete the process of bailing out the bank. Ultimately saddled with a debt of $200,000, the state began disposing of bank obligations on any terms available. In December, 1851, the Central Bank's assets were moved to the treasury. By 1851, the bank had netted a profit of only $50,000 in its entire history, according to Governor George Towns. The *Southern Banner* summed up the opinions of many contemporaries while praising the liquidation process as "prudent and safe." The experiment of state banking, it concluded, "is a poor business."[40]

Georgia's investment in the Central Bank was hardly inspiring in its returns. The state's assumption of the $440,000 sterling loan as a credit was in reality a liability and, when combined with uncollected assets, meant that more than half a million dollars must be added to the bank's

---

For the merchants' reactions, see *Georgia Messenger*, July 8, September 9, September 16, 1841, and June 2, June 23, August 18, September 8, 1842.

39. *Georgia Messenger*, August 18, September 8, 1842, September 4, 1845; *Georgia Senate Journal*, 1842, 9–13; 1843, 93–95; *Acts, Ga.*, 1842, 27–32.

40. *Southern Banner*, February 10, 1843.

losses. Private banks might have been unable to match the Central Bank's performance, even lacking the huge capital stock of the Central Bank, and had to operate without any guarantee of a state bailout. In short, the security of a public institution offered substantial advantages. Even when Central Bank *investment* was compared with private bank returns, the bottom line showed that the bank made little money. Moreover, the real comparison should not have been just alternative investment but investment compared with taxation and opportunity costs. Georgia could have raised far more than $50,000 in taxes from 1829 to 1856 simply by slightly increasing taxes on real estate, slaves, or specific goods, not to mention private bank stock. It would even have been reasonable to expect incremental gains in the private-sector economy, brought about by decreased state-backed competition, to have boosted the value, desirability, and amount of private bank stock and to have raised the necessary revenue without any additional taxes.

Those who pressed for the Central Bank also had to monitor the condition of the Bank of Darien carefully. If the Bank of Darien exhibited sudden serious weaknesses or instabilities, many of the arguments in favor of the Central Bank would evaporate. Third in size among the commercial banks, the Bank of Darien could thank the state for special advantages not enjoyed by its private competitors. Georgia owned half of its stock and appointed half of its directors. Until the Central Bank was made the state depository in 1828, government deposits went to the Bank of Darien. An abundant supply of other states' notes always left the Bank of Darien in a position to redeem in those bills rather than in specie. The availability of these notes actually encouraged the bank to expand its issues when other banks were curtailing and to concentrate on exchange operations. Its creators had intended otherwise, wanting the bank instead "to encourage and facilitate commercial operations between the western and southwestern parts of the state and Darien." The bank did little business until 1841, after several political controversies, when the governor revealed that the bank had engaged in cotton speculation with John Delafield, a New York bank president. Such a violation of its charter cost the Bank of Darien its life. In 1842 the state transferred its assets to the Central Bank. Legally Georgia appeared responsible to the bank's creditors, but the Georgia Supreme Court ruled in *William Robinson et al.* v. *The Bank of Darien* that the state was liable for only half the outstanding bills; the other half was the responsibility of the stockholders.[41]

Finally, despite the weaknesses of both the Bank of Darien and the Central Bank, Georgia's experience in banking proved proportional to its involvement. This involvement was relatively little compared with that of some New South states and quite minor compared with that of the Alabama and Arkansas monopolies. Georgia never held a banking monopoly in the state, and the existing private banks, especially prior to the free-banking law, had good financial connections in New York, making them somewhat stronger and more versatile than the Bank of Alabama, the Union Bank in Mississippi, and others. Georgia never tried to dominate the private banks or the Central Bank or the Bank of Darien. Commercial groups remained strong, and Whigs checked Jacksonian antibank excesses. Likewise, the banks never quite became the political footballs that they did in many states of the New South. Following the passage of the free-banking law and the demise of the state institutions, banking mushroomed in Georgia until the Panic of 1857. Although its development was matched and even exceeded by Georgia's agricultural growth, the commercial sector nevertheless wielded considerable influence. The result was societal tension as the industrialized world closed in.

REGULATORY POLICY IN VIRGINIA

Experiences in Georgia and South Carolina suggest that well-designed public policy played a critical role in the creation and growth of an adequate banking structure. Virginia added further evidence to this hypothesis, producing strong banks with its laws. It, too, chartered a state bank (see Table 5), seeking not a monopoly but a regulatory mechanism. One of the legislature's goals in chartering the Bank of Virginia was to force unchartered banks out of business so that the state could establish a consistent policy for future banks. Certain provisions enabled the Bank of Virginia to create branches at Norfolk, Petersburg, Fredericksburg, Lynchburg, Winchester, and Staunton. With subscriptions limited, the Virginia assembly hoped to spread its control over the banks. Charter provisions limited note issue to three times the capital stock. In a precedent that states of the New South in particular failed to adopt, the state

41. *William Robinson et al.* v. *The Bank of Darien,* 18 Georgia Reports 65, 1843.

legislature reserved inspection rights. (North Carolina adopted the same practice.) Reports featured a simple format, including only capital stock, debts due, deposits, notes in circulation, and cash on hand. Stockholders, by charter provisions, had to keep written records at their meetings. The charter for the Bank of Virginia provided a model for others granted by the state until 1837, when a general banking law was passed.[42]

Increased business in Virginia, as well as a growing need for internal improvements, meant that by the 1830s the capital stock in Virginia banks fell below demand. Either the legislature had to recharter existing banks with more capital or it had to restrict their issues somehow. Anticipating an increased number of applications for charters, the general assembly of 1836–1837 passed a controversial general banking law, simplifying existing charters and expanding the capital of the state's banks by $5 million. Opponents had argued that banks' loans and deposits already exceeded capital and that such increases would only encourage irresponsible lending. The capital increases were tied to several new provisions. Circulation was restricted to five times the banks' reserves; banks could not begin operations until three-fifths of their capital had been paid in; refusal to pay specie could be challenged through lawsuits, wherein plaintiffs could recover 15 percent damages plus costs; and examination statements were to be sent to the governor every three months. Emphasis, however, remained on numbers—loans to capital, and notes to specie—and examinations did not presume to judge loan quality or risk. The state agreed to receive the notes of any specie-paying bank as taxes. Virginia banks could not hold stock in another bank, although they could receive stock in payment of debts due, nor could banks outside Virginia hold stock in any Virginia bank incorporated under the law. Punishment for violations, also unusually strong for the time, could involve the bank's forfeiture of all its stock to the state.[43]

Since 1817, when inadequacies in the bank committee's powers of inspection had led to the embarrassing refusal by the officials of the Farmers' Bank of Lynchburg to cooperate with an investigation, Virginia's

42. Royall, A History of Virginia Banks, 9; Through the Years in Norfolk, 1636 to 1936 (n.p., 1936). Also see Frances Williams, They Faced the Future (Richmond, Va., 1951).
43. Acts, Va., 1836–37, Chap. 83, pp. 68–71. For opposition to the capital increase, see Howard Braverman, "The Economic and Political Background of the Conservative Revolt in Virginia," Virginia Magazine of History and Biography, April, 1952, pp. 266–87.

Table 5. Commercial Banks in Virginia Prior to 1865

Bank	Date(s) Chartered	Capital ($ millions)	Location	Remarks
Bank of Virginia	January, 1804	1.50; 1814: 2.50; 1837: 3.15	Richmond	State owned $.30 of stock that went in Literary Fund for Public Education
Farmers Bank of Virginia	February, 1812	2.00; 1837: 3.01	Richmond	State owned 1,087 shares of stock that went in Literary Fund for Public Education.
Bank of the Valley of Virginia	February, 1817	0.40–0.60; 1834: 0.80; 1837: 1.54	Winchester	
Northwestern Bank of Virginia	February, 1817	0.40–0.60; 1830: 0.30; 1837: 0.80	Wheeling	Survived to current times
Merchants and Mechanics Bank	March, 1834	0.20–0.50; 1837: 0.80	Wheeling	
Exchange Bank of Virginia	March, 1837	1.80	Norfolk	
Bank of Kanawha	1839		Kanawha	Special charter provisions for loans
Trans-Allegheny Bank	October, 1851	0.10	Jeffersonville	Free bank
Bank of Wheeling	October, 1851	0.50	Wheeling	Free bank
Bank of the Old Dominion	January, 1851	0.50	Alexandria	Free bank

Bank	Date		City	
Central Bank	March, 1853	0.50	Staunton	Free bank
Bank of Winchester	July, 1853	0.25	Winchester	Free bank
Monticello Bank	July, 1853	0.30	Charlottesville	Free bank
Bank of Berkeley	September, 1853	0.10	Martinsburg	Free bank
Bank of Rockingham	November, 1853	0.30	Harrisonburg	Free bank
Bank of Scottsville	November, 1853	0.20	Scottsville	Free bank
Bank of Commerce	December, 1853	0.50	Fredericksburg	Free bank
Manufacturing and Farmers Bank	February, 1854	0.30	Wheeling	Free bank
Merchants Bank	March, 1854	0.90	Lynchburg	Free bank
Bank of Fairmont	July, 1854	0.20	Fairmont	Free bank
Bank of Charleston	?	0.30	Charleston	
Bank of Howardsville	?	0.16	Howardsville	
Bank of Philippi	?	0.70	Philippi	
Bank of Danville	?	0.28	Danville	
Farmers Bank of Fincastle	?	0.15	Fincastle	
Bank of Rockinbridge	?	0.12	Rockinbridge	

Sources: (a) Van Fenstermaker, *Development of American Commercial Banking*, Table A-29; Starnes, *Sixty Years of Branch Banking*; (b) individual bank reports made at varying dates in the year; House Executive Document 30, 25th Cong., 1st Sess.; House Executive Document 79, 25th Cong., 2d Sess.; House Executive Document 156, 25th Cong., 3d Sess.; House Executive Document 172, 26th Cong., 1st Sess.; House Executive Document 111, 26th Cong., 2d Sess.; House Executive Document 226, 29th Cong., 1st Sess.; House Executive Document 68, 31st Cong., 1st Sess.; House Executive Document 66, 3zd Cong., 2d Sess.; House Executive Document 102, 33d Cong., 1st Sess.; House Executive Document 82, 33d Cong., 2d Sess.; House Executive Document 102, 34th Cong., 2d Sess.; House Executive Document 87, 34th Cong., 3d Sess.; House Executive Document 107, 35th Cong., 1st Sess.; House Executive Document 112, 35th Cong., 2d Sess.; House Executive Document 49, 36th Cong., 2d Sess.; House Executive Document 77, 36th Cong., 2d Sess.; House Executive Document 25, 37th Cong., 3d Sess.; House Executive Document 20, 38th Cong., 1st Sess.; Senate Executive Document 2, 37th Cong., 2d Sess.

laws demanded increasingly thorough and complete examinations. Most charters also required periodical internal examinations by the directors. Using its portion of the surplus revenue, the state took one-half of the new capital stock of all banks then existing in Virginia. As a condition of receiving this capital, the banks agreed to distribute it among their branches equally. Before the distribution had been completed, the Panic of 1837 struck Virginia.

Postponing the suspension of specie payments during the depression, the Virginia financial institutions finally succumbed from caution more than from distress, although the Northwestern Bank did not suspend. Most banks thus violated their charters and faced forfeiture, but the legislature well understood the banks' plight and, in a special session, passed a relief measure, delaying the forfeiture provisions by almost a year. In the interim, banks tried to reduce their loans and discounts. The special session also postponed the planned capital increases for some banks and appointed a special committee to investigate the solvency of the state's banks. Reporting that Virginia's banks remained solvent, an investigating committee recommended that the relief be extended until April 1839. After learning of action by New York and Philadelphia banks, Virginia's financial community resumed specie payments in 1838, and so no charter forfeitures occurred. A brief upturn in the economy gave way to recession. Philadelphia and Baltimore banks again suspended in 1839, and after a short period of specie loss, Virginia followed, in an action that cost the banks political support and public trust.[44]

During the panic periods antibank Democrats tried seriously to curtail banking in Virginia. Still, the legislature applied the law with great reluctance, as the Democrats saw it. Banks, thundered one Democratic editorial, must "be *obedient* to the laws, not *masters* of the law-making power." Another described the financial system as "eminently defective, and rotten in its operations." When evaluating comments such as these, we may usefully recall the reasoning behind the specie-suspension provisions: the goal was to maintain a sound bank, that is, an acceptable specie-to-bills ratio. Because the perceived northward drain of southern specie threatened to decrease the specie reserves of the Virginia banks to zero, the Virginia legislature acted within the spirit of the law to pre-

44. *Acts, Va.*, 1838, Chap. 106, pp. 78–79; *Virginia House Documents*, 1841–42, Doc. 59, p. 1.

serve the banks' specie until the drain subsided. Moreover, the law was worthwhile in its other aim—to prevent fiat suspension. Then, too, the banks exhibited great concern about suspending, indicating that they hardly controlled the legislature. Virginia's banking record, which featured strong reserve ratios and conservative but responsible management, defused much of the antibank sentiment. The 1837 banking law, then, can be judged a sound measure for its time. Although the panic intervened before the law could be implemented, it eventually discouraged the behavior that the state disliked, and it encouraged sound banking operations.[45]

The state's support of banks came at some cost. In 1840 the banks loaned the state $200,000 to assist in the payment of debts incurred through public-improvement schemes, and they increased the loan by $150,000 in 1843. Perhaps, however, the loan was less altruistic than it might have seemed at first. Bank taxation bills passed in both 1842 and 1843, so that the loans perhaps staved off bank taxation.[46]

Virginia continued with its 1837 banking law until it introduced its own free-banking law in 1851, which did not interfere with existing branch bank charters. Any group desiring a banking charter could deposit with the state treasurer certificates of public debt or bonds of any accepted improvement company in amounts equal to the value of securities deposited. Thirteen independent banks took advantage of this law—although over thirty had received charters—but they found stiff competition from existing financial houses. Free banks paid the same premiums and otherwise followed the rules governing existing banks. These taxes and premiums restricted entry, but the new banks soon discovered that, through the power to create branches, existing banks had substantial advantages. A mother bank easily established branch offices in small towns, whereas an independent bank, faced with high operating costs and premiums, found the going tough. Adding to the free banks' burden, the 1854 legislature created an office of banking clerk in the treasury department and authorized additional fees to pay his salary.[47]

45. Richmond *Enquirer*, June 13, 23, 1837, March 10, 1838, December 21, 1939, October 26, November 19, December 11, 1841; Richmond *Whig*, June 27, 1937; Sharp, *Jacksonians vs. the Banks*, 242–43.

46. *Acts, Va.*, 1843, Chap. 1, p. 6 (not p. 9, as Starnes reported on p. 102); *ibid.*, 1844, Chap. 1, p. 6.

47. *Acts, Va.*, 1851, Chap. 58, p. 43. "Banking capital should always be based upon the active operations and positive value of commerce [but] when loaned to those who are

Free banking brought greater interest in public supervision and examinations of banking. According to one Virginia legislator, "looking to our permanent future policy we should provide some better security for the public than the charter of bank officers," which in the past had generally proved sufficient. Efforts to put these concerns into law, however, were "lost in a maze of unsound remedial proposals." In truth, hardly more regulation was needed. Even historians who lamented the lack of more widespread banking regulation have acknowledged that "banks had large capitals, bank failures were of no consequence [actually, they were completely absent in Virginia], and losses to note holders and depositors of State banks were unknown before 1860."[48]

Branch banking, perhaps because of its strong competition with the independent banks, came under attack in 1854. The charters of the established banks were soon to expire, and if the state chose to switch to a complete independent banking system, the time was ripe. Despite some strong opposition in the general assembly from John Rutherfoord, the existing system won a vote of confidence. Existing banks' charters received a six-year extension. A year later, the state also took a major step in separating itself from banking by deciding to sell its share of all bank stock in order to pay the public debt. Loans from the banks failed to keep the state's deficit from growing, and the sale of bank stock could bring as much as two million dollars. The decision to sell, however, also involved a surrender of Virginia's power to appoint directors, and so the state substituted a law permitting it, at any time, to appoint commissioners with full power to inspect the books.

Overall, Virginia's banking history featured stable and strong banks. Despite the charters granted to thirteen independent banks (thirteen

---

not engaged in trade or enterprise, is an evil to the community upon which it is bestowed" (Richmond *Whig*, March 28, 1851). Hugh Rockoff (*The Free Banking Era: A Re-examination* [New York, 1975], 3) asserted that Virginia did not permit free entry. This statement is only technically true, for there is little evidence that the general assembly refused any application for a charter under free-banking provisions, and indeed the state chartered far more banks than actually began operations.

48. John Rutherfoord, *Speech on Banks* (n.p., 1854); *Virginia House Journal*, 1855–56, 31; *Acts, Va.*, 1855–56, Chaps. 60–75, pp. 48–78; *Acts, Va.*, 1856–57, Chap. 15, p. 22; *Code of Virginia, 1860*, 265–66; *Virginia House Journal*, 1855–56, 13. Also, see Gruchy, *Supervision and Control*, 59. For post-1857 developments in policy, see *Acts, Va.*, 1857–58, Chap. 76, pp. 57–58.

actually went into operation of the thirty-five granted charters), no bank actually failed in Virginia until the Civil War. The banks survived the crisis of 1837–1839 and again of 1857 without failure. Most of them did not even suffer a reduction of capital. Virginia relied heavily on the ex-perience of other southern states as well as on that of northern states in formulating early banking policies. Like their counterparts in Georgia, the Virginia regulators sought to prevent monopoly by maximum diffu-sion of stock—by requiring the opening of stock books at various loca-tions throughout the state. Unlike Alabama and Arkansas, Virginia care-fully limited the powers of the directors by restricting the duration of service, prohibiting interlocking directorates, requiring citizenship for directors, and later making them hold stock in the bank. Branch-banking provisions allowed sound banks to extend capital to needed areas with-out risking the creation of a new, separate bank, which contributed to the fact that no economic division of the state developed to engulf the issue of banks politically.

REGULATORY POLICY IN NORTH CAROLINA

Virginia followed the same pattern as North Carolina, which had also chartered private banks before it entered banking (see Table 6). The State Bank of North Carolina came into being after the Bank of Cape Fear and the Bank of Newbern. Its purpose was to detach the state from northern control. Legislators approved a state bank somewhat reluc-tantly because it had never been shown that the proposed state institu-tion would have any advantages not already enjoyed by the private banks. Its creation demonstrated a need for banking capital more than for state involvement, but ultimately the demand for longer-term credit than had been offered by either private institution proved the tell-ing factor. North Carolina's first state bank, chartered in 1810, had a $1.6 million capitalization, provided for six branches, and could main-tain a circulation of $4.8 million above capitalization. The state reserved the right to take 2,500 shares and provided in the State Bank's charter that no other banks would be established while the State Bank lived. Lawmakers mistakenly anticipated that both the Bank of Cape Fear and the Bank of Newbern would subscribe for stock in the State Bank, per-haps eventually becoming branches. Instead, they treated the State Bank as a rival and competitor. By remaining separate from the state,

Table 6. The Commercial Banks in North Carolina Prior to 1865

Bank	Date(s) Chartered	Capital ($ millions)	Location	Remarks
Bank of Cape Fear	1804	0.25	Wilmington	Capital increased to $0.52 million in 1814; again increased in 1833 with $0.8 million capital; state reserved $.025 million capital stock
Bank of Newbern	1804	0.20	Newbern	Capital increased to $.57 million in 1814; state reserved $.25 million capital stock
State Bank of North Carolina	1810	1.60	Raleigh	
Merchants Bank	1833	0.25	Newbern	
Albermarle Bank	1833	0.20	Edenton	
Bank of the State of North Carolina	1833	1.50	Raleigh(?)	
Bank of Washington	1850	0.40	Washington	
Commercial Bank	1850	?	Wilmington	
Bank of Wadesboro	?	?	Wadesboro	
Milton Savings Institution	1850	0.25	Milton	
Jackson Savings Institution	1850	0.05	Northampton	
Raleigh Savings Institution	1850	0.25	Raleigh	
Mechanics Savings Society	1850	0.02	Weldon	
Bank of Charlotte	1852	0.03	Charlotte	
Farmers Bank of North Carolina	1852	0.50	Elizabeth City	

Bank of Yanceyville	1852	0.20	Yanceyville
Bank of Fayetteville	1854	0.38	Fayetteville
Bank of Clarendon	1854	?	Fayetteville
Bank of Wilmington	1854	?	Wilmington
Savings institution	1854	?	Washington
Savings institution	1854	?	Wilmington
Savings institution	1854	?	Smithville
Bank of Lexington	1859	?	Lexington
Bank of Salisbury	1859	?	Salisbury
Minters and Planters Bank	1859	?	Murphey
Bank of Commerce	1859	?	Newbern
Bank of North Carolina	1859	2.50	Raleigh?
Savings institution	1859	?	?
Savings institution	1859	?	?
Savings institution	1859	?	?
Savings institution	1859	?	?
Mutual Life Insurance and Trust Company	1861	?	?
Bank of Graham	1862	?	Graham
Bank of Lincolnton	1862	?	Lincolnton

Sources: Branston Holder, "The Three Banks of the State of North Carolina, 1810–1812" (Ph.D. dissertation, University of North Carolina, 1937); individual bank reports made at varying dates in the year; *House Executive Document 30*, 25th Cong., 1st Sess.; *House Executive Document 79*, 25th Cong., 2d Sess.; *House Executive Document 156*, 25th Cong., 3d Sess.; *House Executive Document 172*, 26th Cong., 1st Sess.; *House Executive Document 111*, 26th Cong., 2d Sess.; *House Executive Document 226*, 29th Cong., 1st Sess.; *House Executive Document 68*, 31st Cong., 1st Sess.; *House Executive Document 66*, 32d Cong., 2d Sess.; *House Executive Document 102*, 33d Cong., 1st Sess.; *House Executive Document 82*, 33d Cong., 2d Sess.; *House Executive Document 102*, 34th Cong., 2d Sess.; *House Executive Document 87*, 34th Cong., 3d Sess.; *House Executive Document 107*, 35th Cong., 1st Sess.; *House Executive Document 112*, 35th Cong., 2d Sess.; *House Executive Document 49*, 36th Cong., 1st Sess.; *House Executive Document 77*, 36th Cong., 2d Sess.; *House Executive Document 25*, 37th Cong., 3d Sess.; *House Executive Document 20*, 38th Cong., 1st Sess.; *Senate Executive Document 2*, 37th Cong., 2d Sess.

they preserved market forces in the banking development of North
Carolina.[49]

Despite its name, the first state bank was primarily a private institution. Only a portion of its stock was owned by the state. Its private status
was upheld in the *State Bank of North Carolina* v. *Clark and McNeil*,
but the state cultivated its identity as a public institution to gain wider
circulation for its notes. Still, the state retained as many votes as the
largest stockholder, and on the whole, the State Bank's connection to the
state government was considerably closer than the relationship of any private bank with the state government. Many in the legislature and much of
the public regarded the bank as a state institution. North Carolina therefore reinforces the notion that, although a dichotomy existed, Old South
and New South categories represent something of a continuum.[50]

Association with the state had certain advantages. Although the State
Bank's stock escaped taxation, both private banks paid a 1 percent tax.
Moreover, after 1814 both private banks were required to lend the state
10 percent of their paid-in capital. No such requirement fell on the
State Bank.

Anticipating the bank's charter expiration in 1835, and disappointed
with the profits, stockholders in 1828 voted to liquidate the State Bank
of North Carolina. Prevailing views of loan collection held that it was
impossible for a corporation to collect after its charter expired, a view
the legislature shared. An act passed in 1830 that allowed the final
liquidation of the bank. It paid stockholders 94 percent of par when it
closed. The state had received a 9 percent return on its investment.
Even though the stockholders and the state as the major shareholder
expected certain favors, the bank was well managed overall.

With the demise of the State Bank, legislators immediately called for
the establishment of a true state bank, arguing that such intermediaries
had proved successful in Virginia, Louisiana, and Florida. One attempt
to set up such a bank failed when the stock sales fell short because the
state retained half of the directorships. When another bank bill was submitted in 1834 calling for only four of its ten directors to be appointed by
the state, it became law. In line with North Carolina's first experience

49. *Laws, N.C.*, 1804, Chaps. 21 and 22, 1810, Chap. 5; *Fayetteville* (N.C.) *Journal*,
June 10, 1829; *Acts Incorporating the State Bank of North Carolina and the By-Laws*,
30–31.

50. *State Bank of North Carolina* vs. *Clark and McNeil*, 8 North Carolina Reports 36
(1820); *Laws, N.C.*, 1810, Chap. 788.

and in order to decrease loans going to directors, fewer directors were permitted to serve. In spite of such precautions, many of the same people who had run the State Bank became employees of the Bank of the State of North Carolina.[51]

Although the bank had branches in four cities and agencies in six others, it still had no monopoly: the Bank of Cape Fear, with its newly extended charter, continued to compete with it. The legislature also chartered new banks in Newbern and Albermarle, although the latter never opened. Branches of the Bank of the State kept their own books and specie reserves, but the total assets of the bank were computed on the basis of all branch and agency assets. Initial capitalization of the Bank of the State was $1.5 million.

Charter provisions also exemplified the seriousness with which North Carolina legislators viewed corruption. False reports made to the directors, the treasurer, or the legislators were punishable by imprisonment. Penalties for embezzlement included a fine, imprisonment, or thirty-nine lashes! Perhaps confident that the threat alone would deter, policy makers required no regular inspections.[52]

Most of the Bank of the State's battles concerned the issue of increasing its capitalization. An 1854 attempt to raise the capital to $2 million and renew the charter failed because the state insisted on having directorships proportional to stock ownership. Stockholders also opposed provisions that made stockholders liable for twice the amount they held in case of insolvency. In 1857, a second increase attempt that would have raised the capitalization to $3 million failed. Stockholders considered such a capitalization too large. The bank continued in business until its 1860 charter expiration. Eventually the charter was extended to 1868 for note collection, but the bank generally ended its business through 1859, returning 100 percent to its stockholders and paying a 4 percent dividend in its final six months.[53]

51. *North Carolina Legislative Documents*, 1831–1835, Doc. No. 8, 1833; Holder, "Three Banks," 268–79; *Laws, N.C.*, 1833–1834, Chap. 3. The state bank also played a role in some of North Carolina's most important corporation regulation cases. See *State Bank of North Carolina* vs. *Hunter*, 12 North Carolina Reports, 125 (1826); *Ehringhous* vs. *Ford*, 25 North Carolina Reports, 522 (1843).

52. *Laws, N.C.*, 1833–1834, Chap. 5.

53. "Memorial of the Stockholders to the Bank of the State of North Carolina," *North Carolina Legislative Documents*, 1856–1857, Doc. No. 20; Tarboro (N.C.) *Southerner*, July 11, 1857; Raleigh *North Carolina Standard*, July 15, 1857, January 4, February 25, June 16, 1860, July 3, 1861.

Between 1847 and 1860 the state witnessed the incorporation of fourteen new private banks with twenty-six branches. North Carolina seemed to feel a void without a state bank and organized the Bank of North Carolina to replace the Bank of the State. It began operations on November 1, 1859, under management nearly identical to that of the Bank of the State. Many people who owed the old bank transferred their obligations and renewed their notes at the Bank of North Carolina. G. W. Mordecai, president of the Bank of the State, also served as president of the Bank of North Carolina; some other officers had even served in all three state banks.[54]

Charter provisions for the new state bank included a required loan to the state of $200,000, annual taxation of thirty cents per share on all stock owned by individuals, and provision that the state treasurer would collect 4 percent annual interest on all notes in circulation. Comprehensive bylaws, representing an attempt to correct previous state bank abuses, provided for two loan types of varying duration and for investigations of the bank's books by stockholders' committees. The legislature retained inspection rights, and stockholders again made serious attempts to curtail loans to directors, which ultimately succeeded. Unlike almost all other southern states, North Carolina placed the supervision of banking in the hands of the state treasurer rather than the legislature. This final state bank was liquidated at the end of the Civil War, bringing to three the total number of state banks that had concluded operations with relatively little controversy.[55]

In the 1850s North Carolina considered adopting free-banking laws. The general bank-incorporating act appeared simultaneously with an-

54. *Laws, N.C.*, 1848–1849, Chap. 8; *Laws, N.C.*, 1850–51, Chap. 9; *Laws, N.C.*, 1852, Chaps. 4, 5, 6, 8; *Laws, N.C.*, 1854–1855, Chap. 75; *N.C. Legislative Documents*, 1860–1861, Doc. No. 14; *Bankers' Magazine*, February, 1859, p. 661; *House Executive Documents*, 26th Cong., 1st Sess., No. 49, p. 153.

55. *Laws, N.C.*, 1859, Chap. 67; *Charter and By-Laws of the Bank of North Carolina*, pp. 15–22. At no time were any of the state banks to provide even a substantial portion of North Carolina's revenues. Nor were private banks to play a major role in financing state enterprise through their taxes. Revenues came from land taxes, poll taxes, and various licenses, and later both income and inheritance taxes were added. Payments for internal improvements came mostly from the state, for example in the case of the Cape Fear Navigation Company. In smaller, more general improvements, the Board of Internal Improvements relied on tolls. Towns levied taxes for railroad capitalization, and railroads were also aided by tolls. The single exception to this pattern was the Southwestern Railroad Bank, which operated a branch in North Carolina. See Charles Weaver, *Internal Improvements in North Carolina Previous to 1860* (Spartanburg, S.C., 1971 [1903]), 48, 74, 78, 86.

other bill to establish a People's Bank of North Carolina with the whopping capitalization of $10 million, which was also based on the bond security system. Neither bill passed, but the legislature had not been niggardly in dispensing charters. In view of this fact and the branch-banking provisions, it is unlikely that North Carolina would have profited as much from a free-banking act as some of the more monopolistic states. Furthermore, in addition to standard banks of issue, the state chartered at least seven savings banks between 1850 and 1860. Thus North Carolina's system profited by introducing competition and variety from its earliest stages.[56]

Apart from Virginia, North Carolina had the best banking record of the antebellum period. Like Virginia, Georgia, and South Carolina, it welcomed competition. Perhaps even more than their counterparts in Virginia, North Carolina's lawmakers periodically assessed their laws in an objective way, correcting and modifying them. For the Old South states, a balance of regulation and competition was the key to success, and they generally emphasized competition.

Great continuity in its state bank management also benefited North Carolina's banks. Many of the employees of the Bank of the State took jobs with the Bank of North Carolina. A network of family and friends had a hand in the management of all three banks. Stability of this sort enhanced the experience of the officers and employees, contributing to sounder management. It is instructive to contrast this record with that of Mississippi; no employees of the Bank of the Mississippi, and especially no officers, were invited to fill jobs at the Union Bank. Similarly, Alabama's lawmakers failed to draw on the experience of the Royalist bank in Huntsville or to learn "tricks of the trade" from bankers at the Bank of Mobile.

North Carolina and Virginia made clear yet another difference between policy makers and bankers in New South and Old South: lawmakers and bankers in the Old South seemed to understand banking and monetary theory, or at least the theories of the day, much more clearly than their contemporaries in the New South. Members of the committee on corporations, which dealt with banking, for example, exhibited familiarity with most of the banking systems in the United States as well

56. *North Carolina Legislative Documents*, 1854–1855, House Doc. No. 34, p. 311; *North Carolina Legislative Documents*, 1854–1855, House Doc. No. 22, p. 172; *Laws, N.C.*, 1858–1859, Chaps. 73, 74, 75.

as with those in England, Scotland, and Germany. Committee members often quoted from *Bankers Magazine* or from the writings of David Ricardo, H. C. Carey, William Gouge, and other banking theorists.[57]

REGULATORY POLICY IN LOUISIANA

Despite admirable records of the Carolinas and Virginia, Louisiana was generally considered the state in the Old South that was most advanced and progressive in its banking policies. George Green has so thoroughly detailed Louisiana's regulatory history that only a brief review is needed here. Louisiana's highly diversified economy, fine natural port, and proximity to the Mississippi River created a commercial economy with a tremendous demand for banking services. Linking the rural areas to New Orleans, individual entrepreneurs, factors, brokers, and planters often crossed occupational lines to pursue "simultaneous careers in planting, commerce, and finance." The state exhibited the three major types of financial institutions found elsewhere in the South: chartered banks, private unincorporated banks, and free banks (see Table 7). As early as 1804 New Orleans had a bank, established by W. C. C. Claiborne on a grant from the territorial governor. Shortly thereafter, the Bank of the United States opened a branch in the city. When its charter expired, the legislature placed two private banks in operation in its stead, one of which was the highly successful Bank of New Orleans.[58]

Early in Louisiana's history it encouraged competition; it also showed little reluctance to seek a solution to its debts—totaling $121,000 by 1815—through a state bank. Discussion of such an institution lasted several years until the state chartered the Louisiana State Bank, with $2 million capitalization, of which the state purchased $500,000 worth of capital stock and received in return the power to appoint six of the eigh-

57. *North Carolina Legislative Documents*, 1858–1859, House Document No. 22, p. 172.

58. Green, *Finance and Economic Development*, 15, 18–29; Robert Roeder, "Merchants of Antebellum New Orleans," *Explorations in Entrepreneurial History*, 1958, pp. 113–22; Caldwell, *Banking History of Louisiana*, 26–29; *Acts, La.*, 4th Legis., 1st Sess., March 3, 1819, p. 48; *Acts, La.*, 5th Legis. 2d Sess., March 14, 1822, p. 40; *Acts, La.*, 6th Legis., 1st Sess., March 26, 1823, pp. 66–68; *Acts, La.*, 3d Legis., 2d Sess., March 14, 1818, pp. 78–90; *Acts of the Territory of New Orleans*, 86–100, 164–78; *Louisiana House Journal*, 5th Legis., 1st Sess., February 19, 1820, p. 34; *ibid.*, 7th Legis., 2d Sess., 48–76, 83–84.

Table 7. The Commercial Banks in Louisiana Prior to 1865

Bank	Date(s) Chartered	Capital ($ millions)	Location	Remarks
Louisiana	March, 1804	$0.3		Liquidation 1819–1821
First Bank of the United States (branch)	1805	2.0		Charter expired 1811
Planters Bank	April, 1811	0.6		Suspended operations 1820, charter expired 1826
Bank of New Orleans	April, 1811	0.5	New Orleans	Scheduled to expire 1826
Second Bank of the United States (branch)	March, 1823 1817	— —		Renewed to 1847; into liquidation in 1842 Charter expired 1836
Louisiana State Bank	March, 1818	2.0		Became State National Bank in 1870; liquidated 1908
Bank of Louisiana	April, 1824	4.0		Into liquidation 1865
Consolidated Association of the Planters of Louisiana	March, 1827 February, 1828	2.0 2.5	New Orleans	New charter, state bonds issued, capital increased; liquidation begun 1843, completed 1883
City Bank of New Orleans	March, 1831	2.0	New Orleans	Charter expired 1850; assets purchased by Louisiana State Bank
Canal Bank	March, 1831	4.0	New Orleans	Original charter to 1870; reorganized and survived into twentieth century

Table 7. *(continued)*

Bank	Date(s) Chartered	Capital ($ millions)	Location	Remarks
Union Bank of Lousiana	April, 1832	7.0		Into liquidation January, 1844
Citizens Bank of Louisiana	April, 1833	12.0		Original charter to 1884
	March, 1836	—		State guarantees bank bonds; into liquidation 1842
	March, 1852	—		Legislature revives charter; reorganized and survived into twentieth century
Clinton and Port Hudson Railroad Company	1833	0.5		Charter amended to give mortgage banking powers
Mechanics and Traders Bank	April, 1833	2.0		Original charter to 1853
	March, 1850	—		Authorized to begin liquidation; converted to free bank 1853; survived past Civil War
Commercial Bank of New Orleans	April, 1833	3.0	New Orleans	Into liquidation 1843
Atchafalaya Railroad and Banking Company	March, 1835	2.0		Banking operations into liquidation in 1842
New Orleans and Carrollton Railroad and Banking Company	April, 1835	3.0	New Orleans	Banking powers granted to existing company and surrendered 1844

Bank	Date	Capital	City	Notes
New Orleans Gas Light and Banking Company	April, 1835	6.0	New Orleans	Banking powers granted to existing company and surrendered 1845
Exchange and Banking Company	April, 1835	2.0	New Orleans	Into liquidation 1842
New Orleans Improvement and Banking Company	February, 1836	2.0	New Orleans	Banking powers granted to existing company; into liquidation 1842
Merchants Bank of New Orleans	February, 1836	1.0	New Orleans	Into liquidation 1847
Pontchartrain Railroad and Banking Company	March, 1836	—	New Orleans	Banking powers granted to existing company but never exercised
Bank of New Orleans	1835	1.0	New Orleans	First free bank; capital raised to $2 million by 1857
Southern Bank	1853	1.25	New Orleans	Free bank
Bank of James Robb	1857	0.6	New Orleans	Reorganized 1859 as Merchants Bank; free bank
Bank of America	1857	1.0		Free bank
Union Bank	1857	1.5	New Orleans	Free bank
Crescent City Bank	1857	1.0	New Orleans	Free bank

Source: Green, Finance and Economic Development, 22–23.

teen directors. It also had five branch offices outside New Orleans, each capitalized at $100,000.[59]

Credit reduction by the Louisiana State Bank in the 1820s caused the state to charter the Bank of Louisiana, capitalized at $4 million, with half of the stock held by the state in return for $2.4 million worth of bonds. The Bank of Louisiana had five branches in rural areas, each capitalized at $200,000, but four of these closed. In 1828, new demands for agricultural credit led to the charter of the state's first property bank—the Consolidated Association of the Planters of Louisiana. Unable to sell its two million dollars' worth of bonds backed by the mortgages, the bank turned to the state, which rescued it despite heavy opposition. Inundated by demands for bank charters from private sources, lawmakers soon realized that the state had no real obligation to play such a role. Instead they saw advantages in mobilizing "domestic capital in the hands of small traders, mechanics, professional men, and property owners." They therefore chartered ten more banks through 1836, not counting three railroad and banking companies, one gas light and banking company, and an improvement banking company. Many of these had branches, and their total capitalizations added almost $30 million to the state's burgeoning capital. The largest were the $7 million of the Union Bank and the huge $12 million of the Citizens Bank of Louisiana.[60]

Each of the two last-named banks was offered opportunities for state participation. Indeed, lawmakers seemed hypnotized by prospects for profit and mesmerized by appeals for more credit. When the Union Bank proposal appeared in 1832, it represented a doubling of all the capital of state-chartered banks, some of it deemed necessary in anticipation of the demise of the second Bank of the United States. Again, the state planned to issue bonds on the bank's behalf. Eight branches eventually dotted the state, dispensing $1.8 million in capital and reserving yet another $800,000 for loans in parishes outside the operating range of the branches. The Citizens Bank, chartered a year later, was a property bank representing the largest bank in America by capitalization. Bond

59. *Louisiana House Journal*, 6 Legis., 2d Sess., 25, 39–40; ibid., 7 Legis., 1st Sess., 52.

60. *Acts, La.*, 8 Legis., 1st Sess., March 16, 1827, pp. 96–116; *ibid.*, 2d Sess., February 19, 1828, pp. 30–36; *ibid.*, 10th Legis., 1st Sess., 26–62; *Louisiana House Journal*, 8th Legis., 1st Sess., 64–66; *ibid.*, 2d Sess., 33–34; 9th Legis., 2d Sess., 69–70; *ibid.*, 10th Legis., 1st Sess., 21, 26, 30, 33, 36, 42, 47–48, 53, 92–95; Green, *Finance and Economic Development*, 21–22.

sales slowed to a snail's pace, however, until, in 1835, Hope and Company of Amsterdam decided to take three million dollars' worth if the state would guarantee the bonds. Endorsement from the legislature in 1836 meant that the state's underwriting of three property banks totaled "a potential obligation of $21.5 million," or roughly two-thirds of the available capital in the state.[61]

Five banking companies with special improvements or construction responsibilities, chartered in 1835 and 1836, by and large also suffered from an illiquid asset structure. They engaged in the creation and operation of two railroads, the installation of New Orleans city gas streetlights, and construction of two of the city's hotels. When these obviously weak enterprises are added to the true banks in Louisiana, it is evident that the state commanded forty-six million dollars in banking capital by the beginning of the panic, at least on paper.

Shocked by the panic, Louisiana reacted with major banking regulations. Coming early in a decade marked by restrictive regulations, the Louisiana Bank Act of 1842 represented Louisiana's first attempt to reform its regulations and actually to control its banking system. This act was viewed as a model law and was used as a pattern in other states and Congress. Before the 1842 law, among the general rules found in most charters, restrictions on the size and location of branches had the effect of giving the state geographical control of loan distribution. Occasionally provisions required that a portion of funds go toward long-term credit to expand lending to planters. Limits on the amount a single borrower could obtain were sometimes written into the charter.[62]

Attempts to control usury led to the Usury Bill of 1823, which allowed third parties to recover both interest and principal on usurious loans. Merchants reacted so negatively to the bill that the legislature set usury rates quite high—10 percent in 1840, the highest in any southern state—which indicated that the rate reacted to current conditions rather than acted as a ceiling. Louisiana's tendencies appeared to be an index of

61. Green, *Finance and Economic Development*, 24; *Louisiana House Journal*, 10th Legis., 3d Sess., 39, 65–83, 102–11; *ibid.*, 11th Legis., 1st Sess., 4; 12th Legis., 2d Sess., 15–35, 103–105; *Acts, La.*, 10th Legis., 3d Sess., 42–72; *ibid.*, 11th Legis., 1st Sess., 124–36, 151–94; *ibid.*, 12th Legis., 2d Sess., 16–24.

62. *House Journal*, 10th Legis., 3d Sess., 1832, pp. 64, 81–82, 106–108; *ibid.*, 11th Legis., 1st Sess., 1833, pp. 32, 41; *ibid.*, 2d Sess., 1834, pp. 45–46, 76; *ibid.*, 12th Legis., 2d Sess., 1836, pp. 22–25, 30, 103–105. Also see Paul Trescott, *Financing American Enterprise* (New York, 1963), 10–11.

current conditions. By 1850, Louisiana's rate had dropped to 8 percent, still higher than that in half the southern states and no lower than that in any of them. Expanded credit, not stricter laws, eventually drove out usury in Louisiana.

Louisiana banks promoted a number of social welfare and public economic objectives, often at the request or order of the state. More than twenty-four million dollars in state bonds were authorized for banking purposes between 1824 and 1838. Loans from the banks to canal, brick, and railroad companies reflected larger outlays, but the state also mandated loans to finance street pavings, maintain schools and orphanages, and operate hospitals. Promotion of agriculture, frequently cited as evidence of planter domination, certainly played an important role in the state's promotional ventures. The state led most others in developing and promoting property banks. Gradually the banks evolved into mortgage and commercial banks catering to urban clientele. Pure "plantation banks" diminished in number and influence.[63]

Whereas general regulations appeared to fail during the Panic of 1837, the Louisiana legislature passed the Bank Act of 1842. Historians and bankers have praised it at virtually every opportunity. Yet most of the accolades have stressed one section containing its "fundamental rules." Basically, the honored section divided a bank's accounts into cash assets (including specie, "loans on deposits," or commercial paper due in ninety days, all offset by cash liabilities in notes and deposits) and "dead weight" assets or "loans on capital" (in other words, loans that would fall due in a period longer than ninety days). Under the law, banks could not increase their dead weight without maintaining a corresponding cash liability-to-specie ratio of three to one, with two-thirds of the paper payable in ninety days.[64]

Disagreeing with generations of banking historians, George Green offered a sharply critical analysis of the Bank Act. The act initially

63. See the charters of Citizens Bank, Gas Light Bank, Carrollton Bank, Exchange Bank, Merchants Bank, and amendments. For the role of bank profits in the fiscal policy of Louisiana government, see *Acts, La.*, 1813–14, 1821, 1825–29, 1837, 1839, 1846, 1852, and 1859, all of which record state borrowing from banks; *Louisiana House Journal*, 14th Legis., 2d Sess., App.; *ibid.*, 15th Legis., 1st Sess., 53–54, App.; *ibid.*, 2d Sess., App. For a record of the court cases, see *Louisiana Senate Journal*, 8th Legis., 2d Sess., 1828, pp. 62–65; *Louisiana House Journal*, 11th Legis., 1834, p. 4; *ibid.*, 12th Legis., 1st Sess., 1835, p. 6 and App.

64. Provisions of the act are found in *Acts, La.*, 15th Legis., 2d Sess., February 5, 1842, pp. 34ff.

saddled banks with illiquid assets and insufficient reserves. They responded by tightening credit, and "the rigid rules of the Bank Act made the process unnecessarily harsh." Politically, the Democrats benefited from the antibank sentiment, so that the state's banking policy remained in unsympathetic hands for several years. Repudiationist movements, built on the idea that the state's huge delinquent debt had resulted from subsidies to banks and that many state bonds rested in the hands of foreigners, also predominated for a while. Paradoxically, the result was that, in one of the few states where Whigs (who certainly favored government intervention) actually led in banking regulation, the contraction caused by the act served as powder for the opposition's guns.[65]

Worse, as of 1843 the legislature rearranged the Board of Currency, adding to it the Democratic secretary of state and the secretary of the treasury, and the governor placed antibank directors on the boards of property banks. These groups tried to liquidate the Union Bank. In 1845 a constitution was passed that prohibited the creation or rechartering of banks. The General Incorporation Act of 1848 also excluded from incorporation anyone engaged in factorage, brokerage, or exchange business. The effect was to create a monopoly among surviving banks. The state encouraged bank stockholders to buy their banks' bonds back from foreign holders at 40 to 70 percent discounts. Both foreign bondholders and local stockholders paid the price for the state's policy. Baring Brothers of London and Hope and Company of Amsterdam fought to persuade Louisiana to pay all debts at full value and employed a New Orleans agent, Edmund Forstall, for this purpose. Most issues were either repaid or renegotiated by 1847, and the repudiation act of 1843 was repealed.[66]

Tight credit and the oligopoly created in 1845 ultimately prompted

65. Green, *Finance and Economic Development*, 128–29; *House Journal*, 16th Legis., 1st Sess., 3–4; Citizens Bank Minutebook 4, 1841–1842, CBC, Tulane University, 155, 214–19, 234; Smith, Hubbard and Company, to Thomas Smith and Company, June 16, 1842, Smith, Hubbard and Company Correspondence, Tulane University; Thomas Butler to his wife, February 23, 1842, Butler Papers, LSU, Baton Rouge, La. An egalitarian attempt to link the strong banks to the weak ones was also attacked (Robert Palfrey to William Palfrey, March 29, 1842, Palfrey Papers, LSU Archives).

66. Robert Palfrey to Enoch Hyde, July 12, 1842, City Bank Records, LSU; Leslie Murray, "A History of the Whig Party in Louisiana" (Ph.D. dissertation, Tulane University, 1961), 197; *De Bow's Review*, XVI (January, 1854), 78–80; Reginald C. McGrane, *Foreign Bondholders and American State Debts* (New York, 1935), 182–97; *Acts, La.*, 16th Legis., 1st Sess., 56–59, 63; *ibid.*, 2d Legis., 1st Sess., March 16, 1848, pp. 70–77; Green, *Finance and Economic Development*, 131.

another constitutional convention, which reevaluated Louisiana's poli-cies in 1842. Demand for more banking and credit suggested the need for a free-banking law, but Whigs successfully prevented any actions against the chartered banks. The new laws contained some stringent clauses, such as those giving noteholders priority over other bank credi-tors, or a regulation denying the legislature power to sanction specie suspension or refrain from punishing a suspending bank. Limitations on banks joining with public-improvement companies discouraged, but did not completely prohibit, banks from financing such projects. Indeed, when the free-bank act was expanded in 1854 to allow banks to finance the New Orleans, Jackson, and Great Northern Railroad and the New Orleans, Opelousas, and Great Western Railroad, it marked the initial stage of a major return by the banks to the arena of investment.[67]

By the Civil War, a free-banking system was operating within strict rules. Louisiana's subsidization of its banks had given way to a more lim-ited interpretation of state business relationships, derived more from in-ternal trial and error than from out-of-state examples. Torn between the contradictory goals of sound money and easy credit and the antithetical demands of the commercial Whigs and the agricultural Democrats, Loui-siana oscillated between creating banks and expanding their capitaliza-tion on the one hand and trying to ensure adequate specie reserves on the other. Thus Louisiana's policies of experimentation differed from the more single-minded programs followed elsewhere. Yet Louisiana did re-semble states of the Old South in allowing competition at an early date, and the influence of commercial groups gave the state an important counterweight to the planters. Opportunity for corruption at public ex-pense, despite the constant presence of the state's banks in internal-improvement schemes, never reached the epidemic proportions it did in Arkansas, because of both the political balance and the presence of strong and numerous competitors. Moreover, public improvements themselves failed to become the instrument of banking abuse that they became in Mississippi, for which the strong reserve clauses of the bank

67. Green, *Finance and Economic Development*, 132–35; *Acts, La.*, 4th Legis., March 10, 1852, pp. 109–11; *Acts, La.*, 1st Legis., April 30, 1853, pp. 301–11; *Acts, La.*, 2d Legis., 1st Sess., March 16, 1854, pp. 151–52; *Journal of the Convention to Form a New Constitution for the State of Louisiana*, New Orleans, 1852, pp. 28, 46–50, 70–80; *Report of the Joint Committee on Banks and Banking*, 1857, 10–11, 116–34; *Minority Report of the Senate Committee on the General System of Free Banking in the State of Louisiana* (Tulane, 1854).

act can be at least partially credited. Although the plantation's influence prevented Louisiana from being a model state of the Old South in all aspects of its banking policy, it nevertheless exhibited critical assumptions about banking policy that aligned it more closely with other states of the Old South than with those of the New.

DIFFERENCES BETWEEN OLD SOUTH AND NEW SOUTH POLICIES

Expectations about the proper role of regulation in the economy were illustrated in a diversity of policies even outside banking. It is notable, for example, that some states in the Old South, in particular Georgia and South Carolina, never seriously considered ending all taxes on the expectation that their state banks would provide enough state revenue, however desirable or politically popular an end to taxes might have been. Both states had property and slave taxes as well as securities taxes and licenses on businesses and professions. Georgia also taxed railroads and banking capital. State banks in South Carolina and Georgia were thus not instruments for achieving the millennium but rather public institutions tempered by competition of a strong private sector whose primary functions were to support internal improvements and to invest the state's money wisely. Whig attitudes in the Old South reinforced this view: although Whigs favored a national bank, they opposed inflation. This attitude differed greatly from that in most states of the New South, where Jacksonians joined the Whigs in supporting state banks. Still, differences in attitude between the Old and the New South did not break cleanly along partisan lines.

One central difference between the two areas' attitudes derived from the predominance of commerce in the states of the Old South, which contrasted with the agriculture-based economies of the New South. (Thus it could be argued that, outside New Orleans, Louisiana was "New South." Yet such an assertion resembles the argument that, except for New York City, New York was like Pennsylvania.) An important difference marked the two groups' view of the function of money. To the planters it was a flexible medium, available in advance for goods and services to be delivered in the future (an antebellum demand-side equation of a sort). Joshua Martin of Alabama described this attitude when he remarked, "What a glorious business planting is, for we always hope the next crop will bring us out." Merchants generally viewed money as a product of work and as a stable medium of exchange, whose value should remain constant. Banking policy, in the form of solvency requirements and lending provisions, clearly reflected these differences. In short, different world views called for different approaches to banks and money.[68]

The state banks in the Old South were generally created to serve the agricultural demands, but private banking had a longer history and was stronger there, subjecting the state institutions to greater market discipline. Merchants and fledgling industrialists, who shared a view of the national economy that emphasized large markets, division of labor, and a long-term shift to industrialization and manufacturing, encountered increasing hostility from those who still harbored affection for the image of Jefferson's yeoman and clung to ideals of self-sufficiency. Whereas bankers easily fit into the former world view, their attempts to transform the pastoral images of the latter group into policy often directly damaged banks' daily operations as well as the overall regulatory framework, not the least by showing a propensity to place New South banks in the hands of inexperienced directors and officers. Institutions were run, not by self-made businessmen such as Edmund Jean Forstall of New Orleans, who had learned about the characteristics and dangers of borrowing and lending through their own businesses, but by planters and politicians indebted to planters. Likewise, the commercial areas, especially Richmond, Charleston, and New Orleans, all felt the influences of foreign businessmen, who brought a rich heritage of business experience to those cities. These contacts were completely missing in Little Rock, Tuscaloosa, Tallahassee, and rural areas of Mississippi and Florida. More significantly, the world view encompassing capitalistic commercial attitudes was also noticeably absent.

The often unfortunate and occasionally incompetent policies of the New South stand in sharp contrast. Competition there was not encouraged. The resulting concentration of finances in state hands led to abuses of lending facilities. Poor regulation in some cases fostered embezzlement and profiteering. In the New South, the planters' perceptions led them either to ignore the economic change that closed in around them or to combat it openly.

68. Joshua Martin to John Mason, January 28, 1849, George Houston Papers, DU. Thornton presents the clearest elaboration of the distinctions in the two world views (*Politics and Power,* 267–342).

4

PUBLIC POLICY AND BANKING REGULATION IN THE NEW SOUTH

Operating under a framework of laws that encouraged competition, no state in the Old South had witnessed a total collapse of its financial system. Certainly the Old South's financial systems reflected much of the balance evident in its economy. Conversely, some New South states saw their banking systems completely collapse because of their regulatory policies, or they reacted to the panic by radically changing their existing laws. Alabama clearly illustrated a regulatory structure exposed by the panic. Legislative attempts had involved giving the state a virtual monopoly over banking activities within its borders. Alabama's monopoly, in turn, led to a legal case stemming from the panic that set a precedent for laws regarding foreign corporations.

BANKING AND CORPORATE REGULATION: THE BANK OF AUGUSTA V. EARLE CASE

One of the most important cases involving antebellum banking, the *Bank of Augusta* v. *Earle,* filed in 1837, established several important precedents for corporate law in general. Joseph Earle, of Mobile, whose business was apparently suffering, had developed an interesting solution to his cash flow problems. He simply refused to pay a bill of exchange on the New Orleans and Carrollton Railroad Company on the grounds that out-of-state banking corporations violated the Alabama constitution, under which the state bank system had a monopoly (with the single exception of the Bank of Mobile that I have already noted). When Earle refused to pay a similar bill of exchange to the Bank of Augusta, the Georgia bank sued in the Alabama Circuit Court. Earle emerged the victor when the newly appointed Justice John McKinley of Huntsville agreed with him that out-of-state banks were forbidden to do business in Alabama. McKinley also ruled that the international legal theory of comity (one sovereignty honoring another's laws) did not apply and that corporations were, in effect, restricted to the boundaries of their chartering legislative bodies (the so-called restrictive theory of corporations).[1]

When news of McKinley's decision spread, other debtors tested the legal waters regarding out-of-state notes, including one man who refused to honor a bill of exchange on the BUS. Solicitors for the BUS sued, and the case reached the Supreme Court along with the Bank of Augusta's lawsuit against Earle, which was appealed to the Supreme Court on a writ of error, and the case of Earle and the New Orleans company. Justice Roger B. Taney considered all three cases together, taking special care to review both McKinley's interpretation of comity and his judgment prohibiting foreign corporations from operating in Alabama. Daniel Webster of Massachusetts, representing the BUS, argued for the "liberal" interpretation of corporations, that is, that a corporation was free to move across state boundaries as if it were a citizen, although it was freely acknowledged that foreign corporations could not establish any branch banks within the state. Charles Jared Ingersoll, arguing on behalf of Earle, supported the "restrictive" interpretation of corporate charters. Corporations, he maintained, being creations of municipal law, had no contractual powers whatever, unless the law granted such permission.

Emphasis on the principle of comity allowed Taney to avoid choosing between the "liberal" and "restrictive" contract theories. Although corporations were not citizens, in Taney's view, every state accepted comity unless explicitly denied. The court therefore assumed that comity existed otherwise, even if only implicitly. In Alabama's case, although the legislature had specifically prohibited foreign banking corporations, it had not prevented foreign corporations from dealing in bills of exchange within the state. Taney's ambiguous ruling had thus rejected "liberal" theory but allowed "liberal" practice. Some observers, however, viewed

1. Gerard Henderson, *The Position of Foreign Corporations in American Constitutional Law* (Cambridge, Mass., 1918), 42–48; *Bank of Augusta* v. *Joseph B. Earle*, 13 Peters 580 (1839); Eric Monkkonen, "*Bank of Augusta* v. *Earle*: Corporate Growth v. States' Rights," *Alabama Historical Quarterly*, Summer, 1972, pp. 113–30.

the decision as accepting the "liberal" theory while conceding to states the right to reject comity. Alabamians failed to see the brilliance in the decision—Governor Arthur Bagby called it a "palpable and direct encroachment upon the sovereignty of Alabama"—but they might have noticed that Taney had allowed them the escape clause of positive regulation, that is, the court had upheld the rights of states *explicitly* to regulate corporations.[2]

For Alabama, the immediate effects of Taney's ruling were ambiguous as well. Did *Bank of Augusta* v. *Earle* "usher in the corporate age," as Arthur S. Miller stated, and did it establish the "fountain head of the law of foreign corporations in America," as Gerard Henderson suggested? Did these "agrarian actions" wreak havoc in the economy, as Charles and Mary Beard maintained? Two well-known economic historians, Bray Hammond and Stuart Bruchey, without mentioning the case specifically, observed that Taney had ruled on the side of "*laissez faire* and rampant business individualism." Bruchey concluded that Taney's decision strongly encouraged the rise of the business corporation, and in this the Beards agreed. Taney's adroit legal maneuvering allowed him to vote both his "head" and his "heart," simultaneously upholding doctrines of both regulation and states' rights. Perhaps the most telling testament to the southerner's perception of *Bank of Augusta* v. *Earle* decision was the absence of any significant southern protest. Even Alabama's citizens remained unusually quiet about a decision that, if it indeed constituted a license for corporate dominance of the common man, should have rattled the rafters. Alabama's legal and business community realized that Taney had rendered a very favorable decision from its point of view. The decline of the "panic" psychology rendered the issue either irrelevant or unimportant by the 1840s.[3]

2. *Niles Register,* December 28, 1839, p. 278. Taney apparently referred to *Marietta* v. *Pindall* for his opinion of the power of foreign banks to issue notes (2 Rand. [Va.] 465 [1824]). Taney also refused to apply the ruling in the *Bank of the United States* v. *Deveaux,* whereby a corporation was judged on the citizenship of its incorporators, to the Bank of Augusta, realizing that to do so threatened the sanctity of corporate contracts.

3. Arthur S. Miller, *The Supreme Court and American Capitalism* (New York, 1968), 44, 50; Henderson, *Position of Foreign Corporations,* 42, 48; Charles Beard and Mary Beard, *The Rise of American Civilization* (New York, 1927), 689; Hammond, *Banks and Politics,* 337; Stuart Bruchey, *The Roots of American Economic Growth, 1607–1861: An Essay in Social Causation* (New York, 1965), 139; J. Willard Hurst, *Law and the Conditions of Freedom in the Nineteenth Century United States* (Madison, 1956), 15, and *The Legitimacy of the Business Corporation in the Law of the United States, 1788–1970* (Charlottesville, Va., 1970), 64–65, 142.

REGULATORY POLICY IN ALABAMA

At the beginning of the Panic of 1837, Alabama had only three banks: the state-run Bank of Alabama, with its branches in Huntsville, Mobile, Decatur, and Montgomery, and two private banks whose activities were tightly tied to the fortunes of the state bank through laws requiring the banks to sell a portion of their stock to the state (see Table 8). Branch banks of the state bank were in reality independent state-run banks, their only shared trait being that they all had directors elected by the state legislature and that most of them had been capitalized from state bond sales. The private banks, both in Mobile, the Planters and Merchants Bank of Mobile and the Bank of Mobile, eventually lost two-fifths of their stock to the state. When the Bank of Mobile wanted to increase its capital and extend its charter in 1833, the legislature consented only after extracting its two-fifths pound of flesh and establishing a provision that the bank pay a "bonus" to the state of $100,000 in 1839 in lieu of taxes. Still, whereas in Georgia and South Carolina the state banks merely competed with private banks—albeit with a disproportionate potential for capital—the Bank of Alabama dominated the state's finances in every county outside the Mobile area, and even there it had a branch. Alabama's state's financial monopoly ran into trouble almost from its inception.

Efforts to create a state bank in Alabama had commenced in 1820, although three more years passed before the legislature chartered a state bank. Leroy Pope's Planters and Merchants Bank in Huntsville had provided the entire circulating medium for all of northern Alabama but had suspended specie payments during the Panic of 1819 and had not resumed. Pope, a member of a political cadre known as the Royalists, from Georgia, had been a popular figure until the suspension. Thereafter he was the object of consistent political opposition from the state bank forces of Governor Israel Pickens. Still, the capitalization of the state bank took time, as the state needed to build up the money gradually through various receipts and transfers from other funds. Pickens knew that he must keep the Huntsville bank operating in order to supply money and credit to planters until the capitalization of the state bank could be consummated. Among the sources of capitalization, the legislature used sales of land owned by the University of Alabama.

Formative attitudes toward banking held by many Alabamians were observable in Pickens's speeches. For the state to have influence in a bank, Pickens said in 1822, it must have a financial interest proportionate to its control. If pushed, the legislature only had to revoke the bank's charter, as it did in 1825, alleging that the bank was fully capable of paying specie but refused to do so in order to force small farmers to sell their land to the Royalists. Pickens, aided by editor William Long, had persuaded the legislature to neutralize the Planters and Merchants Bank, but he nevertheless resisted more radical legislative attempts to alter the Planters and Merchants charter, concerned that any such amendment would violate the *Logwood* decision and would jeopardize the sanctity of contracts.

No sooner did the Bank of Alabama begin operations than members of the assembly swarmed in with requests for loans and petitions that would establish branches of the state bank in their home towns. Plans to relocate the capital made the conflict over the state bank's main office even more bitter. Although most of these clashes were regional in nature, debtor groups frantically tried to maintain barriers of secrecy from legislative inspection. Ultimately, the assembly denied itself any legal right to examine or inspect the papers of the bank. When the legislature moved the seat of government from Cahawba to Tuscaloosa, the mother branch of the Bank of Alabama moved with it, taking both the political clout and the financial power away from the former Broad River and Royalist strongholds of northern Alabama.[4]

Having won its banking powers, the state jealously guarded its privilege against any new interlopers, such as the St. Stephens Steamboat Company. In 1826 the company entered the banking business, despite the absence of charter provisions giving the company banking powers. Directors elected a cashier, printed notes, and began soliciting deposits and discounting notes and *then* as an afterthought petitioned the legislature for a grant of banking powers. An insulted assembly refused, adding stiffer penalty provisions for violation of the original charter. In defiance of the assembly's decision, the St. Stephens Steamboat Company persisted in its banking operations until the sheriffs arrested the

4. The best analysis of Alabama banking is Thornton, *Politics and Power*, 110–14. Also see Abrams, "The State Bank of Alabama" and Schweikart, "Alabama's Antebellum Banks," 202–21.

Table 8. The Commercial Banks in Alabama Prior to 1865

Bank	Date(s) Chartered	Capital ($ millions)	Location	Remarks
Planters and Mechanics Bank (name changed to Planters and Merchants Bank, February 1818)	December, 1816	0.05; 1823: 0.50	Huntsville	Closed in February 1825; one-tenth of stock reserved for territory
Tombigbee Bank	February, 1818	0.50	St. Stephens	Failed in 1827; two-fifths of stock reserved for territory
Bank of Mobile	November, 1818	0.50; 1834: 1.50; 1835: 1.85	Mobile	One-fifth of stock reserved for territory
Bank of the State of Alabama; Branches: Decatur, Huntsville, Montgomery, Mobile	December, 1823	No limit[a]	Tuscaloosa	Closed by the legislature in January 1845
Planters and Merchants Bank	January, 1836	5.00	Mobile	Failed in October 1842; two-fifths of stock reserved for state
Southern Bank of Alabama	October, 1850	0.834	Mobile	Two-fifths of stock reserved for state
Northern Bank of Alabama	February, 1852	0.834	Huntsville	Two-fifths of stock reserved for state
Bank of Montgomery	August, 1852	?	Montgomery	Organized as first bank under free banking law in Alabama; the free-banking law established capital at between $100,000 and $500,000

Bank	Date	Amount	City	Notes
Central Bank of Alabama	February, 1854	1.50	Montgomery	Two-fifths of stock reserved for state
Commercial Bank of Alabama	February, 1856	1.00	Selma	Bill vetoed by Governor John Winston; passed over veto; two-fifths of stock reserved for state
Eastern Bank of Alabama	February, 1858	0.50	Eulala	Two-fifths of stock reserved for state
Bank of Alabama	February, 1860	2.50	Mobile	Three-fifths of stock may be owned by individuals owning stock in the South and North Alabama Railroad Company; two-fifths of stock reserved for state
Farmers Bank of Alabama	Autumn, 1861	0.10–0.50	Montgomery	Free bank
Bank of Selma	1859/1860	0.10–0.50	Selma	
Planters Bank of Alabama	November, 1861	0.60	Gainesville	Free bank
Western Bank of Alabama	November, 1861	0.60	Tuscaloosa	
Exchange Bank of Alabama	December, 1862	0.60	Opelika	No charter appears; its only mention is in acts
Merchants Bank of Alabama	?	?	?	

Sources: Van Fenstermaker, *Development of American Commercial Banking*, Table A-1; J. H. Fitts, "Sketch of the State Bank of Alabama," *Proceedings of the Second Annual Convention of the Alabama Bankers Association, 1891* (N.p., 1891). Other sources used for 1838–60 data include notes taken from the W. H. Brantley Collection, Stamford University.

ªCreated by deposits of state receipts from various sources specified in the act creating it.

president and eight other directors and officers, who were thereupon prosecuted and convicted.[5]

By 1830, the private competition to the state bank had been cut again; the Tombeckbe Bank entered into bankruptcy in 1829. Still, partly because the Bank of Alabama served primarily the northern part of the state, partly because of the presence of the branch of the BUS in Mobile, and partly because of the Bank of Mobile's own localized strength, a total state monopoly of banking never developed. Competition from the Bank of Mobile, backed by coastal merchant and business groups, remained so strong that a feud developed between it and the state bank, whose support came from the planters of south-central Alabama. The private institution prospered, announcing unprecedented dividends during 1833 and 1834 when other banks in the South were folding. Its conservative lending policies made it extremely solvent. Where the state bank had to deal in long-term agricultural paper, the Bank of Mobile could maintain accounts with the more easily liquidated short-term commercial paper. Economic growth also helped to sustain private banking in Mobile. Even so, by 1831 the demand for capital in the seaport city exceeded the capacity of all three existing banks. Instead of allowing another private bank in Mobile, the assembly continued to guard its semimonopolistic bank by chartering a branch of the state bank there. This branch soon developed a reputation for incompetent management and became the object of rumors about corruption in the ranks of the directors and officers. When the results of the commissioners' investigative reports on the branches were turned over to the assembly in 1834, they "showed the liabilities of the directors and president [of the Mobile branch] as payers and endorsers to their bank to be an enormous sum." Such charges were commonplace, although the extent to which illegal activities characterized any of the activities in the branches remains undocumented. These charges are further obscured by the tendency of Alabamians to label as "corrupt" a number of business and political practices that were normal for the time.[6]

The awarding of loans for political ends also caused the Bank of Alabama no small difficulties. When the planting regions in the Black Belt

5. *Alabama Senate Journal*, 1826, pp. 9, 78; *Alabama Acts*, 1826, p. 90. Also see *The State* v. *Russel Stebbins*, I Stewart 299, in which the Supreme Court upheld the sentence.

6. Brantley, *Banking in Alabama*, I, 295, 313, and Appendix, 372; *Alabama Senate Journal*, 1834, p. 13; *Niles Register*, November 23, 1831.

were starved for capital, the bank busily pursued lending in the northern regions. As the legislature came increasingly under the influence of planters in the 1850s, capital was redirected to the Black Belt at precisely the time when the manufacturing and mining businesses needed it. Regulatory policy toward banking, and especially toward the state bank, also suffered, finding itself consistently bound to a corresponding drive to eliminate direct taxes. As early as 1826, Jesse Garth of the state senate's committee on banking prophesied that Alabamians could one day expect the profits of a state bank to support the government without a direct tax. In 1831 Governor Samuel Moore had reasoned that "banking is a tax because by it a revenue is collected." Governor John Gayle had agreed in 1834, demonstrating that the existing taxation could be replaced by bank earnings. This reliance on bank profits as a source of state income placed an even greater strain on the bank monopoly. While pondering these implications, lawmakers also discovered that additional money could be raised if private banks were chartered. Thus the Alabama assembly faced a dilemma that struck at the heart of Jacksonian precepts: keep the state's near-monopoly on banking and lose revenue or allow other private banks to be chartered and collect more taxes. Leaning toward the latter approach, Alabama legislators abolished direct taxation and then chartered the private Planters and Merchants Bank of Mobile in 1836.[7]

In the "flush times" prior to the panic, the Panglossian view of growth without discomfort, monopoly control without stifled development, and universal access to public funds without strict regulations—all made possible by a state bank—prevailed in Alabama. The arrival of panic conditions in 1837 gnawed at the already weakened corporate foundations of the bank. Alabama's General Assembly sanctioned specie suspension and relieved the banks from forfeitures and penalties caused by suspension. An 1837 law extended the time for paying debts owed the state and the banks.

To rescue the state bank, the assembly floated a $5 million bond issue aimed at bringing in specie. When the first bond issue failed to attract interest, anxious representatives hastily authorized *an additional* $2.5 mil-

---

7. Brantley, *Banking in Alabama*, I, 231, 237, 293, 320–21; II, 196–97; *Alabama Republican*, December 26, 1823; *Alabama Senate Journal*, 1833, p. 24; *Alabama Acts*, 1842, p. 228; Scroggs, "Financial History of Alabama," 36–39; *Alabama Acts*, 1822, p. 89.

lion bond issue. Faced with substantial debts to New York, the Bank of Alabama began making advances on cotton. Entrance into the cotton financing business, however, took place after the general election; in other words, the bank would be so deeply involved in the business by the next election that the new legislature would have a difficult task in extracting the bank even if the cotton venture violated the bank's charter. At first only the Tuscaloosa bank entered the cotton market, but other branches eventually followed suit, as did several private "banking associations."[8]

Mobile merchants intensely opposed the cotton financing, fearing that the Mobile branch in particular would engage in such operations, at which time the state could use its monopolistic power to destroy cotton merchants of the Gulf coast. Their concern was not entirely selfish. Cotton speculation often plunged the most experienced brokers into financial ruin. The inexperienced bank directors had used other people's money as the ante in a serious game of high stakes, knowing little about its rules.

Governor Arthur Bagby recognized the state's precarious position but tended to lay the blame on excessive borrowing by directors and officers. He therefore devoted his energy to establishing a bank examination law and finally succeeded in 1837. This law forbade the presidents and directors to incur a debt from the state bank or its branches, required bank officers to submit a complete statement of their liabilities and securities, and prohibited unlawful banking associations. None of these measures could counterbalance the heavy debts represented by the agricultural paper, and Bagby lost a crucial fight over a year-old law giving the governor the power to appoint commissioners for bank examinations. Legislators sought to rectify what they perceived to be an unfair political situation, not a flaw in economic policy.

Allegations of corruption generally revolved around lending policies. Directors, officers, friends of the bank, and legislators received large portions of available loans. This fact of life in itself hardly constituted corruption because it was commonplace in the antebellum period and also because most of these individuals had attained positions in government through successful agricultural and business careers. These were precisely the individuals who needed capital to pursue entrepreneurial

8. *Alabama House Journal*, 1837 (Annual), 75; *Alabama Acts*, 1837 (Annual), 46.

ventures and who would have applied for and received credit from any bank.[9]

The level of their borrowing still generated more than enough political heat. Following the election of new directors to all of the state bank branches in 1839, the *Flag of the Union* published a record of the liabilities of the newly elected directors. In spite of the 1837 law, directors and former directors owed the state bank more than $3.2 million dollars, and some ninety other individuals owed more than $6 million. A report by the new board of directors of the Mobile branch revealed that its predecessors had advanced almost $200,000 for cotton. The books of the Mobile branch show similar cotton-related advances. Word of these advances persuaded depositors to remove their money. Coming on top of the effects of the panic, the cotton speculations made it plain that the Mobile branch's days were numbered. Public sentiment grew sharply critical. Mudslinging in local papers prompted confessions by former employees, including a former director, who testified that ten employees maintained extended running "overdrafts." The directors, seeing their employees pilloried in public, discharged all the officers.[10]

Losses due to uncollected loans within the state's banking system mounted, steadily draining specie and declining paper circulation. The state bank and its branches had less than $400,000 to circulate, whereas debtors owed the system between six million and eight million dollars. Relief in some form was necessary, and the assembly responded by extending the deadlines by which banks had to resume specie payment, also sounding alarm bells that awoke the protax faction in the legislature.[11]

Occasionally, even when courts rendered judgments against the debtors, sheriffs did not enforce the executions, reported "no property found," or endlessly delayed returning the money to the courts. One examiner reported almost $100,000 worth of executions in the hands of law enforcement officials, most long since overdue. Events of the previous few years, according to rhetoricians of the day, suggested that the sheriffs, too, were a source of corruption.

9. The primary documents on bank lending to directors are *Alabama Senate Journal*, 1835–36, p. 8; *Alabama Senate Journal*, 1839–40, pp. 12, 18; *Alabama House Journal*, 1841–42, pp. 191–95; Bank of Alabama Ledger Books, various years; Bank of Alabama, Mobile Branch, 1833–36, SBA, ADAH.

10. *Flag of the Union*, January 23, 1839; Brantley, *Banking in Alabama*, Appendix, 317.

11. *Alabama House Journal*, 1839, pp. 154–60.

By January 1840, cotton speculation had forced the Tuscaloosa bank, and a month later the Montgomery branch, to suspend specie payments. Only the private Bank of Mobile and the Planters and Merchants Bank continued specie payment in Alabama during this period. Disagreements between the legislature and the newspapers as to which debts owed the bank were "good" or "bad" made it difficult to evaluate the position of the state bank and its branches. At best the bank verged on bankruptcy, and at worst it owed more than $10 million. To be sure, most of the debts were directly traceable to the depressed value of land. When land prices returned in the mid-1840s, the number of debts moving from the bad to doubtful and from doubtful to good categories in the receivers' ledger books was mainly responsible for the legendary financial wizardry of Commissioner Frances Strother Lyon. Alabama needed more immediate help than a ten-year program of land appreciation. Such help was forthcoming when the state supreme court intervened with a decision in *Bates and Hines* v. *The Bank of the State of Alabama*. In this case the bank sued John M. Bates and others for more than $300,000 in reclamations on cotton contracts. The defendants argued that the original transactions were void under the bank's charter. The justices, in line with the *Logwood* decision, upheld the sanctity of contracts, ordering the defendants to pay. Prior to the decision, Alabamians had been beginning to believe that it was acceptable or even desirable to avoid paying debts to the banks.[12]

In 1841 Governor Benjamin Fitzpatrick became the next in a long line of governors who had tried to relieve the legislature of its power to appoint bank directors. Fitzpatrick recommended closing the insolvent Mobile and Decatur branches to rescue the other branches. Results from the latest commissioners' reports showed that the Mobile branch had lost more than $105,000 in its cotton dealings, finally providing the commission with enough evidence to recommend closing it. Momentum in the legislature finally shifted toward dissolution of the bank, and Huntsville and Montgomery were soon on the termination list. The Bank of Alabama declared itself officially out of business, with branches liquidated in separate acts. Rather than repudiate its debt on the banking bonds, the state passed a revenue bill virtually without opposition.

12. *Bates and Hines* v. *The Bank of the State of Alabama*, 2 Alabama Reports (New Series, 1842), 451.

The bank's real weakness had been less in taking bad paper than in failing to respond to the real economic demands. Accordingly, until the death of the state bank, Alabama found itself always one step behind in matching its capital supply to its demand.[13]

Collections consumed the time and energy of the commissioners, who ran aground in the courts. Defendants in the recovery cases had steadfastly opposed the collections, a trend exemplified by two cases that appeared before a circuit court in 1844, with the defendants winning both *Branch of the Bank of the State of Alabama at Mobile* v. *Collins* and *Branch Bank at Mobile* v. *Scott*. Debtors, frantically hoping to escape payment using the old *Craig* arguments against the state note issue, suffered a crushing reversal in 1851 in *Darrington et al.* v. *Bank of Alabama*. Between the legislature and the judiciary, Alabama was rapidly closing loopholes.[14]

New taxes did not eliminate the debt, which was exacerbated by rapidly increased spending that had accompanied the abolition of direct taxation. When legislators realized that the bank could not compensate for lost revenue, they passed additional taxes but still fell short of balancing the state budget. Consequently, given the lack of revenue, by 1848 a new wave of sentiment for repudiating the debt had arisen, but appeals to Alabama's honor succeeded in stemming the repudiationist movement.

Even when regulatory and redistributionist public policy is planned, its results seldom conform to the original goals, and so it was in Alabama. Originally the state sought to raise revenue from the banks: it lost money. The state tried to avoid taxation: between the actual assessed taxes and the impact of inflation, every Alabama citizen paid far more than could ever have been imagined when the bank was formed. The state bank was supposedly to have promoted growth, whereas in fact it directly stifled growth by destabilizing the money supply, stifling credit, and directing the credit supply to areas where demand existed and denying it to areas that were starved for it. The state was to have supplied a check on the accumulation of wealth; in reality it placed huge concen-

13. Separate acts liquidated each bank branch. See *Alabama Acts*, 1842, 11 (Mobile), 37 (Montgomery), 47 (Huntsville), 53 (Decatur), 74–77 (Tuscaloosa).

14. *The Branch of the Bank of the State of Alabama at Mobile* v. *Collins*, 7 Alabama Reports (New Series, 1845), 95; *Branch Bank at Mobile* v. *Scott*, 7 Alabama Reports (New Series, 1845), 107; Brantley, *Banking in Alabama*, II, 232, 396 (n. 5); *John Darlington, Lorenzo James, and Robert D. James* v. *Bank of Alabama*, 13 Howard 12 (1851).

trations of capital in the hands of increasingly unresponsive groups. Insofar as the state intervened to plan, promote, and direct financial and economic policy itself—to a greater degree than that seen in most other southern states—it reduced prosperity, exaggerated inequalities (through wealth transfers via loans and inflation as well as by some inevitable corruption), and eroded the democratic checks available to every consumer in the marketplace.[15]

These arguments suggest a sharp contrast with Bray Hammond's assessment of banking in the early West, where the "antibank, hard money program of the Western agrarians . . . produced, in Indiana, Missouri, and Iowa, some of the best banking in American history—restrained, conservative, and untouched by the enthusiastic belief that credit was the font of every blessing." State monopolies, he argued, left the people in better shape than they would have been if banking had been prohibited, and they were relatively better off with banking prohibited than they would have been if it had been uncontrolled. In stating the former conclusion, Hammond used the example of Arkansas. Yet the regulatory pattern in Arkansas closely followed that of Alabama, with even more unfortunate results.[16]

REGULATORY POLICY IN ARKANSAS

Upon convening in 1836, the Arkansas legislature, anxious to establish a bank, created the Real Estate Bank of the State of Arkansas in its first act (see Table 9) and soon chartered its own state bank with another law. The state controlled the first institution only in a nominal sense. It furnished two million dollars in bonds for capital, appointed some of the officers, and set up a system of reports to monitor the bank, but the state was supposedly not to influence the operations or the policies of the bank. Hoping to aid the agricultural interests, the legislature had given the management of the bank to planters and farmers from the eastern and southern sections of Arkansas. Struggles over the institution's favors, such as those that occurred in Alabama, fell along lines more sectional

15. Egalitarianism and economic policy are treated from the Left by Leszek Kolakowski and Stuart Hampshire, eds., *Main Currents of Marxism*, trans. P. S. Falla (Oxford, 1978), III, 523, 525, 530, and Frank Parkin, *Class, Inequality, and Political Order* (London, 1971); and from the Right by Michael Novak, *The Spirit of Democratic Capitalism* (New York, 1982), 189–95, and George Gilder, *Wealth and Poverty* (New York, 1981).

16. Hammond, "Banking in the Early West," *Journal of Economic History*, May, 1948, pp. 24–25, p. 25 n. 67.

Table 9. A Record of the Commercial Banks Chartered Prior to 1838 in Arkansas

Bank	Date(s) Chartered	Capital ($ millions)	Location	Remarks
Real Estate	October, 1836	2.00	Little Rock	Liquidated, 1850s
Bank of the State of Arkansas	November, 1836	1.00	Little Rock	Liquidated, 1840s

Sources: Van Fenstermaker, *Development of American Commercial Banking,* Table A-2

than partisan. Democrats voted with Whigs to create the state-backed banks. Assisting the main branch located in Little Rock were branches in Helena, Columbia, and Washington. Each bank had a board of directors numbering nine, of whom the state appointed two, whereas a central board generally directed the system's affairs. This central board of twelve had four state-appointed members, meaning that both the local constituencies, and the central directors as a whole, operated mostly outside the control of the state.

Appointment to directorships, and hence access to the bank's favors, generated political conflict that devolved to the clan level. Control over the bank rested with a group of related families, sometimes called the Bourbons and the Seviers. Distribution of stock was critical because stockholders soon discovered that charter provisions allowed them to borrow half the value of the $30,000 worth of stock (the maximum available to each citizen who qualified) if the stockholder produced the correct amount of cash. Under this provision, a stockholder could actually receive $45,000 worth of stock for his original collateral. Apparently no prohibition against borrowing on half the *subsequent* stock existed; stockholders could pyramid on a minimal original investment. When interest on the bonds fell due, the pressures of the panic and poor management caused the bank to suspend specie payments.

On the pretext of relieving hardship, the bank granted new accommodations. Its issues from 1839 to 1840 increased by almost 100 percent, and its loans increased by three million dollars. Burdened further by the new issues and loans, the directors had no chance of meeting the interest on the state bonds. They resorted to the desperate tactic of using the remaining unsold bonds (having a par value of $500,000) as collateral for a New York loan from the North American Bank and Trust Company, hoping to get $250,000. Instead, they received only $121,300. The North American Bank and Trust meanwhile turned the bonds over to London banker James Holford, who paid the New York company $350,000! Because the bank had sold the state bonds below par, and because they had been resold in a speculation of sorts, the state of Arkansas contended that it was not liable for the bonds. Chief Justice English, of the Arkansas Supreme Court, however, ruled the state liable for the full amount (par value) of the bonds because the state had originally allowed the bonds to be sold below par. During this time, the directors generated one of the first challenges anywhere to the constitutionality of the Arkansas bank and to the state bank concept as a whole. On May 7, 1839, the Arkansas Supreme Court ruled in favor of the constitutionality of the bank in *McFarland et al. v. The State Bank*.[17]

On April 2, 1842, the directors of the Real Estate Bank issued a deed of assignment to trustees appointed by the central bank. Each branch was to deliver its records to the trustees. All except the board of directors at Little Rock complied. (Although this was the "central bank," a central board of directors operated as state directors apart from the central bank's directors.) Albert Pike, attorney for the Real Estate Bank, asked for an injunction against the central bank's directors, but the Judge of the Fifth Judicial Circuit, J. J. Clendenin, refused the injunction. Branches that had already agreed, however, had shipped their records to the trustees. Pike then applied to the state supreme court for a writ of mandamus to force Clendenin to grant the injunction. In the interlude between the original refusal by Clendenin and the state supreme court's ruling, however, scandal struck the State Bank when Alexander Boileau, a bank commissioner appointed by Governor Archibald Yell to investigate the Fayetteville branch of the State Bank, reported "a shocking exposé of fraud and embezzlement." His investigation had been made more difficult by the fact that some record books were missing and others were mutilated. Boileau eventually reconstructed the bank's accounts from other records and estimated that it had a $43,000 deficit. This news completely destroyed whatever trust the public still had in either bank. As the State Bank scandal raged, the supreme court delivered its decision on the Real Estate Bank in favor of the trustees, compelling Judge Clendenin to issue an injunction.[18]

17. For material on Arkansas banking, see also Ed Stebbins, "Early Banking in Arkansas," *Arkansas Historical Quarterly*, Autumn, 1954, pp. 409–13; Elsie Lewis, "Economic Conditions in Ante Bellum Arkansas, 1850–1861," *Arkansas Historical Quarterly*, Fall, 1947, pp. 256–74; Ted Worley, "The Batesville Branch of the State Bank, 1836–1839," *Arkansas Historical Quarterly*, Fall, 1947, pp. 286–99. The ruling on the so-called Holford bonds appears in 8 Arkansas Reports 24. It should be noted that the lack of control by the legislature left the state with a virtual banking monopoly and, although it had the effect of sheltering the banks from the effects of the market, left the legislators with little say in their operations.

18. Melinda Meek, "The Life of Archibald Yell: Chapter III, The Chief Executive," *Arkansas Historical Quarterly*, Summer, 1967, pp. 226–43 (quotation on p. 233); *Arkansas Gazette*, May 4, 1842; Walter Brown, "Albert Pike, 1809–1891" (Ph.D. dissertation, University of Texas, 1955), p. 164; Letters from Alexander Boileau, in *Arkansas Gazette*, June 29, 1842, November 4, 1842; Little Rock *Times and Advocate*, August 22, 1842; *James S. Conway et al., ex Parte*, 4 Arkansas Reports 406 (1843).

In trying to separate debtors from their money, a task made more diffi-cult by an 1843 law that required liquidators to get at least two-thirds of the value of property when the foreclosed mortgages were sold, the state became embroiled in a major struggle for control of the trustee-ships. On January 31, 1843, an act of the legislature gave the trusteeship corporate powers. State-appointed trustees appear to have been "frozen out" of the liquidation process. With the state's representatives not par-ticipating—it is not clear whether they were outvoted or just refrained from taking any part at all—tremendous advantages accrued to the trust-ees. They received almost $50,000 worth of slaves on mortgage fore-closures, for example, but the reports of the accountants showed no in-come from slave rentals or sales. The trustees rented real estate valued at $566,255.85 for a total of slightly more than $1,200, and, according to the accountants' reports, merely pocketed the difference. Yet informa-tion on the bank lay mysteriously buried. Even when the trustees were not skimming off money, the Real Estate Bank experienced difficulties in collecting its debts. Albert Pike, the bank's attorney, in an 1843 letter to the trustees of the Washington branch offered the following remarks on collecting: "[Since] the great scarcity of money in the country and the exceeding low price of all kinds of property, rendering it unpopular for many who are perfectly solvent . . . to pay at present without another sacrifice of their property . . . , the Trustees [have been compelled] to go to the full limit of the discretion rested in them." They came to the conclusion, therefore, "that their paramount duty is to secure the debts due the Bank, and not to sue if they can avoid it." The trustees at other branches "have found . . . that suits are always unproductive." When a man had paid all the money he could raise, "it is the duty of the Trustees to give him time upon the residue." Trustees at the Washington branch, he advised, should accept available security, "looking to make its *ulti-mate* payment certain."[19]

19. *Report of the Accountants Appointed Under the Act of January 15, 1855, to Inves-tigate the Affairs of the Real Estate Bank of Arkansas* (Little Rock, Ark., 1856), 38, 42, 45, and *passim; Report of Gordon N. Peay, As Receiver in Chancery of Real Estate Bank, 1st October 1856* (Little Rock, Ark., 1856), pp. 32–37; Albert Pike to the Trustees of the Real Estate Bank, December 27, 1843, Albert Pike Collection, Box 13, No. 16, AHC. Ted Worley ("Control of the Real Estate Bank," 420–21) misunderstood a central point about control of the bank's assets: if the original directors were as corrupt or incompetent as he argued, and if the Real Estate Bank was as closely tied to politics as he maintained, then the fact that the state appointed some trustees merely meant that cronyism had spread into the trust-

Bipartisan support for the creation of the State Bank of Arkansas in 1836 came as the culmination of three years of agitation for banking services. John Ringgold of Batesville and Anthony Davies of Chicot County directed the chartering of the state bank, as they had the Real Estate Bank. Unlike the agricultural institution, however, the state bank had its capital entirely owned by the state. Again, the bipartisan acceptance of this project revealed that Democrats sided with Whigs in the thirteen-to-three state senate vote for the state bank's establishment.[20]

Besides the main state bank at Little Rock, the charter established branches at Fayetteville, Arkansas Post, and Batesville. Later, additional charter provisions established a branch at Washington (Hempstead County). As soon as the main bank and the branches received $50,000 of specie paid in, the banks could begin operations. To compound Treasurer William Woodruff's inability to obtain specie in Natchez and New Orleans, bond sales plodded along at a maddeningly sluggish pace. Determined to open by August 5, 1837, even if its only available funds were the bank notes, most of which had been issued in Ohio and Kentucky, the bank careened into debt from birth. By November, the state's main bank had discounts totaling $320,000, compared with bond sales of $300,000. Branch openings, although legally approved, continued to be delayed for reasons such as delays in the arrival of the necessary books and papers.[21]

It soon became clear that the disease of corruption in the agricultural institution also infected the State Bank. While searching the financial catacombs of the Real Estate bank, special examiner Alexander Boileau discovered that many of the State Bank's books had been taken in an 1841 robbery. When searchers found the missing records later at West Fork of White River, the books had been mutilated. A close inspection revealed that the cashier, William Ball, had entered accounts that came up more than forty-six thousand dollars short, despite a local paper's

eeship. For the legislature's action turning over the bank's asset to the chancery court, see *The State of Arkansas* v. *The Trustees of the Real Estate Bank of the State of Arkansas*, cited in *Senate Journal*, 1854, Appendix, 317–54.

20. Batesville *North Arkansas*, September 6, 1843; Arkansas *Advocate*, October 21, 1836; Little Rock *Arkansas Banner*, March 6, 1844, March 12, 1845.

21. *Arkansas Gazette*, July 25, August 15, 1837, November 7, 1837; Letterbook of the Fayetteville Branch of the State Bank, 1840–46, AHC. During this time the Arkansas Post branch planned a costly bank building with extravagant furnishings (*Arkansas Gazette*, June 19, 1839, October 30, 1839).

claim that "the books were taken away merely to satisfy malice, and for the purpose of injuring the officers of the bank in the eyes of the community." Ball returned from Texas, where his relatives lived, on September 29, 1841, steadfastly denied all charges against him, and departed. No arrest was made. Without mentioning Ball, the legislature had turned out the original board members in 1840 "on account of their prodigality in discounts."[22]

In fact, however, as evidenced by the reports in a letterbook of the Fayetteville branch of the State Bank, the new board of directors so strongly suspected Ball of theft that it resolved to "employ such additional counsel as may be necessary to prosecute or bring suit on the Bond of the late cashier Mr. Ball in order to compel him to account for the several deficits that appear in his several reports." Attorney David Walker received the appointment to help prosecute the crafty former cashier and was retained when the bank selected William Scott as its counsel in 1842. (Lawyer Albert Pike was also on the bank's payroll, under contract to prosecute Ball for $700. Records of the bank, however, do not make clear whether this debt constituted part of Ball's "bookkeeping," his bond, or a separate sum he owed the bank in another legal or illegal context.) Bad luck, or perhaps ineptitude, characterized the board's operations; Scott served less than a year before the board fired him, instructing him to return any bank notes still "in his hands" from collections. Meanwhile, Boileau paid $337.50 in specie and "the same amount in Arkansas paper" to update and correct the books of the bank, yet the records do not specify where Boileau *got* the money or under what authority. Ball's embezzlement prompted the directors to write the central board at Little Rock and ask for clarification of five questions concerning the posting of security for, and liability of, officers.[23]

Although the new board avoided theft, it did not escape incompe-

22. *Fayetteville Witness*, May 1, 1841; Worley, "Arkansas State Bank," 71; Blocher, *History of Arkansas Finances*, 31. Blocher reports that the notes not accounted for amounted to $35,000 (p. 26). See William Campbell, *One Hundred Years of Fayetteville, 1828–1928* (Fayetteville, Ark., 1928), 91; *Arkansas Gazette*, September 1, 1841; Van Buren *Arkansas Intelligencer*, June 17, 1843. William M. Ball was evidently a relative of John Ball, a Virginian, for John called his "couzen [*sic*]," also John, "Uncle Mcly's" (John Ball to sister, February 27, 1856, Ball Family Papers, Virginia State Library, Richmond).

23. Letterbook of Fayetteville Branch, State Bank of Arkansas, letters dated July 2(?), 1841, April 2, July 15, December 12, 1842 (hereinafter cited as Letterbook).

tence. On October 15, 1841, the minutes of the board meeting recorded that the "late clerk of this Bank," Onesimus Evans, "has failed in the discharge of his duties" since the last review of the bank's books. "In neglecting to write them up in a correct and mercantile manner and whereas the said neglect [was] the cause of an increase of the heavy expense to this bank in the employing of some competent person to perform [his] duties," the board resolved to "bring suit for damages against said Evans." This resolution would not have been quite so embarrassing if the board had not tendered its warm thanks to Evans two weeks earlier for his "fidelity and ability in the discharge of his duty as clerk" of the bank.[24]

That Ball and Evans had left their mark on the board became evident in an episode that occurred the following year. The directors authorized the purchase of state bonds and state bank bonds (from other states, for the purchase was to be effected in New York), reasoning that such a bond investment would "release the state from a heavy debt, the interest on which debt, after two years will have to be raised by direct taxation on the people." Without the bond purchase, the directors predicted, the resources of the State Bank would be exhausted in two years. Two directors, C. W. Dean and P. James, were appointed as the bank's representatives (although James Scott replaced James before departure), were given expense money, and were dispatched with $9,934.36. These agents were to receive a commission only if they consummated the transaction. Upon arriving in New York, Dean and Scott met with a representative of S. J. Sylvester, a brokerage house, and deposited their funds in Sylvester's account on March 20, 1844. The agents returned to Arkansas, leaving conditional instructions with Sylvester to purchase the bonds.[25]

By September 4, 1842, six weeks after the agents had traveled from Arkansas, the board had not received word from Sylvester. To guard "against the grasp of speculators," the board appointed Dean again to go to New York to "endeavor to get the money out of Sylvester's hands," returning it "to the vaults of this Bank, or to complete the original de-

24. Letterbook, October 1, 15, 1841.
25. Letterbook, July 15, 1842, March 20, June (date obscured), 1844; and receipts cited in letter from William Paradise to receivers in letterbook, dated March 17, 1844, May 17, 1842, and October 11, 1842, AHC.

sign" by purchasing the bonds. Dean arrived in New York and met with Sylvester himself, who contended that he had made the purchase. Dean "knew to the contrary the purchase had not been made," but Sylvester refused to refund the money. Sylvester claimed that the money had been entrusted to a London firm buying the bonds, however, and promised a refund if the bonds were not purchased. Dean, concerned that he might never recover the money, hired Elijah Payne (also spelled Paine), a New York attorney, to get either the bonds or the refund. Payne got neither because the legislature had ordered the bank liquidated in 1843, and the bank's creditors immediately closed in. One of them, Elisha Riggs, who held bills of the Fayetteville branch, obtained a judgment against the bank and attached the bills while the money was still in Sylvester's possession. He then turned over the problem of collecting to his attorney and agent, William S. Paradise of Philadelphia, who also worked for Aertsen and Riggs Company. Desperate receivers reached a compromise by accepting Paradise's suggestion that a sum sufficient to satisfy the judgment should be paid to Riggs, after which all lawyers' fees could be deducted, "the balance thereof if more than sufficient to be paid to said Bank without delay after the collection."[26]

Panic conditions created problems for the disposal of the bond issue, as they had in Alabama. In Arkansas a repudiationist movement similarly took root. Governor Archibald Yell urged repudiation in his 1842 message, arguing that citizens already felt the oppression of taxation. Furthermore, the state should not tolerate the idea of paying for bonds "illegally and fraudulently disposed of." Democrats charged Whigs with supporting repudiation. The newspapers led the battle. The *Arkansas Banner* purported to uphold the "indestructible virtue of the people" and accused Whigs of "vociferously shouting repudiation." Failing to pay the bonds, it editorialized, "*alias Thieving,* is putting on a bolder face." Still, Arkansas shunned repudiation and joined Alabama in facing squarely up to its debt. By 1848 Governor Thomas Drew had devised a plan to pay on the basis of land sales. Deciding to pay and formulating a plan that satisfied everyone were quite different problems. The state wrestled with its debt until the 1850s, when the *True Democrat* summarized the popular sentiment against the bank, urging that "the bank,

26. Letterbook, September 4, 1842, March 20, June (date obscured), 1844.

its history, and its former unwise management . . . be erased from the history of the State, and the memory of its people."[27]

Both of Arkansas' banks suspended because of the panic. Afterward Governor Yell led the attack to close them. When the legislators conceded that the bond-financing plan had been a failure, Yell suggested other requirements, such as a specie-to-circulation ratio. Over the two-year period from 1840 to 1842, the banks' condition worsened. The legislature, taking Yell's advice, in 1842 passed a law assigning the assets of the Real Estate Bank to receivers and, in January, 1843, an act to place the State Bank in liquidation. Democratic governor Thomas Drew continued the executive attempts to eliminate completely and permanently banks in Arkansas, stating in 1844 that Arkansas' condition and the interests of the public did not justify the use of banking facilities. Actions by the Democrats bore fruit in 1846 when a constitutional amendment, passed by both houses of the legislature unanimously, provided that the state would never again charter a bank.[28]

Liquidating the state bank proved a vastly difficult task. Only liquidation of the Real Estate Bank exceeded it in complexity and corruption. A target date of 1852 for ending the bank's affairs was established. The legislature had already given debtors a considerable period to settle their obligations (an "unnecessary extension," according to Governor John Roane). John Ross, the receiver, estimated that $780,000 owed the bank was "irretrievably lost." Roane claimed that "the great bulk of the loss [was] attributable to the criminal negligence and dishonesty of the officers of the bank," who often failed to sue promptly, costing the bank up to $200,000 by the expiration of the statute of limitations, and more lost by taking inferior security.[29]

Governor Roane noted four specific ways in which the officers contributed to the mismanagement. First, the great number of officers, despite their relatively low pay, caused a constant drain on bank resources.

27. *Arkansas Banner*, February 6, 1844, September 24, 1845; *Arkansas Gazette*, September 22, 1845; *Arkansas Intelligencer*, June 10, 1848; *True Democrat*, February 23, 1859; John S. Roane to General Henry Wilcox, Little Rock, Arkansas, August 26, 1850, Eno Collection, AHC.
28. *House Executive Document*, 26th Cong., 2d Sess., No. 111, pp. 1082–83; *Niles Register*, December 10, 1842; *House Executive Document*, 26th Cong., 2d Sess., No. 226, pp. 898–901; Leonard Helderman, *National and State Banks* (Boston, 1931), pp. 122–24.
29. Worthen, *Early Banking in Arkansas*, 98–111.

Second, the officers failed to burn accumulated paper. A third fault involved the failure of the officers to make timely and regular reports. Finally, the officials were lazy when it came to depositing bonds turned in to them, costing the state money in interest. The state, Roane concluded, "was an immense loser by this operation." The worst misconduct, however, was that of A. E. Thornton, the receiver who had preceded Ross. Thornton, according to Ross's reports, "had received some nine or ten thousand dollars, which he had failed to account for." When this unaccounted sum was brought to his attention, however, Thornton paid the bank, perhaps hoping to cover other blemishes, to no avail. It was discovered that Thornton had defaulted on $14,000, and "that his whole system of book-keeping was a system of fictions. . . . He traded with himself in State bonds and Arkansas bank notes, and his entries . . . were made to suit himself." He also neglected to credit himself with another $23,440 that he had canceled and with another $14,640 worth of bonds and interest he had received from his predecessor. Thornton also received Real Estate bonds, however, and pocketed the interest that accrued during the time he held them. Ross estimated that Thornton took $5,200 in this manner, but a subsequent investigator figured that "the true amount was probably nearer $10,000." Thornton embezzled close to $50,000 and netted far more than $20,000 even by the most conservative estimates (and assuming he repaid the amounts that had been "brought to his attention"). The Thornton affair followed the intrigues of Ball, the incompetence of Evans, and the confusion that had afflicted the bank's activities in New York. It typified the slipshod and corrupt dealings of Arkansas' public banking system. Meanwhile, collection, always difficult, grew virtually impossible in the case of the State Bank because of cronyism and insufficient collateral.[30]

Worse, the bank's money flowed out in suits faster than it came in. James Curran, for instance, owned state notes in the amount of $9,355, for which he instituted ninety-four lawsuits against the bank. After a series of suits, the bank lost $109,720.50 in assets over a debt of $9,355, which even with interest and damages still came to only $20,883.20.

Most of the State Bank's dealings were finally made public in 1858, when, following an act of the legislature, William Gouge and A. H.

---

30. *Ibid.*, 100–102, 112; Letterbook, November 28, 1844. In addition to the other weaknesses of the bank, "the fee bills of the sheriffs and clerks of courts swelled to large amounts" (p. 110).

Rutherford delivered a comprehensive report and accounting of the bank's activities. This examination closely resembled that of the Real Estate Bank. With the state banks gone, and no free-banking act to fill the void, a number of private bankers quietly carried on their businesses in Arkansas until the Civil War. Ultimately, the "attempt to coin the wild lands of Arkansas failed, bankers became suspected, and credit money regarded as a swindle."[31]

Still, there were choices other than rigid state control, monopoly, or abolition. One regulatory option, "free banking," appeared with variations in Virginia, Georgia, Florida, Tennessee, Louisiana, and later Alabama. Basically, free banking used a bond security law whereby a bank had to deposit designated securities—state or federal bonds, for example—with a state authority. The deposit served as collateral for the notes issued by the bank. Virginia used a bond security system without allowing open entry, although Virginia had several banks, and competition was sharp. Critics complained that western state government bonds fluctuated greatly, making them undesirable as securities. Yet the *states* controlled the securities they deemed acceptable, and a state could easily choose to require security paid in the form of federal bonds. The potential capital gains available to the holder of a "risky" bond served as additional protection for those holding bank notes. Hugh Rockoff demonstrated that certain southern bonds—Georgia and Virginia 6 percent bonds, for example—brought fairly high prices and fluctuated along the same general lines as the bonds of many northern states.[32]

31. Leonard Helderman, *National and State Banks* (Boston, 1931), 124.

32. Rockoff, *The Free Banking Era*, 3, 30–32. Free banking devolved into "wildcat banking," according to critics. The "wildcat" theory held that in certain states the banknotes were not backed by bonds completely, because the states permitted the banks to issue notes equal to the par value rather than the market value of the bonds deposited with the state auditor. If the market value of these bonds dropped below their par value, and the notes were not fully backed, the bankers could profit "by quickly going out of business and running off with the bank's assets exchanged for the notes" even at the loss of the bonds (Rolnick and Weber, "Free Banking, Wildcat Banking, and Shinplasters," *Federal Reserve Bank of Minneapolis Quarterly Review*, Fall, 1982, pp. 10–19 [quotation on p. 13]). This enabled enterprising wildcatters to buy highly depreciated state bonds, receive an inflated amount of notes in return, put them into circulation, then close. Rockoff tested this by comparing par-valuation-bond states with high degrees of wildcatting and found a high correlation. Rolnick and Weber found, instead, that most losses in free banks were not caused by fraud but by "substantial drops in the price of the state bonds that made up a large part of bank portfolios" (p. 16). The others closed rather than "failed" ("New Evidence on the Free Banking Era," *American Economic Review*, December 1983, pp. 1080–91).

Contrary to the oft-cited assumptions of some modern historians, and many of the contemporary policy makers in the South, free banking in the southern states of Louisiana and Tennessee, and including Virginia's "conservative variant," produced fairly sound institutions and increased competition. (It should be emphasized that free banking in the United States was not laissez-faire banking or free banking in the sense that Scotland had free banks.)[33]

REGULATORY POLICY IN FLORIDA

On the surface, Florida's laws might have appeared to contradict the position that less regulation is better. Florida lacked banks during its early territorial period, even though the legislature twice passed bills incorporating banks. Both bills met Governor William Duval's veto, with the second overridden only to fall prey to "a technical decision on the size of the majority." By 1833, Duval admitted to the need for some banking facilities while maintaining his "conviction that they were radically defective and that their operation would not benefit the community generally." He willingly permitted the establishment of an institution that might "induce the investment of *foreign capital* in it." Duval's position was the opposite of Thomas E. DeBow, the publisher of *De Bow's Review*, who feared that outside capital controlled the South.[34]

Unable singlehandedly to keep banks out of Florida, Duval watched as the legislature chartered the Bank of Florida at Tallahassee in 1828 (see Table 10) and, following the governor's expected veto, repassed the charter bill in 1829. Authorized to sell stock in shares of $100, not to exceed $400,000, the bank could open for business with $40,000 in specie in the vault (U.S. notes also counted as paid-in security). Florida's

33. Rockoff, *Free Banking Era*, 127; Theodore Mathews, "Statutory Protection of Bank Creditors Prior to the Civil War" (M.A. thesis, University of Chicago, 1930), 242. Rockoff did not explore the reasons these laws were "dead letters," nor did J. E. Dovell, in his *History of Banking in Florida* (Gainesville, 1955), I, 45. Fred Marckhoff reported twelve private unchartered banks in business "at the outbreak of the Civil War" ("Development of Currency and Banking in Florida," 123). Thus Florida, during its banking hiatus from 1845 to 1853, was not truly "bankless." Free banking may have been more successful in Florida than even Rockoff believed, in that private bank agencies had preempted the revised banking law and operated so effectively that no reason to welcome new banks existed.

34. Dovell, *History of Banking*, 11–12; Brevard, *A History of Florida*, I, 202; *Journal of the Legislative Council of Florida*, 1833, p. 3.

situation was unlike that of Alabama. Florida's participation in stock purchases involved a mere 100 shares, although the state retained a high proportional control over the directorships by reserving half of them as legislative appointees. In 1829 the legislature repealed the first charter in order to substitute a charter with a lower capitalization, which allowed the state to levy a territorial tax of 3 percent of the bank's profits.[35]

By 1832, the bank committee of the legislative council had complained about the bank's loan practices, which favored the stockholders and not the general public "for whose benefit it was chartered." To induce more competition, the legislature had chartered the Central Bank of Florida at Tallahassee in 1832, but the plan backfired when the Central Bank absorbed the Bank of Florida. Still, the secretary of the territory, James Westcott, Jr., warned the legislative council in 1832 that the erection of such institutions could not simply create capital. Consequently, Florida substituted state action by planning to issue territorial bonds to finance a number of private banks. These "faith bonds" sold well, in the amount of nearly four million dollars by 1843.[36]

With the arrival of the panic, land values depreciated. Mortgages used as security for bonds fell precipitously. Banks were unable to pay depositors, to collect loans, or to redeem circulation. Mortgages proved of doubtful value as well, leaving the banks in the position of failing to meet their interest payments. The debt, which Florida thus assumed, totaled nearly four million dollars. Yet Florida's banks wanted the state to issue even more bonds. A March, 1841, popular referendum favoring repudiation officially became law in 1842. Repudiation set an ugly precedent for Florida, "denying the competency of a territory to bind the State and the justice of the contract." Popular ire against banks and bankers in the wake of repudiation surfaced in the stringent laws passed in 1843. One provision made directors subject to five years' imprisonment and a $5,000 fine for failure to redeem, with stockholders subject to triple liability. These laws built upon a foundation of the most radical banking regulation of the period, which had been written into the state's

35. An additional seventeen banks received charters between 1828 and 1839 (G. E. Lewis, *Florida Banks* [Tallahassee, 1942], 2), but Dovell reported that six of them never actually organized, and several other charters were purchased by other banks.

36. David Y. Thomas, "A History of Banking in Florida," 7; *Journal of the Legislative Council*, 1832, pp. 82–83; Kathryn Abbey, "The Union Bank of Tallahassee," *Florida Historical Quarterly*, April, 1937, pp. 207–31.

Table 10. The Commercial Banks in Florida Prior to 1865

Bank	Date(s) Chartered	Capital ($ millions)	Location	Remarks
Bank of Florida	November, 1828	0.60	Tallahassee	Purchased in 1832 by Central Bank; no issues made
Bank of West Florida	November, 1829	0.10[a]	Marianna	Capital raised to 0.50 in 1833; withdrew charter 1836
Bank of St. Augustine	1831	0.30	St. Augustine	Did not open
Bank of Pensacola	1831	0.20[b]	Pensacola	Allowable capital up to 1.00
Merchants' and Planters' Bank of Florida	1832	0.60	Magnolia	Failed January 1834
Central Bank of Florida	1832	1.00[c]	Tallahassee	Capital up to 2.00
Commercial Bank of Florida	1833	0.50	Apalachicola	
Union Bank	February, 1833	1.00	Tallahassee	Capital up to 2.00; opened 1835
Farmers Bank of Florida	1834	0.075	Marianna	Moved to Georgia 1835
Bank of Jacksonville	1835	0.075	Jacksonville	Opened 1837
Southern Life Insurance Trust Company	February, 1835	2.00	St. Augustine	Capital up to 4.00
St. Joseph Banking Company	1836	1.00	St. Joseph	Charter annulled by Congress
Florida Insurance and Banking Company	1836	1.00	Pensacola	Charter annulled by Congress

Franklin Bank of Florida	1837	St. Joseph	1.00	Not approved by Congress
Marine Insurance Bank	1837	Apalachicola	0.50	Not approved by Congress
Apalachicola Bank	1839	Apalachicola	—	
Bank of Apalachicola	1839	Apalachicola	0.50	
State Bank of Florida	1851	Tallahassee	1.00	Never opened
Bank of the State of Florida	1855	Tallahassee	0.50	
Bank of St. Johns at Jacksonville	1858	Jacksonville	0.125	Resources moved to Lake City during the war
Bank of Commerce at Fernandina	1860	Fernandina	—	Apparently never opened
Commercial Bank at Lake City	1860	Lake City	—	Apparently never opened
Planters and Merchants Bank at Pensacola	1860	Pensacola	—	Apparently never opened
Bank of Tallahassee	1860	Tallahassee	0.30[d]	
Commercial Bank at Pensacola	1860	Pensacola	—	Apparently never opened
Bank of Fernandina	1861	Fernandina	1.00	Capital never exceeded 0.10
Western Bank of Apalachicola	1861	Apalachicola	—	Apparently never opened

[a]1831.
[b]1835.
[c]1837.
[d]1861.

Sources: Van Fenstermaker, *Development of American Commercial Banking*, Table A-7; Dovell, *History of Banking in Florida*, pp. 13, 44–46, 50–53; Lewis, *Florida Banks*, p. 2.

constitution at its St. Joseph's convention in 1838. The regulations included one that made bank officials ineligible for state offices during their duty or for a period of one year after they left their bank positions. Three months' advance publicity was required before a charter could be granted, and stockholders' liability equaled the amount of their shares. No bank could deal in real estate, insurance, manufacturing, import, or export. Regular reports were required, and the state was prohibited from pledging its faith for any bank liability. These laws, passed in 1838 and submitted to the public for ratification along with all of the other constitutional provisions, went into effect in 1845. By then, the Jacksonians' antibank repudiation fever was running rampant. Florida refused to recognize its debt or the existence of any banks. Banks continued to operate anyway, in the cracks of the laws, but essentially became liquidation agencies. Two formerly powerful banks, the Union Bank and the Southern Life, saw their bills circulating at 80 percent discounts.[37]

Numerous private agents and merchants provided banking operations from 1845 to 1851. They took over transactions involving bills of exchange and small loans, but some even issued their own notes. Eventually the increasing population and growing economy induced the state to charter the State Bank of Florida at Tallahassee, although the conditions that the bank had to meet to qualify prevented the bank from progressing beyond the paper stage. The charter of the state bank seemed to signal the end of the antibank feeling in Florida, for within two years the legislature enacted a general free-banking law.

Yet free banking in Florida did not cause a burst of banking activity, largely because of the widespread activities of private agents from out-of-state banks, which developed and solidified their markets during the "bankless" period, leaving no real market for local banks. Indeed, these small bankers might be viewed as the forerunners of free banking, who only avoided the formal steps involved in filing the bonds with the state's agent. Florida's free-banking law came eleven years too late to have any significant positive effect on either the state's economy or its public regulatory policy. Florida had experienced free banking for a decade before it became official.

37. Helderman, *National and State Banks*, 87–91; Dodd, *Florida Becomes a State*, 316.

REGULATORY POLICY IN MISSISSIPPI

Mississippi combined the two regulatory models of Alabama and Florida, establishing a state bank monopoly in its early years. A Natchez-based group received a charter for the Bank of the Mississippi and ran it as a private bank until the state's first legislature in 1818 converted it into a state bank by issuing a supplemental charter (see Table 11). It then changed its name to the Bank of the State of Mississippi. Its notes were legal tender for all payments to the state, and it operated without the frauds and speculation associated with the State Bank of Alabama. When the state removed its own monopoly by chartering the Planters Bank, however, the directors of the Bank of the Mississippi decided to close their institution in 1832. Liquidation was completed by 1834, and corporate powers ceased on December 31, 1843. A privately owned institution, the Agricultural Bank, formed using the funds of the liquidated Bank of the Mississippi, emerged in 1833 to stand with the Planters Bank as the most important financial institutions of Mississippi. The Planters Bank's willingness to forfeit its original monopoly might seem curious. In fact, the state had succeeded in subscribing to two million dollars' worth of the Planters Bank (two-thirds of the stock). More important, the charter provided for the governor to appoint seven directors to represent the state, thus gaining for it majority control. Mississippi had actually exchanged the charter of a bank over which the state had virtually no control for one in which it owned two-thirds of the stock and had a majority of the directors. It had also traded a bank with an unimpeachable reputation for a financial virgin subject to the manipulations of politicians. Although Mississippians were aware of the difficulties in nearby states, they found the banking to be under the control of Natchez elites. Once the interior groups obtained a political majority, they expanded credit. Clearly the Bank of the Mississippi did not fit their formula for a tool of easy credit expansion wieldable by politicians.[38]

Indeed, stability in the Bank of the Mississippi had stemmed from its conservative lending policy concentrated in the Natchez area. Although its lending was balanced among mercantile and planter groups, the

38. See Marvin Bentley, "The State Bank of Mississippi: Monopoly Bank on the Frontier (1809–1830)," *Journal of Mississippi History,* August, 1978, pp. 297–318.

Table 11. The Commercial Banks in Mississippi Prior to 1865

Bank	Date(s) Chartered	Capital ($ millions)	Location	Remarks
Bank of the Mississippi; name changed to Bank of the State of Mississippi in 1818	December, 1809	0.50[a]	Natchez	Ceased active banking in December 1831
Planters Bank	February, 1830	3.00[b]	Natchez	Capital later raised to 4.0
Agricultural Bank	April, 1833	2.0[c]	Natchez	Capital later raised to 2.5
West Feliciana Railroad and Banking Company	1835	1.00	Woodville	
Commercial Railroad and Banking Company	January, 1836	4.00	Vicksburg	Branches at Clinton and Vernon
Grand Gulf Railroad and Banking Company	January, 1836	2.00	Grand Gulf	Branch at Gallatin
Commercial Bank; name changed to Bank of Natchez in 1837	January, 1836	3.00	Natchez	Branches at Brandon, Canton, Holmesville, Shieldsboro
Commercial Bank	January, 1836	1.00	Columbus	
Commercial Bank	January, 1836	0.80	Rodney	

Bank	Date	Value	Location
Commercial Bank	January, 1836	0.60	Manchester
Citizens Bank of Yalobusha	?	?	Yalobusha
Aberdeen and Pontotoc Railroad and Banking Company			Aberdeen
Mississippi Railroad Banking Company	1836	4.00	Natchez
Mississippi and Alabama Railroad and Banking Company (called Brandon Bank)	1836	4.00	Brandon
Lake Washington and Deer Creek Railroad and Banking Company	January, 1836	1.00	Lake Washington
Tombigby Railroad and Banking Company	1836	1.00	Tombigby
Real Estate and Banking Company of Hinds County	1836	2.00	Holly Springs
Bank of Vicksburg	April, 1837	2.00	Vicksburg
Vicksburg Waterworks and Banking Company	April, 1837	1.00	Vicksburg
Bank of Port Gibson	April, 1837	1.00	Port Gibson
Bank of Lexington	April, 1837	0.80	Lexington

Table 11. (continued)

Bank	Date(s) Chartered	Capital ($ millions)	Location	Remarks
Benton and Manchester Railroad and Banking Company	April, 1837	1.00	Benton	
Northern Bank of Mississippi	April, 1837	2.00	Holly Springs	
Hernando Railroad and Banking Company	April, 1837	1.00		
Citizens Bank of Madison County	May, 1837	1.00	Canton	
Bank of Grenada	May, 1837	1.00	Grenada	

[a] 1818.
[b] 1833.
[c] 1837.

Sources: Van Fenstermaker, *Development of American Commercial Banking,* Table A-17; individual bank reports made at varying dates in the year; *House Executive Document* 30, 25th Cong., 1st Sess.; *House Executive Document* 79, 25th Cong., 2d Sess.; *House Executive Document* 156, 25th Cong., 3d Sess.; *House Executive Document* 172, 26th Cong., 1st Sess.; *House Executive Document* 111, 26th Cong., 2d Sess.; *House Executive Document* 226, 29th Cong., 1st Sess.; *House Executive Document* 68, 31st Cong., 1st Sess.; *House Executive Document* 66, 32d Cong., 2d Sess.; *House Executive Document* 102, 33d Cong., 1st Sess.; *House Executive Document* 82, 33d Cong., 2d Sess.; *House Executive Document* 102, 34th Cong., 2d Sess.; *House Executive Document* 87, 34th Cong., 3d Sess.; *House Executive Document* 107, 35th Cong., 1st Sess.; *House Executive Document* 112, 35th Cong., 2d Sess.; *House Executive Document* 49, 36th Cong., 2d Sess.; *House Executive Document* 77, 36th Cong., 2d Sess.; *House Executive Document* 25, 37th Cong., 3d Sess.; *House Executive Document* 20, 38th Cong., 1st Sess.; *Senate Executive Document* 2, 37th Cong., 2d Sess.

Natchez planters controlled the bank. State officials wanted greater distribution of loans and built an apportionment provision into the charter of the Planters Bank. Bonds used to capitalize the bank sold well at first—two New York stock brokerage houses took $500,000 worth of the bonds—and might have sold even better had not some members of the legislature continued publicly to deplore the legislature's violation of the Bank of the Mississippi agreement. The state's involvement in the Bank of the State of Mississippi "crushed out private initiative and left a public monopoly." Slow sales of stock ensued: by January 8, 1833, Governor Scott reported in his message that "of the two millions worth of stock reserved for the State in [the Planter's Bank], there still remain $1,474,100 yet vacant." Suggesting that state control might be stifling sales, Scott recommended amending the charter to allow private stockholders to have a preponderance in managing the bank.[39]

Private stockholders and politicians alike agreed that banking capital should increase commensurate with increasing crop values. Pressing for an agricultural bank operated "on the principle of the Union or Citizens' Bank of Louisiana, the stock of which to be taken by planters on the mortgage of their lands," Governor Hiram Runnels had called the limited lending of the Planters Bank and its branches "a mockery of banking principles." The constant demand for funds led to renewed efforts at chartering land and improvement banks, often combining internal improvement corporations and banking services. These banks launched Mississippi into a frenzy of finance. Every town became the proud owner of a new banking office, and every internal improvement company the recipient of banking privileges. Banks soon obtained oft-denied authority to deal in real estate. The real estate banks, as in Arkansas, suffered a disastrous year in 1837. One, the Real Estate Banking Company of Hinds County, found itself in court every year after 1839. It had pledged $600,000 worth of real estate in 1838 to secure an advance of $300,000 at 7 percent interest on 5,000 bales of cotton from Edward Boisgerard, a New Orleans agent, who worked through John Delafield, a New York speculator and banker (and Boisgerard's trustee). Delafield would sell the cotton in France to pay the debt and interest. Not only did the bank deliver only 3,206 bales, which sold for only

39. *Mississippi Senate Journal*, 1831, p. 9; *ibid.*, 1833, p. 10; Brough, "History of Banking in Mississippi," 317–40.

$90,364, but the land securing the advance plunged in value. Boisgerard and Delafield then sued the wealthiest directors, and especially the president, Samuel Neill, eventually winning the suits but collecting little. Nearly all of Mississippi's banks faced equally sad situations.[40]

Of the ten-million-dollar total banking capital of the state in 1837, railroad banks had contributed almost two million dollars. Many of these banks also suspended or failed in the panic, causing the state to return to the state bank concept, although many factors influenced the state's decision. Democrats split over the banking issue into one group that saw state banks as a necessary evil and another completely opposed to banks of all types, while the Whiggery supported bank creation enthusiastically but for commercial, not agricultural, purposes. Distrust of banks was gradually tempered by the hope that the banks might help alleviate the financial distress under which the state labored.[41]

Governor Alexander McNutt, who assumed office in January 1838, was determined to reform the Mississippi banking system. He urged the legislature to pass a general banking law, using the banks' specie suspensions (and thus charter violations) to place them "under salutary control." He insisted, for example, that state representatives on the board of the Planters Bank be given their lawful seats. McNutt's recommendations included giving the legislature the power to amend or repeal bank charters "at pleasure." He implored the lawmakers to cancel any charters of banks not paying specie by November 1, 1838.[42]

The worst case in Mississippi was that of the Union Bank, originally authorized by the 1836 legislature. To pay the interest and principal of the bonds used to capitalize the bank, the stockholders mortgaged their property, with the state appointing its own commissioners to appraise property values. Management of the institution was entrusted to thir-

40. *Mississippi Senate Journal*, 1835, p. 21; Record Books of the Real Estate Banking Company of Hinds County, 2 vols., MDAH; *Edward Boisgerard and John Delafield* v. *Samuel Neill*, Case 2650, 1842, Drawer 90; *Edward Boisgerard and John Delafield* v. *Abram McWillie*, case 2654, 1844; Superior Court, Report of Commissioners "A," June 12, 1844; Decree by R. H. Buckner, July 15, 1844, all in MDAH. Also see Thomas Erskine to Samuel McCorkle, September 25, 1837, McCorkle Papers, MDAH.

41. *Mississippi Senate Journal*, 1835, p. 21; *Mississippi House Journal*, 1838, pp. 170–71.

42. Jackson *Mississippian*, January 19, 26, 1838; Alexander McNutt to John B. Nevill, February 14, 1838, Executive Journal, MDAH; Alexander McNutt to William Cannon, June 14, 1838, ibid.; Alexander McNutt to President and Board of Directors of Planters' Bank, September 13, 1838, *ibid.*

teen directors, of whom the legislature picked eight. Hoping to spread the bank's favors around, the legislators divided the state into eight districts each with its own branch. Constitutional requirements stipulated that, prior to pledging the faith of the state to an institution, two successive legislatures had to reenact the charter. Still, as the charter made clear, the state intended the bond issue to be a loan, not a commitment of the state to engage in enterprise jointly. The Union Bank thus became one of the most elaborate forms of state banking in the United States.[43]

Nicholas Biddle contracted to buy the Union Bank bonds through the U.S. Bank in Philadelphia in August, 1838, and quickly moved the bonds on to English and Dutch brokers. Sales of a second group of bonds died, however, leading McNutt to ask that the legislature recall this issue. The governor stated publicly that anyone buying the bonds below par forfeited state backing for the bonds. Furthermore, by selling bonds below par, McNutt later added, the Union Bank had violated its charter. It had from the outset faced charges of mismanagement, with "terms of loans . . . made easy to borrowers, and the worst possible judgment . . . displayed in making advances." When the interest on the bonds became overdue, a repudiationist movement backed by the Democrats took root. Whigs fumed that the governor had appointed "a good Van Buren Anti Bank Anti everything Democrat" to hold the key position on an investigating commission. Directors of the bank antagonized state officials and legislators when they refused to forfeit the bank's charter, as demanded by McNutt. Attempts to control the bank in 1840 ended with a whimper in the defeat of a bill that would have repealed the Union Bank's charter, a failure chalked up to the "corrupt influence" of the banks.[44]

Mississippi's politicians continued the battle over the Union Bank in 1841, when the legislative committee continued to pledge the state's

43. Jackson *Mississippian,* October 13, 1837, and July 19, 1839. For the legislative history of the Union Bank, see *Mississippi Laws,* February 5, 15, 1838, pp. 9–44; *Mississippi Senate Journal,* 1838, p. 312. The branches were located at Aberdeen, Augusta, Liberty, Lexington, Macon, Tillatobo, and Vicksburg.

44. Josiah Campbell, "Planters and Union Bank Bonds," *Mississippi Historical Society Publications,* 1905, p. 496; Brough, "History of Banking in Mississippi," 327–30; Sharp, *Jacksonians vs. the Banks,* 63, 71–73; *Niles Register,* March 7, 1840; Edward Walmough to Levi Woodbury, March 5, 1840, Series 1, Levi Woodbury Papers, Library of Congress; Lorenzo Besancon to J. F. H. Claiborne, February 20, 1840, J. F. H. Claiborne Papers, MDAH; John Stewart to Duncan McLaurin, December 25, 1838, Duncan McLaurin Papers, DU.

honor to the bonds in defiance of the governor's recommendation to the contrary. Democratic repudiators representing the antibank factions of the party captured the next election but split the party. One Whig noted that the "words Whig and democrat [are] thrown aside for the time." The repudiation of the Union Bank bonds later ended. Court actions continued until 1853, when the High Court of Appeals and Errors ruled the original sale of the Union Bank bonds legally valid. Nothing, the court said, could remove the liability that the state had incurred by chartering the bank. Popular referendums, however, favored repudiation.[45]

The issue was moot, because the state's banks were dead, but public interest flagged, and a constitutional amendment of 1847 to prohibit banks failed a referendum. Mississippi Whigs declined in their ability to shape policy, and Mississippi banks had virtually disappeared by the Civil War. Only a pair of banks remained in operation.[46]

Regulatory Policy in Tennessee

Just as Louisiana proved something of a hybrid state in the Old South, Tennessee was the most adaptable of all southern states in its regulatory policies. It was New South in its goals and expectations for its banks and yet Old South in its actual approach. Unlike states with a drive for financing agriculture, Tennessee had a need for internal improvements that made state banks attractive to lawmakers. Lawmakers chartered the Bank of the State of Tennessee in 1838 (see Table 12). Not only did the state anticipate financing its bridges and railroads, but state officials soon added education funding to the expected benefits from the bank. Democrats and Whigs both supported the bank's chartering; Tennessee's opposing groups split along sectional lines as in Arkansas.

Tennessee's banks had suspended specie payments during the panic, giving the Democrats a chance to eliminate them, gain control of a state bank to generate agricultural credit, and exploit their political advantages at the same time. Governor James K. Polk had recommended that banks be required to resume specie payments and be prohibited from

45. John Stewart to Duncan McLaurin, July 22, 1841, Duncan McLaurin Papers, DU; *The State of Mississippi* v. *Hezron Johnson*, 25 Mississippi Reports, 625.

46. Jackson *Mississippian*, August 17, December 6, 1843, March 5, April 30, June 4, September 24, 1845, February 25, 1846.

Table 12. The Commercial Banks in Tennessee Prior to 1865

Bank	Date(s) Chartered	Capital ($ millions)	Location	Remarks
Bank of Nashville	1807	0.20	Nashville	Liquidated in 1826
Bank of the State of Tennessee	November, 1811	Up to 0.40; 1817: 0.80	Knoxville	Operated to 1828; $.02 million capital reserved for state
Fayetteville Tennessee Bank	November, 1815	0.20; 1817: 0.40	Fayetteville	Closed in 1819
Halston Tennessee Bank (name changed to Eastern Bank of Tennessee)	November, 1815	0.20; 1817: 0.40	Jonesborough	Closed in 1819
Franklin Tennessee Bank	November, 1815	0.20; 1817: 0.40	Williamson County	Closed in 1819
Gallatin Bank	November, 1817	0.40	Gallatin	Became branch of State Bank or Nashville Bank
Bank of Kingston	November, 1817	0.40	Kingston	Lasted to 1819
Maryville Bank	November, 1817	0.40	Maryville	Lasted to 1819
Carthage Bank	November, 1817	0.40	Carthage	Lasted to 1819
Rogersville Bank	November, 1817	0.40	Rogersville	
Farmers and Mechanics Bank of Nashville	November, 1817	0.40	Nashville	Lasted to 1819
Winchester Bank	November, 1817	0.40	Winchester	Became branch of Nashville Bank

Table 12. *(continued)*

Bank	Date(s) Chartered	Capital ($ millions)	Location	Remarks
Columbia Bank	November, 1817	0.40	Columbia	Lasted to 1819
Shelbyville Bank	November, 1817	0.40	Shelbyville	Became branch of Nashville Bank
Murfreesborough Bank	November, 1817	0.40	Murfrees-borough	Lasted to 1819
Bank of the State of Tennessee	July, 1820	1.00	Nashville	Lasted to 1832
Union Bank of Tennessee	October, 1832	3.00	Nashville	Lasted to the Civil War; state reserved $1.5 million of capital stock
Planters Bank of Tennessee	November, 1833	2.00	Nashville	Lasted to the Civil War
Farmers and Mechanics Bank	1833	0.60	Memphis	
Farmers and Merchants Bank	1833	?	Memphis	Liquidated in 1847
Bank of Tennessee	1837	0.005	Nashville	Liquidated in 1869
Bank of America	?	?	Clarksville	
Citizens Bank of Nashville		?	Nashville	
Bank of Memphis		?	Memphis	Free bank
Traders Bank		?	Nashville	Free bank; liquidated by 1860
Bank of Union		?	Nashville	Free bank; liquidated by 1860
Bank of Middle Tennessee		?	Lebanon	Free bank; continued after Civil War

Bank	Location	Status
Northern Bank of Tennessee	Clarksville	?	Free bank; liquidated by 1860
Commercial Bank of Memphis	Memphis	?	Free bank; liquidated by 1860
River Bank of Memphis	Memphis	?	Free bank; liquidated by 1860
City Bank	Nashville	?	Free bank; liquidated by 1860
Merchants Bank	Nashville	?	Free bank; liquidated by 1860
Bank of Paris	Paris	?	Free bank; liquidated by 1860
Farmers Bank of Tennessee	Knoxville	?	Free bank; liquidated by 1860
Buck's Bank	McMinnville	?	Free bank; liquidated by 1860
Bank of Dandridge	Dandridge	?	Free bank; liquidated by 1860
Southern Bank	Memphis	?	Free bank; liquidated by 1860
Bank of Nashville	Nashville	?	Free bank; liquidated by 1860
Bank of Jefferson	Jefferson City	?	Free bank; liquidated by 1860
Bank of Tazewell	Tazewell	?	Free bank; liquidated by 1860
Bank of Trenton	Trenton	?	Free bank; liquidated by 1860
Bank of Claiborne	Tazewell	?	Free bank; liquidated by 1860
Bank of Commerce	Nashville	?	Free bank; liquidated by 1860
Exchange Bank	Murfreesboro	?	Free bank; liquidated by 1860

Sources: (a) Ven Fenstermaker *Development of American Commercial Banking*, Table A-27; Campbell, *Development of Banking in Tennessee*; (b) individual bank reports made at varying dates in the year; *House Executive Document* 30, 25th Cong., 1st Sess.; *House Executive Document* 79, 25th Cong., 2d Sess.; *House Executive Document* 156, 25th Cong., 3d Sess.; *House Executive Document* 172, 26th Cong., 1st Sess.; *House Executive Document* 111, 26th Cong., 2d Sess.; *House Executive Document* 226, 29th Cong., 1st Sess.; *House Executive Document* 68, 31st Cong., 1st Sess.; *House Executive Document* 66, 3d Cong., 2d Sess.; *House Executive Document* 102, 33d Cong., 1st Sess.; *House Executive Document* 82, 33d Cong., 2d Sess.; *House Executive Document* 102, 34th Cong., 2d Sess.; *House Executive Document* 87, 34th Cong., 3d Sess.; *House Executive Document* 107, 35th Cong., 1st Sess.; *House Executive Document* 112, 35th Cong., 2d Sess.; *House Executive Document* 49, 36th Cong., 2d Sess.; *House Executive Document* 77, 36th Cong., 2d Sess.; *House Executive Document* 25, 37th Cong., 3d Sess.; *House Executive Document* 20, 38th Cong., 1st Sess.; *Senate Executive Document* 2, 37th Cong., 2d Sess.

paying dividends if they failed to do so. Again, Democrats in the Tennessee House supported the measure, but it failed in the Senate. According to the charter of the state bank, the state would furnish the capital and the legislators were to elect the directors. A county quota system for note distribution was established on the basis of the number of local voters. One of the bank's burdens was the obligation to pay for the support of the school system from the bank's profits to the tune of a hundred thousand dollars per year.[47]

Competition in Tennessee reduced the power of the Bank of the State of Tennessee. Democrats seemed satisfied with their control of the state bank, which did not inherit its predecessor's corruption. The state's regulatory record during the antebellum period demonstrated more stability than the records of its neighbors in the New South because its public financing went into areas other than agriculture and because of the relative strength of Tennessee's commercial groups. Although Bray Hammond contended that banking in Tennessee "had been neither conspicuously bad nor conspicuously good, and free banking did not change the record materially," branching provisions permitted the number of banks in Tennessee to fall from twenty-two in 1839 to fourteen in 1846.[48]

SOUTHERN REGULATORY POLICY IN HISTORICAL PERSPECTIVE

In virtually each state, the New South had ignored the regulatory precedents available in the Old South. Even when John Ringgold, the chairman of the Arkansas joint committee on banking, which first sought to establish state banks, said that "South Carolina, Georgia, and Alabama, have created banks upon their faith and public funds," neither he nor the committee spent any time actually investigating these systems. The older commercial areas, having experienced earlier many of the troubles that plagued the New South's agricultural areas, had developed strong systems in which the state did not try to monopolize banking. Besides avoiding many of the economic misfortunes of Alabama, Arkansas, and

47. Stanley Folmsbee, *Sectionalism and Internal Improvements in Tennessee, 1796–1845* (Philadelphia, 1939), 170–71; *Niles Register,* January 11, 1840, November 6, 1841; William Nichol to Speaker of the Senate, December 23, 1839, Bank Papers, TLA; Nashville *Union,* January 6, 1840; *Tennessee Public Acts,* 1837–38, pp. 153ff.; Emory Hawk, *Economic History of the South* (New York, 1934), 360–61, 379–80; Charles Grier Sellers, *James K. Polk, Jacksonian, 1795–1843* (Princeton, 1957), Chap. 12.

48. Hammond, *Banks and Politics,* 617.

Mississippi in particular, the banking systems of the Old South also seemed to escape the widespread corruption that afflicted states of the New South in one form or another because of both effective regulation and more experience by the participants in business and commerce. We may well ask why the newer areas so deliberately ignored the public policy of the more established southern states. Although a number of factors contributed, the answer probably lies in the Old South's economic goals of a sound currency tied to commerce and, later, industry, goals that differed from those of the New South, which emphasized equal opportunity to obtain credit on agriculture.[49]

Any proper assessment of southern regulatory policy must situate itself in the wider perspective of economic regulatory theory. Neither the theories of James Willard Hurst nor those of Morton Horwitz fit the southern banking experience well. It might seem that supporters of a "capture" theory could adapt it so that southern banking conformed to their views. Yet antebellum southern bureaucracy presented little opportunity for this type of perpetual life in an agency. Actual daily policing of the legislature's laws usually fell under the domain of a committee of the legislature, the treasurer, or a state clerk, although occasionally states created special investigative offices, usually headed by a bank commissioner. These officers owed their jobs to the state assemblies in those states of the New South where the popularity of the state banks was clear, at least initially. Few of these commissioners displayed any inclination to turn in reports showing the state bank in too unfavorable a light.[50]

Other historians have tried to explain southern regulatory development in terms of "deference politics" and "slavocracy interests," but a proper definition of deferential responses to specific situations is needed

---

49. Ringgold's comments are cited in Worthen, *Early Banking in Arkansas*, 41.

50. For theories of regulation, see Thomas McCraw, "Regulation in America: A Review Article," *Business History Review*, Summer, 1975, pp. 159–83 (quotation on p. 160); Harry Scheiber, "At the Borderland of Law and Economic History: The Contributions of Willard Hurst," *American Historical Review*, February, 1970, pp. 744–56 (quotations on pp. 746–49); J. Willard Hurst, *Law and Social Process in United States History* (New York, 1972), 23, 79, 164–67; J. Willard Hurst, *Law and Economic Growth: The Legal History of the Lumber Industry in Wisconsin, 1836–1915* (Cambridge, Mass., 1964), 106–107, 204, 207, 220, 518, 760; Hurst, *Legitimacy of the Business Corporation*, 34, 34 n. 31, 37–38, 46; Hammond, *Banks and Politics*, 594; Marshall, "Strange Stillbirth of the Whig Party," 445–68. A more developed discussion appears in Schweikart, "Banking in the American South," 270–71.

to do so. Would one expect to find a regulatory style for "public interest" corporations based on deference to existing systems in older areas? To some extent, such was the case in Georgia, for example, which modeled its central bank on the South Carolina state bank. Tennessee also looked seriously at precedents—its own—with somewhat less success than either Georgia or South Carolina. An equally reasonable "deferential" approach might have seen policy makers deferring to the wishes of well-known individuals or families. Arkansas, with its "Bourbon" connection in the state bank, provided an example of this type of deference. It was easy to rule and to carve out favored positions in the offices of the bank when a single family dominated the governorship, as the Seviers did in Arkansas. It is virtually impossible to prove deference, for one is never sure of causality. Were individuals deferentially treated because of their money and power, or did they amass money and gain power because others deferred to them?[51]

State-business relationships also had to be shaped by geographical and agricultural forces. Once movement into the New South areas had begun, Black Belt planters and agriculturalists found their banking needs entirely separate from those of coastal and port businessmen. For several reasons they abandoned systems of banking regulation that had proved fairly effective. First, most policy makers of the New South, with the general exception of those in Tennessee, regarded their interests as different from, although tied to, those of the Old South's centers of commerce, such as Charleston, Savannah, New Orleans, and Richmond. Jealousy and a general perception of distinctiveness played an important role in these attitudes. Second, because they assumed that their own areas were different, New South leaders felt obliged to take new approaches to policy. Alexander Gerschenkron has observed such tenden-

51. Harry Scheiber, "Regulation, Property Rights, and Definition of 'The Market': Law and the American Economy," *Journal of Economic History*, March, 1982, pp. 103–109; Scheiber, "At the Borderland," 750; Loewenberg, "'Value-Free' vs. 'Value-Laden' History," 439–54; Scheiber, "Government and the Economy," 135–51, quotation on 150n; Schweikart, "Banking in the American South, 295 n. 81. Rondo Cameron has suggested that "deference" to highly skilled businessmen, in fact, would have made more sense to a developing economy. To "maximize the output of the economy . . . the few really capable entrepreneurs should be placed in positions where they can exercise the greatest leverage," he wrote (Rondo Cameron, "The Banker as Entrepreneur," *Explorations in Economic History*, Fall, 1963, 50–55). A detailed critique of these theories from a non-Enlightenment approach may be found in the entire May 1982 issue of the *Conservative Historians Forum* (ed. Robert Loewenberg).

cies in many underdeveloped countries, which have often followed the pattern of the New South in trying to "catch up" by according the state an expanded role. Third, as the New South tended to be more agricultural and plantation oriented, it rejected the growing capitalist world view and attitudes developing in the Old South's centers of commerce. The New South did not wish to encourage such attitudes. Instead it sought to perpetuate the plantation system. Fourth, as many historians have shown, when they could not create their own credit facilities, the planters in the newer areas relied heavily on bankers, factors, and commission merchants from the Old South. The assertion that such deference existed necessarily entails adherence to either a Marxist view of "subsumed class struggle" (with class distinctions so fuzzy that even a recent Marxist study has abandoned the traditional opposition of planters against yeoman) or a highly selective interpretation of deference that operated on one level but not on another. Either view falls short of a meaningful description of the antebellum South.[52]

Given the antinomies in the politics of the Jacksonians, it should surprise no one that they created contradictory and self-defeating banking regulations everywhere they went, especially in the states of the New South. At the same time, the Jacksonians increased the power of the state governments deliberately, but they also tended unintentionally to expand the authority of the national government and to centralize it further through their banking policies. Banking, then, reflected many of the antinomies associated with egalitarianism and in many ways helped establish the conditions for the Civil War by increasing the potential for the federal government to exercise power of the states. Southerners recognized this tendency, for the southern states had individually fought internal battles regarding banking for years.[53]

52. On development in "backward" countries, see Alexander Gerschenkron, *Economic Backwardness in Historical Perspective* (Cambridge, Mass., 1962). The Marxist arguments are presented in Feiner, "Financial Structures of the Antebellum South." Feiner's work tends to support Thomas Sowell's contention that few economists take Marxism seriously as a method of studying economics; Sowell states, "The Marxian contribution to economics can be readily summarized as virtually zero." See *Marxism: Philosophy and Economics* (New York, 1985), 220.

53. The best approach to the antebellum question of centralization and egalitarianism is Robert Loewenberg's "That Graver Fire Bell: A Reconsideration of the Debate over Slavery from the Standpoint of Lincoln," *St. John's Review*, Summer, 1982, pp. 39–50. Also see Schweikart, "Mormon Connection," 1–22.

5

BANKERS, PLANTERS, AND SOUTHERN SOCIETY

Regulation and politics certainly played an important role in the life of a southern banker, but bankers spent far more of their time in a world of business and competition, characterized by the entire spectrum of business activities. These ranged from the performance of routine and dull daily tasks to the application of management skills needed to swing complicated and challenging entrepreneurial deals. Bankers had to oversee the management and daily operations of their enterprises, to hire competent help when they were unable to handle all the chores themselves, and to weigh long-term rewards against short-term returns.

Bankers had community interests, of course, which occasionally manifested themselves in societal groupings, often with editors, lawyers, and businessmen. Many bankers were, or had been, planters. Yet although bankers may have formed identifiable groups in various states, and although they shared attitudes toward commercialization and industrialization that differed from those of the planters, they did not constitute classes in any narrow Marxist sense. Differences between large-scale factor-bankers, commercial-institutional bankers, and private lenders were occasionally as sharp as those between some bankers and their borrowers. On other occasions the lines were blurred, in which cases the transition from one role to another was as simple as expanding the business or offering a new service. Many southern financial entrepreneurs viewed their mercantile and exchange businesses not as a series of separate, defined "roles" but as inextricably bound together with banking and other services.

Cooperation between bankers on an organized basis was infrequent and generally manifested itself in activity in a political party. Bankers acted monolithically on only a few occasions, usually during a crisis. More typical was cooperation between bankers and the rest of the business community, although again the goals of the two groups were not always compatible. When political and cultural differences, accentuated by business and economic concerns, mixed further with state and ethnic identities, bankers in the South proved to be a very diverse group. Competition was a fact of life at all levels, providing opportunities for increases (or decreases) in wealth, status, or work load. It is therefore very difficult to identify a banker who may be regarded as typical.

SOME TYPICAL SOUTHERN BANKERS

Nathan C. Munroe of Macon was probably as typical a small-town semibanker as existed in rural areas of Georgia. Many bankers in other states undoubtedly led similar lives. Munroe was a farmer, specializing mostly in cotton, and also acted as a factor on a part-time basis. His banking career started in 1843 when G. B. Earhart, the cashier of the Mechanics Bank of Augusta, wrote Munroe, inquiring "on what terms" he would take charge of an agency that the bank planned to establish in Macon. Munroe replied that he would promise to run the agency "faithfully" and in his discretion, giving the agency "such attention as is usual in the conducting of any agency business in Banking." Munroe carefully limited his liabilities, however: "Should it so happen that the funds, property, capital, or other assets of the Agency in my care, should be lost by Robbery, or by Fire, or by any manner where by general or special instructions I should have remitted said funds, I am not to be considered as personally liable or responsible to the Mechanics Bank for any losses incurred under such circumstances." He even took care to cover potential losses due to discounted paper, denying liability for any paper that proved "insolvent at its maturity." Munroe's personal responsibility, he admitted, extended "only to such errors as may occur in telling or counting or paying out the funds of the Agency, being the usual liability of the Tellers of the Banks." The bank agreed to those provisions, acknowledging that Munroe's liability extended "only to such errors as may come in telling or counting or paying out the funds." Paying him $150 a month for his full term of six months, the Mechanics Bank reappointed him in July

1844. He was subsequently reappointed for full-year terms in 1845–1848 and 1850. Although there is no record for 1849, quite probably he served in that year as well. Eight days after Munroe had stated his interpretation of the duties and liabilities, the board of directors made his appointment official.[1]

Munroe's letters reveal many characteristics of bankers and banking in the 1840s. First, he was familiar with banking law, liability, practice, and procedure. He knew, for example, that the liabilities for tellers he outlined were typical or "usual." The fact that he requested in a regular manner, and received, a vacation after two years indicates that the job was demanding and that he might have had outside interests that he ignored because of banking. His pay, good for the period, hardly qualified him as a member of an elite. Indeed, Monroe paid "at his own expense the Salary of his assistant in said Office," doing so from his $150 monthly gross salary. Munroe might of course have supplemented his income from outside sources. Yet he could not pursue other avenues of income too far without jeopardizing the agency business. His easy reappointments indicate that he never sacrificed banking for other activities. Nathan Munroe thus appears to have been a hard-working, reliable, smart, careful southern banker whose income put him at a level above the yeoman farmer but below that of wealthy planters.[2]

To commence operations, Munroe instructed the Mechanics Bank to buy "Books, stationery, fuel & [such]." He also arranged for the use of a portion of the banking office of the Commercial Bank, complete with furniture (for which he reminded the board that it needed to send two hundred dollars) until the agency established its own office. Cutthroat competition obviously did not prevail, or the Commercial Bank would not have aided in any way. Still, the rental rates charged by the Commercial Bank indicated that the institution rented the space with an eye toward profit.[3]

Monroe maintained a harmonious relationship with the mother bank,

1. Nathan C. Munroe to G. B. Earhart, October 17, 1843, Macon, Ga., Banking, MS 1450, Special Collections, UG; Memorandum and letter of appointment to Nathan C. Munroe, October 25, 1843, UG, MS 1450; Memorandum signed by Nathan C. Munroe and A. Sibley, President, July 10, 1844, MS 1450, UG.
2. Munroe to Earhart, October 17, 1843, and reappointments, 1844, 1845, 1846, 1847, 1848, 1850.
3. Munroe to Earhart, October 17, 1843.

but other agents were not as lucky. George Gibbs of Jacksonville, Florida, agent for the Planters Bank of Fairfield, South Carolina, in a notification of a forthcoming inspection, read that he would be responsible for certain bad debts at the agency. He welcomed the president of the bank, J. R. Aitken, and "the lawyers you propose bringing with you." As for the debts, Gibbs offered to go personally to New York to take possession of stock put up for the debt. Gibbs warned, "unless you take the stock offered, you will probably lose the debt." On the other hand, he advised, "if . . . suit has already been commenced . . . , you may look upon the money as lost." Gibbs emphatically demanded that Aitken "direct me to employ *a reliable man* to keep my office open in my absence, [and] supply him with funds so as to *continue the Agency.*" He reasoned that he could not be expected to go after the bank's debts in New York if the agency was to be closed or discontinued during his service. Gibbs then concluded by noting that most of the protested notes were no longer under protest or were not in his possession.[4]

Whereas agents such as Munroe or Gibbs were typical of bankers in the rural western part of Georgia or the sparsely populated northern Florida area, James Rhind of Savannah typified the independent urban banker-businessman. Rhind, a nearsighted cotton farmer whose entertainments consisted of the New York *Home Journal* and imported cigars, began his banking activities with a partner in Augusta under the name of Gardelle and Rhind. Opening his own agency in Savannah, Rhind continued under the name of James Rhind and Company until he dissolved his ties to Gardelle, and the two operations, in 1848. He then returned to Augusta and engaged in banking there. He was appointed cashier of the Savannah branch of the Bank of Augusta in 1853. A year later, a friend and president of the Bank of Charleston, Arthur G. Rose, while congratulating Rhind—"it is the very location and position to suit you"—

4. George Couper Gibbs to James R. Aiken, March 19, 1855, Miscellaneous Manuscripts Collection, Box 15, P. K. Yonge Library of History, University of Florida. Gibbs was fortunate that he avoided further litigation. John Banks, a merchant from Columbus, Georgia, who accepted the presidency of the Planters and Mechanics Bank in 1841 after several years of purchasing stock with his business profits, found that even his business skills could not save the bank. In Georgia, because stockholders were responsible for the ultimate redemption of the stock, Banks represented a readily identifiable target for collection agents, and he spent at least a year contending with them. See John Banks, *A Short Biographical Sketch of the Undersigned by Himself, John Banks* (Anstell, Ga., 1956), 18.

also warned "never let the sweetness of your disposition be ruffled by the thousand and one petty annoyances incidental to business."[5]

Rose agreed to be one of Rhind's "securities to the extent of $5000" (officers usually posted a bond to insure the bank against criminal activity on their part). The sum of $5,000 was the limit to which "certain confidential engagements" would permit Rose to go, a phrase that probably referred to his position as an officer in a competing bank. These special commitments caused Rose to ask that Rhind keep Rose's bonds "separate and distinct from that given by your other securities." Rose noted that this practice was "a usual thing . . . with most Banks." He enclosed a form to execute the agreement.[6]

Although he was a more urbanized private banker than Nathan Munroe, Rhind nevertheless did not seem to be a man of exceptional means. His personal purchases at a general store over a nine-month period in 1849 reflect little extravagance: numerous candles, jars of pickles, coffee, tea, pepper, soap, and a single splurge on eight bottles of champagne and "1 bunch cigars." The total bill of $78.15 made Rhind's yearly purchases at the store modest, although he undoubtedly had accounts at a number of other stores.[7]

Like all bankers, Rhind had one very annoying problem relating to the exchange of drafts and the evaluation of notes. The refusal of a draft could elicit extreme hostility. When Rhind refused the drafts of John McFallows, for example, McFallows demanded an explanation from Rhind. Rhind had apparently not cashed McFallows drafts because of "money due nearly 1 year ago, [and] upon the ground that you 'don't wish to cause undo [sic] engagements to pay money,'" reasoning that McFallows called "an excuse . . . unworthy of you as a businessman, and

5. Arthur G. Rose to James Rhind, May 30, 1854, Rhind-Stokes Collection, MS 1305, Box 1, Folder 6, UG; James Rhind to Arthur Rose, June 6, 1853, MS 1305, Box 1, Folder 5, UG; James Rhind biographical information given in the collection. Also see memo of November 1, 1848, regarding the dissolution of Gardelle and Rhind.

6. Arthur G. Rose to James Rhind, May 30, 1854, MS 1305, Box 1, Folder 6, UG; James Rhind to Arthur Rose, June 6, 1853, MS 1305, Box 1, Folder 5, UG. The bonds of the type posted became the subject of a North Carolina legal case in which the Raleigh agency of the Bank of Cape Fear appealed for payment of a bond on behalf of the cashier. Correspondence from two lawyers involved in the case indicates that the law viewed such a bond as temporary, only for the time of the appointment (John Loomis[?] to William Wright, December 11, 1841, Adelaide Meares Collection, DU).

7. List of items purchased from G. T. and Ben Dooley, April–December, 1849, MS 1305, Box 1, Folder 9, UG.

one I am not disposed to allow." McFallows admitted having been "myself much embarrassed at times, but no one can say that I ever afixed [*sic*] my signature to notes & debts when I owed money, especially when time was given." Disgusted with Rhind, McFallows withdrew "all propositions." Luckily, Rhind had stopped short of giving McFallows money.[8]

Other urbanized bankers included Thomas Branch and Sons in Richmond, a firm that began as a mercantile business and shifted into banking in the 1850s, finally emerging as the Merchants National Bank in 1871. Burke and Herbert, an Alexandria private banking company, closely resembled Branch and Sons. South Carolina banker W. E. Johnson, a businessman and plantation owner from Kirkwood, near Camden, represented yet another type of banker. Camden residents frequently entrusted their proxy votes to him, and directors trusted him to run the bank, deferring policy decisions to him as well. Johnson kept accounts with the Charleston banking house of Conner and Company. His access to markets that most of his neighbors probably lacked accounted for his autonomy in the bank.[9]

BANKERS, CREDIT, AND DEBT

One of the most frequent problems for bankers was debtors who could not pay. In the case of William Smedes of Vicksburg, Mississippi, president of the Southern Rail Road Company, who owed Johnson nearly eight thousand dollars but found it difficult to raise money on the eve of the Civil War, Smedes asked for an extension. He noted that the secession movement had destroyed business confidence. "Whether there will be any restoration of confidence after the worst is known . . . is impossible to say," he wrote, but it was "absolutely impracticable to raise money here at any rate or upon any securities." Smedes reported that the "strongest mercantile houses have gone down," including his own factors' houses. Because he depended upon their credit, Smedes had no

8. John McFallows to James Rhind, April 11, 1853, MS 1305, Box 1, Folder 5, UG.

9. James Branch Cabell, *Branchiana, Being a Partial Account of the Branch Family in Virginia* (Richmond, 1907[?]), 51–68; Thomas Branch to M. J. Hecks, November 25, to L. L. Masters and to Thomas Bass, November 30, 1850, Branch Letterbook, 1850, Thomas Branch Collection, VHS. Special thanks to Lee Shepard and Howson Cole for permission to examine this collection, still uncatalogued as of this writing; *Southern Planter,* cited in Craven, *Soil Exhaustion in Virginia,* 149. "A Century of Banking," *Commonwealth,* February, 1953, pp. 20–21. Also see the records of Atwood and Company, SHC, UNC.

way to obtain quick cash. After this preface Smedes came to the point: "You have doubtless divined the object of this fore face . . . is to solicit the extension of the debt due by me to you."[10]

Unfortunately for both debtor and creditor, the situation worsened. Two months after first asking for an extension, Smedes again wrote Johnson, who had granted the first request. Johnson rescheduled the payments on the loan, which in its original amount came to $8,750, and charged an interest rate of 10 percent over the following year. Smedes restated his "determination to pay every debt I owe in the world as soon as property once more has value." By October, however, and after several letters from Johnson, Smedes finally responded, citing illness as his reason for not corresponding sooner. Johnson had accused Smedes of "a financial scheme," which he had "neither time nor strength to pursue." New Orleans, Smedes replied in defense, "is pursuing a most strange policy, her banks loan nothing; & her commission merchants have nothing to loan, & there is no money, no business, nor prospect of either in the country; not a bank in this state & money not to be had here for any price."[11]

Johnson's efforts to obtain payment from Smedes represented a problem familiar to all bankers at some time but frequently overlooked by historians, namely the difficulty of collecting debts consistently and regularly. The struggle to collect delinquent or unpaid notes constituted a different but no less costly aspect of lending. A banker typically had only two choices: bring suit in court or cut off all credit until the notes were paid. Henry Ewing, for instance, cashier of the Bank of Tennessee, instructed one of the bank's branch managers to bring suit on seven notes belonging to the bank. Ewing instructed J. Currin to "hand over [the notes] to some lawyer." Because the district court was to meet "in Monday week . . . , the writs must be secured immediately." Other references to the time and dates of court sessions throughout the South suggest that a court calendar was standard equipment for a banker. Judgments, even when rendered, could linger in an inactive state for months, given the right action by the debtor. An Arkansas cashier lamented, "In all undisputed cases judgment is obtained in six months

10. William C. Smedes to W. E. Johnson, December 15, 1860, Johnson Papers, SC.
11. William C. Smedes to W. E. Johnson, February 20, October 5, 1861, Johnson Papers, SC.

but, by incurring heavy expenses, and getting the cooperation of the sheriff, payment can be delayed twelve months."[12]

Caution in the extension of credit was, of course, the mark of a good banker. Joseph Baldwin observed that "credit was a thing [in abundance] of course" and "to refuse it . . . were an insult for which a bowie-knife were not too summary or exemplary a means of redress." Most bankers sought to avoid such retribution. Baldwin recalled that the state banks "were issuing their bills by the sheet, like a patent steam printing-press *its* issues; and no other showing was asked of the applicant for the loan than an authentication of his great distress for money." Some individuals succumbed to the pressures. Salomon (Sol) Andrews, who served as a commissioner in New Orleans for a New York bank, and his brother Eliezer, a director of the reasonably stable Bank of Mobile, "died in a suicide pact" over business reverses.[13]

More than one southern banker was an inept businessman. Lending by the Union Bank of Florida in Tallahassee, for example, had spearheaded the speculative surge in plantation lands. When the crisis of 1837 subsided, excessive lending caused the bank to go out of business. The Union Bank's records reveal the extent of its credit to plantation owners. Samuel Parkhill, the second largest stockholder in the Union Bank by 1839, owned 4,400 acres and 80 slaves, on two separate plantations. His death in 1841 left his heavily mortgaged estate in the hands of the Superior Court of Leon County, at which time the Union Bank valued all his property and slaves at $138,300—of which he still owed the bank $94,182. The bank brought suit and in 1846 secured a judgment against Parkhill's estate for $143,782 in principal and interest. Another incident involved Benjamin Chaires, also a large landholder, whose largest purchase of land occurred in 1836 when he bought a plantation from George Fauntleroy for $50,000. The deed records showed, however, that Chaires had paid only $25,000 for the property. Chaires, perhaps conveniently in this case, had been president and founder of the Central Bank of Florida in 1832 (which was absorbed by the Union Bank

12. John Leonard to D. A. Davis, January 8, 1845, D. O. Davis Papers, SHC, UNC; Henry Ewing to J. Currin, June 21, 1839, Bank of Tennessee Papers, Record Group 47, Series 5, Vol. 15–16, Letterbook 1839–41, TLA; Arkansas State Bank Letterbook, January 27, 1841, cited in Blocher, *History of Arkansas Finance*, 21.

13. Baldwin, *Flush Times*, 83; Bertram Korn, *The Jews of Mobile, Alabama, 1763–1841* (Cincinnati, 1970), 43–44.

in 1838). His son Joseph served as a director of the Union Bank until its collapse and then promoted the Bank of the State of Florida together with the son of another famous Floridian subject to large debts, Robert Gamble. Gamble's father, John, moved to Florida from Virginia in 1821. John Gamble soon increased his landholdings by purchasing, in 1835, a second plantation, paying $42,000 plus $5,000 for 69 slaves. Yet Gamble, despite his position as president of the Union Bank from 1833 until its demise in 1843, never paid on his debt. Indeed, when the same tract of land finally came before a public auction in 1845, Gamble bought it for $814![14]

The experience of other Florida planters reflected the availability of credit and the generosity of lending. Joseph Braden, a sugar plantation owner on the Manatee River, also mortgaged much of his property to secure large loans. Many of his mortgages were eventually foreclosed. Jeremiah Powell borrowed to buy his plantations, totaling twenty-seven hundred acres. When he died, the Union Bank again initiated suits against the heirs and the estate only to find that sufficient collateral had not been given. Yet another director in the Union Bank, John Shepard, purchased land costing almost $54,000 with a loan from the bank negotiated on incredible terms: no initial payment, and the four installments were payable from 1861 to 1868, or twenty-three years after the date of purchase! In 1842, Shepard bought a plantation sold by the Union Bank in an auction for $2,236. This property had previously been mortgaged to the bank for $25,000. The Union Bank succeeded in getting the property only after a series of suits against the former owner's widow and only after attaching a portion of the acreage and slaves for $9,000 of the debt. Despite these and other examples of foreclosures, in general the Union Bank failed to collect from its debtors. The attitude spread that repaying a debt was optional; moral obligation had little to do with it.[15]

New South bankers who made the transition from planters to bank officers or directors often lacked business experience in the finer points

14. *Manley et al., Administrators* v. *Union Bank*, 1 Florida 160; *Union Bank* v. *Parkhill's Administrators*, 2 Florida 660; Deed Records, Book H, pp. 325, 505, Book I, p. 172, Book A, pp. 172, 540, Book E, pp. 81, 147, 581, Book F, p. 47, Leon County, Florida; court paper on the mortgage of Benjamin Chaires, November 17, 1836, Leon County; Dovell.

15. Union Bank suits vs. heirs, 1841–45; Deed Records, Book A, pp. 151, 153, 190, 428, Book D, p. 230, Book E, p. 638, Book H, pp. 406–407, Book K, p. 33, Leon County; *Union Bank* vs. *John Shepard*, January 5, 1842.

of credit debt. This deficiency contributed to poor banking practices, such as the failure to secure adequate collateral. Portfolios quickly swung out of balance, and the bankers also overvalued property taken as collateral or honestly overestimated the value of the collateral they themselves put up when they borrowed. The lack of a business background among New South bankers cannot be discounted as having contributed to the poor banking practices. It also contributed to the view that some bankers were under the control of planters. A banker's incompetence often took the form of deliberate favoritism.

Large loans to planters were certainly not confined to the New South. In most areas they formed the stock-in-trade of most bank business. Records of loans to South Carolina planters reveal similarly large amounts. John DeSaussure and Abram Jones borrowed $13,700 from the Bank of Camden, to be repaid in ten months, although DeSaussure and his estate were the liable parties. DeSaussure's record of payments was considerably more faithful than those of his Florida counterparts. Because, in South Carolina as in all other states, one could fall into debt by acting as security for other individuals' notes, it is not surprising to find prominent individuals, such as J. M. DeSaussure, implicated in the debts of others. One notarized document from the Bank of Camden illustrated the process whereby the notary public of the bank, Alexander Johnson, presented the cashier of the bank with a three-thousand-dollar note of J. C. Cantey. The cashier refused, "saying, 'there are no funds in this Bank to pay that note, [and] I will not pay it,'" whereupon the notary went to the post office and deposited notices of nonpayment. Soon thereafter, the note was submitted to DeSaussure, who signed as security.[16]

William B. Johnston left a detailed account of his lending and debts when he died. His assets as a Charleston factor and private banker—notes, stock, and houses—came to more than $22,000 by his own estimate. When they were actually sold, however, they brought only $12,664 (of which $185 were debts yet to be collected). Still, Johnston loaned nearly seventy other individuals a total of almost $6,000. Some of the individuals, as noted by the assignee, were "not found," "Dead in Miss.," "insolvent," or their debts paid to others, "Discount[ed]," the judgment having shifted to others. Still other notes stated only that they

16. Bond (loan) from Bank of Camden to John DeSaussure and Abram Jones, April 28, 1842, William G. DeSaussure Papers, SC; document of nonpayment, September 29, 1841, William G. DeSaussure Papers, SC.

"refused to pay," or the individuals were cited only as to state of last known residence. Johnston's accounts with banks came to $2,744.03, of which all but $878.38 rested with the Bank of Camden. The other bank account, listed only as the "Branch Bank," was probably the branch of the Georgia state bank. Two individual accounts, those of Martin, Starr and Walker and J. M. DeSaussure, held $7,817.28 of Johnston's money, plus interest (dividend) of $101.76. Other sources owed his estate a dividend of $36.65.[17]

Johnston's estate papers are significant because they provide information on a type of banker who loaned money in both a personal capacity and an official one. Johnston had kept sizable accounts with other factors and bankers throughout his life. Although he called Camden home, and not Charleston, his other lending activities suggest little favoritism. He had two debtors from Mississippi, two from Alabama, and one from Tennessee. With but three exceptions, no loans exceeded $100. Johnston had given George Reynolds $4,380. The assignee considered this large debt, and the second largest, $860, solvent. There is no way of telling how much of Johnston's money in the accounts of DeSaussure and other factors was intended as an actual deposit account and how much was, in effect, a personal loan, but it can reasonably be concluded that little of it was personal, for DeSaussure himself was relatively wealthy. Johnston received a hefty dividend from DeSaussure and Martin and from Starr and Walker, however, approaching 13 percent. This sum was many times greater than the puny 1 percent dividends offered by the Bank of Camden and the Branch Bank and above South Carolina's usury rate of 7 percent.[18]

Johnston's only major loss was a loan of $375 to insolvent H. C. Roberts. Added to the other insolvencies and debtors who denied or refused their debts or who were not found, Roberts' debt made a total of roughly $536 not recovered from loans coming to more than $5,940. On loans of more than $100, the ratio of defaults and insolvencies to total loans was 6 percent, but on smaller loans the ratio was 40 percent. Johnston's larger loans were apparently more secure, so that he could more easily afford to extend credit to smaller borrowers who, according to this ratio, represented poorer credit risks. The implication is that the low failure rates in

17. "Assigned Estate of Wm. B. Johnston," October 18, 1851, William Johnston papers, SC. Also see "Second Division of Funds, Feb. 15, 1849," "Fourth Division of Funds, Feb. 1, 1850," 'Fifth Division of Funds, Sept. 21, 1850," *ibid.*
18. "Assigned Estate of William B. Johnston, Oct. 18, 1851," *ibid.*

the postbellum period to which Roger Ransom and Richard Sutch alluded in *One Kind of Freedom* were highly unusual in the antebellum period. The larger borrowers represented greater security to Johnston. He made his greatest dividends—that is, his profit—from his accounts to other factors or from large borrowers such as Reynolds. If we assume that Johnston's practices were to some extent typical, inasmuch as the large loans accounted for the profits, and because they were more secure than a proportionately larger percentage of small loans, the large borrowers in effect subsidized, or at least assured, loans to smaller, and presumably less wealthy, borrowers. Some of these "loans" were in effect deposits that paid interest.[19]

Factors also had to be figured into the antebellum equation. Acting as credit middlemen, factors obtained fairly high interest rates and commissions. Much of the interest, in turn, clearly went to the banker. Although the factor suffered any initial impact from debts in arrears, the banker, too, shared the risk: should one or two of his best factor customers go out of business, the banker would be seriously extended. Still, the presence of the middleman gave the banker a buffer in two separate ways. First, the factor's own interests dictated that he should protect himself through diversification, hence he would lend to several different planters. It was unlikely that they would all collapse except in a general depression. Second, through the factor's own knowledge of his borrowers, the banker gained information on market conditions and a credit rating of sorts on individuals. These information costs prevented interest rates from rising even higher. Conversely, information on small borrowers was not nearly as crucial, for the amounts to be gained or lost were smaller. Thus two or three large planters might keep one factor in business. He, in turn, would be the primary borrower of a single banker, whose other accounts ultimately profited from the planter. Moreover, borrowing from factors often financed permanent additions to the physical capital of the economy.[20]

Virtually every public or private bank had to define its own proper

19. For a comparison with the postbellum period, see Roger Ransom and Richard Sutch, *One Kind of Freedom: The Economic Consequences of Emancipation* (Cambridge, 1977), 130–31. Ransom and Sutch contended that "an anticipated default rate of over 30 percent would be necessary to justify a 60 percent charge for interest" (p. 131).

20. Robert Davis, *The Southern Planter, the Factor, and the Banker* (New Orleans, 1871).

relationship with factors and commission merchants. Only in Arkansas, with its stillborn banking system, did brokers and factors lack strong influence. In other states, however, a major complaint against banks was that they were controlled by the factors or planters, captured by them, or both. In reality, the factors provided necessary information that lowered lending risks. Tennessee's legislature heard complaints that the Union Bank and Planters Bank "unduly favored" certain commission merchants by allowing the factors to act as securities on bills from planters in outlying areas. These merchants, whose reputation was solid and whose credit was sound, therefore provided a service to the banks by transmitting credit information about their customers. Banks rewarded them through increased business and especially dealt extensively with a select group whose members were well known to the planters and banks.[21]

On the surface, it might appear that the factors would have had an interest to protect and might have resisted bank branch expansion. Evidence from Tennessee, especially, contradicts this conjecture, showing activity regarding branch openings to be highly positive, with competition for the six planned branch sites strong, but did the private bankers' usurious rates and the dominance of factors cause the local residents of dozens of towns to request banking services? From the tone of the letters to the legislature, it seems doubtful that such was the case. The many requests made during the years 1838–1840 stressed the potential for growth in the cities, the fine and unimpeachable character of the city fathers, and the benefits that expanded credit would bring to businessman and banker alike. If the factors had such a viselike grip on borrowers, no requests at all for branches of the state bank would have been permitted.[22]

THE BANK OF THE STATE OF MISSISSIPPI
AS A CASE STUDY IN LOAN DEMAND

In states where credit was not abundantly available, the demand for loans, not the practices of factors, played the dominant role in branch establishment. The plight of the Bank of the State of Mississippi shows that credit had become the central issue in that state, even more than

21. *Tennessee House Journal, 1837–38*, 686–87.
22. See, for example, letters with various dates requesting branches of the Bank of Tennessee, Bank of Tennessee, Record Group 47, Box 8, TLA.

solvency or the profits of factors. Despite the brilliant record of its Bank of the State in staying solvent and avoiding corruption or political manipulation, a broad movement spread across all of Mississippi outside of Natchez, the bank's home, for greater access to credit. Perhaps, in line with the theory of the mysterious critic called "Branch Bank," who wrote to the Natchez *Statesman and Gazette* in 1830, the bank was trying to conceal a policy of sending loan business to New Orleans, where interest ran at 10 to 20 percent (compared with the 6 to 8 percent of the Bank of the State), and therefore kept a large portion of its funds in the bank. Increasingly large numbers of bills and notes representing New Orleans borrowings appeared in the bank in the early 1830s, with reported rates as high as 20 percent.[23]

Mississippi factors could not obtain money themselves. Their inability to do so seems to explain the opposition from the interior areas to the Bank of the State's tight credit policies from 1825 to 1830. Those policies also reflected the important auxiliary benefits of trading in New Orleans. There transactions could be consummated more directly, with more market opportunities. Mississippi's lack of a major seaport helps explain the limited influence of local factors. Meanwhile criticism of the bank grew because of its strong reluctance to open a branch in the rapidly developing eastern and central parts of the state. Reaction to Natchez control grew increasingly. By 1830 the directors came to feel the criticism and realized that they had only two options: to open a branch or branches rapidly or to watch idly as the state chartered a new state bank.

The Bank of the State's directors throughout its life were shrewd. Even when they agreed to the creation of a branch in Vicksburg against their will, they carefully requested concessions from the legislature and received them. The Bank of the State, however, had been too late in recognizing the momentum building toward credit expansion. Another group had already succeeded in creating and promoting a new state bank, the Planters Bank. Not only did it feature branches at Vicksburg, Woodville, and Port Gibson, but its loans were to be "apportioned among the senatorial districts," meaning that loans "would be associated directly with political favors." Sections of the state still loyal to the Bank

23. Natchez *Statesman and Gazette*, January 2, 1830. Note that rates of 20 percent still fell well below the 60 percent rates attributed to lenders of the postbellum period by Ransom and Sutch (*One Kind of Freedom*, 130–31).

of the State, including most of the Mississippi River areas, abandoned it soon after the Planters Bank extended the promise of branches.[24]

Difficulties of another kind surrounded the opening of the Planters Bank. A branch of the BUS started operations in Natchez in December 1830, and court challenges to the new Planters Bank persisted. Pressure for greater credit exerted considerable strain on the monopoly exercised by the Bank of the State until the directors finally sought legal shelter, asking for a ten-year extension of their monopoly. They also requested state aid in obtaining an out-of-state loan and insisted on tax exemption. Such demands placed the state in a politically unpopular position, as the directors realized. Hence they offered to pay for these privileges by canceling a $20,000 loan to the state, advanced several years before. Voting on the bill, Mississippi's lawmakers split along sectional lines, with western areas favoring the "new" Bank of the State, some river counties divided over approval for either it or the BUS, and the rest of the state supporting the Planters Bank. This marked the legislature's second violation of its pledge of monopoly, given twelve years earlier to the old bank.[25]

Credit expanded as a result of legislative pressure. In the previous five years, the Bank of the State had increased its loans by 31 percent and had opened a new branch. Its actions had been somewhat effective although contractually questionable. Sentiment, however, had swung sharply to the new bank. By 1831 the directors of the Bank of the State had lost legislative support and had worked out a compromise with the Planters Bank.[26]

The demise of the Bank of the State opened the floodgates to a credit boom in Mississippi. Twenty-seven banks opened between 1832 and 1837, not counting branches, savings institutions, or private banks. Partly as a consequence of the legislature's removal of a stockholder-

24. Weems, "Bank of the Mississippi," 532–33, 535, 538; Bank of the State of Mississippi, "Stockholders' Journal," February 1, 1830. Also see F. Winston, "A Protest," *Mississippi Senate Journal*, January 1830, February 5, 1830.

25. *Mississippi House Journal*, November 1830, pp. 8, 20, 39, 143–44, 219, 243; *Mississippi Laws*, 1826, 26–29.

26. *Mississippi Senate Journal*, November 1831, p. 16. Also see Bank of the Mississippi, "Memorial of the Board of Directors," August 5, 1831; Bank of the Mississippi, "Stockholders' Journal," November 6, 1831; Bank of the Mississippi, "Memorial on Behalf of the Stockholders," presented to the General Assembly, November 18, 1831; *Mississippi Laws, 1831*, 136–38.

liability clause in the Planters Bank charter, stock sales soared, and by 1835 the bank had a paid-in capital of nearly $4 million and capital stock of $4.2 million. Much of the capital stock sales hinged directly on the state's promise to back the bank with its "full faith and credit." The Planters Bank, the private Agricultural Bank and its $2 million in authorized capital, and three railroad banks, the largest of which had an authorized capital stock of $4 million, attested to the boom in banking facilities.[27]

BANKERS AS FACTORS

Of the weapons that could be used against factors and brokers, the states of the New South considered a state bank the most effective. Countless lawmakers, politicians, and self-proclaimed banking authorities had often (but not always) favored state banks as a means to tear capital from the hands of commission merchants. When banks themselves replaced factors as the central financial "danger," the same critics turned on the banks, employing at times identical criticisms. Governor Archibald Yell, of Arkansas, lashed out at the State Bank and the Real Estate Bank in his 1840 inaugural address when it became known that the Batesville branch of the State Bank had flagrantly engaged in the cotton business. He referred to the two banks as brokers and stock jobbers and urged the legislature to teach them a lesson.[28]

Alabama's state financial house, of course, *had* taken over the job of the factors. In so doing it had elicited bitter protests from cotton factors, brokers, and merchants, who resented the competition. Opponents of the state's entrance into cotton speculation realized that the bank's inexperience put it at an immediate disadvantage, but the massive capital of the state system—overwhelming, compared with their own—posed a greater danger to them than any potential undercutting of interest rates. Samuel Hale, editor of the Tuscaloosa *Flag of the Union*, attacked the venture as a means by which the bank could further monopolize lending, giving promissory notes for cotton, expanding note issues, and receiving specie for cotton, without having any intent of exchanging the

27. *Mississippi Laws, 1833*, 126–34, 151–57; *Mississipi Laws, 1824–1838*, 700–701, 751–52. For laws chartering specific Mississippi banks, see Schweikart, "Banking in the American South," 469, n. 33.
28. Blocher, *History of Arkansas Finances*, 22–28.

notes for specie. He warned, "Under the idle and silly pretext of regulating exchange [the State Banks] have depreciated their own paper . . . , and now they go a step farther, and offer to regulate the cotton market—the next year we may expect to see them buying land and negroes, and becoming planters and merchants, as well as regulators of exchange and bankers." Significantly, the attacks on the state's financial system virtually never extended to an all-out attack on banks, bankers, factors, or other lenders.[29]

Illegal activities by the state bank's Tuscaloosa branch apparently encouraged Montgomery's branch to enter into a contract with the Montgomery and West Point Rail Road Company, which was prohibited by the bank's charter. Although the exact nature of that contract remains obscure—indeed, even the bank commissioner who reported on it in 1838 seemed unsure of its terms—it resulted in the payment of forty thousand dollars of its own bills to the branch. The worst violations, however, remained the involvement in the cotton business, which immediately brought a number of associations into the market. The Farmers Banking Association, for example, took advantage of the legal murkiness that allowed the state bank to deal in cotton by issuing its own bills in return for cotton. Brought to court in Marengo County, the Farmers Banking Association found a sympathetic justice, who ruled that "although the Constitution restricts the right of banking to the State and such companies it might incorporate for the purpose . . . , it might be exercised by others with impunity, as the Legislature had failed to provide any mode for preventing it." Governor Bagby ordered proceedings against the association, undoubtedly as a means of employing the law ultimately to force the Tuscaloosa branch out of the cotton business and to make other branches cease their illegal activities.[30]

Banking associations, involved in cotton operations, popped up in Selma and Wetumpka. J. B. Cook's Farmers Banking Association conducted an extensive business in southwestern Alabama. Its bills, known as "Demopolis Money," circulated widely, but in 1838 the legislature finally cracked down on the bank and ordered it closed by July 1839. Much more determined illegal operations fleeced Alabama's yeomen.

29. Brantley, *Banking in Alabama*, II, 134; *Flag of the Union*, October 3, 1838.

30. Mobile *Commercial Register*, September 12, 17, November 16, December 5, 11, 1838; Brantley, *Banking in Alabama*, II, 40–47. See other articles on the bank in the *Register*: May 15, 23, June 29, July 6, August 1, 8, October 3, 5, 17, 20, 26, 27, November 2, 5, 9, 1838; *Alabama Senate Journal*, 1838, pp. 7–15.

One group, the Wetumpka Trading Company, issued its own notes for cotton even though it, as a partnership, faced specific prohibitions against such activity under Alabama's limited-partnership law. This company had northern connections, like many of the trading firms in the South. It, the Real Estate Banking Company of South Alabama, and other institutions like them took on the name "Muggins Banks" or simply "Mugginses." By the time the legislature finally dealt with the Mugginses, many defrauded farmers had lost everything. The Mobile *Register*, reprinting estimates made by the Wetumpka *Argus*, stated that the Trading Company had swindled between $125,000 and $150,000 from the Wetumpka community. In other words, the legacy of the Bank of Alabama included the scores of farmers and planters who suffered from its effects. To some degree, the plight of the yeomen and planters in areas struck by Muggins Banks can be traced to the efforts of the state to drive the factors out of business.[31]

Both Mississippi and Alabama provided useful examples of factor-banker relationships in states of the New South, although their record cannot be applied across the board without qualification. Mississippi showed how pressures for greater credit led to banking expansion, leaving factors much less powerful than they had been under the Bank of the State of Mississippi. Thirsting for loans, Mississippians wanted banks, and factors found themselves "forgotten men" in the process.

The role of the factors has thus led one historian to view the rise of the state banks as "effects of the exigencies of the slave accumulation process" and to assert that the factors were "so immersed in the web of

31. Brantley, *Banking in Alabama*, II, 41–43, 56, 64–69, 78–79, 171; "Bank Commissioner's Report," December 1, 1838, reprinted in Brantley, Appendix, 296–303. The discussion of the railroad appears on p. 299. *Alabama Acts, 1838*, 93, made "banking associations" illegal (Judge Eli Shortrige ruled the Real Estate Banking Company illegal in 1839 (*Flag of the Union*, October 16, 1839); *Alabama Acts, 1837* (Annual), 7–10, set up Alabama's limited partnership law. Also see *Flag of the Union*, September 19, October 24, November 14, December 12, 1838. Courts became packed with suits although apparently not as extensively as in 1820, when, wrote one lawyer from Winchester, Alabama, as a consequence of the Panic of 1819, the "country altho beautiful and flourishing in appearance is under great embarrassments and the dockets of our courts are crowded with suits," referring to the cases involving notes. "Nearly two-thirds of the merchants are broke," he continued. "Some of them make over their property, some run off and some go deranged. I sued a poor fellow about a week ago (a merchant of this place) for 3 or 4,000 dollars and he has run stark mad and taken to the woods" (John Campbell to Col. Claiborne Gooch, May 16, 1820, Claiborne W. Gooch MS, VHS). *Mobile Commercial Register*, January 30, February 13, April 20, July 26, 1839; *Monitor*, April 13, 1842.

Southern social life" that "they did not extend credit to all masters based solely on . . . 'rational' business criteria." Although factors obviously operated within the political economy of the day, they were nevertheless neither captives of the planters nor their captors. Moreover, considerable differences existed between the Mississippi and Alabama state banks as they related to factors. Mississippi, which already had a state bank, chartered another to ensure easier credit. Neither state bank faced serious competition from factors. Quite the contrary; there were apparently not enough local factors to go around. Alabama's state bank pursued cotton ventures to avoid paying specie so that it could continue inflationary lending.[32]

FACTORS' AND BANKERS' CAREERS

Pummeled by state banks encroaching on their business, competing with private and commercial bankers, and maintaining their own reputation and credit in hard times, factors may have seemed headed for extinction in the antebellum southern economy. Yet they still played an important role in getting the banks' credit to those who most needed it—planters—and in giving the banks a valuable commodity: credit information. No wonder an English visitor to Charleston in the 1850s found it astonishing that "as a singular feature of the banking system . . . a broker, who may be a mere man of straw, can get his bills cashed at banks, whereas those of a really substantial planter . . . would not be looked at." Planters, to cash or discount their notes, had to obtain the endorsement of a reputable factor in most areas. These factors usually had a merchant business in the city and used their liquid assets for loans.[33]

A typical factor was John Hagan and Company, of New Orleans, which sent to planters "blank checks"—notes for endorsement in advance so that "if necessary [Hagan and Company] can obtain funds through [the]

32. Susan Feiner, "Factors, Bankers, and Masters: Class Relations in the Antebellum South," *Journal of Economic History*, March, 1982, pp. 61–67 (quotations on p. 65). For examples of brokers engaged in paper exchange, see *Nott v. Papet*, 15 La. 306; *Conrey v. Hoover*, 10 La. Ann. 437; *Betts v. The Planters and Merchants' Bank of Huntsville*, 3 Stewart 18. Also see Albert O. Greef, *The Commercial Paper House in the United States* (Cambridge, Mass., 1938), 17–29.

33. Leonard Wray, "The Culture and Preparation of Cotton in the United States of America, &c." *Journal of the Society of Arts*, December, 1958, p. 82, quoted in Harold Woodman, *King Cotton and His Retainers: Financing and Marketing the Cotton Crop of the South, 1800–1825* (Lexington, Ky., 1968), 115 n. 1.

Bank." This early, far less convenient, and human version of the modern mechanized twenty-four-hour teller nevertheless performed the same function: to give cash or its equivalent to a planter at inconvenient times, especially during the summer, when Hagan and Company "may not find it very convenient to lay out . . . money." Banks cooperated. Peter Hickman's factor, R. W. Estlin and Company, made an arrangement with the Citizens Bank of New Orleans whereby the bank discounted notes for 100 to 120 days at 8 percent to cover the factor until the cotton arrived.[34]

Not all planters maintained constant debts, of course. Some, such as North Carolina sugar planter Lewis Thompson, kept a constant credit balance with his factor from 1851 to 1861. Thompson received 8 percent interest from his factor. As Johnston's records showed, the South Carolinian received even higher rates at times. Still, Thompson had difficulty collecting the interest and commented that "Bogart & Foley ought to have allowed me the *interest* on the money which I left in their hands . . . one *year after*." Thompson's agents eventually handled as much as $100,000 of his money at a given time. As removed as Thompson was from the New Orleans offices of Bogart, Foley, and Avery, he simply had to trust them. In all likelihood, considerable amounts of floating cash and interest due became the investment tools of shrewd factors. Planters also endorsed each other's notes. South Carolina planter J. M. DeSaussure, for example, acted as security for Samuel Gliver on a fifteen-hundred-dollar note filed with the Bank of Camden. Joseph Baldwin, commenting on this practice in Mississippi during the Panic of 1837, recollected that everyone in a community had endorsed his neighbor's note, in return for having his own secured in a like manner. Thus "Mississippi went broke by neighborhoods."[35]

Moreover, brokers, factors, and bankers operated somewhat interchangeably. Certainly a legal public banking business had to receive the sanction of some state agency, even in states with free-banking laws. Yet the transition from one to the other was easy, and all maintained ac-

---

34. Woodman, *King Cotton and His Retainers*, 115.

35. Henry Burgwyn to Lewis Thompson, May 16, 1859, Lewis Thompson Papers, SHC, UNC; Andrew McCollam Papers 1852, *ibid.*; J. Carlyle Sitterson, "Financing and Marketing the Sugar Crop of the Old South," *Journal of Southern History*, May, 1944, pp. 188–99; note of loan to Samuel Gliver, secured by J. M. DeSaussure, Bank of Camden Ledger Book, December 7, 1842, Bank of Camden MSS, SC; Baldwin, *Flush Times*, 89.

counts with each other. Cheraw (South Carolina) private banker William Godfrey was a prominent depositor in the Merchants Bank of Cheraw, but the bank's busiest accounts were those of John Matheson (listed as an "agent"), D. Malloy, and A. Malloy. Accounts such as these seldom dropped below fifteen hundred dollars and occasionally reached twenty to twenty-five thousand dollars.[36]

Perhaps the most typical career move involved a merchant who had cultivated a good reputation and worked his way into a bank directorship. David N. Kennedy of Clarksville, Tennessee, was just such a merchant-banker. Arriving in Clarksville in 1842, he started a dry goods store and two years later was elected a director of the branch of the Bank of Tennessee in that town. He parlayed the directorship into the presidency within a year, then retired in 1851 to take the cashiership for three years. In 1854 he left the state system and used his experience to organize the Northern Bank of Tennessee—a bank that survived the war. The career of Georgia and South Carolina banker George Walton Williams was similar in its development.[37]

Merchants, factors, and bankers seem to have changed places frequently throughout the South. Even a switch from planter to banker to merchant, then back to planter again, was not unusual in the less urban areas. William Johnston and William Godfrey of South Carolina, James Rhind and Seaborn Mays of Georgia, and Benjamin Chaires and John Gamble of Florida were all southern planters turned banker. George Williams and William Johnston provided good examples of factors who moved into banking businesses. The most common shift, especially as the South's urban areas developed, took place when a businessman or merchant moved into factorage or banking, using his goods as security on bank loans, gradually working into the banking business at his own rate or winning an invitation to serve as a director on a bank.[38]

36. Ledger books, February 5, March 24, August 2, 1860, and *passim*, Merchants' Bank of South Carolina, Cheraw, 1859–65, SC.

37. *The Northern Bank of Tennessee*, 1954, pamphlet in TLA. Also see E. Merton Coulter, *George Walton Williams* (Athens, Ga., 1976), 23, 31, 34, 39, 43, 46.

38. Henry Ewing to J. Currin, June 14, 1839, Bank of Tennessee Letterbook, 1839–41, Record Group 47, Series 5, Vols. 15 and 16, TLA. Not all states approved of merchants' being bankers. Henry Ewing, cashier of the main branch of the Bank of Tennessee, wrote to J. Currin of the Columbia branch that five of that branch's recently elected directors were merchants, which, in the opinion of the state attorney general, "is a legal disqualification & renders their appointment a nullity."

EDMOND JEAN FORSTALL: MERCHANT-BANKER EXTRAORDINAIRE

Perhaps the most famous of the merchant-bankers was Edmond Jean Forstall of New Orleans. The son of a merchant, Forstall worked his way from poverty into wealth and entered his own mercantile career at the age of twelve. A self-made man, both vain and arrogant, Forstall worked his way into a partnership in Gordon, Forstall and Company, with an office in Liverpool, and the new partnership associated with the Lizardi brothers of Paris, London, and Liverpool.[39]

Forstall was not known as a full-time banker, but his other seasonal business freed him for financial activities. He had served as a director of the Louisiana State Bank in 1818, so that by 1829 he had a reputation of being familiar with bank practices. That same year Governor Peter Derbigny appointed Forstall to the position of comptroller in the Consolidated Association of Planters of Louisiana. The post gave him a place of power in a large and important property bank. He apparently lost his job after a new group of directors denounced him for being an agent of foreigners.[40]

Forstall viewed his release as a business opportunity and immediately packed for Europe to promote a new property bank with the Barings. Fruitful discussions with that firm led him to help design the new institution; Forstall in fact wrote much of the charter of the proposed Union Bank. It became a reality by 1832, and not unexpectedly, the Barings (and their New York correspondent firm of Prime, Ward, King and Company) took fifty-five hundred of the bank's available seven thousand bonds.[41]

Within two years Forstall was contemplating an association with yet a third property bank, the Citizens Bank of Louisiana. Directors of the

39. Irene Neu, "Edmond Jean Forstall and Louisiana Banking," *Explorations in Economic History,* Summer, 1970, pp. 383–98; Letter from Lizardi, New Orleans, to the Governor of the Bank of England, October 24, 1836, reproduced in Richard Kilbourne, *Louisiana Commercial Law* (Baton Rouge, 1980), 208–209.

40. Thomas Baring to Baring Brothers and Company, New York, June 24, 1829, cited in Neu, "Edmond Jean Forstall," 387; Directors' Minutes, June 9, 1829, CAPL, LSU; Irene Neu, "J. B. Moussier and the Property Banks of Louisiana," *Business History Review,* Winter, 1961, pp. 556–57.

41. Forstall to Baring Brothers and Company, October 4, 1830, June 22, 1850, cited in Neu, "Edmond Jean Forstall," 387; Also see Ralph Hidy, "The Union Bank of Louisiana," *Journal of Political Economy,* April, 1939, pp. 236–37.

Citizens Bank soon chose Forstall to fill a vacancy among them. They appointed him to committees and also asked him to acquire land for the yet-to-be-opened bank, finally asking him, as they had probably always intended, to serve on the committee to negotiate the sales of bank bonds to Europe. With Forstall as the driving force, the legislature in 1836 passed an act to pledge the faith and credit of the state behind the bonds, whereupon Forstall was elected president of the bank.[42]

By 1838, Forstall's tight money policy brought him into conflict with other directors. He thereupon resigned, but a year later he was back on the board again and soon took over the job of selling bonds in Europe as the bank's confidential agent. Forstall's efforts to keep the bank solvent and paying specie failed in 1839 when it suspended, but paradoxically, resumption in 1842 caused the final collapse of the Citizens Bank. Forstall directed the liquidation process until 1843.[43]

Forstall's story fits well in the tale of bankers, factors, merchants, and the rest of the business community not only because he made a well-documented and easily observed transition from merchant to banker but also because, during part of his career, the businesses blended together. While he was president of Citizens Bank, "Forstall routed the bank's foreign business, including further sales of bonds, exchange operations, and specie purchases, through his mercantile house F. de Lizardi and Company of London and Lizardi Hermanos of Paris." He and Johnston were typical southern bankers. Their approach to mercantile or exchange business involved a wide interpretation of the term *service*. Thus the mercantile or exchange activities grew to include banking and lending services and sometimes factorage.[44]

42. Neu, "Edmond Jean Forstall," 386; Directors' Minutes, Citizens Bank, March 23, 25, 27, May 1, November 24, 1835, March 9, 1836, CBC, Tulane University; *Louisiana House Journal*, January 2–30, 1836; *Acts, La.*, 1836, 16–24.

43. Neu, "Edmond Jean Forstall," 388 n. 19; Directors' Minutes, Citizens Bank, February–May, 1839; Grenier, "Property Banks in Louisiana," 245; Forstall to the Directors of the Citizens Bank, Parish of St. James, Louisiana, August 31, 1838, cited in *Report of the Committee of Investigation (selected from the Stockholders) Appointed by the Direction of the Citizens' Bank of Louisiana . . . Oct. 18, 1838* (New Orleans, 1839), 4–7; Edmond Forstall, "Circular to the Stockholders of the Citizens Bank of Louisiana, New Orleans, September 20th, 1838" (*ibid.*, p. 4); Forstall to Thomas Ward, February 11, 1847, cited in Neu, "Edmond Jean Forstall," p. 390 n 26; Forstall to the Stockholders of the Consolidated Association of Planters of Louisiana, February 27, 1847, CAPL.

44. Neu, "Edmond Jean Forstall," 389.

KINSHIP AND BANKING: JEWS IN THE SOUTH

Whatever Forstall's material inheritance, his father apparently gave him the needed training and familial experience. Forstall later put them to good use. Kinship often provided important advantages to young entrepreneurs seeking to enter the banking business. The letters of the Campbell family of Tennessee and Virginia reveal considerable correspondence regarding family businesses, especially the letters in which banker William Campbell asked questions of his uncle David, the governor of Virginia during the post-panic antibank frenzy. Kinship ties for those making the transition from merchants to bankers were especially important for immigrants and for subsequent generations. No ethnic group profited as much from kinship ties as did southern Jews (or northern Jews who traveled south for work). As the histories of many southern Jewish communities show, the arrival of Jews in the South occurred relatively late—after the 1830s—and many of the individuals were actually immigrants who had continued South after arriving in New York.[45]

Kinship appears to have been more important for southern Jewish merchant-bankers than ethnicity. Jewish immigrants tended to move to urban areas, and they brought with them a legacy of European discrimination that often disuaded them from landownership, law, medicine, government work, and many other professions. In the United States they therefore followed occupational routes that had served them successfully in Europe: mercantile businesses and banking. Their entry into banking in the South was thus due to their persecution in Europe (and to de facto discrimination in the United States), not to their race or origin. Once involved in finance, they relied on kinship more than on ethnic ties to improve their businesses.

Jewish bankers and commission merchants were extremely influential in New Orleans banking. Judah Touro, one of the wealthiest and most charitable individuals in New Orleans, was elected to the board of directors of the Bank of New Orleans in 1812. Touro came from Boston and began his career in the Crescent City by entering the shipping business, then moved to a more generalized merchant operation. He usually

45. For an effective and brief review of the pressures on European Jews, see Saul Padover, *Karl Marx: An Intimate Biography,* abridged ed. (New York, 1980 [1928]), 8–9.

eschewed investment in banks or speculation in cotton. Like Touro, Samuel Hermann began his career as a private banker, dealing mostly with commercial transactions, exchange, and bank stock. He eventually added partners to his business, calling it Hermann, Briggs and Company. The company specialized in importing specie from Mexico. Hermann himself became a New Orleans civic leader, leaving banking concerns to his sons. Samuel, Jr., Lucien, and Florian all served as directors of banks. In 1832, Samuel, Jr., was nominated for a seat on the board of the City Bank. His brother Florian joined him on the board of the New Orleans Gas Light and Banking Company in 1837. Lucien, meanwhile, directed the operations of the Carrollton Bank beginning in 1836 and spent some time on the board of the Exchange and Banking Company after he had assisted in organizing and commissioning that bank.[46]

All the Hermanns kept ties to other Jewish banks, forming a network with some disadvantages. During the Panic of 1837, Lucien's firm, Thomas Barrett and Company, collapsed because of its close association and reliance upon the Jewish New York firm of J. L. and S. Joseph's. Hermann, Briggs and Company did not depend solely on Jewish credit; it was the only New Orleans firm to enjoy an open credit of ten thousand pounds with the Baring Brothers, a privilege that the Barings revoked in 1837 because of the panic. Debt riddled Hermann, Briggs and Company, too; its liabilities exceeded six million dollars in 1837. Florian's astute business deals and a major reorganization temporarily reduced this figure to two million dollars by 1839, but then bankruptcy set in.[47]

Yet another Jewish banker, Samuel Kohn, often served as a trustee designated by the courts to oversee the property of bankrupted merchants such as Hermann. Kohn's brother, Joachim, a director of the Mechanics and Traders Bank, was a heavy investor in New Orleans real estate who left banking in 1837. Another Kohn, Samuel's nephew Carl, was elected a member of the board of the Atlantic Insurance Company, a position that ultimately brought him to the presidency of the Union National Bank in the postbellum period. Joachim Kohn joined another Jewish director, Benjamin Levy, on the board of the Mechanics and Traders Bank. Levy had served there since 1835. Levy had run a printing and

46. Bertram Korn, *Jews and Negro Slavery in the Old South, 1789–1865* (Elkins Park, Pa., 1961), p. 13; Bertram Korn, *The Early Jews of New Orleans* (Waltham, Mass., 1969), 81–84.

47. Korn, *Early Jews of New Orleans*, 117–18.

publishing business, producing many business volumes and acts of incorporation for banks.[48]

The presence of Jews as directors reflects the strength of the New Orleans Jews in the financial community. Their kinship patterns probably
explain much about the ease with which they obtained credit. Many
Jewish families had relatives or friends in banking. The connections
often went to New York and Baltimore, passing to the Rothschilds of
France via New York. Moreover, their training in financial matters, developed through kinship systems that stressed knowledge, education,
and the development of the intellect as an aspect of religion, fostered
traits that gave Jews substantial advantages in exchange, brokerage, and
banking. Moreover, the Jewish banking community was not limited to
New Orleans; other major groups were located in Mobile, Huntsville,
Charleston, Richmond, and Atlanta. Jewish financiers could also be
found in other southern cities. Throughout the South, Jews used their
kinship and, secondarily, friendship networks to overcome their immigrant status and to offset their inaccessibility to capital. Not only did
they work hard, they often parlayed businesses as merchants into banks.
Their contacts with Old World families, however, occasionally gave Jews
a source of capital in Europe. Moreover, their financial experience was
built up and maintained at the family level rather than at the individual
level.[49]

Connections, such as those exploited by Jewish bankers, to New York
and other eastern financial markets were certainly not restricted to Jews.

48. *Ibid.*, 120, 125, 148–49.

49. *Ibid.*, 148–49, 179. Also see Leo Shpall, *The Jews of Louisiana* (New Orleans,
1936); Bertram Korn, *Jews of Mobile*, 37, 49; *Mobile Register*, June 21, 1837; Barnett
Elzas, *The Jews of South Carolina* (Philadelphia, 1905), pp. 196, 202–205. For Atlanta
Jews, see Steven Hertzberg, "The Jews of Atlanta, 1865–1915" (Ph.D. dissertation, University of Chicago, 1975), 22. Herbert Ezekiel and Gaston Lichenstein, *The History of the
Jews of Richmond from 1769 to 1917* (Richmond, Va., 1917), 29–31, 43, 48, 67, 130–38,
202–203. For Mississippi Jews, see Leo Turitz and Evelyn Turitz, *Jews in Early Mississippi*
(Jackson, Miss., 1983), and Leo Turitz, *Inventory of the Church and Synagogue Archives
of Mississippi: Jewish Congregations and Organizations* (Jackson, Miss., 1940). On immi-
gration generally, see Thomas Sowell, *Ethnic America* (New York, 1981), pp. 73–78, and
his *The Economics and Politics of Race: An International Perspective* (New York, 1983),
80–92; Frances Butwin, *The Jews in America* (Minneapolis, 1969), 38; J. C. Furnas, *The
Americans* (New York, 1969), 393; Stephen Birmingham, *"Our Crowd": The Great Jewish
Families of New York* (New York, 1967), and Dolores Greenberg, "Yankee Financiers and
the Establishment of Trans-Atlantic Partnerships: A Reexamination," *Business History Review*, January, 1924, pp. 17–35.

Yet Jews' otherwise strong kinship patterns, to the extent that these hold for their banking activities, present some interesting implications for historians dealing with the economic relationship of the North and the South in the antebellum period. According to Charles Beard, the powerful economic (and especially financial) interests in the North struggled unsuccessfully to gain complete domination of the South until the war, when northern control of southern capital became a key issue.

Certainly many southerners believed that their economic fortunes depended heavily upon northern capital markets, although even the most acerbic southern critics stopped short of accusing southern bankers of treason. The complaint against banks by the Camden *Southern Chronicle* was representative: "The plain truth is that the Banks, and the innumerable host of corporate bodies . . . which they force upon us, do oppress and retard our advancement in true science, and . . . improvements in agriculture." William Gregg cited lack of sufficient capital as one of five principal reasons for the failure of the South to compete with northern cotton mills.[50]

Although many southerners centered their attacks on the BUS as a tool of northern interests, others believed that the northern banks indeed had control of the financial system. When New York banks found themselves in difficulty, Charleston, Georgia, and Virginia banks, despite their spectacular soundness, were forced into suspension. Legitimate banking activities were therefore viewed with suspicion in the South, despite the region's generally solid record. The establishment of new banks, for example, in Charleston, Georgetown, and Hamburg from 1835 to 1838, met with criticism. These banks, it was charged, fostered speculation. Virtually all solutions concerning the BUS, including Martin Van Buren's stillborn subtreasury, were evaluated in light of their potential for causing a specie drain to the North. Langdon Cheves feared that such a specie drain might discredit bank paper from solvent banks.[51]

50. Camden *Southern Chronicle*, April 23, 1823; John G. Van Deusen, *Economic Bases of Disunion*, 148; Elwood Fisher, *Lecture on the North and South Delivered Before the Young Men's Mercantile Library Association of Cincinnati, Ohio, January 16, 1849* (Charleston, S.C., 1849); *Speech of Honorable James H. Hammond, at Barnwell, October 29, 1858* (Charleston, S.C., 1858); Greenville, S.C., *Patriot*, November 27, 28, 30, 1837; Charleston *Mercury*, August 14, September 29, 1838.

51. Charleston *Courier*, December 8, 1837, April 21, 1841; J. C. Levy to Nicholas Biddle, December 22, 1838, Biddle Papers, LC; *Niles Register*, December 2, 1837. See also Michael Prichett, "Northern Institutions in Southern Financial History: A Note on Insurance Investments," *Journal of Southern History*, August, 1975, pp. 391–96.

The evidence from Jewish bankers, however, throws a different light on interpretations of the South as a "colony" of the North. Southern Jewish financial intermediaries and bankers obviously owed some debts to northern and European friends and relatives, but these Jewish bankers were quite competitive and were excellent businessmen, by and large, whose interests differed greatly from those of all their northern counterparts except their direct kin. More important, until the very eve of the Civil War, Jewish groups apparently continued to emphasize kinship and religious affiliation. Southern Jews who received aid from northern kinsmen were independent entrepreneurs with good connections in many cases; they were not the tools or pawns of northern capitalists. They displayed little concern that such economic domination might occur, and their allegiance to the South and the Confederacy was complete.

A similar trend developed in the sugar marketing and financing business, one built on both family and friendship (so-called social class factors). Sugar planters, factors, and financiers often switched roles, as evidenced by the experiences of Henry and Charles Leverich, New Yorkers and brothers who, on their annual trips, established connections with planters and shippers all along the Mississippi River. James, their oldest brother, had already become a leading commercial banker in New Orleans. Another brother, William, was a successful merchant and banker in New Orleans. Henry and Charles eventually set up a banking business in New Orleans, handling the investments of their southern clients. Despite their northern source of funds, the Leveriches suffered from increasing competition, which forced the company into the hinterlands to gain new customers and encouraged it more than ever to rely on family ties.[52]

NORTHERN CAPITAL IN THE SOUTH

The experiences of the Leveriches support the proposition that northeastern capital may have been convenient but was hardly the controlling influence in the lives of most planters and factors. Actually the Leverich

52. Morton Rothstein, "Sugar and Secession: A New York Firm in Ante-bellum Louisiana," *Explorations in Economic History*, Winter, 1968, pp. 115–31, especially p. 130 nn. 15–19; Harold Woodman, "Itinerant Cotton Merchants of the Antebellum South," *Agricultural History*, April, 1966, pp. 79–90, and his "Decline of Cotton Factorage After the Civil War," *American Historical Review*, July, 1966, pp. 19–36.

Company seems to have succeeded only to the degree that it relinquished an eastern image, especially as the Civil War neared. Planters shipped directly to New York or Philadelphia markets when they believed New Orleans prices were too high as compared with the eastern prices, and opposition to the North was growing; even Charleston developed a bad name for its alleged ties to the North. Expected profits in the East of course had always balanced with transportation costs. Southern bankers and factors could therefore extract a little additional return and still hold a competitive advantage although it was a declining one because of improvements in transportation and the gradual but steady drop in transportation costs. Also, information savings gave the southerners an important advantage over northern investors in assessing risk, the excellent reports of Dun and Bradstreet notwithstanding. Southerners were not prevented from "colonizing" the North either. Augusta businessman and insurance company owner Gazaway Bugg Lamar founded the Bank of the Republic in New York in 1851. His loyalty to the South showed during the war, when he funneled money and supplies to the Confederacy. Finally, other southerners often demanded northern securities on trade. Thomas Branch once complained to James Hunter of New York that "the collector here [in Petersburg] informed me . . . it will be necessary that I furnish some New York resident as security. . . . I there for have reluctantly to ask you to join me in the bond."[53]

Competition such as that affecting major northern bankers, including Alexander Brown and Son and Jacob I. Cohen and Brothers, in southern financial markets has been seriously underestimated or ignored because writers have often relied on the *Banker's Almanac* or on newspapers as sources for the number of banks in operation. Private bankers often lacked the funds to advertise or had a thriving business built on friendships and stood to gain little through promotion. Newspapers published items about private bankers when they did something illegal or somehow attracted attention but otherwise recorded few legal business activi-

53. For comments on transportation costs, see William G. Hewes to Andrew McCollam, November 15, 1854, Andrew McCollam Papers, 1855, SHC, UNC; William Thompson to Lewis Thompson, January 11, 1858, Box 4, Folder 33, Lewis Thompson Papers, *ibid.;* Kenneth Clark to Thompson, December 17, 1854, Box 3, Folder 19, *ibid.;* Thomas Branch to James Hunter, January 17, 22, February 17, 1850, Branch Collection, VHS; Robert Mathis, "Gazaway Bugg Lamar: A Southern Businessman and Confidant in New York City," *New York History,* July, 1975, pp. 298–313.

ties in any reliable manner. The problem, of course, with trying to count the number of private bankers in the antebellum southern population is that they seldom identified themselves in newspaper ads and were not required to obtain any license or charter to operate. Private bankers are best identified and counted on a state-by-state basis. Richard Sylla compared the *Almanac's* figures with those of the Treasury reports, which identified some, but certainly not all, private bankers. Even in the postbellum period, and in other states, when state governments, through treasurers or bank commissioners, tried to gain a more accurate count of private banks, they still missed a significant portion.[54]

Bankers such as William Johnson, William Johnston, Seaborn Mays, James Rhind, George Williams, and William Godfrey had important—but often unnoticed—effects on the southern economy. First, the most apparent, banking services existed in many areas where it has often been assumed that they did not. In Arkansas, for example, where banking was prohibited by law for more than a decade prior to the Civil War, several private bankers did business. W. B. Wait, perhaps the dean of the Arkansas private bankers, had his operation under way well before the Civil War. S. H. Tucker engaged in exchange operations in connection with his Little Rock mercantile establishment well before 1860, as did B. L. Brittin and Company from 1845 to 1860 in Washington, Arkansas. Edwin Burr and Company had a banking operation in Batesville. In the 1850s, two prominent merchants, H. P. Coolidge and Henry W. Bailey, furnished banking services in Helena until the mid-1850s, when John J. Jackson and Company opened a private banking business, which lasted a few years. In at least two other cities in Arkansas, private bankers plied their trade, despite the fact that they were technically in violation of the law.

The extensive private banking raises important questions about the

54. Richard Sylla, "Forgotten Men of Money: Private Bankers in Early U.S. History," *Journal of Economic History*, March, 1976, pp. 173–88; *Banker's Almanac*, 1853–60. This publication's title varied, as Sylla pointed out. Sylla has estimated that, *at best*, the *Almanac* recorded only five out of six private bankers who were actually in business in the 1850s. Material on Cohen and the Browns appears in W. Ray Luce, "The Cohen Brothers of Baltimore: From Lotteries to Banking," *Maryland Historical Magazine*, Fall, 1973, pp. 288–308; John Killick, "Risk, Specialization, and Profit in the Mercantile Sector of the Nineteenth Century Cotton Trade: Alexander Brown and Sons, 1820–80," *Business History*, January, 1974, pp. 1–16.

fundamental components of monetary analysis in the antebellum period. Monetary data from which most studies are drawn omit private banks and therefore would understate the money supply. Using data from William Johnston's records, for example, and allowing for turnover each year of one-third of his loans, we would conclude that Johnston personally made two thousand dollars a year in new loans. Movements of money stock would plainly be more difficult to trace.[55]

MOBILITY IN BANKING

Infinitely more significant than the fact of competition was the presence of mobility. Bankers could, and often did, move from proprietorships of small stores (or even occasional peddling, in the case of some Jews) to cashierships, then on to the presidency or a seat on the board of directors. Both factors—competition and mobility—suggest that the distinctions between bankers, factors, merchants, and planters could not be established by income, job description, position in society, or other narrow means of identification that are readily employed.

At some times these groups merely reflected the movement of men at different stages of their careers. According to one interpretation, planters, frustrated by factors and unable to meet the increasing financial burdens created by their need to maintain "class" dominance over yeoman farmers, supported the formation of banks that would give them an eternal wellspring of credit. In this view, the ensuing struggle between planters trying to obtain credit led to a "subsumed class struggle" among bankers and factors. In reality, of course, very few planters engaged in banking. Quite the contrary; if competition among financial outlets was present to the degree suggested here, the planters had every reason *not* to pursue banking. Planters preferred factorage to banking, and most bankers came from the ranks of business and merchants. Planters such as Godfrey, Johnson, and Johnston avoided commercial banking because it was time consuming and not as profitable as planting, whereas Williams, Kennedy, Leverich, Branch, and others began their careers in business. Most planters were farmers on a greater scale, but they still had a special

55. Richard Timberlake, Jr., "Denominational Factors in Nineteenth-Century Currency Experience," *Journal of Economic History*, December, 1974, pp. 835–50; Hugh Rockoff, "Varieties of Banking and Regional Economic Development in the United States," *Journal of Economic History*, March, 1975, pp. 174–76, 179–81.

affection for the earth. Indoor work, even as a bank director, would have been a pursuit too refined and cosmopolitan for most of them. Still, one cannot readily categorize either group.[56]

A model of southern society should allow considerable latitude for occupational and professional mobility; it would provide for debtors' emergence as creditors; and it would have to allow for geographical mobility. Differences between southerners were real, however, and planters frequently viewed their interests as distinct from those of merchants. Still, the most fundamental division in southern society was that between the groups which sought to operate in the capitalistic mainstream, and wished to develop commercial and industrial sectors, and the groups that viewed this desire as a threat to autonomy and freedom. In political terms, such distinctions placed the Whigs in the former group and the Jacksonians in the latter. Economically, the commercial elements ultimately found themselves in major disagreement with planters over the shape of southern society in the future. Still, the evidence presented here suggests that these differences hardly defined classes in any Marxist sense, especially because a change in attitude was all that was ultimately required to shift an individual from one group to the other.[57]

Conversely, it would be ludicrous to contend that bankers did not have general career patterns as businessmen or that they did not form associations with other businessmen. One of the more interesting patterns can be seen in the movement of bank officers and directors. Individuals did serve concurrently on two boards of directors, but only infrequently. More commonly, bank directors moved from one board to another. The career patterns of several South Carolina bankers show such movement. J. H. Honour served on the board of the Bank of the State for a year, then took a directorship with the Peoples Bank of

56. Feiner, "Factors, Bankers, and Masters," 63–65. Now, it seems, Marxist theoreticians are trying to have it both ways: if competition existed, it represented only "subsumed class struggle," and if competition did not exist, it meant the triumph of monopolistic capitalism.

57. The issue of "class," as a term used by Marxists, far from being peripheral to this subject, lies at its very core. If "class" in a Marxian sense exists, then Feiner was correct and previous studies of banking (including the present book) are virtually useless because of their concentration on entirely the wrong issues. A thorough discussion of the issues raised by "class analysis" appears in Schweikart, "Banking in the American South," 479–83. Also see Rebecca Allison, "The Force of Argument: George Fitzhugh's Defense of Slavery," *The Conservative Historians' Forum*, May, 1982, pp. 5–13.

Charleston. He had served concurrently on the board and as a trustee of the Trustee Charleston Savings Institution, positions that extended simultaneously through *both* bank directorships. J. B. Lafitte followed a similar one-year pattern, going from the Farmers and Exchange Bank in 1859–1860 to the Peoples Bank in 1860–1865, where he served on the same board with J. H. Honour. These represent only two of many similar career moves by South Carolina bankers.[58]

Careers often traveled a slightly different path. A director in one bank would become an officer—usually the president—of another. Tennessee directors who became officers included R. C. Brinkley and David Molloy. Brinkley, a director of the Memphis branch of the Planters Bank, later assumed the presidency of the Bank of Memphis. Molloy was a director and secretary of the Memphis Life and General Insurance Company. Another director in that company, T. R. Farnsworth, took the cashiership of the De Soto Savings Institution. James Williamson, who began as a director in the Bank of West Tennessee, later became president, a pattern used by E. McDavitt of the branch of the Planters Bank. Tennessee is only an example; such movements occurred with regularity.

Just as important was the way in which cashiers and bookkeepers often moved up the ranks. In the Farmers and Merchants Bank of Charleston, for example, J. S. Davies, who began as early as 1853 in the bank as a bookkeeper, became cashier in 1859, then served as president of the bank during the war. M. D. Strobel, of that same bank, meanwhile, who was a teller while Davies was a bookkeeper, later became cashier during Davies' presidency. Clement Stevens started as a teller with the Planters and Mechanics Bank, working his way into a cashiership and eventually a directorship. Similarly, John Fisher, teller for the Columbia branch of the Bank of the State of South Carolina, moved to the cashiership and finally to the presidency of that bank. Tellers, on the other hand, were not officers, and so the level of movement from these and lower posi-

58. Movements of bankers are discussed in Schweikart, "Banking in the American South," tables 5.4–5.6. Additional materials appear in *ibid.*, 447–50, and in Larry Schweikart, "Antebellum Southern Bankers: Origins and Mobility," in Jeremy Atack (ed.), *Business and Economic History* (Urbana, 1985); in Schweikart, "Entrepreneurial Aspects of Antebellum Banking," in Joseph Pusateri and Henry Dethloff (eds.), *Casebook in American Business History* (New York, 1986); and in Schweikart, "Private Bankers in the Antebellum South," *Southern Studies*, Summer, 1986. In the last-named article, the contribution of the Harmonists, a millennialist society, is examined. The Harmonists had extensive penetration of the South through "agents," who had access to the Harmonists' banking capital of $1 million.

tions to bank presidencies and seats on the boards of directors reflects the high degree of opportunity that existed in South Carolina banking and probably in most southern banking. This occupational opportunity is particularly visible in the number of porters, clerks, "outdoor clerks," and lower-ranked employees who eventually became cashiers.

Indeed, the ability of the "low men on the totem poles" to advance in bank work goes far toward explaining why there was little concern with class. Bankers, after all, were no more often planters or otherwise men of aristocratic airs than they were Jewish immigrants, former peddlers, merchants, brokers, former tellers, or cashiers who came up through the ranks. Opportunity in banking made it a profession of equality more than historians have ever suspected. Jacksonians attacked banks as symbols of aristocracy, but in more ways than one they were testimony that equal treatment was available in the market, even for refugees with a religious taint whose only talents involved an antebellum form of door-to-door salesmanship.

Harsh criticism was heaped on bankers who failed to keep their banks solvent, but woe unto the director who did not extend credit freely and "equally." Officials of the Bank of the State of Mississippi and of many Louisiana banks learned that there was little relief from this antinomic problem of easy credit/solvency. Free banks did not completely solve the problem either. There was consequently a plethora of semibankers, brokers, agents, and other financial merchants who dotted the South or who swept through on regular runs. Other bankers, usually with a state franchise of a monopolistic nature, solved the credit/solvency problem by appropriating as much as possible for themselves and their friends, relying on state bond sales to rescue their institutions in time of trouble. Major exceptions to this pattern involved cotton speculation, even more disastrous.

Entrance into the cotton business, although clearly opposed by many factors who stood to lose their livelihood to the state, nevertheless indicates an even more significant feature of the southern bankers' character, namely the blurring of occupational, social, and income divisions between themselves and the other financial intermediaries. The effort to explain this similarity in Marxist terms has led historians almost to abandon the argument that there was any real class struggle and to concentrate on "subsumed classes" in conflict with each other, in essence admitting the absence of clear conflict between factors, bankers, planters, businessmen, or entrepreneurs of almost any type along class lines. Still, tension and anxiety did exist along somewhat different lines. Ideological differences were present, shaped by Jeffersonians—both planters and nonplanters—who viewed with horror the encroachment of a national and an international economy. It is crucial to understand banking, therefore, in the context of freedom, as it was viewed by the antebellum southerner. Either banks constituted, as the Jacksonians believed, potential threats to equality, convenient but capable of enslaving the unwary southerner, or they were, as the Whigs maintained, important tools for economic progress, which in turn freed the individual. This was the dividing line along which southerners broke. Individual bankers, factors, and planters held one view or the other, depending on their own political philosophy and personal preference, and the view held by the individual may not have been predictable from his occupation. Generally, bankers adopted the Whig view. Over time, planters found themselves ideologically at odds with a widely held definition of freedom that stressed economic growth, world markets, and mobility. Ironically, whereas the bankers are now viewed in some circles as having been "subsumed" by the planters, in reality it was the other way around. Even in the South, the argument that slavery made men free was being drowned out by the sounds of forges, railroads, and industry.

6

INVESTMENTS AND CREDIT

Nearly every writer who has concentrated on southern banking has eventually focused on a single question: did southern banks provide enough credit? This question has usually been pursued with the intent of answering other implied and related questions. Did southern banks encourage or discourage industrial growth in the South? Did they therefore directly help perpetuate slavery or contribute to abolishing it eventually? Any theory of southern economic growth must ultimately ask where and why the southern banker loaned money.

The larger question of the dominance of slave-based plantation agriculture seems to have been generally answered, in some cases since early influential studies on banking took place. Southerners concentrated "on their most rational, profit-maximizing course, cotton monoculture," and attempts to utilize slaves in urban industrial settings appeared feasible only temporarily. By the 1850s, "urbanization had so weakened the ability of masters to capture income earned by slaves that planters were easily able to outbid urban employers for slaves." Thus the investment habits of southern bankers should not be contemplated with the attitude that bankers were the scapegoats for Negro slavery in America. Rather, the objective must be study of their practices to determine whether they responded in a businesslike fashion, when and to what degree moral concerns about investments played a role in shaping investment decisions, and to what degree they foresaw and balanced long-range investments (improving southern production in industrial goods, for example) with short-term profits (agriculture in most cases) as

Table 13.   Abbreviated Sample Balance Sheet of a
Southern Bank, Alabama, 1830–1831
($ millions)

Date	No. of Banks	Assets			Liabilities		
		Loans and Discounts	Notes of Other Banks	Specie	Capital	Circu- lations	Deposits
1831	1	1.23	0.033	0.169	0.739	0.407	0.370
1832	1	1.95	0.190	0.172	1.071	0.565	0.559

Source: All southern monetary data taken from Larry Schweikart, "Banking in the American South, 1836–1865" (Ph.D. dissertation, University of California, Santa Barbara, 1983), table 6.1.

well as with social and political demands. Historians who expect ante-bellum southern bankers as a group to have behaved differently from the rest of the South are concentrating on the wrong questions.[1]

The evidence is scattered, uneven, and less than complete in many cases. Often it can offer examples of banking activity—loans, deposits, collections, or circulation—on only a specific level. A sample balance sheet appears in Table 13. Seldom, except when original account books are located, are the individual accounts available for analysis. The only data available on a larger scale, for example from the U.S. Treasury reports and from congressional and executive documents, suffer from variations in reporting dates and from omissions. They can, however, provide highly informative trend analyses on growth rates for all major banking indicators. The cumulative data for the South, 1834–1861, appear in Table 14; the real comparison of percentage growth in the South, 1834–1861, with that in all other states occupies Table 15; and real percentage growth for all southern states except Arkansas, 1840–1861, and all other states, using variables such as number of banks, loans, deposits, and circulation regressed along time, appears in Table 16. An annual average of southern growth and that of all other states, using the same indicators, appears in Table 17. These indicators usefully show where some of the southern banking assets went, but even these omit private bank operations. Moreover, banks, no matter how efficient or successful,

1. Brownlee, *Dynamics of Ascent*, 248–49; Richard Wade, *Slavery in the Cities: The South, 1820–1860* (Chicago, 1964); Claudia Goldin, *Urban Slavery in the American South, 1820–1860: A Quantitative History* (Chicago, 1974).

Table 14. Cumulative Data, Banking Indicators of Southern States
and All Other States, 1834–1861
($ millions)

Year	No. of Banks	Loans	Deposits	Circulations
1834	38	82.48	14.31	26.15
1835	43	99.12	20.78	36.11
1836	63	143.80	33.64	46.85
1837	81	156.97	29.47	39.71
1838	67	137.89	25.92	43.93
1839	68	127.54	18.98	30.93
1840	92	156.99	22.94	37.03
1841	72	163.00	21.48	45.80
1842	58	139.93	17.10	37.25
1843	48	119.67	17.96	26.42
1844	33	97.71	18.31	26.59
1845	32	99.26	21.28	27.12
1846	34	84.45	23.72	28.31
1847	38	77.45	18.75	26.11
1848	39	92.95	22.65	36.78
1849	43	94.54	21.84	35.16
1850	44	104.11	25.24	45.32
1851	41	91.99	16.76	53.89
1852	39	90.63	23.43	47.87
1853	37	85.72	28.17	40.74
1854	69	109.41	28.01	53.83
1855	93	91.73	24.28	41.81
1856	99	115.45	33.10	46.52
1857	101	121.93	32.85	53.62
1858	126	125.18	33.68	47.45
1859	122	140.40	48.66	64.84
1860	118	152.12	50.56	65.05
1861	105	134.76	42.49	44.77

Note: All numbers have been rounded off.
Source: All southern monetary data taken from Larry Schweikart, "Banking in the American South, 1836–1865," tables 6.1–6.10.

Table 15.   Real Growth of Southern and Other U.S. Banking Indicators,
1834–1861
(percent per annum)

States	Number of Banks	Loans	Circulation	Deposits
Other	3.2	3.0	3.3	4.1
South	2.4	−0.1	1.9	2.4

Note: All numbers have rounded off.
Sources: All southern monetary data taken from Schweikart, "Banking in the American South,"
Tables 6.1–6.10. U.S. totals from Historical Statistics of the United States; Colonial Times to 1970, 2
parts (Washington, D.C., 1975), II, 1020; wholesale price data from the same source. All "other" data
from Larry Schweikart, "Southern Banking and Economic Growth in the Antebellum Period: A Reassessment," Journal of Southern History, February, 1987.

Table 16.   Real Growth of Southern
and Other U.S. Banking Indicators, 1840–1861
(percent per annum)

States	Number of Banks	Loans	Circulation	Deposits
Other	4.3	4.5	3.1	5.9
South	4.5	1.8	4.5	4.1

Note: All numbers have been rounded off.
Sources: All southern monetary data taken from Schweikart, "Banking in the American South,"
Tables 6.1–6.10. U.S. totals from Historical Statistics of the United States; Colonial Times to 1970, 2
parts (Washington, D.C., 1975), II, 1020; wholesale price data from the same source. All "other" data
from Larry Schweikart, "Southern Banking and Economic Growth in the Antebellum Period: A Reassessment," Journal of Southern History, February, 1987.

Table 17.   Comparative Real Annual Average Growth, Southern States
and All Other States, 1840–1861
(percent)

Area	No. of Banks	Loans	Deposits	Circulation
South	4.55	0.18	4.19	3.10
All other states	4.34	4.58	5.90	4.57

Note: All prices adjusted for inflation and deflation, using prices in wholesale price index from His-
torical Statistics of the United States: Colonial Times to 1970, 2 parts (Washington, D.C., 1979).
Source: Larry Schweikart, "Southern Banking and Economic Growth in the Antebellum Period: A
Reassessment," Journal of Southern History, February, 1987.

never financed any more than a small portion of a region's economic growth. Investment choices would thus make a significant difference within that portion.

BANKS AND RAILROAD INVESTMENT

Some students of southern banking have distinguished between the financing of industry and internal improvements. Almost no one doubts that banks contributed heavily to transportation, especially in the development of railroads. To many southerners, railroads epitomized the "campaign for Southern self-sufficiency" and served as a bench mark of industrialization even if they were intended to link interior cotton lands to market. A few case studies of specific contributions by southern banks toward the founding and capitalization of railroads will illuminate the development question. A prime example was the Georgia Railroad (later the Georgia Railroad and Banking Company). Organized in Athens, Georgia, in 1833, the railroad met the challenge of the rival South Carolina Railroad just across the river from Augusta, the terminus of the Georgia road. After two years the directors petitioned for banking privileges, hoping to secure subscriptions and contribute to general finances. When the request was granted, the company included the term *banking company* in its title.[2]

According to one authority on the bank, its "outstanding characteristic . . . was its relative prosperity despite adversity, a condition due largely to the fiscal and social conservatism of the company's officials and directors." James Camak and John King, the company's first presidents, set the tone for the bank's conservatism, refusing to rely too heavily on cotton trade. The Georgia Railroad and Banking Company demonstrated considerable concern over inefficiency and unproductivity, which led it to seek additional sources of trade and revenue. Like other southern railroads, the Georgia company consistently worked to establish a western connection, with its vast trade possibilities. Progress toward this goal was slow because of the Panic of 1837.[3]

2. Robert Starobin, *Industrial Slavery in the Old South* (New York, 1970), 226; W. K. Wood, "The Georgia Railroad and Banking Company," *Georgia Historical Quarterly,* Winter, 1973, pp. 544–61. Also see Max Dixon, "Building the Central Railroad of Georgia," *Georgia Historical Quarterly,* September, 1961, pp. 1–21.

3. Wood, "Georgia Railroad and Banking Company," 548–49; Diane Lindstrom, "Southern Dependence on Interregional Grain Supplies: A Review of the Trade Flow Data, 1840–1860," in Parker (ed.), *Structure of the Cotton Economy.*

To meet its financial needs, the company borrowed large amounts. When the corporation faced financial difficulties, it reverted to austerity and conservatism. More important, it struggled to make operations even more efficient and productive, stressing self-sufficiency through vertical integration and building its own iron foundry next to its Augusta machine shop to furnish wheel castings. By 1848, the Georgia railway was manufacturing its own cars. Soon thereafter it erected a car factory machine shop in Augusta. Once in the business of industry, the company promoted other Augusta manufacturing firms and tried to increase the noncotton trade. The willingness of the directors to compete in markets that the bank deemed critical to the company's health was illustrated by its entry into the steamship business in 1860, which marked yet another attempt to gain better control of the company's trade routes.[4]

Successful as the Georgia Railroad and Banking Company was, few railroads had more impact on the South or generated more publicity than the Louisville, Cincinnati, and Charleston Railroad Company. Like the Georgia Railroad, this project—"one of the great might have beens in American history"—secured banking privileges. Directly competing with the seaboard cities of the North and their Erie canal route, southern proponents chose a railroad scheme that would open "the whole valley of the Mississippi and of the Ohio . . . to an easy, cheap and rapid trade" with Georgia and South Carolina. It would, however, require charters from states through which the road was to pass: North and South Carolina, Tennessee, and Kentucky. To bolster both state and private stock subscriptions there, proponents sought banking privileges.[5]

Debates over the banking powers came before the South Carolina legislature in 1836. Opponents of another bank, led by George McDuffie, feared that a new bank would only cut into the profits of the state bank and thus deprive the state's citizens of a tax benefit. Ignoring McDuffie's pleas, the legislature not only gave the company banking powers by

4. Wood, "Georgia Railroad and Banking Company," 548–51. Also see Peter Stewart, "Railroads and Urban Rivalries in Antebellum Eastern Virginia," *Virginia Magazine of History and Biography*, January, 1973, pp. 3–22.

5. *Charleston Courier*, August 31, 1836; Stuart Sprague, "Kentucky and the Cincinnati and Charleston Railroad, 1835–1839," *Register of the Kentucky Historical Society*, April 1975, pp. 122–35; Macon *Georgia Messenger*, November 10, 1836, Charles Schultz, "Hayne's Magnificent Dream: Factors Which Influenced the Efforts to Join Cincinnati and Charleston by Railroad, 1835–1860" (Ph.D. dissertation, Ohio State University, 1966), 45–47.

chartering the South Western Railroad Bank but obligated the state to buy one million dollars worth of stock in the railroad. The "extraordinarily broad" banking privileges granted to the bank were designed to encourage subscriptions and to pay enough in dividends to keep investors happy until the railroad showed a profit. The flow of money to the railroad was assured by the requirement that no one could own stock in the bank without first holding stock in the railroad.

Abraham Blanding assumed the presidency of the newly formed bank, using the $500,000 in specie imported from England to open for business in 1838. In its early months of operation, before the dual setbacks of Blanding's death in 1839 and the fall in cotton prices in 1839 and 1840, the bank prospered. Meanwhile the company had received short-term loans from Charleston's banks and from the state but suffered another loss of morale when John C. Calhoun resigned from the board of directors in a dispute over the proper route through the mountains. Another worse and ultimately irrecoverable loss struck the company in September, 1839, when Robert Y. Hayne died. The railroad and the bank had each lost its most important spokesmen. An attempt to merge the railroad with the Hiwassee Railroad Company of Tennessee foundered with the grant of banking privileges to the Louisville, Cincinnati, and Charleston company. A new president, James Gadsden, took over the affairs of the railroad company. The railroad languished until the early 1850s, when it finally started to develop its property, but even then it never fulfilled the expectations of its promoters.[6]

The important question for students of southern investment is the degree to which banks—in the case of the Cincinnati-Charleston railroad, a specially created bank—aided in the development of internal improvements. The Southwestern Railroad Bank, operated separately from the

---

6. U. B. Phillips, *A History of Transportation in the Eastern Cotton Belt to 1860* (New York, 1968), 197; Letter of John C. Calhoun to Robert Y. Hayne, October 28, 1838, as published in John Bomar Cleveland, *Controversy Between John C. Calhoun and Robert Y. Hayne as to the Proper Route of a Railroad from South Carolina to the West* (Spartanburg, S.C., 1913[?]), 12; Letters of Mitchell King to James G. M. Ramsey and William F. DeSaussure, October 9, 1839, Mitchell King Papers, SHC, UNC; Folmsbee, *Sectionalism and Internal Improvements*, 194–95; *Charleston Courier*, December 1, 1836 (carrying Governor McDuffie's message of November 28); *Charter of the Louisville, Cincinnati and Charleston Rail Road Company*, 1838, pp. 16–17, 21–26; Phillips, *History of Transportation*, 180–220; *Exposition of the Acts Amending the Charter and Conferring Banking Privileges on the Louisville, Cincinnati and Charleston Rail Road Company: By C. G. Memminger, Commissioner from South Carolina* (Raleigh, N.C., 1836), 8.

railroad, had little to do with railroad policy, although the purpose in creating the bank was to improve stock sales. The refusal of Kentucky to join the system more than offset any influence the bank might have had. Banking seems to have been an instrument of convenience and a means to increase capital, as was clearly the case with the Georgia Railroad and Banking Company. Its bank operated almost independently of the railroad and became so strong that it survived the war and eventually enabled the company to move strictly into banking. A similar arrangement existed in the case of the Georgia Railroad's competitor, the Central of Georgia Company, which also had banking privileges.

Given the objectives of the promoters in creating the banks, perhaps they failed to flood the projects with a rolling tide of capital, but they can hardly be criticized. They viewed railroads as instruments of industrialization and not as tools for the specific benefit of planters. Banks created as a subsidiary of the railroad proved as strong as—or stronger than—their associated railroad companies. The convenient services they rendered cannot be dismissed. Willingness to finance such projects and enthusiasm about financing railroads were also quite different sentiments. Charles Mills, the cashier of the Marine Bank of Georgia, received a loan request in 1855 from W. E. Danell, of the Atchafalaya Railroad Company in Louisiana. Mills explained that the bank was not "desirous of doing local business, particularly at long term." He and the directors believed "any *considerable* amount *locked up* in this way would operate against our ability to make the regular mercantile business negotiations." Danell had presented his case well, though, and so the board agreed to lend fifteen thousand dollars despite the fact that the bank declined all local stock business and confined its discounts to business transactions. Mills expected more than strictly monetary returns, too: "We hope this concession will be appreciated by your community, and that the circulation of [Marine Bank] notes will be increased by a fair portion of the amount of the loan."[7]

CAPITAL INVESTMENT IN SOUTHERN RAILROADS

With profits related almost entirely to business and planting investments, it is little wonder that public finance of railroads in the South exceeded private support and accounted for a much larger proportion of

7. Charles Mills to W. E. Danell, 1855, Charles Mills Letterbooks, SHC, UNCL.

investment than in the North. Commercial groups, led by Whigs, attempted to compensate for the hostility toward large-scale projects by planters. Their efforts met with some success in the Old South and in Alabama after 1850 but failed in most states of the New South. Estimates of the amount vary. Albert Fishlow calculated that investment in railroads totaled $252,100,000 by 1860. Milton Heath estimated that public sources in the South raised $143,602,166 for railroad investment, indicating that southern public investment was quite high. Carter Goodrich, by comparison, has suggested that the average public investment nationwide approached only 25 or 30 percent.[8]

Louisiana, especially, saw private financing of railroads as inadequate, to the degree that the legislature occasionally forced banks to make loans to railroads. In 1835 and 1836, the state's lawmakers coerced the New Orleans Gas Light and Banking Company to aid railroads by purchasing $250,000 worth of bonds of the Clinton and Port Hudson Railroad, lending the company $100,000, and lending the Red River Railroad $150,000. Banks in New Orleans, on the whole, were reluctant to extend loans to railroads; only one offered credit to the New Orleans and Nashville Railroad. The legislature granted banking privileges to railroads in three cases, but like their sister companies in Georgia and South Carolina, the investment value of such privileges proved negligible. Private lenders were quite niggardly about credit to railroads, because "most of the small promoters had to face immensely complex or unforeseen problems . . . , with little or no experience behind them." The prospective return was virtually inestimable because railroads were supposed to improve profits from shipping agricultural goods from the West to markets. Inasmuch as calculating the return on such an undertaking would be extremely difficult today, one can understand the hesitancy of private investors to dole out cash in the 1800s.[9]

Critics of southern railroad building and indirectly of southern bank

8. Albert Fishlow, *American Railroads and the Transformation of the American Economy* (Cambridge, Mass., 1965), p. 397; Milton Heath, "Public Railroad Construction and the Development of Private Enterprise in the South Before 1861," *Journal of Economic History*, Supplement X (1950), 41; James Ward, "A New Look at Antebellum Southern Railroad Development," *Journal of Southern History*, August, 1973, pp. 400–420.

9. *Acts, La.*, 12th Legis., 1st Sess., 1835, pp. 39, 51, 82–86, 193; *ibid.*, 2d Sess., 1836, pp. 3, 12–13; Claude Babin, "The Economic Expansion of New Orleans before the Civil War" (Ph.D. dissertation, Tulane University, 1953), 256; New Orleans *Bee*, November 21, 24, 1836; Merl Reed, *New Orleans and the Railroads: The Struggle for Commercial Empire, 1830–1860* (Baton Rouge, 1966), 11–12.

capitalization missed the point that southern railroad building was to serve commercial groups by linking markets and in passing to promote planting and farming areas. Seeing railroads as fundamental to industrial development, James Ward contended, "The crucial question is whether the southern rail system was always undercapitalized. If it was not, the whole theory that inadequate capital formation was built into southern society crumbles." Evidence compiled from Fishlow and Henry V. Poor's yearly railroad mileage tables refutes the undercapitalization theory. In fact, the South equaled or exceeded northern investment per mile in railways from 1837 to 1842. Its peak year, 1839, boasted a capitalization of twelve thousand dollars *more* than the national average. Southern railroads, however, did suffer from certain idiosyncratic disadvantages. Falling cotton prices, the debt repudiations, and the timing of the South's emergence from the depressions unfortunately coincided with a serious shortage of civil engineers. The latter problem was exacerbated by the Mexican War, and just as the South recovered from this setback, the Crimean War disrupted the overseas money markets that were closely tied to the South. Thus cotton again played a major role in preventing a more vigorous industrialization. Still, banking's contribution to railroad building in the antebellum South has been neglected. A new historical tack must be taken.[10]

BANKS, RAILROADS, STATE INVESTMENT:
SOME CASE STUDIES

First, the role of public investment must be placed in perspective, because state capitalization of projects can occur for a number of different reasons. Again, Alabama provides a useful example of this development. Alabama's laws severely restricted private banking because of the power of the state bank (Arkansas, devoid of banks, lacked railroads until 1860). Even in Alabama, however, the Decatur Branch of the Bank of the State had loaned large sums to the Tuscumbia, Cortland and Decatur Railroad Company. By 1837, the railroad's debt totaled $507,609.35, plus notes

10. Ward, "A New Look at Railroad Development," 412–14, 418, and *passim;* Fishlow, *American Railroads,* 397; [Henry V. Poor], *Manual of Railroads in the United States, for 1869–70* (New York, 1860), xxvi–xxvii. Also see Merle Reed, "Government Investment and Economic Growth: Louisiana's Ante Bellum Railroads," *Journal of Southern History,* May, 1962, pp. 183–201, and William McCain, *The Story of Jackson: A History of the Capital of Mississippi, 1821–1951* (Jackson, Miss., 1953), I, 60.

the railroad had endorsed to the tune of another $295,639.55. Afraid of allegations about mismanagement, the bank's bookkeepers kept these amounts secret as long as possible. The railroad had enjoyed certain privileges from the Decatur bank since the road's inception, and the bank had an interlocking directorate with the road. Intended to go around the Muscle Shoals of the Tennessee River and to take advantage of shipping around that point, the railroad sank into disrepair and debt and eventually resorted to horse-drawn trains. Eventually the inability of the railroad to repay its debt forced the bank to acquire its property in 1843.[11]

Despite the Decatur branch's difficulties with the Tuscumbia, Cortland, and Decatur, other branches of the Alabama state bank attempted to support some railroad investment. Montgomery's branch officers had already entered into an agreement with the Montgomery and West Point Rail Road whereby the bank would circulate the railroad's bills. Governor Bagby vehemently opposed the arrangement. Charles Pollard, president of the West Point Line and an entrepreneur who understood the radical impact that a railroad could have on trade routes, had suggested to the legislature a joint venture with the Tennessee and Coosa Rail Road Company. Pollard succeeded in getting the money from the state despite opposition. Some capital was generated by individuals associated with the Broad River group (once called the Royalists). Federal land grants, necessary to most roads, became the real focal point of entrepreneurial interest. Urban rivalries between Mobile, Montgomery, and northern Alabama further detracted from long-term private banking investment.[12]

These conditions make it difficult to criticize Alabama's private banks for their failure to capitalize railroads. Mississippi's response to railroad investment was just the opposite, and greatly resembled that of Louisianans. Like Louisiana, Mississippi came under heavy criticism for overbanking.[13]

Several railroad banks appeared in Mississippi: three in 1833 and seven

11. *Alabama Senate Journal*, 1839–40, pp. 231–42, 308–21; Wetumpka *Argus*, January 1, 1840; Brantley, *Banking in Alabama*, appendix, 298, 354; Memorial of the Tuscumbia, Courtland, and Decatur Railroad Company, Benjamin Sherrod, president, to the Legislature of Alabama, n.d., Governor's Correspondence: Arthur Bagby, ADAH.

12. *Alabama Senate Journal*, 1838, pp. 109, 114; *Alabama Acts*, 1842, pp. 63, 127; *ibid.*, 1843, p. 136. Also see Thornton, *Politics and Power*, 105, 107, 271–80.

13. Scroggs, "Financial History of Alabama," 117–21.

more in 1836 and 1837, virtually all directed at benefiting planters. Most of these roads sponsored short lines without any real earning power. Their notes passed at increasingly greater discounts. When the crash came, everyone paid. The Mississippi treasury reported in 1842 that the Mississippi Railroad Company (and bank) owed the state $63,030. Nowhere did repudiation harm future development more than in Mississippi. Private capital, especially from overseas, was nonexistent after repudiation. As a result, Mississippi's problem was inflation: private banks capitalizing railroads had virtually no specie to back their issues (Mississippi's regression shows a decline in specie averaging 16 percent annually). From 1819 to 1836, prior to the collapse, Mississippi's loans grew at a 47 percent rate annually. Circulation increased at a rate of 39 percent a year. Undercapitalized in real terms, Mississippi still managed to construct a number of railroads on the basis of a promise that the state would back the bonds supporting the banks. Had the state not repudiated its debts, foreign investors might still have been enticed to inject more capital into the state after its creditworthiness had been reestablished.

Florida, while not booming with railroad construction, participated in the construction of the Alabama, Georgia, and Florida Railroad Company by allowing the private Bank of Pensacola to purchase shares in the railway. Combining this privilege with an increased capitalization for the bank, the legislature further encouraged private investment through tax relief on the stock of the bank and the railroad. Most of the funding came from the Bank of Pensacola, which purchased large blocs of stock, leaving little money for other lending. The Bank of Pensacola's authorized capitalization was $2.5 million, although by 1836 it had only $600,000 in capital. Compared with the Union Bank's $1 million in actual capitalization, this sum was not impressive, although both loaned about the same actual dollar amounts. Most of the Union Bank's funds went into long-term agriculture.[14]

Virginia invested heavily in public improvement schemes between 1830 and 1837, without sufficient revenue to pay the interest. By 1840 the drain on the treasury had grown so great that the banks extended $200,000 worth of loans to the state, a sum that increased to $350,000 by 1843. Philip Nicholas, president of the Farmers Bank of Virginia, had

---

14. *Bank of Pensacola and Alabama, Georgia, and Florida Railroad Company Charters* (New York, 1835).

refused to allow the bank to subscribe to five thousand shares of stock to extend the James River and Kanawha Canal, even though the state tried to lure the bank's stockholders into supporting the company by promising to allow an increase in its capitalization. He argued, instead, for railroads. His successor, William H. Macfarland, supported railroads with equal enthusiasm, serving as the president of the Richmond and Petersburg Railroad. In 1845, Macfarland pioneered a drive to build a railroad from Lynchburg to western Virginia. Four other Virginia banks had loans to the James River and Kanawha Company by 1859: the Bank of Phillipi, the Bank of Rockbridge, the Bank of Rockingham, and the Bank of Scottsville. In the latter's case, the state had guaranteed the bonds.[15]

South Carolina's heavy backing of railroads caused some observers to call the building of the railways a "mania" in the late 1840s. Despite the setbacks incurred by the Louisville, Cincinnati, and Charleston, South Carolinians still dreamed of an iron link to the Mississippi Valley. An opportunity arose for the Bank of the State to support railroads in 1850 when it paid $202,000 to the South Carolina Railroad Company for stock taken by the state. In 1854, the Blue Ridge Railroad seemed to kindle the fires of westward transportation lines lit by Hayne's "magnificent dream." Again the Bank of the State was there with financial support. The bank frequently advanced funds to the state government to purchase stock in various railroads.[16]

Louisiana, a hotbed of improvement banks of all types, ironically, experienced little success with the railroad improvement-bank mechanism. Much of the slow movement in the improvement-bank-related construction stemmed from the unfortunate timing of the operations (most of them suffered from the panic). Three railroad banks held a paper railroad capitalization of one million dollars by 1840, little of it financed through improvement banks. Among the railroads operating with banking privileges in Louisiana, the New Orleans and Carrollton (of the *Bank of Augusta* v. *Earle* fame) received banking powers in 1835 but languished after the depression. The Atchafalaya Railroad and Bank-

15. Frances Williams, *They Faced the Future*, 20–27; "Notice of Meeting and Form of Power of Attorney," Bank of Virginia, April 16, 1833, VHS.
16. *South Carolina Reports and Resolutions*, 1851, 32; *ibid.*, 1857, 10; *ibid.*, 1859, 299; S.C. *Statutes*, XIII, 70–71, 193–94, 202–208, 371–74.

ing Company (chartered 1835) never constructed its railroad. Although the Clinton and Port Hudson Railroad used its mortgage banking powers (which it received in 1833) to aid in early construction, it succeeded in completing its line only through a $500,000 loan in 1839 directly from the state.[17]

INVESTMENT THROUGH IMPROVEMENT BANKING

Despite the illiquidity of the Louisiana improvement banks and their failure during the Panic of 1837—described by one historian as "building America through bankruptcy"—they were not inherently unsound or inflationary. Success, demonstrated by the Canal Bank, awaited the improvement bank capable of acquiring sufficient liquid assets and diversifying its portfolio. The major problems with liquidity lay in the need to sell the bank's respective canal, hotel, or railroad, a sometimes difficult undertaking, and the commitment to one project, which prevented diversification.[18]

Illiquidity in such ventures as canals caused strained debtor-creditor relationships wherever they appeared. A loan by the Planters Bank of Savannah, Georgia, to the Savannah, Ogeechee, and Alatahama Canal Company was ignored by the bank for some time while directors hoped the company would find a way to make payments. Finally, in 1841, the bank informed the directors of the canal company that the bank could "no longer conceal from itself the pecuniary embarrassment in which the Canal Company is now placed." Calling for the canal company to surrender its charter to the bank or to make "a last appeal for further aid in completing the works which have been commenced," the president of the bank recommended that he appoint a board to discuss with the city council and other banks a plan to surrender the canal company's assets. The case dragged on for a year until a court assigned a judgment against

17. *Louisiana Documents*, 14th Legis., 2d Sess., 1840, pp. 43, 49, 192; Edwin Odom, "Louisiana Railroads, 1830–1880: A Study of State and Local Aid" (Ph.D. dissertation, Tulane University, 1961), 19.

18. Green, *Finance and Economic Development*, 34; Robert Roeder, "Merchants of Ante-Bellum New Orleans," 113–22; Merl Reed, "Boom or Bust: Louisiana's Economy During the 1830's," *Louisiana History*, 1963, 35–53. Nor was the image of the improvement banks greatly enhanced by the type of promoters who became involved with them—"in one case, a theatrical impressario founded such a bank" (Roeder, "Merchants," 120).

the company. In 1846, an individual named Amos Scudder purchased the apparently as yet uncollected judgment.[19]

Railroads and canals also received investments from other banks, making the risks somewhat more bearable. Six banks in the 1830s contributed $400,000 in stock or bond investments in the railroad banks. An additional $492,000 found its way into railroad and canal companies that lacked banking privileges. Together the railroad banks and the private banks financed 40 percent of Louisiana's total expenditure on railroad construction and equipment prior to 1840.[20]

One of the most successful improvement institutions was the Canal Bank of New Orleans, chartered on March 5, 1831, with four million dollars in capitalization. Promoters Maunsel White and Beverly Chew conceived of the project, which sought to construct a major navigation canal. This enterprise met its goal of a completed canal at under half the estimated cost. The bank's stock was oversubscribed. Within six years after White had first contacted Chew about his idea, the company had turned the completed canal over to the state. Business at the bank continued strong until a crisis in 1841, when by mutual consent all of the banks in New Orleans suspended specie payments. Glendy Burke, a director of the Canal Bank, realized that the bank lacked sufficient cash in the vault to meet the demand, and suspension meant the forfeiture of the charter. Burke put up his own money at the counters "until the run was stopped, everybody satisfied and order restored." Integrity, according to one bank legend, stretched all the way to the German porter, who "stood so well" that "his single assurance given to friends—that the bank was all right—dissipat[ed] a gathering at the time of the Atchafalaya Riot." A bank with such a strong commitment by its directors, and one with such inspiring legends, plainly stood a good chance of surviving the war, as indeed it did.[21]

Except for the Canal Bank and the Citizens Bank, most internal-

19. Statement of May 7, 1841, "Condition of the Savannah, Ogeechee, and Alatahama Canal Company," Planters Bank Papers, Folder 1, SHC, UNC; statement of Canal Company, June 8, 1841, ibid.; sale of assignment, January 16, 1842, ibid.

20. Robert Roeder, "New Orleans Merchants, 1790–1837" (Ph.D. dissertation, Harvard University, 1959), 351–61; Louisiana Documents, 46, 106, 117, 123, 127, 144, 156, 167, 186.

21. J. P. Thompson, "Early Financing in New Orleans, Being the Story of the Canal Bank, 1831–1915," Louisiana Historical Society Publications, 1913–14, 11–61.

improvement investments had been liquidated by 1850. Only three banks remained in the improvement business, and apparently the Louisiana legislature planned to separate the activities of banks and internal improvements altogether by stipulating in the 1852 constitution that banking privileges were to be denied to improvement companies. Free banks quickly filled the void left by the 1852 laws.[22]

James Robb, the outstanding banker of New Orleans, had campaigned for greater rail connections to the west and north. He envisioned linking the new system of free banks to railroad financing, using the city to issue bonds in order to purchase stock in the current major railroad undertakings, the New Orleans, Jackson, and Great Northern; the New Orleans and Mobile; and the New Orleans, Opelousas, and Great Western. Free banks, according to this plan, would buy the city bonds. The city issued more than $3.5 million worth of bonds (to augment its already outstanding debt of $3 million), and the free banks responded, purchasing more than $2 million while the Louisiana State Bank took $328,750. Consequently, the participation of the free banks represented a significant share, perhaps as much as 15 percent, of the $7.1 million spent by Louisiana on railroads in the 1850s, although it remained far below the 40 percent investment that banks had made in the previous decade. Under this system, however, a participating bank's role was much sounder because the city bore the risk. Free banks held only small proportions of railroad stocks. As a result they gained greater liquidity.

Many states passed internal-improvement bills to issue bonds for railroad and bridge projects, several of which failed or languished. In light of such results, it should not be considered odd that banks chose not to lend to such operations. Private banking capital aided some railroads, and state banks assisted many more. Even when state chartering of railroad banks got completely out of hand, as it did in Mississippi, the net result was not entirely negative for the state; once the railroad lines had been laid, they remained after the bankruptcy of a particular railroad company. (This statement was not true where the repudiation of state bonds was involved because once the state's credit was gone, it was gone

22. Citizens Bank Minutebook 6, Vol. 100, 1846–51, pp. 70, 314–15, CBA, LSU; Citizens Bank Minutebook 8, Vol. 58, 1856–68, pp. 217–18, CBC, LSU; *Report of the Joint Committee of Banks and Banking*, 1857, pp. 89, 98, 106, 112, 116, 136; Harry Evans, "James Robb, Banker and Pioneer Railroad Builder of Antebellum Louisiana," *Louisiana Historical Quarterly*, 1940, 170–258; *Minority Report of the Senate Committee on the General System of Free Banking in the State of Louisiana*, 1854.

forever. The inability of Florida and Mississippi to win foreign credit in the Civil War attested to this fact.) The negative factors usually outweighed the positive. Planters and businessmen suffered under the burden of excess and devalued notes churned up by the railroad banks and private banks in general and often paid for this inflation by going broke themselves, even when some elements of society profited from the permanent capital investment of these companies.

INVESTMENT IN INDUSTRY

Investment in other areas was forthcoming, if to a much lesser degree than in railroading. *De Bow's Review* reported that banks and local businessmen were capitalizing factories and mills in Georgia and Virginia. The paucity of manufacturing firms, however, could not always be blamed on lack of capital: in 1850 James Hammond estimated that during each of the previous twenty years an average of $500,000 in capital had left South Carolina for greener investment pastures. Hammond blamed the exodus on the attitude of the people. Elwood Fisher, in his 1849 lecture to the Young Men's Mercantile Library Association of Cincinnati, condemned attempts to industrialize, arguing that the agricultural South diversified the American economy. If the South developed industry, he argued, it would only cause competition. As late as 1845 editorials still criticized corporations as "the least efficient of all industrial contrivances": the "banking system applied to business." Hammond's contention that southerners had capital enough to "perform the manufacturing for the world" represented an exaggeration not only in language but in conception. That capital had largely migrated north in relatively small amounts, widely diffused. It was not as if South Carolina's banks consciously and deliberately transferred huge sums past the Mason-Dixon Line, although it was common to keep notes in northern banks paying interest at 4 percent.[23]

Concentrating on solvency, especially after the 1837 depression,

23. Philip Davidson, "Industrialism in the Ante Bellum South," *South Atlantic Quarterly*, October, 1928, pp. 405–25; *De Bow's Review* vol. 29, p. 494; Elwood Fisher, *Lecture on the North and South*, 31–32; Chauncey Boucher, "The Ante Bellum Attitude of South Carolina Towards Manufacturing and Agriculture," *Washington University Studies*, July, 1915, pp. 243–50; *Charleston Mercury*, January 6, 1845; *Greenville* (South Carolina) *Southern Enterprise*, March 1, 1860. Of course, southern banks maintained much higher specie reserves than northern banks (Thomas Kettell, *Southern Wealth and Northern Profits* [New York, 1860], 96).

southern bankers looked to short-term loans and discounting of paper as their primary sources of profit, a strategy characteristic of northern bankers, too. Historians of the development process, such as Alexander Gerschenkron, have suggested that the role of banks in the process of industrialization involves "deliberate attitudes on the part of the banks . . . [under which] banks were primarily attracted to certain lines of production to the neglect, if not virtual exclusion, of others." Southern bankers made a conscious effort to support agriculture and commerce, for reasons of profit, risk, and social attitudes. Even so, long-term loans were not, according to Gerschenkron, a necessary factor in aiding industrial development. A "device of formally short-term but in reality long-term current account credits" could be used, as in Germany, or capital could accrue "from earnings in trade . . . , modernized agriculture, and later from industry itself."[24]

Long-term loans had to be carefully considered. Often an industrialist interested in entering the manufacturing field found it easier to collaborate with a group of planters and businessmen on an individual basis than to seek aid from a bank. One of the most famous attempts of planters to enter manufacturing with the informal aid of a banker involved the Nesbitt Manufacturing Company of South Carolina. It had received a charter under the name Wilson Nesbitt and Associates in 1835, with capital of $100,00, to extract and process iron ore and soon had land with mineral deposits in Spartanburg and blast furnaces. It reorganized as Nesbitt Manufacturing Company in 1836. Franklin H. Elmore, soon to be president of the Bank of the State of South Carolina, subscribed to stock and acted as an agent to secure a loan, approaching Charles Colcock, who was president of the Bank of the State at the time. The Bank of the State loaned $50,000, and the Insurance Trust Company of Charleston added a $30,000 loan, making the final capitalization somewhat larger but still inadequate. Elmore served as a director in the company and played the critical role in the search for capital.[25]

Meanwhile, the company fell on hard times, becoming virtually bank-

24. Gerschenkron, *Economic Backwardness*, 14–15.

25. *Reports and Resolutions, South Carolina*, 1840, 200; *Compilation of All the Acts, Resolutions, Reports and Other Documents* (Columbia, 1848), 541–44; "Speech of J. E. Henry in the House of Representatives," Greenville *Mountaineer*, February 19, 1841; *Reports and Resolutions, South Carolina*, 1849, 111–12, 173–74, 203; *ibid.*, 1841, 127.

rupt by 1844 and having paid nothing at all on either the principal or the interest of its debt. The company was given a five-year "adjustment period" to reach full production, during which time Nesbitt Manufacturing would pay interest. At the end of the five years the company would pay on the $120,000 principal.[26]

Concurrent with the attack on the Bank of the State made by "Anti-Debt" in 1848–1849, opponents raised the question of loans to Nesbitt Manufacturing Company as an indication of scandal; the columns of the *South Carolinian* reported the controversy. Of greater significance, and wielding considerably more power, was the 1849 joint committee of the legislature that investigated the bank. Following the passage of a resolution requiring the bank to place the contract regarding Nesbitt Manufacturing Company's debt in the proper form, the board of directors initiated property sales to alleviate the debt. Sales eventually generated almost enough to cancel the debt without resorting to other security, but Nesbitt Manufacturing had become a sordid affair in the minds of many South Carolinians. Many observers were convinced that the debt involved outright corruption.[27]

Other states used their state banks to finance and support various projects. The various cases ran the gamut from Tennessee's heavy involvement in state-sponsored improvements to more reserved conduct on the part of North Carolina. Although North Carolina's bank assisted the state's railroads by purchasing $500,000 worth of Raleigh and Gaston Railroad bonds, it rarely invested in other projects apart from the standard practice of purchasing stock of other banks for security. In Elizabeth City, at least, the lack of confidence in banks may have retarded industrialization and slowed urban growth somewhat. Tennessee, on the other hand, expected its state bank to pay annually $1 million for the support of common schools, plus $18,000 for the support of academies. The state had issued $4 million in internal improvement bonds, upon which the bank was expected to pay interest. Governor Aaron Brown, in his 1847 speech to the legislature, described the record of the bank in

26. *Reports and Resolutions, South Carolina*, 1849, 173–74; 203–208; *ibid.*, 1845, 42, 205; *ibid.*, 1846, 27–28.

27. *South Carolina Senate Journal*, 1848, pp. 105–106, 169; *South Carolinian*, May 22, 1849; *Reports and Resolutions, South Carolina*, 1849, 111–17, 134, 167; *Reports and Resolutions, South Carolina*, 1849, 116–17, 134, 193–94; *ibid.*, 1850, 30–31; Lesesne, *Bank of the State*, 94–97.

positive terms. Its aid to the state's education gave "the friends of education . . . abundant cause to be well pleased with its promptness and fidelity in the fulfilment of its obligations." He viewed the experiment as
successful "and must have a strong tendency to dissipate the fears of
those who have looked to its failure as inevitable." [28]

From 1839 to 1847 the bank paid more than $1 million to the schools
and academies and another $2.1 million to schools and in interest. An-
other million dollars' worth of interest was paid on state bonds, of which
the state had invested an unknown amount in internal improvements.
From 1845 to 1847 the state ran a deficit, causing the legislature to decide to liquidate the affairs of the bank. No specific investments had
caused the problem; rather, the state had expected more from the bank
than its profits could deliver. Criticism of the bank centered more on the
political nature of the loans to individuals than on the bank's failure to
promote industry.

Occasionally a unique opportunity for investments appeared, as in the
Georgia town of Auraria, where the discovery of gold brought a movement in 1830 to establish a mint there. Its completion in 1837 contributed to the growth of the town, which had meanwhile developed a need
for a bank. At an 1833 tavern meeting a proposal for such an institution
noted that the naturally available gold would make Auraria's bank notes
stronger than those of its competitors located in Tennessee, North Carolina, and South Carolina. Banking opportunities in the South seldom
went unfilled for long, and before Auraria could organize a bank, the
Pigeon-roost Mining Company received a charter to begin financial
operations. Because the company's notes could not legally circulate as
money, though, the mining company never fully became a bank. [29]

Aurarians' efforts to establish their own bank also failed because the
Bank of Darien established a bank there, although not without difficulty.
Thomas Bowen had been acting as the agent for the Bank of Darien. In
1834 he was entrusted with 14,950 pennyweights of gold for delivery in
Savannah. Bowen had the conscience to write from Charleston, explain-
ing that "he could not withstand the temptation, that pursuit would be

28. *Laws, N.C.*, 1838–1839, chap. 29; *North Carolina House Journal*, 1847–1848,
24–42.
29. E. Merton Coulter, *Auraria: The Story of a Georgia Gold-Mining Town* (Athens,
Ga., 1956), 25–27.

useless, and that his creditors might make the best of the goods he left behind." Auraria received its branch despite Bowen's escapades, but bankers there failed to connect sufficiently with the mining operations or otherwise to invest in them.[30]

FACTORS AFFECTING INVESTMENT POLICIES

By and large, private banking capital did not frenetically search out investments, either in industry or in railroads. Partly to blame was the anticorporate attitude held by a large segment of southern society. Large accumulations of capital, as Thornton showed, and corporations specifically, elicited little but suspicion from southerners. Although he declined to assign such attitudes a primary role in retarding industrialization in other countries, Alexander Gerschenkron noted that attitudes "patently unfavorable to entrepreneurship greatly reduced the number of potential entrepreneurs and thereby reduced the rate of economic development in the country." Many planters who shared ownership or control in banks experienced frustration and confusion. If they had been asked, these planters would have explained that they opposed investment in industrial projects because of the financial risks involved. They did not easily recognize their real fear: an industrialized and commercial world that had no room for planters in the Jeffersonian tradition.[31]

Until the benefits of state-backed railroads became apparent, many planters opposed public capitalization as well. In Georgia, for example, the question of state involvement remained central to the political discussion of the antebellum period. Quite commonly, banking functions were viewed strictly in terms of exchange—as a facilitator for commerce: lending often remained a job for individual exchange merchants.[32]

John Caldwell's New Orleans Gas Light and Banking Company illustrated another problem, that of state restrictions and regulations. Capitalized at six million dollars and rechartered from an earlier gas company that had held a monopoly, Caldwell's Gas Bank was required to establish branch banks and subsidiary gas companies in a number of rural spots, such as Port Hudson, Springfield, Napoleonville, and Harrisonville.

30. Savannah *Georgian*, May 3, 1834.
31. Gerschenkron, *Economic Backwardness*, 62.
32. Milton Heath, "Laissez Faire in Georgia, 1732–1860," *Journal of Economic History*, Supplement, December, 1943, pp. 78–100.

Louisiana authorities also insisted that the bank subscribe to 500 shares of stock in the Barataria and Lafourche Canal Company. Yet another stipulation forced the bank to lend $150,000 for the construction of a railroad from Alexandria to Cheneyville. Other banks experienced similar restrictions on their investments.

Yet some banks needed no prodding to lend to a variety of borrowers, especially in New Orleans. The Citizens Bank gladly financed residential and commercial construction and owned stock in the Lake Borgne Navigation and Canal Company, which was engaged in building a railroad. Activities so numerous and diversified were sufficient to overextend a prosperous bank and were dangerous for a bank with a questionable capital base. The Exchange and Banking Company concentrated its investment in the St. Charles Hotel, whereas the New Orleans Improvement and Banking Company offered real estate loans and financed construction of the St. Louis Hotel. Five banks combined to finance and operate more than four million dollars' worth of investment property in the 1850s. With every bank specializing, it was not surprising that the Mechanics and Traders Bank aimed to attract the manufacturing interests. Such frenzied investments proved the exception rather than the rule. More often than not, banks served as the intermediaries for large-scale projects, which were generally financed through stock and bond issues.

George Green, in his study of Louisiana's banks, concluded that they "devoted a negligible proportion of their resources to the support of manufacturing." As of January, 1840, four New Orleans banks had invested $290,000 in the local steam cotton presses owned by two New Orleans firms, but evidence regarding any other industrial investment is scarce. Any industrial loans that existed were "hidden in the totals of loans on mortgage or personal security," but they clearly represented amounts small enough not to attract attention.[33]

Yet Louisianians did not ignore manufacturing or technology whenever it fit the profitable agricultural framework. Census data for 1840 showed New Orleans' manufacturing capital at $6.4 million, although it dropped to $5 million in 1850. By 1860, it had again risen to $7.2 million. Other examples indicate that southerners were willing to adopt agriculturally related technology. Louisiana led the nation in the industrial use of

33. Green, *Finance and Economic Development*, 33–34.

steam power in 1838, most of it involved in raw sugar refineries or cotton presses. These steam engines required repair and maintenance and fostered the development of foundry and machine shop businesses.[34]

LENDING VERSUS OTHER BANKING FUNCTIONS

In the banking systems of Louisiana and South Carolina, any need for industrial capital took a second place to the other two major functions of banks, lending for commercial and agricultural purposes and the maintenance of a sound, convertible currency. This set of priorities was rational in terms of the need for a stable circulating medium and in light of local politics, given the influence of agricultural groups. In essence, business groups had to choose between sound currency for trade and inflated money for industrial investment, because planters and agricultural groups maintained a demand for loans. Their needs could not be ignored politically. Businessmen in the large commercial areas therefore favored sounder money and less investment capital. Indeed, to an extent the twin goals of soundness and credit creation created a dilemma for most states in the antebellum times. Arkansas, Alabama, Florida, and Mississippi all stressed the credit-generating powers of banks, but frequently, as in South Carolina, Louisiana, and to a lesser degree Alabama and Tennessee, the population divided between commercial groups and the planting sectors as to which banking function should take precedence according to occupational needs. Charleston and New Orleans found themselves constantly trying to satisfy interior demands for agricultural credit while simultaneously maintaining sound currency for commercial groups. Mobile, Natchez, and Memphis also experienced these pressures, although to a lesser extent because of the credit-generating abilities of the state banks. Alabama found the separation of the two functions somewhat easier in that the state bank served the agricultural credit demand, whereas the Bank of Mobile looked more to commercial business. In Mississippi the antagonism toward the Bank of the State was directed toward the tight control of credit—maintained in the interest of solvency—by the directors of that bank.

No one would argue that the directors, stockholders, and bankers did

---

34. United States Bureau of the Census, *Compendium of the Sixth Census of the United States* (Washington, D.C., 1840), 241–49; *House Documents*, 23d Cong., 2d Sess., No. 38, 3:196–204: *Senate Documents*, 52d Cong., 2d Sess., No. 38, 1893.

not pursue their own self-interests in these instances, but how did they interpret their self-interests? Did they deliberately seek oligopoly, or was their central concern with solvency (hard money) and convertibility? In Alabama and Arkansas, a monopolistic group freely issued money; it did so because, in its view, in so doing it provided the means by which to maintain individual autonomy.[35]

MANUFACTURERS, MERCHANTS, AND BANKERS

Southern businessmen had other characteristics that contributed to a lack of investment in manufacturing. Antebellum manufacturing firms that successfully produced for markets outside their local area had to develop a partnership with merchants in which, in almost all cases, "the merchants dominated the partnership." Even in the North, long-term investment credit appeared only slowly; unusual collateral or guarantees were needed before lenders parted with their money. Sales of mass securities, as an additional form of capital that might encourage banking investment, could be facilitated only through the grant of a corporate charter, nor did any mechanisms spare the South as a stock exchange. Southern manufacturers, therefore, followed a common pattern: know a merchant, become one, or marry one. To become a merchant, as is evident from the ease with which Jews entered mercantile businesses after beginning as peddlers, was the frequent choice, although one that might have been socially distasteful to proud yeoman farmers.[36]

The paradox whereby merchants could obtain money though manufacturers could not was rooted in two separate attitudes held by bankers. First, some bankers saw personal wealth as the ultimate security for a loan, and merchants themselves had usually become bankers. Analysis of New York, Philadelphia, and Baltimore bank directors and officers revealed that more than two-thirds of them came from a mercantile back-

35. Harold Livesay and Glenn Porter, "The Financial Role of Merchants in the Development of U.S. Manufacturing, 1815–1860," *Explorations in Economic History*, Fall, 1971, pp. 63–87; Joseph Klein, "The Development of Mercantile Instruments of Credit in the United States," *Journal of Accountancy*, (1911), 437. Also see Jonathan Hughes, "Entrepreneurial Activity and American Economic Progress," *Journal of Libertarian Studies*, Winter, 1979, pp. 361–70.

36. Ernest Lander, Jr., "The Iron Industry in Ante-bellum South Carolina," *Journal of Southern History*, 1954, pp. 337–55; William Johnston Estate papers, SC. For the role of southern bankers as entrepreneurs, see Schweikart, "Entrepreneurial Aspects of Antebellum Banking."

ground. The same could probably be said of virtually all the private bankers. In the South, where occupational mobility in financial commerce was common, this generalization applies even more. Middlemen had access to their accumulated business profits and to the deposits of the public, a point as true for the factor and commission merchant as for nothern middlemen. Merchants also needed opportunities to make their capital grow. George Williams, Jacob Cohen, and others who moved into banking did so to find a useful employment for their capital. Second, however, bankers associated manufacturing investment with considerable risk. It was not yet an area in which southern bankers felt comfortable lending.

Risk avoidance was also present in the dearth of manufacturing investments by southern banks. High, reliable, and steady rates of return in agriculture made ventures into manufacturing investment suitable only for speculators. The creation of state banks expressly designed to make long-term property and mortgage loans virtually guaranteed that manufacturing interests would have to turn to merchants, northerners, or Europeans to obtain capital. Private banks in competition with state banks, which already had advantages in capitalization and political support, were thus dissuaded from embarking on any risky business ventures. The state banks should have invested in manufacturing if any banks did, for they could absorb some losses, but the state banks had generally been created to make agricultural loans. Moreover, southern agriculture's profitability kept capital in the fields and out of the furnaces.

States in the New South had troubles of their own making that kept banks from lending to industry. Alabama, through the cotton speculations of its state bank, consistently either lost money or inflated the currency. Arkansas' banks barely lasted long enough to support any industry, even if there had been one, and the private bankers who replaced the state banks eschewed investment risks in industry, preferring agriculture. Tennessee fought through a series of political battles involving banking and committed itself to backing the Louisville, Cincinnati, and Charleston Railroad only to see it fold. The drain on the state bank for educational purposes, combined with the unbusinesslike appropriation of bank profits to bail out state spenders, prevented any financing of industry. Late-developing Florida had a capital vacuum due to its debt repudiation, as did Mississippi. The railroad binge in Mississippi fell prey to inflation, stifling industrial development there.

Problems unique to states in the New South exaggerated the invest-ment tendencies found over the South as a whole. Agriculture constantly presented either a more lucrative investment or a more secure one and sometimes both. Investments that were forthcoming generally involved agriculturally related projects: railroads and canals for transportation or textile mills to process cotton. The kinship and friendship networks, woven together with the various occupational roles of the merchant-banker-planters, meant that when investment banks appeared they were increasingly specialized. Risk to the banks increased because there were fewer opportunities to diversify. In short, most of the South's industrial-investment shortages were decisions of choice, but the bias toward agri-cultural lending reflected a reasonable market response. That single bias explains most of the absence of industrial or manufacturing capital in the South. Again, however, some problems stemmed from the type of bank-ing system established, less in Arkansas or Florida, where there would have been virtually no industry regardless of the particular financial structure, than in Tennessee and perhaps Alabama. Tennessee's prox-imity to major trade areas gave it significant advantages, which could have developed far more with industrial investment. Alabama's port of Mobile offered it a chance to develop a shipbuilding industry. Alabama industrialists had started to exploit mining regions in the north in the 1850s. In both cases the confusion and inefficiency that resulted from the state bank hampered these beginnings.

Movement into industrial development had begun in the states of the Old South, with Virginia, South Carolina, and the city of New Orleans leading the way but at a gradual pace. Opportunities were often missed, as in the case of the Kanawha Valley of western Virginia, where banks failed to finance important coal-mining operations. Virginia's greatest hope for investment banking lay in its proximity to Baltimore, with the corresponding Cohen connection, in which railroad links and commer-cial businesses might spill over. These never developed, because of the war.

Another obstacle confronted greater investment in these states of the Old South. Dominance by businessmen and commercially oriented forces in the cities encouraged people to favor sound money rather than easy credit. With such an attitude entrenched, high-risk enterprises would not easily obtain credit. If states of the Old South had followed the policies of the New South, more investment capital would have been available, but the chances of an inflation-related panic would have been greater. In Mississippi, for example, the flurry of railroad building, made possible in part by the mushrooming number of banks, encountered inflation during the Panic of 1837 and collapsed. Old South conservatism also developed through the attitude that banks themselves were important investments, as some states discovered. Individuals viewed bank stock as an important generator of income, as seen in the correspondence of such prominent investors as Robert E. Lee.[37]

Industrialism did not have a large body of vocal advocates, either. Spokesmen for industrialism, led by the South Carolinians and bankers such as James Robb, were peculiar to the overall intellectual climate. Overall, bankers adopted Whig attitudes that favored diversification, industrialization, and expansion of the commercial sector, but many of the influential economic theorists of the day and respected southern teachers and scholars rejected attitudes that would have required the South to copy the North. Virginia's intellectual community, or at least that part of it concerned with economics, for example, emphasized agriculture in true Jeffersonian style. Thinkers such as John Taylor, George Tucker, Thomas Dew, and George Fitzhugh all developed their economic philosophies around agriculture without envisioning its demise or replacement. Dew and Tucker supported internal improvements and a national banking system for what they could provide to agriculture. These men varied in their acceptance of industry—Tucker had once recommended dismissing arguments against manufacturing—but their central arguments for agriculture eventually reduced to a defense of slavery, culminating in George Fitzhugh's conclusion that, to be completely free, men had to become totally enslaved.[38]

For commentators such as Fitzhugh, industrialism and the visible working of the market posed a threat to the ideals of the Jacksonians. Given the intellectual impact of this tradition cumulatively, its general acceptance in the South meant that industrial investments represented a challenge to certain views of freedom. Even many upwardly mobile, independently thinking, cosmopolitan, promarket southern bankers were unprepared to launch such a challenge. Obviously, the effects of this tradition differed from state to state and at all times were seen in attitudes and long-term results rather than in outright invocation of these doc-

37. Robert E. Lee to Obed. Waite, February 4, 1839, Lee Papers, VHS.
38. Genovese, *Political Economy of Slavery*, 21.

trines. Directors did not decide loans after long discourses about the role of agriculture in maintaining a slave economy; the attitude was ingrained by society and was reaffirmed in the intellectual movement. To its credit, that movement stressed the aspects of agriculture that best enhanced freedom, such as individual landownership and yeomanry. Most southerners "bought" this portion of the package and accepted, rejected, or ignored the accompanying intellectual extensions. Southerners did not, therefore, follow either profits or prophets entirely, but rather, in pursuing profits, southerners often unknowingly demonstrated their social and ideological biases.[39]

Southern investment tendencies with some deviations thus represented both economic good sense over the short term and a widespread attitude toward freedom that brought trouble in the long run, even within the South. With this background, the southern banker who risked his money in manufacturing investments stood to lose both economically and socially. Bankers who did manage to break out of the mold reflected a rare entrepreneurial spirit not common among their fellow businessmen. That is not to say that they did not respond to market forces. Even John Maynard Keynes emphasized the importance of "animal spirits" when it came to making investment decisions. Eugene Genovese interpreted this common background and the accepted intellectual assumptions in the banking system as "an illustration of an ostensibly capitalist institution that worked to augment the power of the planters and retard the development of the bourgeoisie." He correctly considered southern banks "not sources of industrial capital but 'large-scale clearing houses of mercantile finance.'" Southern bankers loaned money "for outlays that were economically feasible and socially acceptable," but they operated in a society in which "socially acceptable" investments included slavery, whereas bankers in the North had different social constraints.[40]

The fact that many bankers were planters, who for personal, selfish reasons sought to preserve a slave society, must be considered with the

39. For a detailed discussion of Fitzhugh's position and his relationship to the foundation of southern investment strategy, see Schweikart, "Banking in the American South," pp. 533–35, 563n, 564n. See especially the comparisons of Fitzhugh to the radical abolitionists that are drawn in Robert Loewenberg, *Freedom's Despots: The Critique of Abolition* (Durham, N.C., 1986), and his "Marx's Sadism," *St. John's Review*, Autumn/Winter), 1982–83, pp. 57–67, and Rebecca Allison, "Force of Argument," 5–13.

40. Genovese, *The Political Economy of Slavery*, 21.

equally important fact that many bankers were *not* planters. Frequently these bankers, like many other southern businessmen, cared little about the continuation of slavery per se except as it furthered their businesses and protected the society they knew. Their letters generally ignore the subject. Bankers who were not planters, such as merchant-bankers and interregional immigrants, including Jews, formed a sizable segment of the southern banking community. Yet when the war came, they almost unanimously supported the Confederacy. Were their actions contradictory or paradoxical? They may be considered so only if the goal is to put all bankers into a homogeneous group—the bourgeoisie, as Genovese would have it. Most southern bankers probably believed in white racial superiority. A majority probably accepted slavery as inevitable in the South for the foreseeable future. Certainly most of them followed exactly the same lending procedures as their northern counterparts by selecting economically feasible investments that were also socially acceptable. A crucial difference existed, however, in that slavery was *both* economically feasible and socially acceptable in the South.

How, then, should bankers in the South be viewed? Thousands of individuals—in this case, bankers—pursued their individual interests in a diverse series of entrepreneurial moves. There is therefore no contradiction in the fact that most of them funded agriculture first and foremost or that they failed to be subsumed into the planter groups. Some bankers were quite willing to accept the noncapitalistic institution of slavery by putting it more or less out of their minds.

When we study finance and economic development, it is important to remember that a particular financial system is not primarily devoted to goals of growth and development. A number of other objectives, including price stability, employment, and soundness, shape formal financial policy and the overall development of financial structures. Bankers, however, shared a broadly held view that threatened the position of small farmer and planter alike, one that anticipated the expansion of the commercial and capitalist economy. Thus, several important investment influences, such as peer group and societal pressures, intergroup competition, familial and personal obligations and responsibilities, regional and sectional loyalties, and, of course, racism or other so-called non-market factors must also be added. Any of these goals, and various combinations of them, "may often lead to financial changes that inhibit economic development." Some—the demand for easy credit and sound money—might be contradjctory. Others (for example, the "planter mentality") may exist to varying degrees in different individuals so as to counteract a number of other forces or another ideology. Another important fact that is often taken for granted is the role of individual incentives. A southern banker had as his primary goal not "development" as such but rather short-term and long-term returns at an individual level.[41]

Finally, one must take care not to imagine that industrialists and manufacturing groups did not exist. The historian's task (as opposed to that of the cliometrician) is to explain what happened and not to dwell upon what might have happened. Most private bankers in the South succeeded because as merchants they had extended credit to other merchants. In the North, their money eventually sought investment. The crucial difference was that in the North the manufacturers and industrialists had already demonstrated their products or ideas and needed only money to put them into large-scale practice. Southern industrialists did not exist in great numbers when southern banking capital sought investments. Although widespread demonstration of industry on a consistent basis had yet to occur throughout the South, no one doubted the profitability of southern agriculture as an investment. Over a longer period, "relentless focus on cotton was economical because the demand for American cotton was strong; the real price of cotton was increasing up to the early 1920s." Care must be taken when comparing the investment tendencies of northern bankers, who had short-term, long-term, *and* social rewards for investing in manufacturing and industry, with those of southern bankers, who had only the most long-term remuneration for such investments.[42]

MEASURING SOUTHERN BANKING AND ECONOMIC GROWTH

Despite the tendencies described above, the South as a whole had begun a modest growth in manufacturing capital and manufacturing. From 1850 to 1860 the investment in manufacturing increased by almost three

41. Hugh Patrick, "Financial Development and Economic Growth in Underdeveloped Countries," *Economic Development and Cultural Change*, 1966, 174–89; Lester Chandler, *Central Banking and Economic Development* (Bombay, 1962), 2–5; John Gurley and Edward Shaw, "Financial Structure and Economic Development," *Economic Development and Cultural Change*, 1967, 257–68.
42. Brownlee, *Dynamics of Ascent*, 250.

dollars per capita, a rise almost matched by the so-called cotton South taken as a subregion. Compared with growth in the rest of the United States, the South's growth in both manufacturing capital and manufacturing value was minuscule: overall per capita U.S. growth reached almost ten dollars in the decade, whereas New England capital rose by almost twenty-five dollars per capita.[43]

This philosophical, social, and regional setting makes it easier to determine the degree to which the South developed economically and hence to what degree its banks contributed. One approach measured financial development in terms of banking density, calculating the number of bank offices and branches per ten thousand population. Applying this measurement to nations in a comparative study, Rondo Cameron defined the levels of density over 1 as "high," 0.5 to 1 as "moderate," below 0.5 as "low," and below 0.1 as "very low" (one office per 100,000 population). It might be possible to apply the data on a regional or state level. Louisiana, except for its burst of banking in the late 1830s, generally remained in the low-density category.

Banking density admittedly provides only a crude index and fails to allow "for variations in bank size or in income levels of the economy." These numbers have a more serious flaw in that they rely upon poor estimates of the numbers of banks in operation—an underestimate in most cases especially. Furthermore, they make almost no allowance for the numerous private bankers and also fail to take into account the few existing mutual savings associations or insurance companies with investment potential. In the South these omissions were probably quite important, as suggested by the frequent references to private bankers in the newspapers and manuscripts of the day. Having recognized this shortcoming, we will still find it of interest at a later point to apply this crude index to other states.[44]

Another ratio for determing the dynamics within an economy compares bank money to yearly state income and would be expected to rise during economic growth. John Gurley and Edward Shaw, using this barometer, found a standard ratio 10 percent or less in the poorest countries and 30 percent in the advanced countries in their studies. Yet this

43. See Gavin Wright, *The Political Economy of the Cotton South* (New York, 1978), 110, and North, *Economic Growth of the United States*, 258.
44. Green, *Finance and Economic Development*, 49–51; Rondo Cameron et al., *Banking in the Early Stages of Industrialization* (New York, 1967), 296–300.

measurement failed when applied to Louisiana's case because of the "inflationary excess" of the years 1836–1840. Before applying the model further we should recall that these "excesses" were massive by comparison with Mississippi, Alabama, and Arkansas. Green argued for discarding the Gurley-Shaw approach in favor of a more complex analysis, beginning with an estimate of "the annual issues of all financial assets, both by ordinary borrowers and by banks or other financial intermediaries," and leading to "a ratio of aggregate debt, or financial assets, to income." Because the data on personal notes, mortgages, and other securities were not available, and because some estimates placed the total amount of external finance handled by intermediaries at one-third or less, that method proved difficult. Green therefore assembled the total bank issues of securities (deposits, notes, and capital stock) and doubled the ratio of bank resources to income.[45]

Compared with modern "poor" countries, with their ratios of 0.5, Louisiana is well ahead. More accurately, Louisiana falls into the moderately prosperous range, where we would find present-day Mexico, Turkey, or Brazil, with ratios in the 1 to 1.5 range. Louisiana's levels suggested an adequate system overall, but the lack of financial growth experienced in the 1840s implied problems. Still, real income continued to grow, and an even more expansionary financial system might have increased Louisiana's growth. That Louisiana was too restrictive can be concluded from the money/income ratio and the monetary contraction between 1837 and 1843. Thereafter the restrictions of the Bank Act of 1842 established more comprehensive requirements to attain the desired goal of "sound money." Citing "exceptionally high profit margins" of New Orleans banks, even those poorly or inefficiently operated, Green claimed Louisianians suffered from inadequate finance between 1840 and 1853. Private unchartered banks sprang up to fill the need; planters, merchants, and businessmen sought credit from foreign sources or from other states.

Louisiana's banks made a significant contribution even when we allow for the free banks, because much of Louisiana's bank money moved into Texas, Arkansas, Mississippi, and Missouri, where banks were few and far between. Missouri had just three banks by 1860 and until the mid-

1850s had only one. Arkansas, of course, had none. Texas had several private bankers but no chartered banks before 1855. Mississippi had lost whatever banks it had in 1858; new ones did not appear until after the Civil War. Louisiana supported four states plus itself.[46]

Banking expansion also independently caused the real economy to grow by forcing specie out of circulation and into vaults, where it acted as a "high-powered" reserve. Attracting large amounts of savings, for example, Louisiana banks brought in nearly twenty million dollars of development capital. Free banks brought in somewhat less, fifteen million dollars. The period prior to 1837 resulted in the greatest investment spending, thanks to the chartering of property banks and internal-improvement banks.[47]

The discussion of investment has in the past been somewhat muddled by "big push" or "takeoff" theories of development. Development in this sense is almost always viewed in terms of industry. Yet in the era following World War II, evidence from New Zealand, Canada, and Denmark has indicated that an area may "develop"—that is, attain high levels of per capita income—and still rely heavily on an agricultural base. Robert Gallman and others have shown that southern planters produced much more of their own food than was previously believed and were self-sufficient in fact. Yet they were not diversified enough to maintain profitable industrial capacity, nor should they have aspired to such diversification: diversification in and of itself did not necessarily represent progress in antebellum Louisiana or in the rest of the South. Evidence offered by Richard Easterlin placed Louisiana's per capita income above the national average from 1840 to 1860, indicating that the economy was productive. Conversely, the Louisiana economy grew at a relatively slow rate compared with the growth in national per capita in-

46. Timothy Hubbard and Lewis Davids (*Banking in Mid-America: A History of Missouri's Banks* (Washington, D.C., 1969), 66) claimed there were fifty private bankers in Missouri in 1860; the *Banker's Almanac* listed only twenty-six. In other words, even knowledgeable private sources underestimated the total by as much as 50 percent. For data on Texas, see Joe Ericson, *Banks and Bankers in Early Texas, 1835–1875* (New Orleans, 1976), 30–79. Ericson estimated that there were 2,638 private lenders in 1858 by examining tax returns, with total loans of $3 million, a level equal to that of Alabama in 1833 or Louisiana before 1820. Thus Texas would have been a drain on either Louisiana or Missouri. Missouri, likewise, suffered, having only the state bank until 1857.

47. Alexander Porter to Dussuau De La Croix, April 27 and July 31, 1819, Louisiana State Bank Collection, LSU; Richard Eastin to Richard Relf, March 1, 1820, *ibid.*; Letterbook of St. Martinsville Branch, Louisiana State Bank, *ibid.*

Table 18.   Growth Rate of Nominal Banking Indicators,
Southern States, 1819–1861 (percent per annum)

State	Loans	Specie	Circulation	Deposits
Alabama	5.0	5.0	7.0	6.0
Florida	5.0	−0.4	−1.0	−0.5
Georgia	2.0	2.0	3.0	4.0
Louisiana	0.5	6.0	4.0	5.0
Mississippi	−21.0	−16.0	−16.0	−23.0
N. Carolina	2.0	4.0	3.0	3.0
S. Carolina	6.0	6.0	5.0	5.0
Tennessee	5.0	7.0	6.0	7.0
Virginia	3.0	4.0	3.0	3.0
Cumulative	3.0	5.0	4.0	4.0

Source: Schweikart, "Southern Banking and Economic Growth."

come. All things considered, the local bankers and planters availed themselves of the South's comparative advantage and made the only economic decisions they could within the limits of their antebellum setting. Some general observations can be made about the rest of the South.[48]

Growth rates based on the monetary data for individual southern states in three periods—1819–1861, 1819–1836, and 1840–1861—appear in Tables 18, 19, and 20, respectively, and regression analyses for nine southern states (Arkansas, for obvious reasons, excepted), with loans, circulation, specie, and deposits identified. The data for Louisiana from 1819 to 1861 suggest that "soundness" was the bench mark of Louisiana policies. Specie grew at an enviable 6 percent annual rate, but circulations stayed at a 4 percent average, only slightly exceeded by deposits at 5 percent. Loans scarcely grew, however, contrary to Green's findings on this point. As in many southern states before the panic, growth proceeded in all categories at a far greater rate. Even loans aver-

48. Robert Gallman, "Self-sufficiency in the Cotton Economy of the Antebellum South," *Agricultural History,* 1970, 5–23; Richard Easterlin, "Regional Income Trends, 1840, 1950," in Seymour Harris (ed.), *American Economic History* (New York, 1961), 528, 545; *De Bow's Review,* May, 1851, p. 589; U.S., Bureau of the Census, *Compendium of the Tenth Census of the United States* (Washington, D.C., 1880), XIX, 252–53, 256.

Table 19. Growth Rate of Nominal Banking Indicators,
Southern States, 1819–1836 (percent per annum)

State	Loans	Specie	Circulation	Deposits
Alabama	20.0	14.0	20.0	14.0
Florida	39.0	34.0	15.0	29.0
Georgia	6.0	6.0	5.0	6.0
Louisiana	12.0	14.0	17.0	21.0
Mississippi	47.0	78.0	39.0	73.0
N. Carolina	−2.0	−2.0	−2.0	−2.0
S. Carolina	5.0	6.0	4.0	9.0
Tennessee	4.0	−4.0	5.0	4.0
Virginia	6.0	3.0	6.0	6.0
Cumulative	6.0	2.0	5.0	7.0

Source: Schweikart, "Southern Banking and Economic Growth."

Table 20. Growth Rate of Nominal Banking Indicators,
Southern States, 1840–1861 (percent per annum)

State	Loans	Specie	Circulation	Deposits
Alabama	0.0	0.8	0.6	4.0
Georgia	3.0	4.0	6.0	7.0
Louisiana	−0.9	5.0	4.0	4.0
Mississippi	−33.0	−6.0	−27.0	−33.0
N. Carolina	7.0	8.0	8.0	7.0
S. Carolina	3.0	0.5	5.0	3.0
Tennessee	2.0	3.0	6.0	7.0
Virginia	4.0	3.0	4.0	7.0
Cumulative	0.5	3.0	3.0	4.0

Source: Schweikart, "Southern Banking and Economic Growth."

aged 12 percent annual growth before the Panic of 1837. Overall, however, the evidence supports Green. When the money going to nearby states is taken into account, Louisiana's growth rates as measured by its banking statistics are impressive.

Mississippi, Louisiana's New South neighbor, suffered greatly by comparison. From 1819 to 1858 Mississippi averaged losses of 21 percent, 16 percent, 16 percent, and 23 percent for loans, specie, circulation, and deposits, respectively. The inflation that struck Mississippi can be seen in the period 1819–1836, however, when circulation grew by almost 40 percent, loans increased by 47 percent, and deposits expanded by 73 percent. Although specie appeared to keep pace by averaging an annual 78 percent growth, it started from virtually zero, reaching one million dollars. Loans went from one million dollars to twenty-four million dollars during the same period. From 1840 to 1858 the loan pattern showed a complete reversal, the rate dropping by an average 33 percent per year. By 1858 there was, again, no specie in Mississippi.

Alabama, meanwhile, had regained ballast and was again steaming ahead by the time of the Civil War, in terms of its banking growth. Overall, from 1819 to 1861 it showed healthy 5, 5, 7, and 6 percent annual increases in loans, specie, circulation, and deposits, respectively. Growth in the pre-panic period proved typically greater in all categories than after. Specie almost kept pace in the early period, and so Alabama did not experience quite the inflation that Mississippi had. From 1840 to 1861, however, Alabama seems to have experienced only slight circulation and specie growth, although data are missing for three years. The state's banks, however, had almost recovered to 1845 levels by 1860 only to collapse with the war.

Florida's record obviously prohibits a long-term regression of the entire antebellum period because banking did not begin in the territory until 1833 and expired, for all practical purposes, in 1845. The reappearance of chartered banks in 1860 would tend to skew any regression that included the decade of the 1850s. If we analyze the active banking years, loans and specie grew at better than 30 percent annual rates, and deposits reached nearly 30 percent. Circulation reached only half that level of growth. Again, the regression must be used in the context of the data. Specie all but disappeared from Florida in 1842. No further specie levels were recorded until 1860. In the 1830s, however, Florida experienced a noticeable boom, which the banks fueled with excessive loans. Even when specie had all but disappeared, circulation and lending remained high.

Tennessee, which had the unique ability to attract specie, had a specie growth ratio of more than 7 percent. Other categories fell between 5 and 7 percent. Again, more rapid growth before 1836 than after characterized Tennessee, where the tendency was for Tennessee banks to reduce loans rather than circulation when they were concerned about soundness.

Much more modest and consistent rates of growth characterized Georgia, where circulation grew at an annual 3 percent clip, specie and loans trailed only slightly at 2 percent, and deposits increased at a 4 percent rate across the 1819–1861 period. Georgia's consistency is largely explained by the restraint Georgia demonstrated in its issues and loans from 1819 to 1836. Georgia's growth scarcely matched the inflationary excesses of the New South and likewise did not have to contract in the post-panic decade. From 1840 to 1861, loans continued to grow at a respectable rate (3 percent), specie increased at a 4 percent rate, and circulations and deposits exceeded 6 percent. Matched against the data, the regression appears to reflect genuine trends. Georgia had solid, consistent, fairly uninflated money growth during the antebellum period.

North Carolina witnessed similar but somewhat slower growth in all categories, generally falling in the range of 2 to 4 percent. North Carolina virtually reversed the 1819–1836 trend, however, growing at a rather slow rate of 1 to 2 percent. This slowness reflected the paucity of banks in North Carolina and the presence of three major banks that exercised cautionary policies. Perhaps because North Carolina did not suffer quite as much in the panic as other states, it embarked on a post–panic program of vigorous expansion of loans and deposits, with circulation exceeding those rates and reaching an 8 percent annual growth. Only specie failed to keep pace, trailing at a 3 percent level. This trend proved peculiar to North Carolina, which always seemed to suffer from a lack of specie. Still, North Carolina after the panic easily maintained a level of growth equal to that of other states in the Old South.

In South Carolina, where more banks operated, an equally consistent but considerably stronger rate of growth occurred. All major indicators increased at levels of at least 5 percent, with loans and specie attaining 6 percent ceilings. Prior to 1836, rates increased somewhat slower except for deposits, which ballooned along at a 9 percent level. Contraction set in during the 1840–1861 period but still expanded at acceptable 3 percent levels. South Carolina maintained enough banking growth to furnish its economy with capital for its entire half decade before the war.

The same could be said for Virginia, with its 3 percent annual expansion in loans, circulation, and deposits. Virginia, in fact, experienced a 4 percent specie growth, making its circulation and lending statistics even more favorable. Like most other states of the Old South it grew at faster rates before the panic than after, but overall, Virginia seldom dropped below 4 percent growth in any category except specie, which managed 3 percent growth.

Overall, every state in the Old South, as well as Alabama, and Tennessee displayed growth in major banking statistics during the antebellum period, usually in the area of 4 to 5 percent annually. In these cases growth was usually legitimately backed by specie, and real growth was not far removed from nominal levels.[49]

Using Cameron's "crude index" of bank density indicators (see Table 21), it would conversely appear that no southern state consistently attained high or even moderate levels of density. Mississippi reached moderate levels during the 1840s before inflation caught up with bank chartering. Georgia managed even higher levels prior to 1837. Despite these apparent low levels, two factors must be considered when the data are analyzed. First, branches accounted for much of the bank activity in North Carolina, Virginia, and Georgia. In each case, density levels including branches were considerably higher (seven times greater in Tennessee in the 1850s and six times greater in Virginia during the same period, for example). Although these density figures still place most states in the low category, density growth is evident, and by 1860 most of the states were rapidly closing on moderate levels of density. Second, private banks are not included in these density figures. If the figures are adjusted to take into account estimated private banks, these levels suggest that banking services were far more available to southerners than scholars have previously suspected, with moderate levels reached on average.[50]

49. See Schweikart, "Banking in the American South," figures 6.1–6.30 and 6.31–6.40, a, b, c, d.
50. Richard Easterlin, "Interregional Differences in per Capita Income, Population, and Total Income, 1840–1850," in *Trends in the American Economy in the Nineteenth*

Other major indicators show steady growth in loans per population in Alabama, Georgia, North Carolina, South Carolina, Tennessee, and Virginia from 1850 to 1860. Similar growth characterized these states in the loans-plus-circulation category compared with population over the same decade. Statistics including 1840 tend to reflect the boom-generated inflation, even when some of the effects of the panic were felt, but when we allow for this deviation, overall growth in these categories is evident since 1820.

One factor negatively affecting the density statistics, however, is the strain put on the banking systems of Tennessee and Louisiana by neighbors lacking banks, such as Texas, Arkansas, Missouri, or Mississippi, from 1858 until the war. Their influence would tend to drive upward all banking density ratios.

Yet another approach to determining the effectiveness of southern banking is to employ a ratio of southern bank money to per capita income. Richard Easterlin estimated individual state per capita income levels for the year 1840 on a state-by-state basis. The attendant problems of that year's monetary data have already been mentioned. Nevertheless, his data on per capita income can suggest different ratios from those set by the other models. Although prosperous states such as Louisiana, South Carolina, Georgia, and Virginia all had high ratios of bank money to income, so did Mississippi, where capital was highly inflated. In Alabama and Florida, states that experienced considerable inflation, the ratios were relatively low. Yet so was Tennessee's, and in Tennessee inflation was relatively controlled. According to the Gurley-Shaw theory of development, the money-to-income ratio should rise if economic development is taking place. In the case of the existing data, economic development is difficult to measure, using Easterlin's 1840 data on a state-by-state basis, because his 1860 data are regional. Nevertheless, some broad conclusion can be drawn about the Atlantic seaboard states, which

Century, Vol. XXIV of *Studies in Income and Wealth* (Princeton, 1960), 73–140. Also see Easterlin's "Regional Income Trends." For these estimates of numbers of private bankers, see Schweikart, "Entrepreneurial Aspects," table in note 32; for the density ratios adjusted for private bankers, see Schweikart, "Banking in the American South," table 6.14. On southern banking growth in general, see Schweikart, "Southern Bankers and Economic Growth in the Antebellum Period: A Reassessment," *Journal of Southern History*, February, 1987. Other sources of capital for Southerners also appeared through the banking activities of millenialist societies such as the Humanists. See Larry Schweikart, "Private Bankers in the Antebellum South," *Southern Studies*, Summer, 1986.

Table 21. Indicators of Money Supply and Banking in Relation to Population,
1820–1860

Year	Loans per Capita ($)	Loans + Circulation per Capita ($)	Density*a*	Density*b*
		Alabama		
1820	3.83	4.75	0.03	0.03
1830	3.35	5.35	0.04	
1840	83.2	105	0.05	0.11
1850	3.9	7.23	0.01	0.01
1860	14.1	21	0.08	0.08
		Florida		
1820				
1830				
1840	86.8	170	0.74	1.29
1850				
1860	3	4.28	0.14	0.14
		Georgia		
1820	15.4	23.9		
1830	12.2	18.1	0.19	0.19
1840	20.8	25.2	0.30	0.53
1850	12.6	23.6	0.12	0.19
1860	16	24.3	0.23	0.27
		Louisiana		
1820	45.3	48.4	0.19	
1830			0.13	0.13
1840	130.8	157.1	0.45	1.33
1850	45.4	55.4	0.13	0.56
1860	50	66.4	0.16	0.18
		Mississippi		
1820	18.5	24.2	0.13	
1830	15.3	20.6	0.07	0.07
1840	132.7	173.7	0.61	1.01
1850	0.18	25.2	0.01	1.01

Table 21.   (continued)

Year	Loans per Capita ($)	Loans + Circulation per Capita ($)	Density[a]	Density[b]
		North Carolina		
1820	2	2.9	0.01	
1830	5.7	7.5	0.04	0.04
1840	3.65	5.2	0.03	0.13
1850	6	9.9	0.04	0.21
1860	12.3	17.9	0.13	0.29
		South Carolina		
1820	4.8	7.1	0.01	0.01
1830	4.8	6.9	0.01	0.01
1840	31	38.5	0.20	0.23
1850	31.2	44.4	0.17	0.20
1860	37.5	54	0.25	0.28
		Tennessee		
1820	8.1	9.1	0.07	0.07
1830	0.33	0.36	0.01	0.01
1840	3.4	4.3	0.04	0.26
1850	9	12.9	0.03	0.21
1860	10.6	15.5	0.14	0.28
		Virginia		
1820	8.3	11.1	0.04	0.04
1830	7.16	10.5	0.01	0.01
1840	5.49	7.9	0.05	0.26
1850	16.3	24.4	0.05	0.32
1860	20.4	33	0.19	0.53

[a] Per 10,000 inhabitants.
[b] Including branches.
Source: Schweikart, "Southern Banking and Economic Growth."

declined considerably from 1840 to 1860. Even if we allow for tremendous growth in the data for Maryland and the District of Columbia, this area would display a significant decline. Thus either the Gurley-Shaw model is inadequate or these states failed to develop in any reasonable fashion. Other statistics presented here suggest an altogether different conclusion. The Easterlin data would include Florida, which had just established an infant banking system, further skewing the evidence. Consequently, the Gurley-Shaw model falls short of explaining southern development. Using much more detailed data, George Green reached the same conclusions about Louisiana as a single state. A broader estimate, based on Easterlin's regional data for 1840 to 1860, suggests larger ratios, but the data apply here in at best a tentative way.

The available data suggest that southern financial growth occurred at a rate and with enough soundness to have supported any activities that entrepreneurs wished to pursue. Southern growth also took place in a setting in which bank density was edging toward "moderate" levels of growth in terms of Rondo Cameron's scale. The money-to-income ratio was rising from 1840 to 1850, a statement that runs somewhat counter to the Gurley-Shaw model of development. It does seem safe to argue that southern states differed widely in their development history, and perhaps Easterlin's inclusion of Texas, Kentucky, Maryland, or other states served to muddle the regional data more than to illuminate them. At any rate, the availability of banks and real capital in the South from 1819 to 1861 should persuade historians to pursue political, social, or other noneconomic reasons for the failure of manufacturing to develop in the South. Too much real capital existed for manufacturing-oriented entrepreneurs to ignore if they chose to invest in industry, and the returns to such investment were quite good. Moreover, the availability of banks and real capital should lay to rest arguments that try to explain southern banking growth narrowly, in terms of "class" alliances between planters and bankers: if anything, bankers and planters, who may have been allies in the 1820s and 1830s, gradually adopted vastly different views of the world and contradictory philosophies. Although these differences began to appear in the 1840s and 1850s, planters, and much of society, were still committed to the continuation of slavery. Industrial and manufacturing investment did not take place because of attitudes about the place of slavery in society (and also that of the plantation) and because the returns to risk (both economic and societal) for cotton were too great to ignore.

7

BANKERS, THE CONFEDERACY
AND THE END OF AN ERA

The South greeted the decade of the 1850s with optimism, buoyed by the final disappearance of the lingering effects of the Panic of 1837. King Cotton led the recovery, its production running at levels nearly double those of the 1840s and its export value increasing. Increased wealth brought new opportunities for investment in nonagricultural areas, too. Railroad building, backed by the planter groups, which saw new opportunities to send their crops to market, resumed at an intensified pace. Entrepreneurs in manufacturing areas gained from high rates of return that only increased over the decade. The discovery of gold in the United States hinted at the start of an economic golden age.

Banking reflected this apparent prosperity in many ways. Almost all states witnessed growth in the availability of loans, notes, and specie, even in proportion to the population. Deposits grew by an average annual rate of 15 percent per state in states where banks reported in every year. Clearly, however, some states, including Florida, Arkansas, and Mississippi, had so seriously damaged their banking systems that recovery proved nearly impossible. Alabama, the lone exception among the New South states in having suffered near collapse with a state bank, experienced a rebirth, whereas Tennessee, as the New South state with the least government involvement and the most competition, returned to normal banking growth after the panic. Given Alabama's example, however, Mississippi and Florida could hope for some life in their moribund systems, and indeed both made some attempts at recovery. Their burdens, however, were perhaps only slightly greater than Alabama's. That state's return to financial health was nothing short of miraculous.

The Second Alabama Banking System

At the start of the 1850s, state banking in Alabama was in decline. The state bank and its branches were in liquidation at the hands of trustee Frances Strother Lyon. Lyon's considerable talents in wrapping up affairs of the bank have been almost universally praised. The joint commit-tee of the legislature in 1849 noted that, under his conduct and manage-ment of the affairs of "our hitherto miserably mismanaged State Bank and branches . . . , a new era has occurred . . . ; a brighter sun has shone on our prospects." Under his eye, the trustees sold the banking house at Huntsville for $15,000, marking the final disposition of that branch, which joined the Decatur and Montgomery branches in liquida-tion, for which the state had received $19,000 total. Steady retirement of both the state debt, incurred by the state bank, and its bank note issues had proceeded alongside the contraction of outstanding note issues. Only $189,000 in state notes remained unredeemed by 1857, although the state treasury still held almost $850,000. By that same date the state had reduced its debt of more than $15 million to slightly more than $3.4 million. Lyon, often hailed as a financial wizard, had inherited a great deal of good fortune. Many of the debts, unpayable earlier because of economic troubles, were repaid when prosperity and land values were restored.[1]

Changes from the antibank mania of the early 1840s were first appar-ent in the address to the legislature made by Governor H. W. Collier. During the legislative session in 1849, several new resolutions for char-

1. *Alabama Senate Journal*, 1849, p. 133; *Biennial Report of the Commissioners and Trustee to Settle the Affairs of the State Bank and Branches, to the General Assembly* (Montgomery, 1857), 2–3, 6; Willis Brewer, *Alabama: Her History, Resources, War Record, and Public Men* (Montgomery, Ala., 1872), 363. For material on the second bank-ing system, consult the Montgomery *Flag and Advertiser*, November 28, 1849, January 23, 30, February 6, April 17, May 29, October 16, 1850, March 5, 1851, October 6, 1852, March 30, September 28, 1853, March 29, July 12, November 15, December 6, 13, 1854, February 7, March 14, 21, September 5, November 14, 1855, October 21, 28, November 4, 18, December 2, 9, 30, 1857; Rufus Clements to Jefferson Franklin Jackson, June 30, 1847, in J. F. Jackson Papers, Report of W. Ledyard and D. Kane, 58, December 5, 1840, Correspondence, Mobile branch, SBA, Report of the Commissioners from the Branch Bank at Montgomery, February 1846 through January 1847, SBA, Minute Book of the Mo-bile branch of the Bank of Alabama, March 5, 1846, SBA, all in ADAH.

tering banks had been offered. Local capitalists wanted avenues of investment, the governor argued, and it was the legislature's duty "to yield to them the field of operation, instead of permitting others to enjoy its benefits at our cost." Collier offered a free-market alternative to state involvement. "We must remember," he urged, "that those evils were superinduced by a reversion of the order of nature" and that the system used by the state "is universally considered to be eminently false and deceptive." Collier suggested major reforms in the banking laws, especially the passage of a free-banking act.[2]

Collier's address signified an important departure from the old-line Jacksonian party dogma. Alabama was as Democratic as ever, even though in the year 1849 the Whigs held a slight majority in the state senate. Still, the state never elected any but a Democratic senator, so that Collier by his very election represented a general change in attitude. The lesson learned by many Alabamians was that private banks operating and responding to market pressures were far preferable to state organs susceptible to political control. Legislators passed the free-banking act in 1850, indicating that they preferred a few effective regulations that allowed the market to function rather than elaborate rules that unintentinally interfered with it. The legislature did not give up its charter powers. Indeed, eight of the ten new banks established in Alabama from 1850 to 1861 were chartered.[3]

On the other hand, no one would deny that the state's lawmakers had gained practical experience in writing banking law. More professional examinations were conducted, higher specie ratios were expected, and the first sign of trouble brought quick reaction. Panic conditions during 1857 forced two of the new banks to suspend. Quickly investigating the situation, the legislature determined that "the condition of said banks is sound and entitled to public confidence." Rather than take extreme measures against either bank, the assembly set a date for resumption, and the banks complied.[4]

Two concerns guided the legislators during the rebirth of banking in

2. *Alabama Senate Journal,* 1849, pp. 173–80.
3. Albert Moore, *History of Alabama* (University, Ala., 1935), 314. See table 3.1.
4. *Alabama Acts,* 1857–58, p. 22; *Alabama Senate Journal,* 1857–58, pp. 13–27, 61, 92, 117; *Alabama House Journal,* 1859, p. 21. These two banks, plus one other, again suspended in 1861. Also see *Report of the Commissioners Appointed by the Governor to Examine the Southern Bank of Alabama* (Montgomery, 1851), 6–7; Huntsville *Southern Advocate,* February 18, 1852, September 6, 1854.

Alabama. First, they sought to drive out of circulation all shinplasters and small notes, especially those issued in other states. The Mobile *Register*, for example, expected the Southern Bank of Alabama to "do what the friends of banks promised that they would . . . , drive out of circulation this abominable shin plaster currency with which we are now infested, to the annoyance and disgrace of the community." Jacksonianism had not revived; the concern, as manifested in an 1853 law addressing the problem, related to the currency of banks in other states. With passage of the 1853 code, no bank could circulate bills under five dollars from an out-of-state bank. Attempts to repeal the law yielded to a bill that permitted the Bank of Mobile and the Northern Bank of Alabama to issue such bills. A practical, "Alabama first" approach to business had caught on. In chartering more banks and passing the free-banking law, the assembly hoped to achieve a second objective, that of preventing the Bank of Mobile from gaining a permanent monopoly there. The Southern Bank of Alabama competed vigorously. Most of its notes circulated in the Mobile area.[5]

Once Alabama had passed its free-banking law, it entered into a period of liberally granting charters within the constitutional limitations. Yet between 1850 and 1860 only one free bank was formed and that by "Georgia capitalists." Why this puzzling situation? If, as Collier and many Alabamians contended, the state was starved for credit, why did not more free banks appear? Alabama had adopted a free-banking law virtually identical to those of other states, so its requirements were no more harsh. Rather, as the relatively slow reaction to free-banking laws in Virginia and Florida suggests, southerners generally hesitated to use free-banking incorporation when they could receive state charters. Charters still meant "special privilege" in many southerners' minds, even when everyone could obtain one, as with modern incorporation laws. Some stockholder liability provisions served as a disincentive to form free banks. Florida's free-bank law made stockholders liable for stock twelve months after the transfer of ownership and also made their private property liable on a pro rata basis. The only free banks organized before 1860 were the Bank of Montgomery, which commenced operations on October 12, 1852, and the Bank of Selma. The former proved as

5. Mobile *Register*, November 21, 1850; Montgomery *Daily Alabama Journal*, November 18, 20, 1853; Huntsville *Southern Advocate*, December 17, 1851, January 21, July 21, 1852.

strong as most chartered banks and continued operations into the war, whereas the latter had just begun business in late 1859. Alabama ended the decade optimistically, with its financial structure finally restored to the point where it could encourage and assist economic growth.[6]

ARKANSAS AND PROHIBITION

Whereas Alabama's financial community was recovering, Arkansas' prohibition against banking had remained in place because of the tremendous political power of the Seviers, driving all business into the hands of a few private bankers or to neighboring states. Sometimes the private bankers succeeded in business because of their connections in adjoining states, or even the North. W. B. Wait, of Little Rock, made an annual trip east in the summer, laden with depositor transactions. Wait's honesty was legendary—he often traveled with thousands of dollars from customers and even from competitors. S. H. Tucker lamented that a close personal friend of his nevertheless did business with Wait because the friend considered Wait "a leetle the safest." Wait maintained his business until after the war, becoming an officer in the First National Bank of Arkansas. Tucker also remained in private banking until 1870.[7]

Private bankers appeared throughout the state, not just in Little Rock, and their timing roughly coincided with the demise of the state banks. B. L. Brittin and Company, in Batesville, did an exchange business in the 1850s, whereas John Jackson and Company of Helena established a private bank there "in 1854 or 1855" only to close within a few years. Several other Helena merchants also offered exchange services. The first private bank in Pine Bluff, opened by Samuel Jack in 1861, closed after two years. A bank in Camden created by Judge John Brown also opened in about 1858 and closed in 1862 or 1863. Brown sold "Mexican dollars and Tennessee paper" and also dealt in "undercurrent money." The need for exchange was so great as to make one editor remark in passing that "all sorts of money goes tolerably here." Despite the need for banks, and the mediating effect of the private bankers, no chartered banks were permitted in Arkansas until after the war.[8]

6. Huntsville *Southern Advocate*, August 18, October 13, 1852; Thomas, "History of Banking," 116–18.

7. Worthen, *Early Banking in Arkansas*, 144–45.

8. *Ibid.*, 118–23. Judge John Brown's Diary, March 8, 17, April 30, May 8, 1858, cited in Elsie Lewis, "Economic Conditions," pp. 256–74; *Acts Passed at the Tenth Session of*

BANKING REVIVAL IN TENNESSEE

Among the remaining states of the New South, only Tennessee witnessed a revival of banking. Mississippi languished with poor credit and a few insignificant banks and left its banking to Louisiana or Tennessee. Florida, although swarming with agents and private bankers, could provide incentive for only two public banks to open by 1860, one of them an insurance company. Still, Tennessee boomed, especially after 1853: the bank population had risen from three to twenty-two by 1856. As many as forty-five branches operated that year. The Panic of 1857, although reducing the number of branches by five, had no lasting impact on the banks themselves. A net loss of only one bank by 1859 was recorded. Much of the strength of the "new" Tennessee banks during the panic resulted from a 0.50 reserve ratio in 1856, an unusual level, given the lower ratios of the years preceding 1856. This ratio, and the phenomenon of Tennessee's rising specie levels in the Panic of 1837, suggest that the state's banks immediately took precautionary measures at the first sign of trouble by reducing deposits—not circulations—and yet, when the Panic of 1857 set in, Tennessee's banks were able to increase their deposits more than sixteenfold.[9]

Tennessee was one of five southern states to adopt a true free-banking law (Virginia had a derivative), although many of the Jacksonian hard-money advocates still lurked in the shadows of the legislature, ready to renew their assaults on banks. Some had softened their views or had molded the free-banking concept to fit their own understanding of it. David Campbell, the Virginia governor during the wave of antibank sentiment in the 1830s, provides an interesting example of a politician with a genuine interest in banking and a more-than-passing knowledge of the subject. His nephew William had become involved in the Bank of Middle Tennessee. William regularly wrote his uncle for advice on financial affairs, especially banking. In 1852, William asked for David's opinion on the Tennessee free-banking law. David, the moderate Jacksonian during the bank controversy, found the system "better than our present systems in Virginia and Tennessee." He regretted, however, that "in a great

---

the *General Assembly of Arkansas, 1854–1855* (Little Rock, Ark., 1855), 107–108; *Acts Passed at the Twelfth Session of the General Assembly of Arkansas, 1858–1859* (Little Rock, Ark., 1859), pp. 300–301; *Arkansas Whig*, February 8, 1855.

9. See Schweikart, "Banking in the American South," tables 6.1 through 6.10.

revolution they would have to stop payment." Notes accepted by the state for debt would have to be made legal tender—"the greatest pecuniary calamity" that could occur—other temporary solutions were equally unacceptable. Campbell, arguing that gold and silver should constitute a bank's capital and that banks should be restricted in their issues to "money in the vaults," then concluded, "That is the free bank doctrine." (Certainly neither Virginia nor Tennessee had free-banking laws based on this principle.) [10]

Even in the best of conditions, a poor banker could destroy a good bank, and a good banker could ensure the success of a poor one. Campbell, who took control from his partners during the Panic of 1857, had little time to hone his business skills, but he concentrated attentively on banking and developed his skills in a short time, often traveling on instinct. Other individuals, such as Charles Furman of the Bank of the State of South Carolina, were more established bankers with skills acquired during years spent as cashier and at other positions. Furman collected many of the debts classified as "doubtful" that remained from the last administration of F. H. Elmore, an action that quickly won him friends in the legislature. Under his direction the bank had turned profitable by the late 1840s. [11]

Because the bank had another fine year in 1852, and because of an alliance with several private banks seeking recharters (and eight new applicants), the bank under Furman received a recharter until 1871. He turned the bank toward railroad investment, lending more than $200,000 to the Blue Ridge Railroad Company and later paying the interest on the state's purchase of one million dollars' worth of stock, for which the state had issued bonds. Furman's management could not control the international forces that brought on the panic. In fact the Bank of the State was the first in South Carolina to suspend, but his administration before and during the panic displayed the value of having businessmen, not politicians, at the helm of business enterprises.

Ten new banks had received charters by mid-decade in South Carolina, providing adequate competition for the state bank, leaving the

10. David Campbell to William Campbell, February 20, 1852, David Campbell Papers, DU. David's financial advice may have been better received because of his occasionally astute political observations: the border states, he predicted in 1857, will "never-never" join in a confederacy (David Campbell to William Campbell, January 30, 1857, *ibid.*).

11. *Reports and Resolutions, South Carolina,* 1850, pp. 32–34, 200.

state with a net gain of seven new banks when three failed. Still, the state's banking system demonstrated substantial growth in its loans per capita, circulation per capita, and banking density. A temporary contraction in Charleston in 1854 led to a flurry of letters in local papers, but in most of the state an expansion was evident. In 1857, the panic caused a short legislative furor, resulting in the passage of a stringently worded but lightly enforced law.[12]

BANKING GROWTH IN THE 1850S

Virginia also struggled to bring its banking capital to levels that would meet the needs of its population, a task considerably easier than in regions of the New South where population still grew at substantial rates. Perhaps because of the widespread concern over state stagnation, Virginia permitted new corporate forms to appear during the 1850s. To meet the need for increased capital, Virginia enacted a form of free-banking law in 1851 whereby state bonds or those of any improvement company acceptable to the state could serve as a deposit with the state to allow the bank to issue an equivalent amount of notes. At the time, none of the six existing branch banks or the Bank of Kanawha suffered any revision of their charters. As had been hoped, free banks first appeared in the outlying, growing, newer areas. New branches of existing banks soon added to the growing capital in the state, so that by 1860 Virginia had the highest banking density, if branches were included, of any southern state, and one of the highest in southern history. Louisiana, in 1840 (when New Orleans still had banks hanging on from the Panic of 1837) remained higher, but only Georgia in 1840 could approach Virginia in availability of banking services as they operated in 1860. In reality, even with branches, few states could approximate the density level offered by Virginia.[13]

Branch banking in the state—which had the most highly developed private branch system in the South—kept some free banks from opening. Unable to cope with higher costs in less populated areas, the free

---

12. Schweikart, "Banking in the American South," tables 6.8 and 6.12; John Cunningham, *Suggestions on the Causes of the Present Scarcity of Money and in Favor of Essential Reforms in Our Banking System* (Charleston, N.C., 1854); J. D. Allen, *The Banking System: A Speech* (Columbia, S.C., 1857).

13. *Virginia Laws*, 1851, Chap. 58, p. 43; Schweikart, "Banking in the American South," table 6.12.

bank had to either raise its interest and exchange rates or go under. Branches, on the other hand, could share in the larger profits of mother banks in more populated areas. A belief that such branch practices offered unfair advantages to certain banks apparently led to a drive to abolish the branch system and replace it entirely with independent banks. John Rutherfoord headed the antibranch group, citing the existing order as being responsible for "rise and depression . . . in the price of labor . . . [and] of every article the laborer is compelled to purchase." He did not elaborate as to why independent banks would be less likely "to multiply and enlarge schemes of speculation" than branches. Accordingly, members of the assembly dismissed his plea. Until the Panic of 1857, loans had grown at an annual rate of 5 percent since 1850, and circulation had grown slightly faster (6 percent), increasing by $3.7 million since 1850. Although it has been suggested that banks in the Old Dominion had contributed to "a great period of inflation . . . highly conducive to reckless trading, overimportation, stock speculation and other . . . dangerous consequences of inflation," this hardly seems to have been the case. Specie perhaps failed to keep pace with note issue, although from 1850 to 1854, when it reached its peak point of the decade, it marched along at an annual growth rate of 7 percent. All in all, Virginia, on the eve of the war, could look back upon a decade marked by generally wise legislation and adequate, if not notable, growth in its banking system.[14]

Like their counterparts in Virginia, Louisiana's new entrepreneurs placed a growing demand for money on the state's banking system at the beginning of the decade. Memories of the panic had lingered until the mid-1840s, and antibank planks had been incorporated in the 1845 state constitution. Louisiana's temporary repudiation of its bonds ended in 1847, marking the real beginning of the recovery stifled only a bit in the last years of the 1840 decade. Then the state's remaining banks were able to satisfy credit demand and curbed some of the expansion. A swing toward expansion was taking place, culminating in the 1852 state constitution, which contained provisions allowing the legislature again to charter

14. John Rutherfoord, *Speech on Banks* (1854) and *Speech on the Banking Policy of Virginia* (1859), pamphlets in Virginia State Library, 1854; Schweikart, "Banking in the American South," table 6.10. See also the *Minority Report to the Committee on Banks* (Richmond, Va., 1853), Doc. 60, and the speech in support of banks by James Caskie to the Senate Committee on Banks (Richmond, Va., 1856). A more detailed discussion of southern banking growth in the 1850s appears in Schweikart, "Secession and Southern Banks," *Civil War History*, June, 1985, pp. 111–25.

banks. Contemporaneous legislative action gave the Citizens Bank permission to return to normal operations, and Louisiana also enacted a free-banking law. Under the new law, seven free banks had opened in New Orleans by 1857, doubling the available banking capital. It is also noteworthy that Louisiana had reduced foreign holdings in the state's banks by $18.5 million since 1837, even allowing for European losses on the stocks of liquidated banks, which may have reduced that amount by several million.

Tennessee also entered a period of expansion, the cornerstone of which was a twofold process by which the state's Bank of Tennessee was eliminated and a free-banking law was passed. The free-banking law was based on a modified "market value"—rather than par value—standard. Should the bonds placed on deposit decline in price below par in New York and remain below par for thirty days, the free bank had to post additional bonds. Of the bonds on deposit, three-fourths had to be state bonds.[15]

Liquidating the Bank of Tennessee involved less difficulty than similar actions in Alabama or Arkansas. Major concerns had developed regarding the ability of the bank to compete with private banks. The bank's own bad debts had reduced its capital by one million dollars in 1849, making remote the possibility that it would finance other state activities in the future. Thus in 1857 Governor Andrew Johnson recommended closing the bank. He was not driven by a love for free banks—he viewed them as part of a national banking system grounded in error—but liquidation of the Bank of Tennessee would set an example. Coincidentally, and almost concurrent with the Panic of 1857, the Bank of Nashville also closed, and a diarist noted that there was "great excitement, money panic here in full force."[16]

The closing of the Bank of Tennessee in 1857 marked its demise legally, but with the waning of its power in the late 1840s, the state's banks had prospered from 1850 to 1857. Capital had increased by almost $1.5 million, deposits had grown at a rate of better than 30 percent annually, circulations had risen at a 7 percent yearly rate, and loans were growing at a 12 percent annual rate. Eighteen new banks had opened since the beginning of the decade. Another eighteen branches operated

15. Tennessee *Public Acts*, 1851–52, Chap. 113; *ibid.*, 1855–56, Chap. 88. See also the *Report on the Condition of Banks to the Governor* (pamphlet in TLA, 1858).
16. John Lindsley Diary, September 28, 1857, TLA.

in the state on the eve of the panic. Shifting its policy toward competition, Tennessee had finally seen the banking growth it had expected from the outset. This growth did not simply reflect the overall prosperity enjoyed by the country, because Florida, Mississippi, and Arkansas had managed to miss these "good times" by enacting poor regulatory policies. The policy framework encouraged prosperity and was integral to it.

Alabama, Louisiana, and Tennessee had each emerged from periods of different duration in which banks were viewed suspiciously, and an era in which state involvement through a state bank or tight state restrictions on banks was an integral part of the banking system. Each made a transition toward more liberalized banking regulations, and all three adopted free-banking laws; usually the transition reflected pent-up demand for money and an economic stifling. When these and other southern states, most notably Virginia and South Carolina, released the investment surge that had been contained, banks played their part in the boom years of development experienced by the South in the 1850s. Only a panic like that of twenty years earlier could threaten the recovery.

Partly conditioned by the Panic of 1837, the public immediately suspected that banks were at least partially to blame for the monetary failure when New York banks suspended on October 14, 1857. One reason for feeling that banks were at fault was that the suspension of specie payments was believed to be a problem of the banks themselves or at least a malfunction of the international money market. Although railroad bond prices dipped and northern cereals sat in warehouses, the South suffered little. Cotton exports rose steadily from 1857 to 1860. Cotton had experienced no drop in European demand, and railroads in the South hauling it continued to show profits and to pay dividends. Railroad expansion, which had cooled in the West, continued relatively unchecked in the South.[17]

17. James Huston, "Western Grains and the Panic of 1857," *Agricultural History*, January, 1983, pp. 14–32; James Gibbons, *The Banks of New-York, Their Dealers, the Clearing House and the Panic of 1857* (New York, 1864), p. 373; Peter Temin, "The Panic of 1857," *Intermountain Economic Review*, Spring, 1975, pp. 1–12; Fishlow, *American Railroads*, 114–15; *Harper's Weekly*, August 22, 1857; *Annual Report of the Secretary of the Treasury*, House Executive Document 2, 36th Cong., 2d Sess., 1860, p. 471; Kettell, *Southern Wealth and Northern Profits*, 86–87. Also see E. Wicker, "Railroad Investment Before the Civil War," in *Trends in the American Economy in the Nineteenth Century*, vol. XXIV of *Studies in Income and Wealth* (Princeton, 1960), 506.

Distress in the Northwest probably stimulated the panic, and financiers had to curtail lending to avoid a specie drain. A contraction in the money supply followed, but this disruption, having only regional causes, soon disappeared. Consequently the South, which had contracted its loans and circulation in 1858, had resumed more normal levels by late 1858 and 1859. Throughout the South, a similar pattern appeared in the panic years. Increasing circulations, deposits, and loans all reached high levels in 1856 and 1857, dropping in 1858, then rebounding strongly in 1859. Specie expanded from 1857 to 1859. Banks cut back loans and circulation in 1858, but by the following year all categories had nearly reached and in some cases had exceeded pre-panic levels. The southern banking economy grew steadily and suffered little from the Panic of 1857, but the panic nevertheless "was a phenomenon which evoked from Southerners an open discussion of their economic views."[18]

Some strong pillars of the old Jacksonian antibank platform were occasionally refurbished, without widespread support. Probably the most popular figure to revive the hard-money theme was Governor Joseph E. Brown of Georgia. Brown threatened to enforce the 1840 law in Georgia that required annulment of the charter of any bank that had suspended specie payments. Admitting that the Georgia House was disposed "to put pretty hard terms on the banks," Brown wondered whether the measures would be "hard *enough*." Brown viewed banks as the possessors of a myriad of "almost unlimited privileges" and dredged up the perennial Jacksonian question, "Shall the banks govern the people or shall the people govern the banks[?]" After the depression eased across much of the country, and when Georgia banks and most others had resumed specie payments, Brown smugly congratulated himself for the resumption: "The banks in this state have found themselves unable to keep up the war on me . . . and have now engaged in a war with S.C. bankers," and, in a partisan note, added, "I am with the Ga. banks in that fight."[19]

18. James Huston, "The Panic of 1857, Southern Economic Thought, and the Patriarchal Defense of Slavery," *Historian*, February, 1984, pp. 163–86 (quotation on p. 163); Schweikart, "Secession and Southern Banks," p. 116, table 3.

19. Milledgeville *Federal Union*, November 10, 1857; Joseph Brown to [?], December 9, 1857, to Augustus R. Wright, May 24, 1858, both in Hargrett Collection, Atlanta Historical Society; *Georgia House Journal*, 1857, pp. 416–17; *Georgia Senate Journal*, 1857, p. 169. See, for Brown's escapades and the plight of the Georgia banks, Savannah *News*, November 9, 11, December 25, 1857; Milledgeville *Federal Union*, December 8, 1857,

Several elements—an initial panic psychology, the recovery of the southern banks, and especially the fear of northern-backed federal action that could further threaten states' rights—were thoroughly addressed in the letters of southern bankers. Charles Mills, cashier of the Marine Bank of Georgia, had proudly observed the growing economy in 1855 ("our circulation continues larger than I had expected by our account") and worried about the first sign of trouble, related to events in Europe, in late 1856. Writing to his agent, R. Patten, at Columbus, Mills stated soberly, "It cannot have escaped your observation that money has become scarce and appreciated in value in Europe and the Northern States." Indeed, although he did not know that the South as a whole had been losing specie since earlier in the year, he knew that the interest rates were up, and he urged his agent to guard against any further specie or note drains northward. He chastised Patten for undertaking an extension of business that would send more money to New York, which Mills insisted was "contrary to my views" and "contrary to my instructions." A few days later, Mills allowed Patten to return to doing business, but only after he had resolved points of difference between the agency's books and those of the Savannah bank. Mills had protected his agent, possibly even glossing over illegal activities, as he expressed concern to a friend that the law might step in to investigate Patten. Throughout 1856 and early 1857, Mills maintained a cautious attitude toward the economy, reminding W. H. J. Walker that "money matters are, as you say, *Easy*," yet no one making such a statement ever "held *over due paper*." Another time, Mills denied a request by a branch manager, L. A. Bowers, to start an insurance business at the branch, fearing that the distractions to normal business would be too great.[20]

Again, the letters of David Campbell to his nephew William, a banker in Tennessee, provide a rich account of a free bank in the Panic of 1857.

July 27, December 14, 1858, December 4, 1860; Atlanta *Constitutionalist*, October 24, December 1, 27, 31, 1857; Augusta *Daily Constitutionalist*, January 1, 5, 10, July 28, November 5, 1858, November 4, 9, 1859; Savannah *Republican*, October 22, 1857; Savannah *Morning News*, December 25, 1857; Joseph Brown to Lewis, December 9, 1857, to George Hillyers, January 8, 1859, to Ira Foster, January 11, 1859, all in Hargrett Collection.

20. Charles Mills to Ed. Radeford[?], July 17, 1855, Charles Mills Letter Books, SHC, UNC; Charles Mills to R. Patten, October 28, 1856, October 31, 1856, *ibid.*; Charles Mills to W. Dickenson, [?], 1857, and to L. G. Bowers, November 24, 1857, *ibid.* The date in the letter to Dickenson was probably an error, because it read January 26, 1857, and appeared before the Bowers letter in the letterbook.

William took over management of the Bank of Middle Tennessee in the autumn of 1857, although he had been instrumental in the bank's affairs several months earlier. Apparently both David and William had suspected that a crash was forthcoming, but William, "taken by the great prosperity of the country," yielded to his business associates. William's bank had spread its assets too thinly, having too large a circulation and buying too many bonds. Early in September the bank had $160,000 in circulation. When the crash came, it "forced us far out at sea with little cash on hand." Fortunately, the bank maintained good credit, especially with the Bank of Tennessee. In an October 12 letter to David, William said that the panic had reached Tennessee around the first of October, and since that time he had "actively engaged in sustaining the credit of our bank." Under Campbell's guidance, the bank reduced more than fifty thousand dollars of its outstanding circulation. William promised to continue "to reduce its notes and pay its depositors." He assumed blame for discounting too heavily on available deposits and admitted that the bank would be in danger if a general suspension occurred. In that event, the bank could pay its liabilities but risked heavy losses in the depreciation of state bonds, "for which there is now no sale at any price."[21]

William's greatest concern was new legislation, although he never made it clear whether he thought the state or the federal laws posed the greater threat. To David, William predicted that banks would "probably be so legislated as to cripple all the banks & the Free Banks in particular." (Indeed, a year later, Georgia Governor Joseph Brown warned against a banking monopoly that would control the state and "make the people the subjects of [its] power.") William further anticipated being "compelled to wind up our bank in some short period of time" and therefore the bank was "most actively engaged in taking up our own paper & taking up bonds with it." Many "of the democracy," he continued in another letter, "are for the most violent measures towards the banks, and would like to see all banks liquidated." Fortunately, he concluded, there were enough conservatives amongst them to "save the country from disaster."[22]

The younger Campbell "learned a valuable lesson," pledging that if

21. William Campbell to David Campbell, October 12, 27, December 7, 1857, Campbell Papers, DU.
22. William Campbell to David Campbell, October 12, 27, December 7, 1857, *ibid.*; Brown, quoted in Huston, Milledgeville *Federal Union*, November 9, 1848.

his business were to survive he would quit banking or "reduce it to a very small business" that would be safe. Pessimism shrouded his commentaries, however (the "prospect ahead is . . . gloomy"), and he indulged in self-pity ("I cannot engage in any business but [that] it turns out badly on me") to the point of sounding like a scorned lover: "This shall be the last enterprise in the way of making money that I will ever engage in preferring to stay at home and . . . depend on the small income from a farm." Yet, he conceded, "our depositors are quiet, and the county takes our paper readily."[23]

With the coming of the new year, William could report to his uncle that "the crisis has passed with us" and that the bank could resume specie payments. "We can now breath [sic] easy," he cautiously concluded, yet the bank would not discount bills but would only collect and pay off demand "until things look better." Although his own business by mid-July was "now easy," William still carefully watched the unwelcome development of animosity among members of the Tennessee banking community brought about by the failure of some to resume specie payments. They were, as he reported, in an "ill natured condition towards each other." Their failure to reach a harmonious understanding made business unsafe. William assured David that he would avoid risk until the problems had resolved themselves. The possible failure of certain banks, he believed could be corrected by a more widespread adoption of free banking.[24]

Campbell's experiences seem to have been commonly shared throughout the South. Several bankers wrote to merchants in the North, such as Atwood and Company, "We have no exchange and cannot remit" or "Owing to the scarcity of money in this country we have not been able to make collections so as to pay our note yet." Such problems were not, of course, universal. Besides the strong specie reserve position of the Bank of Middle Tennessee, to which Campbell alluded, the Georgia Railroad Bank had enough specie to redeem its liabilities in coin, as did several other southern banks.[25]

23. William Campbell to David Campbell, October 12, 17, 1857, David Campbell to William Campbell, October 22, November 4, 1857, Campbell Papers, DU.
24. William Campbell to David Campbell, January 6, 11, May 20, July 17, 1858, *ibid.*
25. J. W. Smith, Union Bank of Tennessee, Memphis Branch, to Atwood and Company, November 5, 1857, Atwood and Company, Papers, SHC, UNC; O. Gillespie and Company, to Atwood and Company, October 9, 1857, *ibid.*

SOUTHERN BANKING AT THE END OF THE PANIC OF 1857

At first glance, banks in the South appeared to react to economic pressures after the depression, recovering by 1859 and then slipping again (see Tables 22 and 23). Upon closer examination, however, it appears that political events shaped the reaction of southern banks in 1860. Relatively speaking, southern banks stood in a much stronger position than they had twenty years earlier, yet they still relied on the northern banking system to remain solvent if they were to maintain specie payments. Bankers closely watched events in the North, even in such small towns as Elizabeth City, North Carolina, where the editor of the local paper explained the anticipatory suspension by the Farmers Bank in terms of the "many banks up North" that failed, predicting there is "bound to be a run on the [local] bank."[26]

Where the Panic of 1837 had decimated southern banks, its successor scarcely thinned the ranks at all. Alabama had two additional banks added to its numbers in 1858. All of its institutions showed notable growth in loans, specie, circulations, and deposits from 1857 to 1859. Most of Arkansas's private bankers either started business soon after the panic or survived it. Georgia had eighteen banks in 1856; in 1859 the count had increased by eight. In terms of active banks it would appear that the "post–depression" of 1860–1861 had a greater impact, for nine of those twenty-six had disappeared by 1861. Even so, the years 1858 and 1859 saw substantial expansion in loans, specie, and other categories. A similar pattern appeared in Louisiana, where by January 1859 circulations, specie, and deposits all exceeded their pre-panic levels. Only loans failed to keep pace, indicating the conservatism with which the Forstall-influenced bankers viewed drawing on their capital base. By late 1859, even loans in Louisiana had surpassed the 1857 levels.[27]

Along the Atlantic seaboard, things were somewhat different (see Table 24). North Carolina suffered from a lack of specie and, as a result, issued notes with restraint. Its reserve ratios remained at levels of 15 percent—a level too low to warrant huge note issues—apparently because North Carolina was unable to attract specie. South Carolina likewise cut back on its loans and circulation from 1857 to 1859, although it had begun to draw specie by 1859 in sufficient quantities to boost its

26. Elizabeth City *Democratic Pioneer*, September 29, 1857.
27. See Schweikart, "Banking in the American South," tables 6.1 through 6.10.

Table 22. Southern Bank Statistics, 1856–1861 ($ millions)

Year	No. of Banks[a]	Loans[b]	Specie[b]	Circulation	Deposits[b]
1856	100	121.22	19.36	41.63	34.75
1857	101	135.24	17.19	81.04	36.46
1858	123	116.36	20.16	44.12	31.78
1859	122	133.31	28.97	61.60	46.23
1860	119	141.47	26.91	51.69	42.27
1861	104	119.87	22.39	40.58	38.17

[a] Louisiana data may include branches.
[b] Millions of dollars.
Note: Data include all states that reported each year: Louisiana data are for January 1861; Mississippi reported only in 1858; Florida reported only in 1860–61; Arkansas did not report in any year.
Source: Schweikart, "Southern Banking and Economic Growth."

Table 23. Adjusted Bank Statistics, 1856–1861

Year	No. of Banks[a]	Loans[b]	Specie[b]	Circulation	Deposits[b]
1856	100	121.22	19.36	41.63	34.75
1857	101	135.24	17.19	81.04	36.46
1858	121	115.97	20.16	43.96	31.23
1859	122	133.31	28.97	61.60	46.23
1860	112	141.01	26.88	51.51	42.15
1861	102	119.45	22.34	39.73	37.71

[a] Louisiana data include branches.
[b] Millions of dollars.
Note: Data include all states that filed reports, 1856–61 (Georgia, Louisiana, Alabama, North Carolina, South Carolina, Tennessee, Virginia); Louisiana data are for January 1861.
Source: Schweikart, "Southern Banking and Economic Growth."

sagging reserve ratios. Virginia's banks labored under a similar slight specie loss, which the state's bankers furiously fought to minimize by slicing circulation. They succeeded to a point, keeping their reserve ratios between 0.157 and 0.178 until 1861. Only Tennessee, that wonderful magnet, seemed to attract specie regardless of the circumstances

Table 24.   Reserve Ratios of the Old South, 1859–1861

State	1859	1860	1861
Georgia	0.22	0.23	0.18
Louisiana	0.47	0.38	0.58
North Carolina	0.15	0.22	0.14
South Carolina	0.20	0.15	0.18
Virginia	0.17	0.16	0.17

Source: Schweikart, "Southern Banking and Economic Growth."

and held almost $800,000 more in 1859 than in 1857 despite the fact that it had *lost one bank*.[28]

The great growth experienced by the southern banking community still fell short of bringing the South to a state in which capital for investment purposes was abundant, especially when we consider the drain exerted on the states in the Old South and Tennessee by the states in the New South that had collapsed during the Panic of 1837. Alabama climbed back, but banking services were still catching up to the state's population growth; in neighboring Mississippi the banking system never caught up with demand. Restricted or undeveloped banking in Texas and Missouri placed an additional burden on southern banks that had remained healthy. Still, a drop in the indicators in 1860 suggests that politics, not economics, played the crucial role, with the presidential election of 1860 taking center stage.

THE ELECTION OF 1860 AND THE SOUTHERN ECONOMY

Any southerner who believed that the responding southern economy would eventually—if not soon—put it in a position to compete in secondary markets with northern manufactured goods (and, of course, no one doubted the ability of the South to dominate the primary markets of sugar, rice, tar, indigo, and cotton) espoused one of two general lines of thought on southern economic strategy. One view held that the South's ability to hold its own in the manufactured areas and maintain its overwhelming dominance in some raw materials or staples might offset the North's fisheries, lumber, grain, livestock, and, most of all, its superi-

28. Schweikart, "Secession and Southern Banks," table 3; Temin, "Panic of 1857," 11.

ority in industrial goods. With the West gaining a comparative advantage in livestock, grain, and corn, to the North's detriment, this view was certainly not implausible. Alternatively, southern optimists could speak of cotton as king and argue for a fuller use of resources to advance the South's comparative advantage in the cotton trade. Whereas the former group stressed more of a cooperative notion about the Union, the second saw the sections as inherently competitive to such a degree that sections were less interdependent than they were dominant or dominated.[29]

Compounding problems in economic theory was the paradox of growing support for a commercialized economy in the South and the apparent conflict between slavery and free-market mechanisms. This some southerners tried to solve through the patriarchal defense of slavery, most elaborately argued by George Fitzhugh, whose labor theory of value was certainly accepted by Georgia Governor Brown. Yet discussions about southern banking regulations in the 1850s, particularly the growing number of advocates for repeal or modification of usury laws, "revealed a decided preference for the theory of free trade." As one historian explained, "By their adherence to free trade principles, Southerners disclosed that they had not yet accepted the economic reasoning of George Fitzhugh."[30]

Bankers, who dealt with slavery in some cases on a daily basis in their processing of loan applications from planters, in assessing the integrity of planters' or factors' notes, and, more frequently, in real estate assessment or foreclosure procedures, had somewhat barren contact with the actual institution. Thomas Branch supported the Union until 1861, but his son, James R. Branch, was probably more typical of the urban southern banker who, despite limited personal contact with slavery, enlisted in the Confederate army. He eventually led an artillery brigade. The

29. See "William Gregg of South Carolina," De Bow's Review, 1851, 348–52. James H. Hammond, who warned that an interruption in the cotton supply "could bring the whole world to our feet. . . . Cotton is King" (Congressional Globe, 34th Cong., 1st Sess., March 4, 1858, appendix, 70), and Henry Wise of Virginia, who had proclaimed in 1825 that the South needed "no standing armies, no navy—because 'Cotton is King'" (James Hambleton, A Biographical Sketch of Henry A. Wise: With a History of the Political Campaign in Virginia in 1855 [Richmond, Va., 1856], 348), shared this particular view. Also see Thomas O'Conner, "Lincoln and the Cotton Trade," Civil War History, March, 1961, pp. 20–35.

30. Huston, "Panic of 1857," 170, 174; Georgia House Journal, 1857, pp. 416–17; Georgia Senate Journal, 1857, p. 169. I draw much of the discussion on Fitzhugh from Robert Loewenberg's Freedom's Despots and his "John Locke and the Antebellum Defense of Slavery," Political Theory, May, 1985, pp. 266–91.

record shows that few, if any, bankers supported the Union once war had erupted. Determining their positions prior to the war is somewhat more difficult. No official record survived them (as it did politicians) except that which the bankers chose to leave in the form of letters, but something of their attitude is known from numerous individual biographies.[31]

M. C. Mordecai, for example, a director in two banks in South Carolina from 1840 to 1860, supported the secession movement wholeheartedly. Mordecai founded the *Southern Standard*, a secessionist paper, and was an active member in the States' Rights party. Isaac Mordecai (apparently not a close relative), a former director of the Bank of the State, favored the Union. William Johnson, president of the Camden Bank, also participated in the States' Rights party. Young L. G. Harris and Asbury Hall, prominent bankers in Athens, Georgia, supported the unionist platform. In the same city T. R. Cobb and his brother, Howell, were devoted secessionists. Henry Marston, the old-line Whig planter-banker from West Feliciana Parish, Louisiana, joined the Constitutional Union party in 1860. David Levy Yulee of Florida, long involved in banking activities there, was a staunch states'-rights supporter. William Macfarland, president of the Farmers Bank in Richmond, was a unionist who attended the secession convention. In Tennessee, Bank of Tennessee officials were sympathetic to the cause of the Confederacy.[32]

More examples could be found for either position, but if bankers were preoccupied with the slavery question, few evidenced such concern in their personal letters until secession was at hand. Even then, they were principally concerned with the practical effects of secession on business. A new spirit of cooperation arose, tied to the economic shocks suffered by the South as a result of Lincoln's election. Jasper Rim, president of the Planters Bank of Fairfield in Winnsboro, South Carolina, advised William Lyles of Mobile that "[we] expect to be able to help you along from time to time, the Legislature having just suspended the 1/3 gold [specie reserve] Act until Jan. '62." Rim hoped Alabama would join the

31. Cabell, *Branchiana*, 64–68. James R. Branch was probably *not* expressing the postbellum attitude of southern bankers when he participated in a party given in 1869 for freedmen. The party, held in an area accessible only by a wooden bridge, drew so many guests (and several hecklers) that the bridge collapsed, killing Branch in the process.

32. Stith Cain, "A History of Branch Banking in Tennessee" (M.A. thesis, University of Virginia, 1935), 129. Henry Young, Christopher Memminger, and John H. Honour were members of the South Carolina Secession Convention. See John May and Joan Faint, *South Carolina Secedes* (Columbia, S.C., 1960), 128–231.

states of Georgia, Florida, and South Carolina "in the formation of the 'Confederacy of Columbia.'" After secession, conditions worsened rather than improving. Rim complained to L. D. Baker in December, 1861, that his bank had "loaned out money liberally, and now very few meet their paper." Secession also contributed to a banking contraction in other ways. "We are obliged (i.e. morrally [*sic*]) to contribute towards the defence of the State, and have done so," Rim explained to Baker, who had petitioned for a loan.[33]

L. S. Webb of the Windsor Branch of the Bank of North Carolina expressed his view that times were hard. "We have to use our [Virginia] Exchange almost entirely to redeem our circulation," he wrote, responding to a loan request. Nevertheless Webb would "try to husband our resources so as to let you have as much as the $5,000, if you don't want it too soon."[34]

Distress associated with the postelection depression was widespread. One businessman petitioned Rim for relief from collections in Mobile. Apparently, unnamed bankers in Mobile extended considerable credit to the borrower until the fall of 1860, at which time "they became alarmed" and demanded repayment. The merchant had purchased a bond at the outset, however, which served as security. Instead it sank the transaction in rather murky surroundings. Claiming that the bank had advanced one thousand dollars that he then paid, the bank insisted on collecting his other debts, for which the merchant offered the bond. Meanwhile, the bond's value had deteriorated to the point where the merchant somewhat desperately reported being threatened "with authority from Washington." Collecting on such a bond itself signified a state of serious concern over bank debts, but the fortunate debtor did not have to worry about the threats from Washington for long—at least not about those implied by the bank.[35]

The unfortunate circumstances of William Smedes, president of the Southern Rail Road Company, related earlier, stemmed directly from the 1860 contraction in the South. Writing William Johnson from Vicksburg

33. Jasper Rim to William Lyles, November 13, 1860, and to L. D. Baker, January 10, 1861, James Quarles Collection, Folder 2, SHC, UNC.

34. L. S. Webb to P. Henneberg, November 23, 1860, Bank of North Carolina Letter and Account Book, Vol. 14, Windsor Branch, SHC, UNC.

35. ? to W. D. Lesser, Agent of the Bank, in James Quarles Collection, Folder 2, SHC, UNC. This letter is highly obscured and illegible (perhaps indicative of the author's desperation?). The date is illegible but is sometime in late 1860 or 1861.

in December, 1860, he worried that "the people here are wild with de-
termination instantly to secede, & I have no doubt but that will be the
decree of the convention soon after its session on the 7th of January
next." Smedes was unsure whether any restoration of confidence in the
economy would occur, but the uncertainty made it impossible to raise
money at all. Factors, including his own, were failing in droves. Their
credit had been helpful, he recalled, but even with suspension they
were in such poor shape that "their acceptances would be of but little
avail . . . for the purpose of effecting a loan."[36]

Smedes kept fairly well-to-do company. One member of his firm,
Adam Griffin, was the treasurer of New Orleans, whereas one of Smedes's
sureties, a Mr. Reading, was estimated by Smedes, "even after a pro-
tracted civil war, as worth half a million dollars." Given such financial
partners, Smedes might have been tempted to disregard the effects of
war. Neither he, in Vicksburg, nor Johnson, in South Carolina, lived in
areas dominated by people who were political moderates in any sense of
the word. He maintained an optimistic outlook for peace "before the
year is out." At that time, confidence restored, "money [would] be abundant & property salable." Hardly sounding like a wild-eyed secessionist,
Smedes closed a letter to Johnson with the hope "that we may live to see
this revolution over, & all our difficulties adjusted."[37]

South Carolina, the hotbed of secession, by no means spoke with a
single voice on the secession issue prior to the election. The bankers
in Charleston who supported John C. Breckinridge included George
Williams, who sponsored a meeting in the city on behalf of his candi-
date. Once Lincoln had won the election, Williams joined many other
disillusioned former unionists, helping to promote a mass meeting on
November 12 to ratify the legislature's call for a secession convention.

In the states that seceded first, banks immediately felt the effects.
South Carolina's legislature requested $400,000 from the state's banks
on November 12, of which the Bank of Charleston was called upon to
furnish $100,000. Some three weeks remained before the convention
would take place, but it was abundantly clear that the forthcoming po-

36. William C. Smedes to William Johnson, December 15, 1860, William Johnson
Papers, SC.

37. *Ibid.*; William C. Smedes to William Johnson, February 20, 1861, William Johnson
Papers, SC.

litical difficulties would interrupt normal trade channels, and so South Carolina banks suspended, an action that especially embittered those proud banks that had not suspended during the Panic of 1857, including the Bank of Charleston. South Carolina's exit from the Union on December 20 set in motion similar conventions in six other states. New Orleans banks, still meeting their obligations in specie, contracted operations in anticipation of Louisiana's secession. With a goal of converting cash assets into specie, New Orleans banks reduced their paper from 74 percent on October 6, 1860, to 57 percent by April 6. They increased specie and reduced loans, deposits, and circulation. In South Carolina, where specie suspension took place virtually concurrently with secession, a different path was taken. There banks did not decrease their loans and circulation as did those in New Orleans, a luxury made possible by the suspension.[38]

Contraction exacerbated the depressed conditions in New Orleans and even touched outlying areas, as described by Smedes. Factors, "swamped with cotton," and buyers willing to purchase it were nearly totally unable to obtain New York bills of exchange, although London bills were available at 15 percent discounts. All through the Mississippi Valley a feeling of panic spread. One diarist recorded seeing a Natchez man "worth not less than $150,000" being "carted off to the Lunatic Asylum at Jackson having been deranged by the present political excitement & immagines himself ruined & poor." Panic had a foundation in reality. During the first two weeks of December, more than thirty New Orleans factorage houses, whose liabilities exceeded thirty million dollars, suspended.[39]

Debtors sometimes took the opposite attitude and used secession as an excuse to escape their obligations. By this reasoning the first tempting target, northern creditors, had no right to expect payment, "because the north is disloyal to the constitutional rights of our section of the country." Southern banks with northern correspondents saw the logic of this argument only too well. They, too, might be undeserving of payment or at least of some part of the debt earmarked for the North. No

38. John Schwab, *The Confederate States of America, 1861–1865: A Financial and Industrial History of the South During the Civil War* (New York, 1968 [1901]), 124–26.
39. B. L. C. Wailes, *Diary*, January 1, 1861. Also see John Bettersworth, *Confederate Mississippi* (Baton Rouge, 1943).

one could be "persuaded out of [money]." A Mississippi merchant lamented, "I am ruined—my country is ruined," all because of the "accursed secession movements."[40]

Southern states that remained in the Union might have been expected to avoid some of the unsavory effects of secession. With their correspondent relationships intact, their debtors had fewer excuses to avoid payment. Every state that had not seceded before the first shells hit Fort Sumter had plenty of banks, most of which were in sound condition. North Carolina, for example, managed to reduce its circulation and increase its deposits, but as ever, seemingly, its specie level dropped. Decreases in loans during 1860 were followed by a ten-year high mark of fourteen million dollars' worth in 1861. Consequently North Carolina banks seem not to have been squeamish about lending and made no obvious effort to obtain cash on the eve of war. Moreover, the high level of deposits reveals that North Carolinians felt confident about placing their money in banks. In Louisiana the situation was much the same. As late as December, 1861, depositors continued to keep large amounts in the state's banks, but loans had dropped and circulation had tailed off drastically since 1859. Louisiana had an advantage over North Carolina in that, as a major specie import point, it always maintained much higher specie levels (also because of the reserve requirements in the Louisiana bank laws). Moreover, there is overall little to suggest that bankers engaged in any drastic measures to move money into their banks in anticipation of war.[41]

A "nation" preparing for war would take advantage of the correspondent relationships in the North to decrease holdings in notes of other banks, especially northern banks and would also owe a great deal more to northern banks if directors anticipated a way to escape redeeming the notes. The South did not act in this manner, however. Smedes's letter implies that knowledgeable businessmen and bankers believed the war

40. Thomas Webber, *Diary*, January 3, 4, February 28, March 15, 18, 28, 29, 1861, DU.

41. A fuller discussion of southern banking during secession appears in Schweikart, "Secession and Southern Banks," 118–25. For a more detailed critique of the philosophical positions of the Jacksonians, see Schweikart, "Banking in the American South," Chaps. 4 and 7, and Schweikart, "How the Jacksonians Opposed Industrialization," *Reason Papers*, April, 1987. Also see Robert Loewenberg, "A New Exodus," *Midstream*, February, 1983, pp. 39–43 (quotation on page 42); Loewenberg, "That Graver Fire Bell," 41; Thornton, *Politics and Power*, Chap. 5; James Stewart, *Holy Warriors* (New York, 1976), 152; Robert Loewenberg, *An American Idol: Emerson and the "Jewish Idea"* (Washington, D.C., 1984).

would be over within a short period of time and that normal trade relations would resume. Thus although the economy entered a recession brought on by southern bankers' fears and uncertainties surrounding the formation of their republic, as of late 1860 and early 1861 few of them wished to risk damaging their contacts in the North. Moreover, it appears that they generally saw little reason to gain control of the money system, perhaps thinking that the Confederate government's monetary and fiscal policy could perform better than it eventually did. Until secession, southern banking had made monumental strides toward furnishing a solid banking structure capable of promoting economic growth. It had breezed through the Panic of 1857 with little trouble, and two New South states had reversed their politices to encourage banking. Florida and Mississippi still struggled; even without the war it was quite possible that another decade would end before Mississippi could boast of even the most remedial banking system. Arkansas seemed likely to remain mired in Jacksonian financial attitudes for at least as long. Still, the overall impressive growth of the banking sector had vindicated the advocates of the market and had generated the capital needed for industrial growth.

Anticipation of war in late 1860 and early 1861 sufficed to cause most New Orleans banks to cut back on loans and try to contract the amount of outstanding bank notes. Like banks in many southern states, they attempted to convert their cash assets into specie as quickly as possible. Although banks in the rest of the South moved at a somewhat slower rate than those in Louisiana, none of them ignored the potential threat posed by secession, and certainly none "increased their . . . circulation" willingly in early 1861. Virginia held steady, expanding loans only slightly; Tennessee, South Carolina, North Carolina, Georgia, and Alabama all reduced circulations and loans from 1860 to 1861. Louisiana's high reserve ratios reflected both its high prewar specie levels, which were a reaction to the Panic of 1857, and the capture of the New Orleans offices of the U.S. Customs House and its specie reserves in 1861.[42]

Not only did banks in seceding states have their own positions to guard, but in some cases the states themselves were not on sound financial footing at the time of secession. Florida still had a large amount of bonds to pay off, through the provisions of an 1856 internal-improvements act,

---

42. See Richard Todd, *Confederate Finance* (Athens, Ga., 1954), p. 126; Schweikart, "Banking in the American South," tables 6.1 through 6.10.

which totaled over $500,000. The legislature added to this five days after secession by issuing $500,000 in state treasury notes. As many as ten private banks may have done business in Florida at the outset of hostilities, but only the small Bank of the State of Florida at Tallahassee and the Bank of Fernandina bore the brunt of most of the rules and burdens. From 1860 to 1861, the legislature chartered four more banks, none of which commenced operations. On paper, the Bank of Fernandina, with its authorized $1 million in capitalization, appeared larger than its Tallahassee counterpart with its small $130,000 capitalization. Neither was in a position to help the Confederacy, or even the state, in 1861.[43]

Mississippi also had problems. Like Florida, Mississippi had repudiated its foreign bond-related debts, and it, too, needed money. In Mississippi's secession convention, delegates searched for ways to raise extra revenue, considering huge surtaxes and other tax measuers directed at the exchange of money. Authorizing a loan of one million dollars at 10 percent interest, the state issued notes with redemption dates staggered three years apart. The state had to convince the public that the notes would be honored. Given Mississippi's history of repudiation, this was an altogether different and more difficult task. Passage of the loan required an enforcement mechanism, and again the faith of the state was pledged, with the addendum, "no law shall be passed to impair [the] validity and obligation [of the faith of the state]." Skeptics of course recognized that, to void the first law, all that was needed was an act nullifying the ordinance amendment. These drawbacks notwithstanding, the sound Richmond firm of Thomas Branch and Sons saw enough return in bonds to be offered by Mississippi for it to express interest in purchasing some.[44]

Not only did the state have a terrible credit rating, but practically no money was available in Mississippi in 1861. Local banks had disappeared by 1860. One contemporary told the governor that "nearly all our whole money circulation is composed of Tennessee bank notes—all of which are now [February 1861] in a state of suspension." Worse, no gold or silver was in any of the private, noncharted banks in northern Missis-

43. David Thomas, "Florida Finance in the Civil War," *Yale Review*, November, 1907, pp. 311–18.

44. Coker, "Cotton and Faith," 71–74; *Journal of the State Convention*, January, 1861, p. 128; Thomas Branch & Sons to John Pettus, January 22, 1862, MDAH. Taxation became a heavy burden when added to the contributions already made by citizens (G. W. Brame to John Pettus, November 28, 1861, MDAH).

sippi, so that virtually no one could invest in Mississippi treasury notes there because they could be purchased only with specie or with the notes from specie-paying banks. As a "consequence of the depreciation of Tennessee money," the secretary of the treasury was told that "we cannot pay our debts and make loans to the Confederate government with the same money." Notes of Tennessee and Louisiana banks also lacked consistency of value: each bank's notes rose and fell, according to its own worth. Individual Mississippi counties had issued scrip to pay for local work, and a variety of private mercantile and banking house notes circulated, causing general exchange values to fluctuate even more.[45]

Alabama had also seceded immediately, but conditions were not as bad in that state because Alabama had carefully cultivated and nurtured its banking system during the 1850s. Some antibank provisions in the 1861 constitution appeared. New banks were to be chartered by a two-thirds vote of the legislature, rather than by a simple majority, and the same majority would be needed to sanction the suspension of specie payments. It was somewhat ironic that the banks had acted on the request of the governor to suspend (so as to have specie for a state emergency) on December 17, 1860, and the state legislature ratified the suspension, adding the requirement that the suspending banks subscribe to specified amounts of state bonds and pay for them in coin if asked to do so.[46]

Suspension cost Alabama banks dearly. They had to accept Confederate treasury notes at par and provide a two-million-dollar loan to the state. Each bank was required to contribute proportionally according to its capital. (A year later the Northern Bank of Alabama had to make a similar "contribution" in order to suspend.) Banks in South Carolina and Georgia suspended in November, more out of a tendency to follow Virginia than from any direct threat. Virginia, in turn, suspended on November 20 and 21, 1860, because New York banks had done so. Although North Carolina and Tennessee did not join the Confederacy immediately, banks there suspended as well.[47]

45. O. Davis to Governor John Pettus, February 4, 1861, G. W. Brame to John Pettus, Governors' Series, MDAH; Coker, "Cotton and Faith," pp. 74, 116–17; W. M. Sea, J. W. Clapp, and W. Goodman to C. G. Memminger, May 27, 1861, cited in Coker, "Cotton and Faith," pp. 124–25; Bettersworth, *Confederate Mississippi*, 95; G. W. Brame to Governor John Pettus, November 28, 1861, Governors' Series, Box 47, MDAH.
46. Thornton, *Politics and Power in a Slave Society*, 431.
47. Minute Book of the Northern Bank of Alabama, January 29, 1862, SBA, ADAH.

Secessionist bankers had not yet realized that their businesses were being viewed as a policy instrument in the hands of the Confederate secretary of the treasury, Christopher G. Memminger. The German-born lawyer had fought numerous court battles for South Carolina banks. He had also registered a dissent from the big three Charleston banks in the legal scuffle over the legislature's right to revoke charters for suspension after the Panic of 1837. Memminger's 1837 legal brief had fostered some distrust and antagonism on the part of his bankers. Because he was not, and had not been, a banker, he lacked collegial ties that could have buttressed his efforts. Still, to obtain the bankers' aid, he dispatched emissaries to plead the treasury's case in bankers' association meetings. More important, he felt "compelled to direct that bank paper . . . be taken at its value in coin" but as late as April 1861 offered only Confederate stock as a backing for the new notes issued by the state banks until the government could print its own notes.[48]

The loan whose success Memminger sought to ensure was the fifteen-million-dollar loan of February 28, 1861, also known as the first Confederate loan. It empowered the secretary to issue fifteen million dollars' worth of bonds bearing 8 percent interest, payable in ten years. In this manner, the Confederacy hoped to raise a substantial quantity of specie. Investors, unfortunately, hardly had the 5 percent in specie due on purchase let alone the remaining 95 percent.

Memminger needed to have the banks ally themselves with the new nation out of both a deeper ideological commitment and a greater economic bond, especially when it was evident that the planters could not support the loan. Banks could accommodate the government by performing a myriad of administrative duties, substantially reducing the need for an onerous and unpopular bureaucracy. Memminger suggested that banks could play a more direct part in the loan for minimal cost. Bankers responded, interest in the loan grew, and by June, half of the subscriptions had been taken. Banks often subscribed themselves for large amounts. So many bank notes came in that the Confederate gov-

48. Schwab, *Confederate States of America*, 7–8; Todd, *Confederate Finance*, 27. Historians differ in their opinions of Memminger. The standard biography is Henry Capers, *The Life and Times of C. G. Memminger* (Richmond, Va., 1893). Criticism appears in Schwab, *Confederate States of America*, 4, and J. B. Jones, *A Rebel War Clerk's Diary at the Confederate Capital* (Philadelphia, 1866). More favorable treatments are found in Emory Thomas, *The Confederate Nation, 1861–1865* (New York, 1979), and Todd, *Confederate Finance*, 1, who called Memminger "shrewd, thrifty, and industrious."

ernment sent many of them back. The vast bulk of the loan went out in the banking-rich areas of New Orleans, South Carolina, and Georgia; the rest of the states altogether subscribed for less than half. With the banks turning some of their coin over to the government, which used it to purchase goods from Europe, southern banks saw their specie reserves decline. A few banks in Mobile that discounted Confederate paper because it could not be converted readily into specie felt Memminger's pressure enough to relent and notify depositors that Confederate currency would be received for all debts made after September 10, 1861. The irony was fitting, however. Gone was the Jacksonian love affair with specie (as one authority on Confederate monetary policy noted, "Confederate officials considered gold and silver as barbarous relics").[49]

To facilitate loan subscriptions, bankers also donated their offices and their time as administrators. Memminger had to win their allegiance and to demonstrate that as an outsider he understood their predicament. Once he had done so, bankers joined the struggle with great dedication. Memminger's successor, George Trenholm, upon taking office in 1864 commented to Secretary of War J. A. Seddon that "the conduct of these institutions has been loyal and patriotic in the extreme."[50]

Cooperation was not the same thing as control, however, and the possibility that the banks might refuse to help at some future point troubled some Confederate officials. One alternative, a national bank, fit poorly with either the southern view of independence or the lingering strains of Jacksonianism. Still, as early as April, 1861, William Murdock suggested such an institution to Jefferson Davis. The proposed Bank of the Confederate States would be capitalized at $14 million, with $1 million coming from each of the original seven Confederate states and an additional subscription of $7 million for the public, the shares to be sold for $100 each. Under the plan, the Confederate States of America hoped to circulate from $25 million to $40 million in notes and to open a branch in each state. A "Confederate National Bank" inspired no great enthusiasm in the Confederate cabinet, which quickly dropped the idea.

George Trenholm, a Charleston merchant and exporter, performed the functions of a central financial agent at the outset of the war. Trenholm sat

49. James Morgan, *Graybacks and Gold: Confederate Monetary Policy* (Pensacola, 1985), 5, 133.

50. Todd, *Confederate Finance*, 21. Todd agreed with Trenholm's assessment, calling the aid rendered to the treasury by the banks "immeasurable."

as a director in two companies, John Fraser and Company, of Charleston, and Trenholm Brothers, which had opened an office in New York in 1853. Later in the war, thoughts turned to establishing a bank in London. Emile de Erlanger, the Parisian who supplied the South with its only major foreign loan, and J. H. Schroeder and Company, of London, made overtures toward establishing a Confederate bank in London in June 1864, capitalized at ten million pounds. This idea failed to take root, forcing individual states to seek foreign aid on their own by the final year of the war. South Carolina's legislature in December 1864 incorporated a bank with notes payable in Paris, for which French citizens were to subscribe an amount of fifty-two million francs. This attempt, too, failed beneath the crumbling structure of the South and the ever-constricting blockade.[51]

State banks controlled note issues until Confederate money appeared. Suspension allowed banks wishing to increase their circulation to do so, and southern legislators extended their blessings to the suspension in subsequent state ordinances. In some cases, suspension was legalized by a loan from the banks to the state.

Another reason for the states to encourage suspension rather than fight it was the expected dearth of specie, which was already felt in some areas. Requirements for circulating mediums of any sort were especially great in Mississippi and Arkansas, although areas as well stocked with money as Virginia reported heavy demand. Legislatures immediately targeted small-note-issue laws for repeal with enthusiasm so widespread that Arkansas withdrew its fifteen-year-old prohibition against circulation of bank notes. Memminger opposed coinage, and the Confederacy made only one feeble stab at passing a shinplaster law. Thus the object of the Jacksonians' fervor in the 1830s—the shinplaster—was embraced wholeheartedly during the war.[52]

Banks began to feel the pressures from the suspension by the autumn of 1861. Mississippi toyed with plans to reestablish its banking system, which drew protests to the governor, including one from a writer who urged Governor Pettus to veto any bank bill "and thereby save the state from utter ruin. . . . If the people opposed [the] establishment [of banks] in times of peace, how much greater will be their opposition now?" The

51. Samuel Thompson, *Confederate Purchasing Operations Abroad* (Chapel Hill, 1935), 5–9; *Charleston Courier*, January 11, 1865.
52. Morgan, *Graybacks and Gold*, 13, 18.

discounting of notes and interest rates was of course on everyone's mind. Tennessee's Committee on Banks wrote William Campbell, concerned about the reports that "the issues of The Bank of Middle Tenn. are selling in this market at seventy five cents on the dollar" and wanted to know whether "this depreciation results from the failure of the Bank to redeem at its counter its own notes in currency." Attempts by the Tennessee legislature could not correct the problems caused by suspension, mainly because of the widespread effects. A customer and shareholder of the Farmers Bank of Virginia, Hugh Grigsby of Norfolk, received a letter from the cashier, A. Sunstall, explaining that the bank could not meet Grigsby's accommodation note for one thousand dollars. The times, Sunstall explained, have "occasioned a *very large amount* of our discounted paper to be in [an unredeemable] situation, and consequently the earnings of the Bank [are] largely reduced."[53]

Grigsby maintained his business relationship with the bank. In November, 1862, J. Adams Smith of the Farmers Bank related that Grigsby's notes would probably not be cashed anymore, as "we are not cashing checks on the office in Norfolk." The banker offered to act as Grigsby's purchasing agent for Confederate bonds, and the bank continued to deal with Grigsby until the end of the war. In its shortcomings the bank was typical of most southern banks. Paper circulation was steadily increasing without a corresponding rise in specie reserves.[54]

Grigsby's correspondence also reveals that the deep-seated confidence that filled the Confederacy in its early months now alternated between bravado and anxious concern. Cashier Sunstall, as early as November 1861, worried that the South "treated [its] enemies with too much *respect & forbearance; they should receive only what is due to despots & Tyrants & that speedily.*" Less than two weeks later, Sunstall noted that "Lincoln's devils appear to be making desperate efforts in all directions to accomplish something to make capital for his forthcoming message to his rump Congress." Conviction regarding the righteousness of the southern cause may have led to some optimism, but southern banks had not sealed themselves off from the North completely. An end to hostilities might bring about a return to normalcy. Even barring an extended war,

53. G. W. Brame to John Pettus, November 28, 1861, Governors' Series, MDAH; B. W. Frazier to William Campbell, October 24, 1861, Campbell Papers, DU; A. Sunstall to Hugh Grigsby, November 12, 1861, Hugh Blair Grigsby Papers, VHS.
54. J. Adams Smith to Hugh Grigsby, November 15, 1862, Grigsby Papers, VHS.

there were advantages to maintaining a northern correspondent bank. The Merchants Bank of South Carolina, which had featured William Godfrey and Charles DeSaussure on its account ledgers, did not cease its relationship with Gazaway Lamar's Bank of the Republic in New York until well into July, 1861. Lamar had supported Georgia even before the war, offering the Bank of the Republic's services to Georgia governors Howell Cobb and Herschel Johnson. He sold bonds for the state, and Johnson pronounced Lamar's bank the "agent of the State" in 1856. Three months after secession the Merchants Bank of South Carolina kept New York deposits of more than $100,000, although the Yankee depositor gradually reduced its deposits after hostilities actually commenced until less than $20,000 remained in July, 1861. It is not certain that the relationship ended then, either—only that the surviving ledger books ended at that date. Lamar used his bank as a front to finance the sale of muskets to South Carolina and later sold arms to Georgia. Just prior to the attack on Fort Sumter, Lamar oversaw the printing of the first Confederate treasury notes. After Sumter, northern agents prevented further printing, but Lamar destroyed the plates before they fell into the clutches of the police.[55]

Money stocks greatly increased with these infusions of notes. Eugene Lerner's estimates placed the 1864 level at eleven times that of 1861. One historian estimated the level of money stocks for five southern states from 1861 to 1864, noting that, despite the elevenfold increase, "the rise in the stocks of money was thus limited because banks sharply increased their reserve ratios as the war continued." Georgia banks, according to Lerner's estimate, held 47 percent reserves in June, 1862, and 69 percent a year later. The Bank of the Valley in Virginia increased its reserves from 41 percent in 1861 to 56, 57, and 66 percent, respectively, in 1862, 1863, and 1864. Substantial increases occurred in the reserves of the Bank of South Carolina and the Bank of Fayetteville.[56]

55. A Sunstall to Hugh Grigsby, November 12, 1861, Grigsby Papers, VHS; A. Sunstall to Hugh Grigsby, November 21, 1861, ibid.; Merchants Bank of South Carolina, Ledger Books, 1859–1865, various dates, 1860–1861, SC; Herschel Johnson to Gazaway Lamar, March 17, 30, 1854, Governors' Letterbook, 1847–1861, UG; Mathis, "Gazaway Bugg Lamar," pp. 303, 307, 310. Lamar also participated in New York's "free city" movement.

56. Eugene Lerner, "Money, Prices, and Wages in the Confederacy, 1861–1865," in Ralph Andreano (ed.), The Economic Impact of the Civil War (rev. ed.; Cambridge, Mass., 1967), 31–60 (quotations on 32–33). Lerner's data must be used with care. His monetary estimates came from only a few states and often from just a few banks in a state. For South

With a general increase in prices, the real value of money declined by one-third as of 1863, a drop linked to the drop in the South's real output. Banks themselves seemed to survive the hostilities, with little interruption of regular business, until federal troops appeared on their doorsteps. They paid dividends regularly, and few failed. As the war progressed, however, business declined. Fewer young men brought in deposits; fewer farmers needed exchange on New York. Optimism died slowly, however. In July, 1862, banker Theodore Honour, at the time president of a Charleston insurance company, expressed doubts about an early end to the war. He still thought "the yanks are getting pretty tired . . . , and we are beginning to feel some of [the] *blessings* [from Northern fatigue]." Dismissing hopes of aid from foreign sources as "bosh," Honour grimly recognized that the Confederacy "*must conquer a peace by the strong* [hand]. . . . And we will do it, but not in a day, or perhaps a year or two."[57]

Economic distress had also set in by late 1862. William Smedes, president of the Southern Rail Road Company, describing his prewar financial situation, thought he had "an independence. I see now my family likely to be left with nothing but an inheritance of debt." Conditions in Vicksburg had deteriortaed: "trade with New Orleans is at an end; personal security is regarded as nothing; & . . . land and negroes have no market value." No money was available because "good securities cannot be given." Wartime conditions prevented Smedes from even visiting some of his properties. Smedes of course related all the distressing news he could to banker William Johnson to beg a further extension on the repayment of his debt.[58]

The problems and insecurity caused by enemy troops forced Charleston and Camden bankers to exercise greater care in sending money. One banker sending interest on treasury notes to a customer had to place the money in an iron chest, assigned to the firm of Russell and Jones, "with directions . . . to deliver it to you should any accident occur to me." The

Carolina, he used only the Bank of the State, an institution subject to less market pressure than any other. Other problems exist as well. Tennessee, for example, was treated like Louisiana, even though Tennessee had unique specie trends, whereas Alabama banks were assumed to behave like Georgia banks.

57. Theodore Honour to Pat [?], July 28, 1862, Theodore Honour Papers, SC.

58. William Smedes to William Johnson, November 26, 1862, William Johnson Papers, SC.

banker feared that he might be detained. Local military authorities expected an attack that would cut off transportation into Charleston.[59]

One of the best accounts of the war's progress and its effect on banking
came from Theodore Honour, an employee of the Bank of Charleston,
whose correspondence to his wife, Beckie, described the daily pressures
on southern banks. Honour was stationed at James Island, South Carolina, while his wife remained in Secessionville. At first, Honour was
much like any other soldier, asking his wife and friends to help manage
his personal affairs. He told Beckie, for example, that he had intended to
invest in Confederate bonds, hoping to use the interest for home improvements and furnishings.[60]

As the war turned against the South, Honour devoted more of his attention to money matters on the home front, directing his wife to make
more frequent money transactions and having her purchase "8 per cent
Bonds" (probably Virginia bonds). He also expressed concern about the
33 percent tax on money, effective on April 1, 1864. Because of it,
he reasoned, he should purchase bonds: "it is better for me to pay now
130 dollars [each] for 8 per cents or even a little more."[61]

Early in 1864, Honour was directed to take a leave from the front and
to return to duty with the Columbia branch of the Bank of Charleston.
Upon arriving, he "was greeted very warmly by all the officers from the
President and Cashier down to the Porter, and at nine o'clock I took my
place in the Bank, and soon [it] felt like old times again." Honour "made
arrangements to eat at the Congress House" for $150 per month. By the
end of March, 1864, after a month's service, Honour related that "the
Bank has done so much for me that I feel sure . . . now that I have a
chance I shall devote all my energies to it." Honour earned his pay, telling his wife, "I have been very hard worked since you were here . . . ,
[am] at my desk in the bank untill very late at night."[62]

Banks had to help disperse Confederate note issues. When this process was scheduled to occur, the banks had to close temporarily to balance all the books before the influx of new notes. On March 17, 1864,

59. E. Jones to E. W. Bonney, April 1, 1863, William DeSaussure Papers, SC. For
Honour's investments, see Schweikart, "Banking in the American South," 656, and Theo-
dore Honour to wife, Beckie, February 4, 1864, Theodore Honour Papers, SC; Theodore
Honour to John DeSaussure, February 1864, *ibid.*

60. Theodore Honour to Beckie, February 22, 1864, *ibid.*

61. *Ibid.*, March 3, March 17, 1864.

62. *Ibid.*

Honour noted that the "bank will close up business on Saturday until the first of April," during which time "we are now, and will be untill for some time to come as busy as bees in a tin bucket." Employees had to open new ledgers "in preparation for the rush of business when the new bills are issued." Honour's deep affection for his wife led to frequent visits, a benefit of being away from his unit. Wartime disruptions in transportation caused him to adjust his schedule, and sometimes a simple weather disturbance made him late for work. Usually, John Cheesborough, the bank's cashier and acting officer, tried to accommodate the employees when they wanted to see their families on holidays. Not all absences were welcome at the bank. Once Honour walked in at eight o'clock to find "all hands hard at work and Cheesborough mad as piper because I had absented myself for the day." His return to the bank after two years in the army made Honour's burden "peculiarly heavy," and he admitted "prefer[ring] camp again to such constant hard work." Again, Honour caught himself: "I must not grumble as I am under great obligations to the Bank."[63]

Army personnel frequently moved into and out of civilian bank jobs. John Cheesborough, who was transferred out of a combat unit in April, 1861, while he was still cashier in Charleston, compalined that "the stores on King St. & elsewhere are all now shut up at 2 o'clock." Every "effective man from the age of 16 to 60," he reported, "was part of a military detachment. Cheesborough's record of the war paralleled that of his employee, Honour, except that Charleston appeared to be more abandoned than Columbia in the early parts of the war. On August 14, 1861, Cheesborough noted to his wife that "the stores are almost universally closed in the afternoons," and he found it "very dull here."[64]

He grew increasingly anxious about rumors of approaching Yankees but remained confident that "we are going to whip them." His anxiety turned to restlessness in August, 1862: "The monotony of my dull life is immeasured—every day is like its predecessor—very little to do and plenty of time to do it in." Unfortunately, he explained to his wife, "while I have very little to employ me, my presence for various reasons is almost indispensable, not only for the business of the bank directly,

63. *Ibid.*, March 17, 22, April 5, 1864. Also see letter to Beckie of April [n.d.] and April 14, 1864, *ibid.*
64. John Cheesborough to wife, Lou, August 7, 14, September 27, 1861, June 6, 20, 1862, John Cheesborough Papers, SHC, UNC.

but also for matters connected with public finances." His view of his own worth to the bank was not inflated. James Sass, president of the bank, told him in a letter that "my presence here is so important I must not think of returning home."[65]

The approach of enemy troops caused a constant drain on the Confederacy's manpower. By 1863, bled white, the army called for new conscriptions that threatened to take the last few officers in the bank, leaving Cheesborough to wonder "how are then we to get on?" Certainly death was a reality to any banker in the field. Egbert Jones, a director of the Northern Bank of Alabama, was killed in battle near the end of the war. Employees left behind worked to keep their banks in good shape throughout the conscriptions. Cheesborough, plagued by the personnel drain, spoke of going to Richmond in April, 1865, to meet with Memminger, possibly to rectify the conscription problem. Union soldiers in the general area, besides threatening the actual security of the bank, posed an imporant psychological problem. In late 1862 the entire financial community in South Carolina was alarmed by the appearance of counterfeit treasury notes, "which the Yankees or some other scoundrels have managed to get into circulation." All banks around Columbia had some. In 1862, Union soldiers captured and circulated unissued notes from the Northern Bank of Mississippi at Holly Springs. It was also becoming a real possibility that, in case of defeat, all Confederate money would have no value. Judge John Campbell of New Orleans warned his wife, "In the event of the restoration of Northern rule, Confederate money may be worthless. I proceed on that assumption." He advised her to spend Confederate money first.[66]

As Union troops neared, southern banks scrambled to protect their assets, especially specie reserves. In August, 1865, the assets of the Northern Bank of Alabama were sent to Augusta for safety. Just as real a danger as capture by the enemy was destruction in battle through deliberate or accidental means by enemy forces or even by Confederates trying to deny the Yankees an important supply depot. Confederate Gen-

---

65. John Cheesborough to wife, June 9, 25, August 22, 24, 1862, July 15, 27, 1863, *ibid.*

66. *Ibid.*, August 25, 1862, August 5, December 7, 1863, April 25, 1864; Minutebook of the Northern Bank of Alabama, August 9, 1865, SBA, ADAH; Bettersworth, *Confederate Mississippi*, 104; Elisabeth Doyle, "Greenbacks, Car Tickets, and the Pot of Gold," *Civil War History*, December, 1959, pp. 347–62, p. 355. Also see Thomas W. Knox, *Campfire and Cotton-Field* (Chicago, 1865), 231, 232.

eral Richard Ewell wreaked havoc on Richmond by deliberately torching a warehouse; the blaze soon spread to the major downtown area. J. L. Bacon wrote, "Every Bank in the city is of course consumed." Bacon tried to see his banker on main street "and was told by the guard placed over the vault by the military authorities that the vault had been broken into this morning, and various things taken from it," including a number of items of silver placed in the bank's keeping. Illness of both the president and cashier of the Exchange Bank exacerbated its already substantial fire-related losses.[67]

Conditions such as those in Richmond were experienced in Atlanta and Columbia. Reports of approaching Union troops sent bankers scurrying out of town with their specie. One cashier, A. Talley, wrote to Captain E. A. Williams, president of the Exchange Bank at Clarksville, Virginia, informing Williams that he had received a letter from J. E. Haskins, "advising me as a friend and as a *director . . .* to return to Clarksville and deposit the specie of the Bank in our vault." Talley agreed it was probably the "very best we can do in our present condition as a nation . . . vanquished" and asked for directions from Williams, or he would "act accordingly."[68]

Wartime conditions called for increasingly drastic measures directed toward saving the assets of the banks. Specie from Richmond banks, sent in care of bank officials to Washington, Georgia, for a final distribution of Confederate funds, was captured by Federals, who "decided to help themselves to it as a reward for their faithful service." Of the money that was recovered, at least one bank in Richmond used the funds to reopen. On another occasion, David Kennedy, of the Northern Bank of Tennessee, loaded the bank's specie and bills into saddlebags at the approach of Federal troops and rode cross-country by horse to the Mississippi. There he boarded a steamer to New Orleans, and from there he sent the assets to England. At the end of the war he retrieved the money and used it to reopen the bank.[69]

Stories such as Kennedy's have become the legends revered by modern-day banks that survived the war. Burke and Herbert, in Alex-

67. Minutebook of the Northern Bank of Alabama, August 9, 1865, SBA, ADAH; John Bacon to John Stewart, April 4, 1865, VHS.

68. A Talley to E. A. Williams, 1865, Edwin A. Williams Papers, VHS.

69. Morgan, *Graybacks and Gold*, 122–23; Lewis Shepherd, "The Confederate Treasure Train," *Confederate Veteran*, June, 1917, pp. 257–58; *Northern Bank of Tennessee* (N.p., 1954), pamphlet in TLA.

andria, Virginia, saved its money with a similarly desperate and clever plan. One of the partners, Arthur Herbert, was serving in the Seventeenth Virginia Regiment, but the other, John Burke, hearing of the Union forces' entry into the city, took his bank's specie to his house and hid it under his wife's clothes. Soldiers searched the house but declined to dig through Mrs. Burke's clothes. Burke contacted Sarah Tracey, who, on her routine run from Alexandria to Washington, D.C., delivered the money to Washington bankers Corcoran and Riggs. Likewise, Samuel Smith, cashier of the Exchange Bank of Richmond, transported securities to temporary safety in an oak chest.[70]

New Orleans bankers especially scurried to ship specie out of the city. Benjamin Butler, whose invading forces entered the Crescent City in May, 1862, promised protection to any banker who obtained specie and hoped to encourage local bankers to actively pursue ways of retrieving gold and silver by arguing that a good specie backing would make the notes of local banks sounder. Because most of the gold and silver had been sent out by that time, New Orleans banks issued unbacked notes.

Butler had allowed continued circulation of Confederate money after he seized the city, but on May 27, 1862, he ordered all Confederate money suppressed. Then local banking issues fell short of demand, and shinplasters, streetcar tickets, and even labels from olive oil bottles passed as currency. Counterfeiters leaped at the opportunity to ply their trade. Butler also prevented banks from passing their losses on to customers when they had ordered depositors to withdraw their deposits before the twenty-seventh. This proved popular because it left banks holding a great deal of Confederate money. Butler's greatest coup came when he dispatched an armed detail to the Dutch consulate to confiscate $800,000 in silver placed in the care of consul Amedie Conturie by the Citizens Bank of New Orleans.[71]

Overall, Butler stood for that which bankers in any occupied southern city feared—arbitrary rule by a northerner bent on imposing Yankee capital and industry. Northern speculators descended on New Orleans in droves. Butler's replacement, General N. P. Banks, hardly endeared

70. "A Century of Banking," *Commonwealth*, February, 1953, pp. 20–21; Richard Smith, *Recollections of Banks and Bankers Since 1865* (Richmond, Va., n.d.), 1.

71. Gerald Capers, *Occupied City: New Orleans Under the Federals, 1862–1865* (Lexington, Ky., 1965), 85–86, 101; Doyle, "Greenbacks, Car Tickets," 347–62. Said one report, "The banks confine their operations to the payment of depositors' checks and the renewal of maturing obligations" (*New Orleans Daily True Delta*, May 4, 1862).

himself to the local citizens; he allowed the local merchants who had taken an oath of loyalty to receive goods and to drive competitors out of business. Such ethics were also applied to financial institutions. General Banks ordered greenbacks to be accepted without depreciation. Both the Louisiana State Bank and the Bank of Louisiana were placed in receivership when they resisted and continued to discount U.S. Treasury notes.[72]

Although Butler had taken Confederate funds deposited in the banks and had ordered the release of impounded Union funds, he had worked to secure bankers' assistance in managing the economic system and some of his own personal investments. General Banks, on the other hand, assumed an adversary stance from the start and tried to use the discounting of notes to liquidate the banks. His specially created commission was ostensibly to search out specie; it was also to investigate assets and liabilities of all local banks and insurance, gas, and railroad companies, to look into the amount of stock held by the directors, and to investigate the backgrounds of the stockholders as well as the loyalty of the stockholders and officers to the government of the United States.[73]

State auditor A. P. Dostie, at Banks's urging, found some statutes of banking law that all New Orleans banks had violated. He returned the report to Banks with a request that the general not interfere with liquidation proceedings, a request with which Banks happily complied. Local financial institutions united to resist, and they engaged in prolonged court battles when proceedings were actually begun. All problems for the New Orleans financial institutions virtually ceased overnight with Banks's departure. A period filled with impending disaster thus ended on a note of optimism.[74]

Throughout the rest of the Confederacy, the military picture deteriorated. The economic outlook was even worse. Banks lucky enough to escape Yankee invasion felt increasing pressure from their own government for monetary support of the war. An 1863 tax of 8 percent was

72. Doyle, "Greenbacks, Car Tickets," 357.
73. *Ibid.*, 359; Benjamin Butler to New Orleans Canal and Banking Company, June 18, 1862, in the *Private and Official Correspondence of General Benjamin F. Butler During the Period of the Civil War* (Norwood, Mass., 1917), I, 613; Benjamin Butler to Edwin M. Stanton, December 4, 1862, in *War of the Rebellion: A Compilation of the Official Records of the Union and Confederate Armies* (130 vols.; Washington, D.C., 1886, 1890–1901), Ser. I, Vol. XV, p. 603.
74. *New Orleans Tribune*, December 15, 1864.

placed on all money and currency on hand or on deposit, and a 1 percent tax on capital held in any fashion that was not employed cut into the banks' slim profits. In 1864 this heavy tax was reenacted, along with additional provisions. Still another tax, on business profits, accompanied these two. On top of all of these taxes, licensing taxes on banking itself (of varying rates), a 5 to 15 percent income tax, and a 5 percent tax on bank-owned property itself also went into effect. Any banker who sat down to compute the combined effects of taxflation would have been staggered to see that his $5.09 million in assets, after inflation and taxes, came to $1.82 million. Confederate taxes wreaked still other miseries on the banker. Stocks, held by the bank for the purpose of making a profit, were taxed on their earnings. In the case of the hypothetical bank, if the stock earned 8 percent, then the earnings tax would have exceeded $1,900. Barely 36 percent of a typical bank's assets (*not* counting its Confederate notes) would survive the Confederate taxflation by 1864.[75]

Desperation set in during the closing months of the war. Government officials argued for more revenue. The legislature passed a bill that added even more taxes. Duties on specie and foreign credits jumped to 20 percent, all other interest was taxed at 5 percent, new rates on profits were enacted, the property tax rate increased by 3 percent (but on the level of *1860 valuation*), and, as the utter hopelessness of the cause became apparent, the Confederate Congress increased the tax on specie and foreign money to 25 percent. The real tax burden imposed on banks was somewhat greater than has been suggested because it included state and local taxes in addition to those levied by the Confederacy.

The absence of a specie-backed currency quickly encouraged agitation for a cotton-based currency. In May and August of 1861, a one-million-dollar loan allowed planters to receive twenty-year, 8 percent bonds in return for produce, especially cotton. "King Cotton," however, was at best a poor substitute for specie—even in normal southern commerce—and at worst it was as inflation prone as the paper it sought to back. Europeans could purchase cotton directly on the open market, drastically driving Confederate bond prices down. Unable to buy European goods using bonds, the Confederacy turned to confiscation. Commandeering officials paid for goods but at prices one-half to one-tenth the market

75. Schwab, *Confederate States of America*, 291–300; Lerner, "Wages and Prices in the Confederacy," 41. The hypothetical bank chosen was the Bank of Mobile, November 27, 1847, balance sheet given in Brantley, *Banking in Alabama*, II, 371–72.

value, forcing individuals to hide those very goods in secure places. Meanwhile, where cotton was defined as money, or was used as a backing for it, expanding cotton production actually multiplied the inflation rate. The more cotton was available, the more individuals used it as a "specie reserve" to circulate more of their notes. Some individual states had already authorized their own cotton currency.[76]

Cotton increasingly became its own medium of exchange—its own specie—often used as a reserve for note issues. Lerner seriously underestimated the money stock, and the velocity of this "money" was much faster than he suspected. Thus despite mammoth efforts by the southern banks to increase their reserve ratios, they could not hope to affect the money stock greatly; rather banks, by having specie, made bank notes dearer, and these notes were therefore spent less freely than any of the other types of money. The taxflation burden constituted a form of impressment exacted on southern capital. An interesting intertwining of banks and Confederate finances also involved the attempts of the South to sell in Europe bonds not related to cotton. Many Europeans, especially in the financial community, recalled that Jefferson Davis, while a senator from Mississippi, had actively urged the state to repudiate its bonds issued on behalf of the Union and Planters banks. Not a few Europeans had lost money in that venture, as they had under similar conditions in Florida. Although Louisiana paid its foreign bondholders during the same depression, it did so reluctantly and in such a way that many of them received less than full payment. Mississippi had the worst reputation of all. An 1859 investor's guide warned, "The name of Mississippi is a byword and reproach upon American state credit." Certainly Florida and other states trailed not far behind in terms of investor trust. Northern agents relished reprinting the speeches of Mississippians and Floridians on these matters and distributed them whenever possible to British businessmen. Mississippi's problems in this regard grew to such proportions that some individuals attempted to have the state make token payments on the twenty-five-year-old Union and Planters bond debts. Governor Pettus rejected these overtures, and no Mississippi bonds at all could be negotiated abroad.[77]

George Williams curtailed much of his banking business during the

76. Lebergott, "Why the South Lost," 59–73; Jackson *Mississippian*, April 9, 15, 1863.
77. Lebergott, "Why the South Lost," 68 n. 41; Coker, "Cotton and Faith," 202; G. Holland to John Pettus, January 20, 1862, Governors' Series, Box 48, MDAH.

war but continued his mercantile operations. Developing a fine prewar reputation in Liverpool and London, he imported goods needed in the Confederacy during the war from the North via England. He and his partners occasionally engaged in outright blockade running. Although he and most other businessmen received criticism for profiteering, he purchased fifty thousand dollars' worth of clothing for Confederate soldiers, for which he paid gold and was reimbursed in Confederate notes. Early in the war Williams bought $100,000 worth of stock in the Bank of South Carolina in an attempt to become its president. A controversy over note issue kept him from attaining the presidency. He therefore turned his attention to his original George W. Williams and Company, a private banking firm. On June 1, 1865, he formally opened a bank, which continued operations into the late 1870s. Between the time of his failure to attain the presidency of the Bank of South Carolina and the opening of his "Banking House," Williams spent time in Washington trying to arrange the establishment of a national bank in Charleston as part of the National Banking Act. This merchant-banker, who had lost thousands supplying clothes to Confederate soldiers, in 1864 was rationalizing a transaction whereby he would have had to place one-third of the proposed bank's capital in U.S. bonds! He attended a New York meeting to arrange final details of the chartering. When the bank received its national charter in 1865, Williams was a director.

Pressures to deal with the victorious Union government eventually required all southerners to acknowledge defeat, although Williams might be blamed for throwing in the towel more than a year early. As soon as an area was conquered, the U.S. Treasury moved in to demand reports from the surviving banks. When this reality set in, other occupied areas, such as Tennessee, learned that greenbacks constituted just another form of currency to exchange, with luck at a profitable rate, although this situation soon changed with passage of the National Bank Act. Campbell's Bank of Middle Tennessee had survived the war with thirty-two thousand dollars more in resources than in liabilities. In late 1863, Saul Mottley, cashier of the Bank of Middle Tennessee, expressed a basic disagreement between the two men over bank policy. Mottley wanted to try to keep the value of the bank's paper up, whereas Campbell wanted to see it depreciate to a 50 percent discount, mainly because he did not wish to lose specie. Mottley proposed another plan: "selling the gold for [greenbacks] and then selling the greenbacks for Planters and Union Bank [notes] which we can readily take our paper up with." Mottley urged Campbell to go to Nashville and sell gold at "the best premium you can in Greenbacks." Mottley wondered whether Campbell objected to U.S. securities because of his loyalty to the Confederacy. Campbell replied that he "never desired the establishment of the Southern Confederacy" and could not see what that had to do with objecting to U.S. securities on economic grounds.[78]

Campbell, and perhaps Williams, showed the confusion and divided loyalties that bankers in all areas of the South must have felt but especially in places occupied well before Appomattox. Responsibility to the institution often conflicted with loyalty to the cause. After the Union forces arrived, further resistance led to greater economic hardships on friends, neighbors, and local customers. Many of them sought to hang on. The Northern Bank of Alabama, for example, planned its liquidation as early as October, 1865, but persevered until December 26, 1883. It sold its building and physical assets to the National Bank of Huntsville. In April, 1866, Theodore Say, the cashier at the Northern Bank, took a job with the institution that had purchased his old bank. For most bankers, the reality of Union victory dawned, and to allow the Yankees to dominate the postwar banking business seemed too great a concession. As a result, quite often southern bankers continued the war on a different plane, saving their resources for battle in the marketplace at a later date. After Lee's surrender, Confederate defeat was irrefutable, but given the contradictory strains under which the bankers and the banking system had been placed, their efforts for the cause were above the call of duty.[79]

The outbreak of hostilities in 1861 ended a particularly promising period for southern banks. When the war thoroughly destroyed southern finances, bankers were among the most resilient survivors. A few managed to keep their banks in operation through the entirety of the war, although the number that recovered sufficiently to do a thriving busi-

78. Salmon Chase to cashier of the Bank of Middle Tennessee, September 18, 1863; Statement of Bank of Middle Tennessee, January 1865 (there is reason to believe that this date's last digit, obscured as it is, should be a 3); Saul Mottley to Governor W. B. Campbell, August 3, 8, 1863, all in Campbell Papers, DU.

79. Minutebook, Northern Bank of Alabama, October 30, 1865, SBA, ADAH. Also see February 19, 1862.

ness into the 1870s was limited. The more successful institutions surviving 1865 (ones that had entered the wartime period as bona fide banks and not as other businesses) included the Bank of Charleston and the Southwestern Rail Road Bank in South Carolina; the Farmers Bank of Virginia (which became Planters National Bank), the Exchange Bank of Virginia (which became part of First National Bank of Alexandria), the Bank of the Old Dominion (which became part of Citizens National Bank), and the Farmers Bank of Alexandria, whose directors formed the First National Bank of Alexandria in 1864; the Banks of Northern and Middle Tennessee; and, in Georgia, the Georgia Railroad and Banking Company and the Central Railroad and Banking Company. George Williams, Burke and Herbert, Thomas Branch, and a half-dozen Arkansas private bankers used the postwar situation to move from private banking to chartered banking, although they encountered a newer banking system than the one of private note issue in which they had competed in the antebellum years. No banks survived in Arkansas, Mississippi, Florida, or North Carolina (although ten private bankers were listed in *Bankers Magazine* as being in business in October, 1865, in North Carolina). At least five private bankers, including Webb, had worked in the large North Carolina chartered banks. Only a few banks held on in Louisiana and Tennessee. The national bank system that ensued after 1864, when it finally moved into the occupied South, drove a number of bankers out of formal banking and into private lending. Southern bankers "went underground," diversified into mercantile trade, or, if pressed, went west.[80]

Certainly, though, the South had been hit hard. Currency declined by more than thirty-five million dollars in volume. Banking capital dropped from sixty-one million dollars in 1860 to seventeen million dollars in 1870. Although much banking capital had only deserted chartered institutions for private banks, the losses in assets held by banks in the form of Confederate securities were still enormous. Any chance

---

80. Ransom and Sutch, *One Kind of Freedom*, 109; H. H. Mitchell, "A Forgotten Institution: Private Banks in North Carolina," *North Carolina Historical Review*, (1958), 34–49. Ransom and Sutch erred in the number of banks that survived. They found only one—"George Williams"—that survived the war in South Carolina. Several South Carolina banks remained in business for a few years, and if we allow for reorganizations, the number doing business in 1870 was between three and eight of the original chartered banks. Ransom and Sutch also completely ignored private bankers.

of the South's recovery depended on some measure of capital inflow after the war. Instead, the North's newly enacted banking system contracted the amount of money available to it.[81]

Radical Republicans, to finance the war, created the national banking system and after the war expanded it to the South. It soon provided a convenient means for subjugating the prostrate Confederacy. Ironically, the Radicals' reconstruction efforts were aimed at the freedmen, who stood to lose most of all from the new system. Under the National Bank Act, many individuals could not aspire to acquire specie reserves and capital to become bankers—which might have been possible under the old banking system—and issue notes to compete in banking directly. The resulting restriction in credit availability worked to the disadvantage of blacks, nor was it likely that the greatly restricted credit market helped them. Although few southern bankers would have been likely to lend to freedmen at the same rates available to whites initially, under a system of private note issue and circulation, opportunities for freedmen to establish records for trustworthiness and credit would soon have created incentive for white southern bankers to break ranks. Continuing the system of private note issue would have been even more advantageous to the northern carpetbaggers trying to help the freedmen or even make a profit, because they would have extended loans when white southerners would not. This was not the case with a system of national banks because they were fewer in number (a result of capitalization requirements) than the private banks.

Richard Sylla, Roger Ransom, and Richard Sutch have all argued that the restrictions of the National Banking Act curbed entry into southern banking and that national banks lacked important mortgage lending powers. Capitalization restrictions, as well as application requirements (enforced more stringently on former Confederates), made entry difficult. An imposed monopoly, arising not from the paranoia of southern Jacksonians but from the Radicals' programs, worked to the detriment of the South.[82]

---

81. James Sellers, "The Economic Incidence of the Civil War in the South," in *The Economic Impact of the Civil War*, 98–108.

82. Richard Sylla, "Federal Policy, Banking Market Structure, and Capital Mobilization in the United States, 1863–1913," *Journal of Economic History*, December, 1969, pp. 659–65; Ransom and Sutch, *One Kind of Freedom*, 107–13.

Ultimately the similarities between the Whig/Republican and Jacksonian/Democrat programs returned to haunt the South. Emancipation, the most beneficial and significant of the Republican accomplishments, lost much of its immediate impact when Republicans attempted to crush or control the southern economic institutions. Local merchant-bankers quickly found market opportunities to lend within the new framework, just as freedmen sought out opportunities to borrow and engage in sharecropping. Southern Democrats gave their full efforts to attempts to disfranchise blacks politically, suspicious that the freedmen now had the potential to achieve economic equality but thanks to their Jacksonian influences were unaware that Republicans made economic equality more difficult. The financial system of the South was the first segment of the economy to experience the dangers associated with property guarantees lost when the slaves were freed through violence rather than through legal process. If freedmen achieved only "one kind of freedom," the reason was that they were being reenslaved by a centralizing economic ideology, not by the market conditions of the South. Only the private bankers in the South, acting solely for personal gain, prevented such a reenslavement.

Where any distinction or difference was viewed by the Jacksonians as an impediment to equality, banks stood as the enemy in rank with all other healthy manifestations of capitalism and, ultimately, with the very categories of sex, race, age, and talent. Thus the affinity of Fitzhugh for northern abolitionists and the similarities between hard-money Jacksonians and greenback Republicans is less mysterious than is generally thought.

Contributing in the war what they had, and often more than duty required, the banks of the South united in a final sacrifice to the Confederacy and the Jacksonian ideal. More important, the prewar accomplishments of southern banking deserve to be interpreted on the basis of the industry's performance since the Jacksonian era. Judged by that standard, the bankers of the antebellum South recovered from a costly and deep-seated threat from the Jacksonians. Southern financiers did not generate an industrial revolution in the South, nor did they generally intend to do so. Working in an environment that viewed slavery as necessary for equality among whites, and as one that viewed business opportunities in corporate form as potential engines of oppression, southern banks struggled to bring to fruition a commercialization of southern society. Unquestionably, some accommodations to planters were necessary. Yet in an age dominated by the central question of American history, besieged at different times by fellow southerners and by federal occupation forces, trying to respond to market incentives and still look toward longer-range goals, the southern banker left a credible banking record and at times an admirable one.

APPENDIX

SOUTHERN STATES

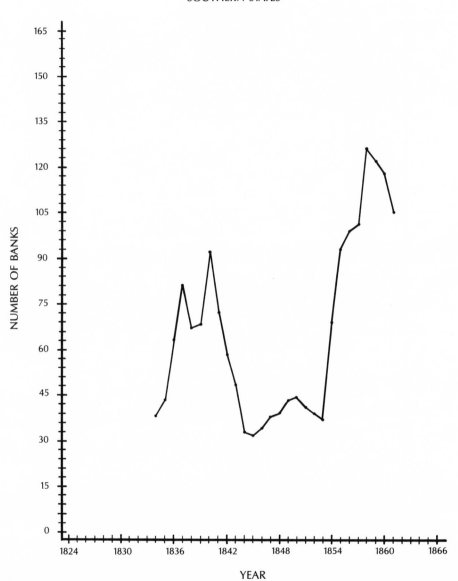

SOUTHERN STATES
CIRCULATIONS

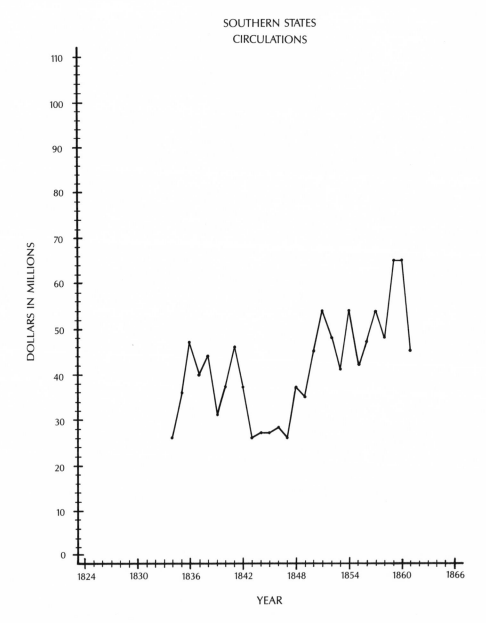

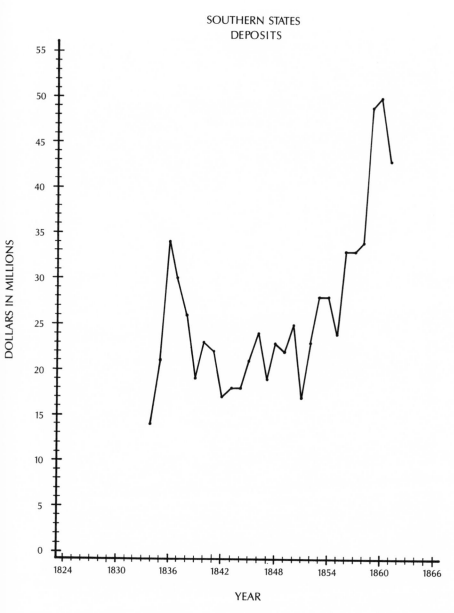

SOUTHERN STATES
DEPOSITS

DOLLARS IN MILLIONS

YEAR

SOUTHERN STATES
LOANS

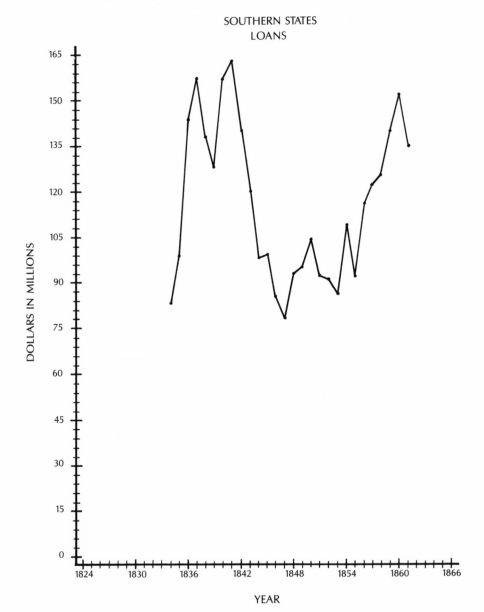

DOLLARS IN MILLIONS

YEAR

BIBLIOGRAPHY

ARCHIVAL MATERIALS

Alabama Department of Archives and History, Montgomery
  C. C. Clay Papers.
  James Dellet Papers.
  J. F. Jackson Papers.
  Perry Collection.
  State Bank of Alabama Collection.
Arkansas History Commission, Little Rock
  Eno Collection.
  Fayetteville Branch of the State Bank. Letterbook, 1840–46.
  Albert Pike Collection.
Atlanta Historical Society, Atlanta, Ga.
  Hargrett Collection.
Duke University, Durham, N.C.
  David Campbell Papers.
  George Houston Papers.
  Joseph Jones Papers.
  Duncan McLaurin Papers.
  Adelaide Meares Collection.
Leon County, Tallahassee, Fla.
  Deed Records.
Library of Congress, Washington, D.C.
  Baring Brothers Manuscripts.
  Nicholas Biddle Papers.

J. F. H. Claiborne Papers.
Franklin H. Elmore Papers.
J. H. Hammond Papers.
James Kent Papers.
Riggs Family Papers.
William C. Rives Papers.
Martin Van Buren Papers.
Levi Woodbury Papers.
Louisiana State University, Baton Rouge, Hill Memorial Library
　City Bank Records. Canal Bank Collection. Consolidated Association of the
　　Planters of Louisiana. Directors' Minutes.
　City Bank Records. Canal Bank Collection. Louisiana State Bank, St. Martin-
　　ville Branch. Letterbook.
　Robert Palfry Papers.
　Alexander Porter Letter.
National Archives, Washington, D.C.
　Correspondence of the Provost Marshal General.
　Letters Received by the Secretary of the [Confederate] Treasury.
　Records of the War Department, Department of the Gulf.
South Caroliniana Library, Columbia, S.C.
　Bank of Camden Manuscripts and Ledger Book.
　William G. DeSaussure Papers.
　Theodore Honour Papers.
　William Johnson Papers.
　William Johnston Papers.
　Merchants Bank of South Carolina Letter Books.
　Yates Snowden Collection.
Tennessee Library and Archives, Nashville
　Bank of Tennessee Letterbook, 1839–41.
　Bank of Tennessee Papers.
Tulane University, New Orleans, Howard-Tilton Memorial Library
　Citizens Bank. Directors' Minutes.
　Citizens Bank. Minutebook.
　De la Vergne Family Papers.
　Smith, Hubbard, and Company Correspondence.
University of Florida, Gainesville, P. K. Yonge Library
　Miscellaneous Manuscripts Collection. Box 15. George Gibbs to James Aiken,
　　March 19, 1855.
University of Georgia Library, Athens
　Circular Letter to the Banks of Georgia. February 8, 1829.
　Governor's Letterbooks.

Nathan Munroe Papers.
Rhind-Stokes Collection.
University of North Carolina Library, Chapel Hill, Southern Historical Collection
    Atwood and Company Papers.
    Bank of North Carolina (Windsor Branch) Account and Letter Book.
    Duncan Cameron Papers.
    Farish Carter Papers.
    John Cheesborough Papers.
    D. O. Davis Papers.
    Dromgoole Papers.
    William Gaston Papers.
    Hardee and Zacharie Papers.
    Mitchell King Papers.
    Edwin L'Engle Papers.
    Andrew McCollam Papers.
    James McDowell Papers.
    Charles Mills Letter Books.
    Planters Bank Papers.
    James Quarles Collection.
    Lewis Thompson Papers.
    James Webb Papers.
Virginia Historical Society, Richmond
    Branch and Co. Collection.
    Claiborne W. Gooch Papers.
    Hugh Blair Grigsby Papers.
    Lee Family Papers.
    John Stewart Letter.
    Edwin A. Williams Papers.
Virginia State Library
    Ball Family Papers

GOVERNMENT DOCUMENTS

Alabama. *Biennial Report of the Commissioners and Trustee to Settle the Affairs of the State Bank and Branches, to the General Assembly.* Montgomery, 1857.
————. *House Journal.* 1837, 1839–40, 1849–50.
————. *House Journal.* 1820–36.
Louisiana. *Journal of the Convention to Form a New Constitution for the State of Louisiana.* New Orleans, 1852.
————. *Minority Report of the Senate Committee on the General System of Free Banking in the State of Louisiana.* 1854.

————. *Report of the Committee of Investigation (Selected from the Stock-holders) Appointed by the Direction of the Citizens' Bank of Louisiana.* N.d.

————. *Report of the Joint Committee on Banks and Banking.* 1857.

————. *Report of the Majority and Minority of the Financial Commission of New Orleans . . .* New Orleans, 1864.

————. *Senate Journal.* 1828.

Mississippi. *House Journal.* 1830.

————. *Laws.* 1826–38.

————. *Senate Journal.* 1830–38.

North Carolina. *Acts Incorporating the State Bank of North Carolina and the By-Laws.* N.d.

————. *Charter and By-Laws of the Bank of North Carolina.* N.d.

————. *Exposition of the Acts Amending the Charter and Conferring Banking Privileges on the Louisville, Cincinnati and Charleston Railroad Company, by C. G. Memminger, Commissioner from South Carolina. Letter of C. G. Memminger, Esq., Special Agent from South Carolina, to the Governor of North Carolina.* Raleigh, N.C., 1836.

————. *Laws of North Carolina.* 1804–55.

————. *Legislative Documents of the House of Representatives of North Carolina.* 1831–61.

South Carolina. *The Bank Case: A Report of the Proceedings in the Cases of the Bank of South Carolina and the Bank of Charleston.* Charleston, S.C., 1844.

————. *Charter, Bank of Charleston.* 1834.

————. *A Compilation of All the Acts, Resolutions, Reports, and Other Documents in Relation to the Bank of the State of South Carolina.* Columbia, S.C., 1848.

————. *House Executive Document No. 226.* N.d.

————. *House Journal.* 1851–52.

————. "Message of Governor J. H. Hammond." *Senate Journal.* 1843.

————. *Senate Journal.* 1843–57.

————. *South Carolina Reports and Resolutions.* 1838–59.

————. *South Carolina Statutes.* N.d.

Tennessee. *House Journal.* 1837–38.

————. *Public Acts, 1851–52.*

————. *Report of the President of Bank of Tennessee to the House of Representatives, October 5, 1843.* Nashville, 1843.

U.S. *Annual Report of the Secretary of the Treasury.* House Executive Doc. 2, 36th Cong., 2d Sess., 1860.

U.S. Congress. House. *Condition of State Banks,* Doc. 79, 26th Cong., 1st Sess., 1840.

————. *House Executive Document*, No. 78, 23d Cong., 2d Sess.

————. *House Executive Document*, No. 65, 24th Cong., 2d Sess.

————. *House Executive Document*, No. 30, 25th Cong., 1st Sess.

————. *House Executive Document*, No. 79, 25th Cong., 1st Sess.

————. *Report of the Commissioners Appointed by the Governor to Examine the Southern Bank of Alabama*. Montgomery, 1851.

————. *Senate Journal*. 1826, 1838, 1839–40, 1841–41, 1849–50.

Arkansas. *Acts Passed at the Tenth Session of the General Assembly of Arkansas, 1854–1855*. Little Rock, Ark., 1855.

————. *Acts Passed at the Twelfth Session of the General Assembly of Arkansas, 1858–1859*. Little Rock, Ark., 1859.

————. *Journals of the Special Session of the General Assembly of the State of Arkansas*. 1838.

————. *Report of Gordon N. Peay, As Receiver in Chancery of Real Estate Bank, 1st October 1856*. Little Rock, Ark., 1856.

Florida. *Journal of the Legislative Council of Florida*. 1838–65.

Georgia. *Acts of the General Assembly of Georgia*. 1819–66.

————. *Journal of the Senate of the General Assembly of Georgia*. 1832.

————. *House Journal*. 1832–60.

————. *Report of the Commissioners Appointed to Investigate the State Finances*. Milledgeville, Ga., 1839.

Louisiana. *Acts of Louisiana*. 1819–59.

————. *Acts of the Territory of New Orleans*. N.d.

————. *Documents and Letters Relative to the Investigation on Banks by the Joint Committee of the Senate and House of Representatives of the State of Louisiana*. 14th Legis., 2d Sess., 1840.

————. *House Executive Document*, No. 471, 25th Cong., 2d Sess.

————. *House Executive Document*, No. 156, 25th Cong., 3d Sess.

————. *House Executive Document*, No. 227, 25th Cong., 3d Sess.

————. *House Executive Document*, No. 49, 26th Cong., 1st Sess.

————. *House Executive Document*, No. 172, 26th Cong., 1st Sess.

————. *House Executive Document*, No. 111, 26th Cong., 2d Sess.

————. *House Executive Document*, No. 172, 26th Cong., 2d Sess.

————. *House Executive Document*, No. 226, 26th Cong., 2d Sess.

————. *House Executive Document*, No. 226, 29th Cong., 1st Sess.

————. *House Executive Document*, No. 68, 31st Cong., 1st Sess.

————. *House Executive Document*, No. 66, 32d Cong., 2d Sess.

————. *House Executive Document*, No. 102, 33d Cong., 1st Sess.

————. *House Executive Document*, No. 82, 33d Cong., 2d Sess.

————. *House Executive Document*, No. 102, 34th Cong., 2d Sess.

————. *House Executive Document*, No. 87, 34th Cong., 3d Sess.

————. *House Executive Document*, No. 107, 35th Cong., 1st Sess.

————. *House Executive Document*, No. 112, 35th Cong., 2d Sess.

————. *House Executive Document*, No. 49, 36th Cong., 2d Sess.

————. *House Executive Document*, No. 77, 36th Cong., 2d Sess.

————. *House Executive Document*, No. 25, 37th Cong., 3d Sess.

————. *House Executive Document*, No. 20, 38th Cong., 1st Sess.

U.S. Congress. *Register of Debates*. Washington, D.C. 1824–37.

U.S. *Congressional Globe*. 1833–73.

U.S. Department of Commerce. Bureau of the Census. *Compendium of the Sixth Census of the United States*. Washington, D.C., 1840.

————. *Compendium of the Tenth Census of the United States*. Washington, D.C., 1880.

U.S. *Legislative Proceedings*. 1841.

U.S. *Legislative Documents, 1862–1863*. Doc. No. 20.

U.S. *Legislative Documents, 1869–1870*. Doc. No. 19.

U.S. *Letters from the Assistant Treasurers*. Philadelphia, 1857.

U.S. *Reports and Resolutions*. 1838, 1839, 1855, 1857, 1858, 1859.

U.S. Senate. *Executive Document*, No. 38, 52d Cong., 2d Sess. 1893.

————. *Senate Documents*, 24th Cong., 1st Sess. Secretary of the Treasury Reports, 1835–36.

U.S. *War of the Rebellion: A Compilation of the Official Records of the War of the Union and Confederate Armies*. Washington, D.C., 1886, 1890–1901.

Virginia. *Acts of the General Assembly of Virginia*. 1836–57.

————. *Auditor's Report of the State of Virginia*. 1849.

————. *Code of Virginia*. 1860.

————. *House Documents*. 1841–42.

————. *House Journal*. 1855–56.

————. *Laws*. 1851.

NEWSPAPERS AND MAGAZINES

Alabama Republican. December 26, 1823.

Arkansas *Advocate*. October 21, 1836.

Atlanta *Constitutionalist*. October 24, December 1, 27, 31, 1857.

Augusta *Chronicle and Sentinel*. 1840–49.

Augusta *Daily Constitutionalist*. 1858–59.

Bankers' Magazine. 1859.

Batesville *North Arkansas*. September 6, 1843.

Camden *Southern Chronicle*. April 23, 1823.

Charleston *Courier*. 1836–65.

Charleston Mercury. 1838–45.
Charleston Patriot. May 17, 1837.
Charleston *Times.* February 27, 1813.
Darien Gazette. September 7, 1824.
De Bow's Review. 1851–54.
Elizabeth City *Democratic Pioneer.* September 29, 1857.
Fayetteville (N.C.) *Carolina Observer.* July 26, 1837.
Fayetteville (N.C.) *Journal.* 1829–36.
Fayetteville (N.C.) *Witness.* May 1, 1841.
Georgia *Messenger.* 1833–46.
Greenville (S.C.) *Mountaineer.* 1839–41.
Greenville (S.C.) *Patriot.* November 27, 28, 30, 1837.
Greenville (S.C.) *Southern Enterprise.* March 1, 1860.
Harper's Weekly. August 22, 1857.
Hunt's Merchant Magazine. 1840–60.
Huntsville (Ala.) *Southern Advocate.* 1852–54.
Jackson *Mississippian.* 1838–63.
Jackson *Southron.* 1841–43.
Jackson *Statesman.* July 22, August 5, 13, 19, October 21, 1843.
Little Rock *Arkansas Banner.* 1844–45.
Little Rock *Arkansas Gazette.* 1836–45.
Little Rock *Arkansas State Gazette.* February 17, 1841.
Little Rock *Arkansas Whig.* February 8, 1855.
Little Rock *Times and Advocate.* August 22, 1942.
Little Rock *True Democrat.* February 23, 1859.
Memphis *Daily Appeal.* 1847–48.
Milledgeville *Federal Union.* 1857–60.
Mobile *Commercial Register.* 1838–39.
Mobile *Morning Advertiser.* March 8, 1842.
Mobile *Register.* 1843–50.
Montgomery *Daily Alabama Journal.* November 18, 20, 1853.
Montgomery *Flag and Advertiser.* 1847–57.
Nashville *Union.* January 6, 1840.
Natchez (Miss.) *Statesman and Gazette.* January 2, 1830.
New Orleans *Bee.* November 21, 24, 1836.
New Orleans *Daily True Delta.* May 4, 1862.
New Orleans *Delta.* May 4, 1862.
New Orleans *Tribune.* December 15, 1864.
New York *Herald.* November 2, 1857.
New York *Journal of Commerce.* August 29, 1838.
Niles National Register. 1831–40.

North Carolina Journal. 1834–37.

Philadelphia *Financial Register*. July 11, 18, October 10, 24, 1838.

Raleigh *North Carolina Standard*. 1857–61.

Raleigh *Register*. 1837–38.

Richmond *Enquirer*. 1837–41.

Richmond *Whig*. 1837–51.

Russell's Magazine. August, 1858.

Savannah *Georgian*. May 3, 1834.

Savannah *Morning News*. December 25, 1857.

Savannah *News*. 1857.

Savannah *Republican*. October 22, 1857.

Southern Banner. February 10, 1843.

Southern Recorder. August 8, September 26, 1829.

Tarboro (N.C.) *Southerner*. July 11, 1857.

Tuscaloosa *Flag of the Union*. 1838–40.

Tuscaloosa *Monitor*. 1842–45.

Van Buren *Arkansas Intelligencer*. 1843–48.

Washington *Globe*. March 28, 1834.

BOOKS

Allen, J. D. *The Banking System: A Speech*. Columbia, S.C., 1857.

Allston, R. F. W. *Memoir on the Introduction and Planting of Rice in South Carolina*. Charleston, S.C., 1843.

Ambler, Charles. *Thomas Ritchie: A Study in Virginia Politics*. Richmond, Va., 1913.

Anderson, T. J. *Federal and State Control of Banking*. New York, 1934.

Andreano, Ralph, ed. *The Economic Impact of the Civil War*. Rev. ed. Cambridge, Mass., 1967.

Arrington, Alfred. *The Lives and Adventures of the Desperadoes of the South-West*. New York, 1849.

Atack, Jeremy, ed. *Business and Economic History*. Urbana, 1985.

Baldwin, Joseph. *Flush Times of Alabama and Mississippi: A Series of Sketches*. 1853; repr. New York, 1957.

Baxter, Maurice G. *Daniel Webster and the Supreme Court*. Amherst, Mass., 1966.

Beard, Charles, and Mary Beard. *The Rise of American Civilization*. New York, 1927.

Benton, Thomas Hart. *Thirty Years' View*. 2 vols. New York, 1859.

Bettersworth, John. *Confederate Mississippi*. Baton Rouge, 1943.

Birmingham, Stephen. *"Our Crowd": The Great Jewish Families of New York.* New York, 1967.

Blair, William. *A Historical Sketch of Banking in North Carolina.* 1899; repr. New York, 1980.

Blocher, W. D. *History of Arkansas Finances.* Little Rock, Ark., 1876.

Bodfish, H. Morton, ed. *History of Building and Loan in the United States.* Chicago, 1931.

Bonner, James. *Milledgeville: Georgia's Antebellum Capital.* Athens, Ga., 1978.

Brantley, William. *Banking in Alabama, 1816–1860.* 2 vols. Birmingham, Ala., 1961, 1967.

Brevard, Caroline. *A History of Florida.* De Land, Fla., 1924.

Brewer, Willis. *Alabama: Her History, Resources, War Record, and Public Men.* Montgomery, Ala., 1872.

Broule, Henry. *The Role of the State in American Economic Growth.* New York, 1959.

Brown, C. K. *A State Movement in Railroad Development.* Chapel Hill, 1928.

Brownlee, W. Elliot. *Dynamics of Ascent: A History of the American Econmoy.* 2d ed. New York, 1979.

Bruchey, Stuart. *The Roots of American Economic Growth, 1607–1861: An Essay in Social Causation.* New York, 1965.

Butwin, Frances. *The Jews in America.* Minneapolis, 1969.

Cabell, James Branch. *Branchiana, Being a Partial Account of the Branch Family in Virginia.* 1907; repr. Richmond, Va., 1979.

Caldwell, Stephen. *A Banking History of Louisiana.* Baton Rouge, 1935.

Cameron, Rondo, et al., *Banking in the Early Stages of Industrialization.* New York, 1967.

Campbell, Claude. *The Development of Banking in Tennessee.* Nashville, Tenn., 1932.

Campbell, William. *One Hundred Years of Fayetteville, 1828–1928.* Fayetteville, Ark., 1928.

Capers, Gerald. *Occupied City: New Orleans Under the Federals, 1862–1865.* Lexington, Ky., 1865.

Capers, Henry. *The Life and Times of C. G. Memminger.* Richmond, Va., 1893.

Cardozo, J. N. *The Charter of the Bank of Charleston, December 17, 1834 and Renewal of Charter, December 20, 1853.* Charleston, S.C., 1871.

———. *Reminiscences of Charleston.* Charleston, S.C., 1886.

Carothers, Neil. *Fractional Money.* 1930; repr. New York, 1967.

Chandler, Alfred, Jr. *The Visible Hand: The Managerial Revolution in American Business.* Cambridge, Mass., 1977.

Chandler, Lester. *Central Banking and Economic Development.* Bombay, 1962.

Chapman, John, and Ray Westerfield. *Branch Banking*. New York, 1942.

Chronicles of the Farmers' and Merchants' Bank of Memphis (1832–1847). By Jesse, the "Scribe." Edited by James Roper. Memphis, 1960.

Claiborne, J. F. H. *Mississippi, as a Province, Territory and State, with Biographical Notices of Eminent Citizens*. Hattiesburg, Miss., 1880.

Clark, W. A. *The History of Banking Institutions Organized in South Carolina Prior to 1860*. Columbia, S.C., 1922.

———. *Statutes at Large of South Carolina*. Vol. XI. N.p., 1873.

Clay, C. C. *A Digest of the Laws of the State of Alabama: Containing All the Statutes of a Public and General Nature, in Force at the Close of the Session of the General Assembly, in February, 1843*. Tuscaloosa, Ala., 1843.

Cleveland, John Bomar. *Controversy Between John C. Calhoun and Robert Y. Hayne as to the Proper Route of a Railroad from South Carolina to the West*. Spartanburg, S.C., 1913.

Cohen, Henry. *Business and Politics in America from the Age of Jackson to the Civil War: The Career Biography of W. W. Corcoran*. Westport, Conn., 1971.

Cohen, Stanley, and Ratner, Lorman, eds. *The Development of an American Culture*. Englewood Cliffs, N.J., 1970.

Cole, Arthur. *The Whig Party in the South*. Washington, D.C., 1913.

Coleman, Peter. *Debtors and Creditors in America: Insolvency, Imprisonment for Debt, and Bankruptcy, 1607–1900*. Madison, 1974.

Cooper, William. *The South and the Politics of Slavery, 1828–1856*. Baton Rouge, 1978.

Cornely, Robert, and Claude Murphy. *Georgia Obsolete Currency: A Checklist*. N.p., 1962.

Coulter, E. Merton. *Auraria: The Story of a Georgia Gold-Mining Town*. Athens, Ga., 1956.

———. *George Walton Williams*. Athens, Ga., 1976.

Craven, Avery. *Soil Exhaustion as a Factor in the Agricultural History of Virginia and Maryland, 1606–1860*. Gloucester, Mass., 1965.

Cumming, Mary. *Georgia Railroad and Banking Co., 1833–1945*. 1945; repr. Augusta, Ga., 1957.

Cunningham, John. *Suggestions on the Causes of the Present Scarcity of Money and in Favor of Essential Reforms in Our Banking System*. Charleston, N.C., 1854.

Daly, Charles. *Jews of Charleston*. New York, 1893.

David, Paul, et al. *Reckoning with Slavery*. New York, 1976.

Davis, David Brion. *The Problem of Slavery in the Age of Revolution, 1770–1823*. Ithaca, N.Y., 1975.

———. *The Problem of Slavery in Western Culture*. Ithaca, N.Y., 1966.

Davis, Edwin. *Louisiana: The Pelican State*. Baton Rouge, 1959.

Davis, John P. *Corporations: A Study in American Economic Development of Great Business Combinations*. New York, 1905.

Davis, Robert. *The Southern Planter, the Factor, and the Banker*. New Orleans, 1871.

Dawson, William. *A Compilation of the Laws of the State of Georgia, Passed by the General Assembly, Since the Year 1819 to the Year 1829, Inclusive*. Milledgeville, Ga., 1831.

Dean, Sidney, ed. *History of Banking and Banks*. Boston, 1884.

Dew, Thomas R. *A Digest of the Laws, Customs, Manners and Institutions of the Ancient and Modern Nations*. New York, 1853.

———. *Lectures on the Restrictive System: Delivered to the Senior Political Class of William and Mary College*. 1829; repr. New York, 1969.

Dodd, Dorothy. *Florida Becomes a State*. Tallahassee, 1945.

Donald, David, ed. *Why the North Won the Civil War*. Baton Rouge, 1960.

Dorfman, Joseph. *The Economic Mind in American Civilization*. 3 vols. New York, 1946.

Dovell, J. E. *History of Banking in Florida, 1828–1954*. 3 vols. Gainesville, Fla., 1955.

Duncombe, Charles. *Duncombe's Free Banking: An Essay on Banking, Currency, Finance Exchanges, and Political Economy*. 1841; repr. New York, 1969.

Dworkin, Ronald. *Taking Rights Seriously*. Cambridge, Mass., 1977.

Eaton, Clement. *The Growth of Southern Civilization*. New York, 1961.

Eidelberg, Paul. *On the Silence of the Declaration of Independence*. Amherst, Mass., 1976.

Elmore, F. H. *Defense of the Bank of the State of South Carolina*. Columbia, S.C., n.d.

Elzas, Barnett. *The Jews of South Carolina*. Philadelphia, 1905.

Ericson, Joe. *Banks and Bankers in Early Texas, 1835–1875*. New Orleans, 1976.

Ezekiel, Herbert, and Gaston Lichenstein. *The History of the Jews of Richmond from 1769 to 1917*. Richmond, Va., 1917.

Fenstermaker, J. Van. *The Development of American Commercial Banking*. Kent, Ohio, 1965.

Fish, Carl Russell. *The Rise of the Common Man*. 1927; repr. New York, 1969.

Fisher, Elwood. *Lecture on the North and South Delivered Before the Young Men's Mercantile Library Association of Cincinnati, Ohio, January 16, 1849*. Charleston, S.C., 1849.

Fishlow, Albert. *American Railroads and the Transformation of the American Economy*. Cambridge, Mass., 1965.

Fitzhugh, George. *Cannibals All! or, Slaves Without Masters*. Edited by C. Vann Woodward. Cambridge, Mass., 1960.

———. *Sociology for the South; or, the Failure of Free Society*. 1854; repr. New York, 1965.

Fogel, Robert, and Stanley Engerman. *Time on the Cross*. Boston, 1974.

Folmsbee, Stanley. *Sectionalism and Internal Improvements in Tennessee, 1796–1845*. Philadelphia, 1939.

Foner, Eric. *Free Soil, Free Labor, Free Men: The Ideology of the Republican Party Before the Civil War*. New York, 1970.

———. *Politics and Ideology in the Age of the Civil War*. New York, 1980.

Friedman, Milton, and Rose Friedman. *Free to Choose: A Personal Statement*. New York, 1979.

Friedman, Milton, and Anna Schwartz. *A Monetary History of the United States, 1867–1960*. Princeton, N.J., 1963.

Furnas, J. C. *The Americans*. New York, 1969.

Garrett, William. *Reminiscences of Public Men in Alabama for Thirty Years*. Atlanta, 1872.

Genovese, Eugene. *The Political Economy of Slavery*. New York, 1961.

Germino, Dante. *Political Philosophy and the Open Society*. Baton Rouge, 1981.

Gerschenkron, Alexander. *Economic Backwardness in Historical Perspective*. Cambridge, Mass., 1962.

Gibbons, James. *The Banks of New-York, Their Dealers, the Clearing House, and the Panic of 1857*. New York, 1864.

Gilder, George. *Wealth and Poverty*. New York, 1981.

Goldin, Claudia. *Urban Slavery in the American South, 1820–1860: A Quantitative History*. Chicago, 1974.

Goodrich, Carter. *Government Promotion of American Canals and Railroads, 1800–1890*. New York, 1909.

Gouge, William. *A Short History of Paper Money and Banking in the United States*. Philadelphia, 1833.

Govan, Thomas. *Nicholas Biddle*. Chicago, 1959.

Grant, Joseph, and Lawrence Crum. *The Development of State-Chartered Banking in Texas*. Austin, 1978.

Gray, Lewis. *History of Agriculture in the Southern United States to 1860*. 2 vols. Washington, D.C., 1933.

Greef, Albert O. *The Commercial Paper House in the United States*. Cambridge, Mass., 1938.

Green, E. L. *George McDuffie*. Columbia, S.C., 1936.

Green, George. *Finance and Economic Development in the Old South: Louisiana Banking, 1804–1861*. Stanford, Calif., 1972.

Griffen, William. *Ante-bellum Elizabeth City: The History of a Canal Town.* Elizabeth City, N.C., 1970.

Gruchy, Allen. *Supervision and Control of Virginia State Banks.* New York, 1937.

Haines, Charles G., and Foster H. Sherwood. *The Role of the Supreme Court in American Government and Politics, 1835–1864.* Berkeley, Calif., 1957.

Hallom, John. *Biographical and Pictorial History of Arkansas.* Albany, 1887.

Hambleton, James. *A Biographical Sketch of Henry A. Wise: With a History of the Political Campaign in Virginia in 1855.* Richmond, Va., 1856.

Hamilton, James. *Reminiscences of James A. Hamilton.* New York, 1869.

Hammond, Bray. *Banks and Politics in America from the Revolution to the Civil War.* Princeton, 1957.

Hammond, Mathew. *The Cotton Industry: An Essay in American Economic History, Part I: The Cotton Culture and the Cotton Trade.* New York, 1897.

Handlin, Oscar, and Mary Handlin. *Commonwealth: A Study of the Role of Government in the American Economy: Massachusetts, 1794–1861.* New York, 1947.

Hawk, Emory, *Economic History of the South.* New York, 1934.

Heath, Milton. *Constructive Liberalism.* Cambridge, Mass., 1954.

Hegel, G. W. F. *The Phenomenology of Mind.* 2d ed. Translated by J. B. Baillie. New York, 1964.

Helderman, Leonard. *National and State Banks.* Boston, 1931.

Henderson, Gerard. *The Position of Foreign Corporations in American Constitutional Law.* Cambridge, Mass., 1918.

Hofstadter, Richard. *The American Political Tradition.* New York, 1948.

Hollander, Jacob, ed. *Minor Papers on the Currency Question, 1809–1823, by David Ricardo.* Baltimore, 1932.

Holt, Michael. *The Political Crisis of the 1850s.* New York, 1978.

Horwitz, Morton. *The Transformation of American Law.* Cambridge, Mass., 1979.

Hubbard, Timothy, and Lewis Davids. *Banking in Mid-America: A History of Missouri's Banks.* Washington, D.C., 1969.

Hughes, Jonathan R. T. *Fluctuations in Trade, Industry, and Finance.* Oxford, England, 1960.

Hugins, Walter. *Jacksonian Democracy and the Working Class.* Stanford, Calif., 1960.

Hurst, J. Willard. *Law and the Conditions of Freedom in the Nineteenth Century United States.* Madison, 1956.

———. *Law and Economic Growth: The Legal History of the Lumber Industry in Wisconsin, 1836–1915.* Cambridge, Mass., 1964.

————. *Law and Social Process in United States History.* New York, 1972.

————. *Legitimacy of the Business Corporation in the Law of the United States, 1788–1970.* Charlottesville, 1970.

Hutchinson, A. *Code of Mississippi: Being an Analytic Compilation of the Public and General Statutes of the Territory and States with Tabular References to the Local and Private Acts, from 1795 to 1848: With the National and State Constitutions.* Jackson, Miss., 1848.

Jaffa, Harry. *Crisis of the House Divided: An Interpretation of the Issues in the Lincoln-Douglas Debates.* New York, 1959.

————. *Liberty and Equality.* New York, 1965.

Jennings, Dudley. *Nine Years of Democratic Rule in Mississippi: Being Notes upon the Political History of the State, from the Beginning of the Year 1838, to the Present Time.* Jackson, Miss., 1847.

Jones, J. B. *A Rebel War Clerk's Diary at the Confederate Capital.* Philadelphia, 1866.

Kahn, Alfred. *The Economics of Regulation.* 2 vols. New York, 1970–1971.

Kammen, Michael. *People of Paradox: An Inquiry Concerning the Origins of American Civilization.* New York, 1972.

Kardelj, Edvard. *Socialism and War.* New York, 1960.

Keating, John. *History of the City of Memphis and Shelby County.* 2 vols. Syracuse, N.Y., 1888.

Kelly, Alfred H., and Winfred A. Harbison. *The American Constitution: Its Origins and Development.* New York, 1963.

Kent, James. *Commentaries on American Law.* 10th ed. Boston, 1860.

Kettel, Thomas. *Southern Wealth and Northern Profits.* New York, 1860.

Keyes, Emerson. *A History of Savings Banks in the United States.* 2 vols. New York, 1876.

Kilbourne, Richard. *Louisiana Commercial Law.* Baton Rouge, 1980.

Klement, Frank. *The Copperheads in the Middlewest.* Chicago, 1960.

Klibansky, Raymond, and H. J. Paton, eds. *Philosophy and History: Essays Presented to Ernst Cassirer.* 2 vols. New York, 1963.

Knox, John Jay. *A History of Banking in the United States.* New York, 1900.

Knox, Thomas W. *Campfire and Cotton-Field.* Chicago, 1865.

Kojève, Alexander. *Introduction to the Reading of Hegel: Lectures on the Phenomenology of the Spirit.* Assembled by Raymond Queneau. Edited by Allen Bloom. Translated by James Nichols. Ithaca, N.Y., 1969.

Kolakowski, Leszek, and Stuart Hampshire, eds. *Main Currents of Marxism.* 3 vols. Translated by P. S. Falla. Oxford, 1978.

————. *The Socialist Idea: A Reappraisal.* New York, 1974.

Kolko, Gabriel. *Railroads and Regulation, 1872–1916.* Princeton, 1965.

——. *The Triumph of Conservatism: A Reinterpretation of American History, 1900–1916.* New York, 1963.

Korn, Bertram. *The Early Jews of New Orleans.* Waltham, Mass., 1969.

——. *Jews and Negro Slavery in the Old South, 1789–1865.* Elkins Park, Pa., 1961.

——. *The Jews of Mobile, Alabama, 1763–1841.* Cincinnati, 1970.

Laffer, Arthur, and Jan Seymour, eds. *The Economics of the Tax Revolt.* New York, 1979.

Lamar, Lucius Q. C. *A Compilation of the Laws of the State of Georgia Passed by the Legislature from the Year 1810 to the Year 1819, Inclusive.* Augusta, Ga., 1821.

Lawrence, Joseph. *Banking Concentration in the United States.* New York, 1930.

Lee, Susan, and Peter Passell. *A New Economic View of American History.* New York, 1979.

Leggett, William. *Democratick Editorials: Essays in Jacksonian Political Economy by William Leggett.* Edited by Lawrence White. Indianapolis, 1984.

Lesesne, J. Mauldin. *The Bank of the State of South Carolina: A General and Political History.* Columbia, S.C., 1970.

Levy, Leonard. *The Law of the Commonwealth and Chief Justice Shaw.* Cambridge, Mass., 1957.

Lewis, G. E. *Florida Banks.* Tallahassee, 1942.

Loewenberg, Robert. *An American Idol: Emerson and the "Jewish Idea."* Washington, D.C., 1984.

——. *Equality on the Oregon Frontier: Jason Lee and the Methodist Mission, 1834–1843.* Seattle, 1976.

——. *Freedom's Despots: The Critique of Abolition.* Durham, N.C., 1986.

Maddex, Jack, Jr. *The Virginia Conservatives, 1867–1879.* Chapel Hill, 1970.

Maddox, Robert. *The New Left and the Origins of the Cold War.* Princeton, 1973.

Marx, Karl, and Frederick Engels. *The Civil War in the United States.* 1937; repr. New York, 1961.

——. *The Communist Manifesto.* New York, 1948.

McCain, William. *The Story of Jackson: A History of the Capital of Mississippi, 1821–1951.* 2 vols. Jackson, Miss., 1953.

McCardell, John. *The Idea of a Southern Nation.* New York, 1979.

McFaul, John. *The Politics of Jacksonian Finance.* Ithaca, N.Y., 1972.

McGrane, Reginald C. *Foreign Bondholders and American State Debts.* New York, 1935.

——. *The Panic of 1837.* New York, 1965.

May, John, and Joan Faint. *South Carolina Secedes*. Columbia, S.C., 1960.

Meigs, William. *The Life of Charles Jared Ingersoll*. Philadelphia, 1847.

Menn, Joseph. *The Large Slaveholders of Louisiana, 1860*. New Orleans, 1964.

Meyers, Marvin. *The Jacksonian Persuasion*. Stanford, Calif., 1960.

Miles, Edwin. *Jacksonian Democracy in Mississippi*. Chapel Hill, 1960.

Miller, Arthur S. *The Supreme Court and American Capitalism*. New York, 1968.

Mises, Ludwig Von. *Human Action*. 2d ed. New Haven, Conn., 1963.

Montgomery, W. J. *Historical Outline of Banking in South Carolina from Colonial Days to the Present Time*. N.p., 1907.

Moore, Albert. *History of Alabama*. University, Ala., 1935.

Moore, Barrington, Jr. *The Social Origins of Dictatorship and Democracy*. Boston, 1966.

Moore, John. *Agriculture in Ante-bellum Mississippi*. New York, 1958.

Morgan, James. *Graybacks and Gold: Confederate Monetary Policy*. Pensacola, 1985.

Murray, Paul. *The Whig Party in Georgia, 1825–1853*. Chapel Hill, 1948.

National Bureau of Economic Research. *Trends in the American Economy in the Nineteenth Century*. Vol. XXIV of *Studies in Income and Wealth*. Princeton, 1960.

Nevins, Allan. *The Emergence of Lincoln: Douglas, Buchanan, and Party Chaos, 1857–1859*. Vol. I. New York, 1950.

———. *Ordeal of the Union: A House Dividing*. Vol. II. New York, 1947.

Newmeyer, R. Kent. *The Supreme Court Under Marshall and Taney*. New York, 1968.

Nichols, Roy. *The Disruption of American Democracy*. 1948; repr. New York, 1967.

Nicholson, A. O. P. *Statute Laws of the State of Tennessee, of a General Character; Passed Since the Compilation of the Statutes by Caruthers and Nicholson, in 1836, and Being a Supplement to that Work, with the Several Titles Arranged in Alphabetical Order*. Nashville, Tenn., 1846.

Nisbet, Robert. *The Quest for Community*. New York, 1953.

North, Douglass. *The Economic Growth of the United States, 1790–1860*. Englewood Cliffs, N.J., 1961.

Novak, Michael. *The Spirit of Democratic Capitalism*. New York, 1982.

Nye, Russel B. *William Lloyd Garrison*. Boston, 1955.

Oakes, James. *The Ruling Race: A History of American Slaveholders*. New York, 1983.

Padover, Saul. *Karl Marx: An Intimate Biography*. 1928. Abridged ed. New York, 1980.

Parker, William, ed. *The Structure of the Cotton Economy of the Antebellum South*. Berkeley, Calif., 1970.

Parkin, Frank. *Class, Inequality, and Political Order*. London, 1971.

Payne, Peter, and Lance Davis. *The Savings Bank of Baltimore, 1818–1866: A Historical and Analytical Study*. Baltimore, 1954.

Pease, William, and Jane Pease. *The Web of Progress: Private Values and Public Styles in Boston and Charleston, 1828–1843*. New York, 1985.

Pessen, Edward. *Jacksonian America: Society, Personality, and Politics*. Homewood, Ill., 1969.

Phillips, U. B. *A History of Transportation in the Eastern Cotton Belt to 1860*. New York, 1968.

———. "The Southern Whigs, 1834–1854." In *Essays in American History Dedicated to Frederick Jackson Turner*. New York, 1910.

[Poor, Henry V.] *Manual of Railroads in the United States, for 1869–70*. New York, 1860.

———. *Money and Its Laws: Embracing a History of Monetary Theories, and a History of the Currencies of the United States*. New York, 1877.

Pope, William. *Early Days in Arkansas*. Little Rock, Ark., 1895.

Primm, James N. *Economic Policy in the Development of a Western State, Missouri, 1820–1860*. Cambridge, Mass., 1954.

Prince, Oliver. *A Digest of the Laws of the State of Georgia, etc.* 2d ed. Athens, Ga., 1837.

Private and Official Correspondence of General Benjamin F. Butler During the Period of the Civil War. Norwood, Mass., 1917.

The Proceedings of the Agricultural Convention and of the State Agricultural Society of South Carolina from 1839 to 1845. . . . Columbia, S.C., 1958.

Pusateri, C. Joseph, and Henry Dethloff, eds. *Casebook in American Business History*. New York, 1987.

Ransom, Roger, and Richard Sutch. *One Kind of Freedom: The Economic Consequences of Emancipation*. Cambridge, 1977.

Raquet, Condy, ed. *Free Trade Advocate and Journal of Political Economy*. Philadelphia, 1829.

Redlich, Fritz. *The Molding of American Banking: Men and Ideas*. 1947; repr. 2 vols. New York, 1968.

Reed, Merl. *New Orleans and the Railroads: The Struggle for Commercial Empire, 1830–1860*. Baton Rouge, 1966.

Remini, Robert. *The Election of Andrew Jackson*. Philadelphia, 1963.

———. *Andrew Jackson and the Bank War*. New York, 1967.

———. *Andrew Jackson and the Course of American Freedom, 1822–1832*. New York, 1981.

———. *Martin Van Buren and the Making of the Democratic Party*. New York, 1959.

Report of the Accountants Appointed to Investigate the . . . Real Estate Bank of Arkansas. Little Rock, Ark., 1856.

Richardson, James, ed. *A Compilation of the Messages and Papers of the Presidents*. Washington, D.C., 1907.

Riggs, John. *The Riggs Family of Maryland*. Baltimore, 1939.

Rightor, Henry, ed. *Standard History of New Orleans*. Chicago, 1900.

Robertson, Alexander. *Alexander Hugh Holmes Stuart: A Biography*. Richmond, Va., 1925.

Rockoff, Hugh. *The Free Banking Era: A Re-examination*. New York, 1975.

Rothbard, Murray. *Man, Economy, and State*. 2 vols. Princeton, 1962.

———. *The Panic of 1819*. New York, 1962.

Rowland, Dunbar, ed. *Mississippi: Comprising Sketches of Counties, Towns, Events, Institutions, and Persons, Arranged in Cyclopedic Form*. 3 vols. Atlanta, 1907.

Royall, William. *A History of Virginia Banks and Banking Prior to the Civil War*. New York, 1907.

Sandoz, Ellis. *The Voeglinian Revolution: A Biographical Introduction*. Baton Rouge, 1981.

Schlesinger, Arthur, Jr. *The Age of Jackson*. Boston, 1945.

Schwab, John. *The Confederate States of America, 1861–1865: A Financial and Industrial History of the South During the Civil War*. 1901; repr. New York, 1968.

Schweikart, Larry. *A History of Banking in Arizona*. Tucson, 1982.

Sellers, Charles Grier. *James K. Polk, Jacksonian, 1795–1843*. Princeton, 1957.

Sharkey, Robert. *Money, Class, and Party: An Economic Study of Civil War and Reconstruction*. Baltimore, 1959.

Sharp, James. *The Jacksonians versus the Banks: Politics in the States After the Panic of 1837*. New York, 1970.

Shenton, James. *Robert John Walker: A Politician from Jackson to Lincoln*. New York, 1961.

Shpall, Leo. *The Jews of Louisiana*. New Orleans, 1936.

Smith, Alfred. *Economic Readjustment of an Old Cotton State: South Carolina, 1820–1860*. Columbia, S.C., 1958.

Smith, Julia. *Slavery and Plantation Growth in Antebellum Florida, 1821–1860*. Gainesville, Fla., 1914.

Smith, Richard. *Recollections of Banks and Bankers Since 1865*. Richmond, Va., n.d.

Smith, T. C. *Parties and Slavery*. Boston, 1907.

Snavely, Tipton. *George Tucker as a Political Economist*. Charlottesville, Va., 1964.

Solzhenitsyn, Alexander. *Warning to the West*. New York, 1980.

Sowell, Thomas. *The Economics and Politics of Race: An International Perspective*. New York, 1983.

———. *Ethnic America*. New York, 1981.

———. *Marxism: Philosophy and Economics*. New York, 1985.

Spiller, Robert, and Alfred Ferguson. *The Complete Works of Ralph Waldo Emerson*. 12 vols. Cambridge, Mass., 1971, 1979.

Starnes, George. *Sixty Years of Branch Banking in Virginia*. New York, 1931.

Starobin, Robert. *Industrial Slavery in the Old South*. New York, 1970.

Stewart, James. *Holy Warriors*. New York, 1976.

Stoney, Samuel. *The Story of South Carolina's Senior Bank*. Charleston, S.C., 1955.

The Story of the South Carolina National Bank. N.p., n.d.

Strauss, Leo. *Liberalism, Ancient and Modern*. New York, 1968.

———. *Natural Right and History*. Chicago, 1953.

Strauss, Leo, and Joseph Cropsey, eds. *History of Political Philosophy*. 2d ed. Chicago, 1972.

Sumner, William. *A History of Banking in the United States*. New York, 1896.

Sumner, William Graham. *Andrew Jackson*. Rev. ed. Boston, 1899.

Swisher, Carl B. *Roger B. Taney*. New York, 1935.

Taylor, George. *The Transportation Revolution*. New York, 1951.

Taylor, John. *New Views of the Constitution of the United States*. Washington, D.C., 1823.

Taylor, Lyon. *Letters and Times of the Tylers*. 3 vols. Richmond, Va., 1884–85.

Teck, Alan. *Mutual Savings Banks and Savings and Loan Associations: Aspects of Growth*. New York, 1968.

Temin, Peter. *The Jacksonian Economy*. New York, 1969.

'37 and '57: A Brief Popular Account of All the Financial Panics in the United States. New York, 1857.

Thomas, Emory. *The Confederate Nation, 1861–1865*. New York, 1979.

Thompson, Samuel. *Confederate Purchasing Operations Abroad*. Chapel Hill, 1935.

Thornton, J. Mills, III. *Politics and Power in a Slave Society: Alabama, 1800–1860*. Baton Rouge, 1978.

Timberlake, Richard, Jr. *The Origins of Central Banking in the United States*. Cambridge, Mass., 1978.

Tocqueville, Alexis de. *Democracy in America*. 2 vols. New York, 1945.

Todd, Richard. *Confederate Finance*. Athens, Ga., 1954.

Trescott, Paul. *Financing American Enterprise*. New York, 1963.

Tucker, George. *The Laws of Wages, Profits, and Rent Investigated*. 1837; repr. New York, 1964.

———. *The Theory of Money and Banks Investigated*. 1839; repr. New York, 1964.

———. *Progress of the United States in Population and Wealth in Fifty Years as Exhibited by the Decennial Census*. 1843; repr. New York, 1964.

Turitz, Leo. *Inventory of the Church and Synagogue Archives of Mississippi: Jewish Congregations and Organizations*. Jackson, Miss., 1940.

Turitz, Leo, and Evelyn Turitz. *Jews in Early Mississippi*. Jackson, Miss., 1983.

Tyler, Samuel. *Memoir of Roger Brooke, LL.D., Chief Justice of the Supreme Court*. Baltimore, 1872.

Van Deusen, Glyndon. *The Jacksonian Era, 1828–1848*. New York, 1959.

Van Deusen, John. *Economic Basis of Disunion in South Carolina*. New York, 1970.

Van Vleck, George. *The Panic of 1857: An Analytical Study*. New York, 1943.

Voegelin, Eric. *From Enlightenment to Revolution*. Edited by John Hallowell. Durham, N.C., 1975.

———. *The New Science of Politics*. Chicago, 1952.

———. *Order and History*. 4 vols. Baton Rouge, 1956–74.

Wade, Richard. *Slavery in the Cities: The South, 1820–1860*. Chicago, 1964.

Watson, Harry. *Jacksonian Politics and Community Conflict*. Baton Rouge, 1981.

Weaver, Charles. *Internal Improvements in North Carolina Previous to 1860*. 1903; repr. Spartanburg, S.C., 1971.

Welfling, Weldon. *Mutual Savings Banks*. Cleveland, 1968.

White, Eugene. *The Regulation and Reform of the American Banking System, 1900–1929*. Princeton, 1983.

Wilhite, Virgil. *Founders of American Economic Thought and Policy*. New York, 1958.

Williams, Frances. *They Faced the Future*. Richmond, 1951.

Williams, George. *History of Banking in South Carolina*. Charleston, S.C., 1900.

Williams, William. *The Roots of the Modern American Empire*. New York, 1969.

Wish, Harvey. *George Fitzhugh: Propagandist of the Old South*. Baton Rouge, 1943.

Woodman, Harold. *King Cotton and His Retainers: Financing and Marketing the Cotton Crop of the South, 1800–1825*. Lexington, Ky., 1968.

Worthen, W. B. *Early Banking in Arkansas*. Little Rock, Ark., 1906.

Wright, Gavin. *The Political Economy of the Cotton South*. New York, 1978.

Young, Mary. *Redskins, Ruffleshirts, and Rednecks*. Norman, Okla., 1961.

ARTICLES

Abbey, Kathryn. "The Union Bank of Tallahassee." *Florida Historical Quarterly,* April, 1937.

Abernethy, Thomas. "The Early Development of Commerce and Banking in Tennessee." *Mississippi Valley Historical Review,* December, 1927.

———. "The Origins of the Whig Party in Tennessee." *Mississippi Valley Historical Review,* December, 1927.

Adams, William. "The Louisiana Whigs." *Louisiana History,* Summer, 1974.

Alexander, Thomas. "Thomas A. R. Nelson as an Example of Whig Conservatism in Tennessee." *Tennessee Historical Quarterly,* March, 1956.

Alexander, Thomas, et al. "The Basics of Alabama's Ante-bellum Two-Party System." *Alabama Review,* Winter, 1966.

———. "Who Were the Alabama Whigs?" *Alabama Review,* Spring, 1963.

Allison, Rebecca. "The Force of Argument: George Fitzhugh's Defense of Slavery." *Conservative Historians' Forum,* May, 1982.

Bateman, Fred, and Thomas Weiss. "Manufacturing in the Ante Bellum South." In *Research in Economic History,* edited by Paul Uselding. Greenwich, Mass., 1976.

Bentley, Marvin. "The State Bank of Mississippi: Monopoly Bank on the Frontier (1809–1830)." *Journal of Mississippi History,* August, 1978.

Bernard, Jesse. "George Tucker: Liberal Southern Social Scientist." *Social Forces,* December, 1946.

Boucher, Chauncey. "The Ante Bellum Attitude of South Carolina Towards Manufacturing and Agriculture." *Washington University Studies,* July, 1915.

Boyd, William. "Currency and Banking in North Carolina, 1790–1836." *Historical Papers, Trinity College Historical Society,* Series 10. Durham, N.C., 1914.

Braverman, Howard. "The Economic and Political Background of the Conservative Revolt in Virginia." *Virginia Magazine of History and Biography,* April, 1952.

Brough, Charles. "The History of Banking in Mississippi." *Mississippi Historical Society Publications,* 1900.

Brown, Richard. "The Missouri Crisis, Slavery, and the Politics of Jacksonianism." *South Atlantic Quarterly,* Winter, 1966.

Brown, Thomas. "The Southern Whigs and Economic Development." *Southern Studies,* Spring, 1981.

Browne, Gary. "Eastern Merchants and Their Southwestern Collections During the Panic and Deflation, 1837–1843." *Southern Studies,* Winter, 1980.

Cameron, Rondo. "The Banker as Entrepreneur." *Explorations in Economic History,* Fall, 1963.

Campbell, Claude. "Banking and Finance in Tennessee During the Depression of 1837." *East Tennessee Historical Society Publications*, 1937.

———. "Branch Banking in Tennessee Prior to the Civil War." *East Tennessee Historical Society Publications*, 1939.

Campbell, Josiah. "Planters and Union Bank Bonds." *Mississippi Historical Society Publications*, 1905.

"A Century of Banking." *Commonwealth*, February, 1953.

Davidson, Philip. "Industrialism in the Ante Bellum South." *South Atlantic Quarterly*, October, 1928.

Dew, Thomas R. "The Improvements of the James and Kanawha Rivers— Mischievous Effects to the West." *Farmers' Register*, June, 1835.

———. "Of the Influence of the Federative, Republican System of Government upon Literature and Development of Character." *Southern Literary Messenger*, March, 1836.

———. "Professor Dew on Slavery." In *The Pro Slavery Argument*. 1853; repr. New York, 1968.

Dixon, Max. "Building the Central Railroad of Georgia." *Georgia Historical Quarterly*, September, 1961.

Doyle, Elisabeth. "Greenbacks, Car Tickets, and the Pot of Gold." *Civil War History*, December, 1959.

Eason, Thomas. "Historic Institutional Change in the Mississippi Economy." *Journal of Mississippi History*, November, 1973.

East, Dennis. "The New York and Mississippi Land Company and the Panic of 1837." *Journal of Mississippi History*, 1971.

Easterlin, Richard. "Interregional Differences in Per Capita Income, Population, and Total Income, 1840–1850." In *Trends in the American Economy in the Nineteenth Century*. Vol. XXIV of *Studies in Income and Wealth*. Princeton, 1960.

———. "Regional Income Trends, 1840, 1950." In *American Economic History*, edited by Seymour Harris. New York, 1961.

Evans, Harry. "James Robb, Banker and Pioneer Railroad Builder of Antebellum Louisiana." *Louisiana Historical Quarterly*, 1940.

Falkner, Roland. "The Private Issue of Token Coins." *Political Science Quarterly*, June, 1901.

Feiner, Susan. "Factors, Bankers, and Masters: Class Relations in the Antebellum South." *Journal of Economic History*, March, 1982.

Fenichel, Allen. "Growth and Diffusion of Power in Manufacturing, 1838–1919." In *Output, Employment, and Productivity After 1800*. Vol. XXX of *Studies in Income and Wealth*. New York, 1966.

Fenstermaker, Van. "The Statistics of American Commercial Banking, 1782–1818." *Journal of Economic History*, September, 1965.

Fisher, J. L. "Early Banking History of Salisbury." In *The Wachovia*. Winston-Salem, N.C., n.d.

Fishlow, Albert. "The Trustee Savings Banks, 1817–1861." *Journal of Economic History*, March, 1961.

Formasino, Ronald, and William Shade. "The Concept of Agrarian Radicalism." *Mid-America*, January, 1970.

Gallman, Robert. "Self-sufficiency in the Cotton Economy of the Antebellum South." *Agricultural History*, January, 1970.

Gatell, Frank. "Spoils of the Bank War: Political Bias in the Selection of Pet Banks." *American Historical Review*, October, 1964.

Govan, Thomas. "An Ante-Bellum Attempt to Regulate the Price and Supply of Cotton." *North Carolina Historical Review*, October, 1940.

Green, George. "The Louisiana Bank Act of 1842." *Explorations in Economic History*, Summer, 1970.

Greenberg, Dolores. "Yankee Financiers and the Establishment of Trans-Atlantic Partnerships: A Reexamination." *Business Historical Review*, January, 1924.

Gurley, John. "Financial Structures in Developing Economies." In *Fiscal and Monetary Problems in Developing States*, edited by David Krivine. New York, 1967.

Gurley, John, and Edward Shaw. "Financial Structure and Economic Development." *Economic Development and Cultural Change*, April, 1967.

Hammond, Bray. "Banking in the Early West: Monopoly, Prohibition, and Laissez Faire." *Journal of Economic History*, May, 1948.

Handlin, Oscar, and Mary Handlin. "Origins of the American Business Corporation." *Journal of Economic History*, May, 1945.

Harbeson, Robert. "Railroads and Regulation, 1877–1916: Conspiracy or Public Interest?" *Journal of Economic History*, June, 1967.

Harrison, Lowell. "Thomas Roderick Dew: Philosopher of the Old South." *Virginia Magazine of History and Biography*, October, 1949.

Hayek, F. A. "Toward a Free Market Monetary System." *Journal of Libertarian Studies*, Spring, 1979.

Heath, Milton. "Laissez Faire in Georgia, 1732–1860." *Journal of Economic History*, Supplement, December, 1943.

———. "Public Railroad Construction and the Development of Private Enterprise in the South Before 1861. *Journal of Economic History*, Supplement 10, September, 1950.

Heilbroner, Robert L. "What Is Socialism?" *Dissent*, Summer, 1978.

Hidy, Ralph. "The Union Bank of Louisiana." *Journal of Political Economy*, April, 1939.

Higham, John. "Hanging Together: Divergent Unities in American History." *Journal of American History*, June, 1974.

Hite, James, and Ellen Hall. "The Reactionary Evolution of Economic Thought on Antebellum Virginia." *Virginia Magazine of History and Biography*, October, 1972.

Holdsworth, John. "Lessons of State Banking Before the Civil War." *Academy of Political Science Proceedings*, Fall, 1971.

Hughes, Jonathan. "Entrepreneurial Activity and American Economic Progress." *Journal of Libertarian Studies*, Winter, 1979.

Hughes, Jonathan, and Nathan Rosenberg. "The United States Business Cycle Before 1860: Some Problems of Interpretation." *Economic History Review*, 2d ser., April, 1963.

Hummel, Jeffrey. "The Jacksonians, Banking, and Economic Theory: A Reinterpretation." *Journal of Libertarian Studies*, Summer, 1978.

———. "The Monetary History of America to 1789: A Historiographical Essay." *Journal of Libertarian Studies*, Winter, 1978.

Huston, James. "Abolitionists and an Errant Economy: The Panic of 1857 and Abolitionist Economic Ideas." *Mid-America*, January, 1983.

———. "The Panic of 1857, Southern Economic Thought, and the Patriarchal Defense of Slavery." *Historian*, February, 1984.

———. "Western Grains and the Panic of 1857." *Agricultural History*, January, 1983.

Jaffe, Louis. "The Effective Limits of the Administrative Process: A Reevaluation." *Harvard Law Review*, May, 1954.

Killick, John. "Risk, Specialization, and Profit in the Mercantile Sector of the Nineteenth Century Cotton Trade: Alexander Brown and Sons, 1820–80." *Business History*, January, 1974.

Klein, Joseph. "The Development of Mercantile Instruments of Credit in the United States." *Journal of Accountancy*, 1911.

Kuzminski, Adrian. "The Paradox of Historical Knowledge." *History and Theory*, Fall, 1973.

Lander, Ernest, Jr. "The Iron Industry in Ante-bellum South Carolina." *Journal of Southern History*, 1954.

Lebergott, Stanley. "Why the South Lost: Commercial Purpose in the Confederacy, 1861–1865." *Journal of American History*, June, 1983.

Lerner, Eugene. "Money, Prices, and Wages in the Confederacy, 1861–1865." In *The Economic Impact of the Civil War*, rev. ed., edited by Ralph Andreano. Cambridge, Mass., 1967.

Lewis, Elsie. "Economic Conditions in Ante Bellum Arkansas, 1850–1861." *Arkansas Historical Quarterly*, Fall, 1947.

Livesay, Harold, and Glenn Porter. "The Financial Role of Merchants in the Development of U.S. Manufacturing, 1815–1860." *Explorations in Economic History*, Fall, 1971.

Loewenberg, Robert. "Emerson and the Genius of American Liberalism." *Center Journal*, Summer, 1983.

————. "Freedom in the Context of American Historiography." *Center Journal*, Fall, 1982.

————. "John Locke and the Antebellum Defense of Slavery." *Political Theory*, May, 1985.

————. "Marx's Sadism." *St. John's Review*, Autumn/Winter, 1982–83.

————. "A New Exodus." *Midstream*, February, 1983.

————. "The Proslavery Roots of Socialist Thought." *Conservative Historians' Forum*, May, 1982.

————. "That Graver Fire Bell: A Reconsideration of the Debate over Slavery from the Standpoint of Lincoln." *St. John's Review*, Summer, 1982.

————. "'Value-Free' versus 'Value-Laden' History: A Distinction Without a Difference." *Historian*, May, 1976.

Longaker, Richard. "Andrew Jackson and the Judiciary." *Political Science Quarterly*, 1956.

Luce, W. Ray. "The Cohen Brothers of Baltimore: From Lotteries to Banking." *Maryland Historical Magazine*, Fall, 1973.

MacAvoy, Paul. "The Regulation-Induced Shortage of Natural Gas." *Journal of Law and Economics*, April, 1971.

McCain, William. "The Charter of Mississippi's First Bank." *Journal of Mississippi History*, 1939.

McGraw, Thomas. "Regulation in America: A Review Article." *Business History Review*, Summer, 1975.

Macesich, George. "Sources of Monetary Disturbances in the United States, 1834–1845." *Journal of Economic History*, September, 1961.

McPherson, Elizabeth. "Unpublished Letters from North Carolinians to Van Buren." *North Carolina Historical Review*, April, 1938.

McWhiney, Grady. "Were the Whigs a Class Party in Alabama?" *Journal of Southern History*, November, 1957.

Mandle, Jay. "The Plantation States as a Sub-region of the Post-bellum South." *Journal of Economic History*, September, 1974.

Marckhoff, Fred. "The Development of Currency and Banking in Florida." *Coin Collector's Journal*, September–October, 1947.

Marshall, Lynn. "The Strange Stillbirth of the Whig Party." *American Historical Review*, January, 1967.

Martin, Albro. "The Troubled Subject of Railroad Regulation in the Gilded Age—A Reappraisal." *Journal of American History*, September, 1974.

Martin, David. "Metallism, Small Notes, and Jackson's War with the B.U.S." *Explorations in Economic History*, Spring, 1974.

Mathis, Robert. "Gazaway Bugg Lamar: A Southern Businessman and Confidant in New York City." *New York History*, July, 1975.

M. B. R. "The Adoption of the Liberal Theory of Foreign Corporations." In Association of American Law Schools, *Selected Essays on Constitutional Law*, Vol. V: *The Nation and the States*. Chicago, 1938.

Meek, Melinda. "The Life of Archibald Yell: Chapter I, Early Life." *Arkansas Historical Quarterly*, Spring, 1967.

———. "The Life of Archibald Yell: Chapter II, The Congressman from Arkansas." *Arkansas Historical Quarterly*, Summer, 1967.

———. "The Life of Archibald Yell: Chapter III, The Chief Executive." *Arkansas Historical Quarterly*, Summer, 1967.

Meyer, John. "The Economics of Slavery in the Ante Bellum South." *Journal of Political Economy*, April, 1959.

Miles, Edwin. "Francis Leech's 'The Mammoth Humbug'; or, The Adventures of Shocco Jones in Mississippi, in the Summer of 1839." *Journal of Mississippi History*, January, 1959.

Millsaps, R. W. "History of Banking in Mississippi." *Sound Currency*, March, 1903.

Minarik, Joseph. "Who Wins, Who Loses from Inflation?" *Challenge*, January–February, 1979.

Mitchell, H. H. "A Forgotten Institution: Private Banks in North Carolina." *North Carolina Historical Review*, 1958.

Monkkonen, Eric. "*Bank of Augusta* v. *Earle:* Corporate Growth v. States' Rights." *Alabama Historical Quarterly*, Summer, 1972.

Murphy, Earl. "The Jurisprudence of Legal History: Willard Hurst as Legal Historian." *New York University Law Review*, November, 1964.

Neu, Irene. "Edmond Jean Forstall and Louisiana Banking." *Explorations in Economic History*, Summer, 1970.

———. "J. B. Moussier and the Property Banks of Louisiana." *Business History Review*, Winter, 1961.

Nisbet, Robert. "Eric Voegelin's Vision." *Public Interest*, Winter, 1983.

O'Conner, Thomas. "Lincoln and the Cotton Trade." *Civil War History*, March, 1961.

Patrick, Hugh. "Financial Development and Economic Growth in Underdeveloped Countries." *Economic Development and Cultural Change*, January, 1966.

Posner, Richard. "Theories of Economic Regulation." *Bell Journal of Economics and Management Science*, Autumn, 1974.

Prichett, Michael. "Northern Institutions in Southern Financial History: A Note on Insurance Investments." *Journal of Southern History*, August, 1975.

Redlich, Fritz. "American Banking Growth in the Nineteenth Century: Epistemological Reflections." *Explorations in Economic History*, Spring, 1973.

Reed, Merl. "Boom or Bust: Louisiana's Economy During the 1830's." *Louisiana History*, 1963.

————. "Government Investment and Economic Growth: Louisiana's Ante Bellum Railroads." *Journal of Southern History*, May, 1962.

Reznick, Samuel. "The Influence of Depression on American Opinion, 1857–1859." *Journal of Economic History*, May, 1942.

Richman, Sheldon. "The Anti-War Abolitionists: The Peace Movement's Split Over the Civil War." *Journal of Libertarian Studies*, Summer, 1981.

Robertson, Alexander. "Manifesto of Seventy-nine Cotton Planters of Adams County, Mississippi in Favor of Protection to American Manufacturers." *The Plough, the Loom, and the Anvil (American Farmers Magazine)*, November, 1848.

Rockoff, Hugh. "Money, Prices, and Banks in the Jacksonian Era." In *The Reinterpretation of American Economic History*, edited by Robert Fogel and Stanley Engerman. New York, 1972.

————. "Varieties of Banking and Regional Economic Development in the United States." *Journal of Economic History*, March, 1975.

Roeder, Robert. "Merchants of Antebellum New Orleans." *Explorations in Entrepreneurial History*, 1958.

Rolnick, Arthur, and Warren Weber. "Free Banking, Wildcat Banking, and Shinplasters." *Federal Reserve Bank of Minneapolis Quarterly Review*, Fall, 1982.

————. "Inherent Instability in Banking: The Free Banking Experience." *CATO Journal*, Winter, 1986.

————. "New Evidence on the Free Banking Era." *American Economic Review*, December, 1983.

Rothstein, Morton. "Sugar and Secession: A New York Firm in Ante-bellum Louisiana." *Explorations in Economic History*, Winter, 1968.

Ruffin, Minnie, and Lilla McLure. "General Solomon Weathersby Downs (1801–1854)." *Louisiana Historical Quarterly*, January, 1934.

Russel, Robert. "A Reevaluation of the Period Before the Civil War: Railroads." *Mississippi Valley Historical Review*, December, 1928.

Scheiber, Harry. "At the Borderland of Law and Economic History: The Contributions of Willard Hurst." *American Historical Review*, February, 1970.

————. "Government and the Economy: Studies of the 'Commonwealth' Policy in Nineteenth-Century America." *Journal of Interdisciplinary History*, Summer, 1972.

————. "The Pet Banks in Jacksonian Politics and Finance, 1833–1841." *Journal of Economic History,* June, 1963.

————. "Regulation, Property Rights, and Definition of 'The Market': Law and the American Economy." *Journal of Economic History,* March, 1982.

————. "The Road to *Munn:* Eminent Domain and the Concept of Public Purpose in the State Courts." *Perspectives in American History,* 1971.

Schweikart, Larry. "Alabama's Antebellum Banks: New Evidence, New Interpretations." *Alabama Review,* July, 1985.

————. "Antebellum Southern Bankers: Origins and Mobility." In *Business and Economic History,* edited by Jeremy Atack. Urbana, 1985.

————. "Banking in the American South, 1836–65, Dissertation Summary," *Journal of Economic History,* June, 1985.

————. "Entrepreneurial Aspects of Antebellum Banking." In *American Business History Case Studies,* edited by Joseph Pusateri and Henry Dethloff. New York, 1987.

————. "How the Jacksonians Opposed Industrialization." *Reason Papers,* April, 1987.

————. "The Mormon Connection: Lincoln, the Saints, and the Crisis of Equality." *Western Humanities Review,* Winter, 1980.

————. "Private Bankers in the Antebellum South." *Southern Studies,* Summer, 1986.

————. "Secession and Southern Banks." *Civil War History,* June, 1985.

————. "Southern Banking and Economic Growth in the Antebellum Period: A Reassessment." *Journal of Southern History,* February, 1987.

————. "Tennessee's Antebellum Banks: Part I." *Tennessee Historical Quarterly,* Summer, 1986.

————. "Tennessee's Antebellum Banks: Part II." *Tennessee Historical Quarterly,* Fall, 1986.

Sellers, Charles, Jr. "Andrew Jackson versus the Historians." *Mississippi Valley Historical Review,* March, 1958.

————. "Banking and Politics in Jackson's Tennessee, 1817–1827." *Mississippi Valley Historical Review,* June, 1954.

————. "Who Were the Southern Whigs?" *American Historical Review,* January, 1974.

Sellers, James. "The Economic Incidence of the Civil War in the South." In *The Economic Impact of the Civil War,* edited by Ralph Andreano. Rev. ed. Cambridge, Mass., 1967.

Shepherd, Lewis. "The Confederate Treasure Train." *Confederate Veteran,* June, 1917.

Sioussat, St. George. "Some Phases of Tennessee Politics in the Jackson Period." *American Historical Review,* October, 1908.

Sitterson, J. Carlyle. "Financing and Marketing the Sugar Crop of the Old South." *Journal of Southern History,* May, 1944.

Sprague, Stuart. "Kentucky and the Cincinnati and Charleston Railroad, 1835–1839." *Register of the Kentucky Historical Society,* April, 1975.

Stebbins, Ed. "Early Banking in Arkansas." *Arkansas Historical Quarterly,* Autumn, 1954.

Stewart, Peter. "Railroads and Urban Rivalries in Antebellum Eastern Virginia." *Virginia Magazine of History and Biography,* January, 1973.

Stigler, George. "The Process of Economic Regulation." *Antitrust Bulletin,* Spring, 1972.

———. "The Theory of Economic Regulation." *Bell Journal of Economics and Management Science,* Spring, 1971.

Stigler, George, and Claire Friedland. "Can Regulators Regulate? The Case of Electricity." *Journal of Law and Economics,* October, 1982.

Stromberg, Joseph. "The War for Southern Independence: A Radical Libertarian Perspective." *Journal of Libertarian Studies,* Spring, 1979.

Sylla, Richard. "American Banking and Economic Growth in the Nineteenth Century: A Partial View of the Terrain." *Explorations in Economic History,* Winter, 1971–72.

———. "Economic History 'von unten nach oben' and 'von oben nach unten': A Reply to Fritz Redlich." *Explorations in Economic History,* Spring, 1973.

———. "Federal Policy, Banking Market Structure, and Capital Mobilization in the United States, 1863–1913." *Journal of Economic History,* December, 1969.

———. "Forgotten Men of Money: Private Bankers in Early U.S. History." *Journal of Economic History,* March, 1976.

———. "Monetary Innovation in America." *Journal of Economic History,* March, 1982.

Temin, Peter. "The Panic of 1857." *Intermountain Economic Review,* Spring, 1975.

———. "Steam and Waterpower in the Early Nineteenth Century." *Journal of Economic History,* June, 1966.

Thomas, David. "Florida Finance in the Civil War." *Yale Review,* November, 1907.

Thompson, J. P. "Early Financing in New Orleans, Being the Story of the Canal Bank, 1831–1915." *Louisiana Historical Society Publications,* 1913–14.

Timberlake, Richard, Jr. "Denominational Factors in Nineteenth-Century Currency Experience." *Journal of Economic History,* December, 1974.

———. "The Specie Standard and Central Banking in the United States Before 1860." *Journal of Economic History,* September, 1961.

Tucker, George. "The Bank of the United States." *American Quarterly Review*, March, 1831.

————. "A Discourse on the Progress of Philosophy and Its Influence on the Intellectual and Moral Character of Man." *Southern Literary Messenger*, April, 1835.

Venit, Abraham. "Isaac Bronson: His Banking Theory and the Financial Controversies of the Jacksonian Period." *Journal of Economic History*, November, 1945.

Wallin, Jeffrey. "History or Interpretation? David Brion Davis on American Slavery." *Conservative Historians' Forum*, May, 1982.

Ward, James. "A New Look at Antebellum Southern Railroad Development." *Journal of Southern History*, August, 1973.

White, Lawrence. "Regulatory Sources of Instability in Banking." *CATO Journal*, Winter, 1986.

Wicker, E. "Railroad Investment Before the Civil War." *Trends in the American Economy in the Nineteenth Century*. Vol. XXIV of *Studies in Income and Wealth*. Princeton, 1960.

Williams, Walter. "Government Sanctioned Restraints That Reduce Economic Opportunities for Minorities." *Policy Review*, July, 1978.

Williamson, Jeffrey. "International Trade and United States Economic Development, 1827–1843." *Journal of Economic History*, September, 1961.

Wilson, James Q. "The Dead Hand of Regulation." *Public Interest*, Fall, 1971.

Winston, F. "A Protest." *Mississippi Senate Journal*, January-February, 1830.

Wood, W. K. "The Georgia Railroad and Banking Company." *Georgia Historical Quarterly*, Winter, 1973.

Woodman, Harold. "Decline of Cotton Factorage After the Civil War." *American Historical Review*, July, 1966.

————. "Itinerant Cotton Merchants of the Antebellum South." *Agricultural History*, April, 1966.

Worley, Ted. "Arkansas and the Money Crisis of 1836–1837." *Journal of Southern History*, May, 1949.

————. "The Arkansas State Bank: Ante-bellum Period." *Arkansas Historical Quarterly*, Spring, 1964.

————. "The Batesville Branch of the State Bank, 1836–1839." *Arkansas Historical Quarterly*, Fall, 1947.

————. "The Control of the Real Estate Bank of the State of Arkansas, 1836–1855." *Mississippi Valley Historical Review*, December, 1950.

Wray, Leonard. "The Culture and Preparation of Cotton in the United States of America, &c." *Journal of the Society of Arts*, December, 1958.

DISSERTATIONS AND THESES

Abrams, David. "The State Bank of Alabama, 1841–45." M.A. thesis, Auburn University, 1965.

Babin, Claude. "The Economic Expansion of New Orleans Before the Civil War." Ph.D. dissertation, Tulane University, 1953.

Brown, Walter. "Albert Pike, 1809–1891." Ph.D. dissertation, University of Texas, 1955.

Cain, Stith. "A History of Branch Banking in Tennessee." M.A. thesis, University of Virginia, 1935.

Coker, William. "Cotton and Faith: A Social and Political View of Mississippi Wartime Finance, 1861–1865." Ph.D. dissertation, University of Oklahoma, 1973.

Ecke, Melvin. "The Fiscal Aspects of the Panic of 1857." Ph.D. dissertation, Princeton University, 1951.

Feiner, Susan. "The Financial Structures and Banking Institutions of the Ante Bellum South, 1811 to 1832." Ph.D. dissertation, University of Massachusetts, 1981.

Fontenot, Elfa. "Social and Economic Life in Louisiana, 1860–65." M.A. thesis, Louisiana State University, 1933.

Freeman, Lorimer. "The Central Bank of Georgia." M.A. thesis, University of Georgia, 1919.

Govan, Thomas. "The Banking and Credit System in Georgia." Ph.D. dissertation, Vanderbilt University, 1936.

Grenier, Emile. "The Early Financing of the Consolidated Association of the Planters of Louisiana." M.A. thesis, Louisiana State University, 1938.

Hertzberg, Steven. "The Jews of Atlanta, 1865–1915." Ph.D. dissertation, University of Chicago, 1975.

Holder, Brantson. "The Three Banks of the State of North Carolina, 1810–1872." Ph.D. dissertation, University of North Carolina, 1937.

Mathews, Theodore. "Statutory Protection of Bank Creditors Prior to the Civil War." M.A. thesis, University of Chicago, 1930.

Murray, Leslie. "A History of the Whig Party in Louisiana." Ph.D. dissertation, Tulane University, 1961.

Odom, Edwin. "Louisiana Railroads, 1830–1880: A Study of State and Local Aid." Ph.D. dissertation, Tulane University, 1961.

Payne, Wayne. "The Commercial Development of Ante-Bellum Elizabeth City." M.A. thesis, Old Dominion University, 1971.

Pulwers, Jacob. "Henry Marston, Ante-bellum Planter and Businessman of East Feliciana." M.A. thesis, Louisiana State University, 1955.

Roeder, Robert. "New Orleans Merchants, 1790–1837." Ph.D. dissertation, Harvard University, 1959.

Schultz, Charles. "Hayne's Magnificent Dream: Factors Which Influenced the Efforts to Join Cincinnati and Charleston by Railroad, 1835–1860." Ph.D. dissertation, Ohio State University, 1966.

Schweikart, Larry. "Banking in the American South, 1836–65." Ph.D. dissertation, University of California, Santa Barbara, 1983.

Scroggs, William. "The Financial History of Alabama, 1819–1860." Ph.D. dissertation, Harvard University, 1907.

Segrest, Robert. "History of Banking in Georgia Before 1856." M.A. thesis, University of Georgia, Athens, 1933.

Stegmaier, Mark. "The U.S. Senate in the Sectional Crisis, 1846–1861: A Roll-Call Voting Analysis." Ph.D. dissertation, University of California, Santa Barbara, 1975.

Weems, Robert. "The Bank of the Mississippi: A Pioneer Bank of the Old Southwest, 1809–1844." Ph.D. dissertation, Columbia University, 1952.

PAMPHLETS AND UNPUBLISHED MANUSCRIPTS

"Annual Report of the Engineer-in-Chief." Georgia Railroad and Banking Company. Augusta Georgia, April 15, 1842.

"Anti-Debt." *The Railroad Mania and Review of the Bank of the State of South Carolina: A Series of Essays by "Anti-Debt."* Charleston, S.C., 1848.

Bank of Mississippi. *Memorial on Behalf of the Stockholders.* N.p., November 18, 1831.

Bank of the Mississippi. *Memorial of the Board of Directors.* N.p., August 5, 1831.

Bank of Pensacola and Alabama, Georgia, and Florida Railroad Company Charters. New York, 1835.

Banks, John. *A Short Biographical Sketch of the Undersigned by Himself, John Banks.* Anstell, Ga., 1956.

Charter of the Louisville, Cincinnati and Charleston Railroad Company. Charleston, S.C., 1838.

"Fair Play." *Reply to "Anti-Debt" on the Bank of the State of South Carolina.* Columbia, S.C., 1848.

"Gallatin." *Thoughts on Banking with Reference to the Trade and Currency of the United States.* Richmond, 1841.

Harrison, Joseph. "Banking in Georgia: Its Development and Progress." Citizens Southern and National Bank. Savannah, Ga., n.d.

Letter of William Gregg to Thornton Coleman, June 8, 1858. Charleston, S.C., 1858.

Meeting of the South Carolina Banks. South Caroliniana Library. Columbia, S.C., n.d.

Minutes of the Convention of Banks. Charleston, S.C., 1841.

Northern Bank of Tennessee. N.p., 1854.

"Report of the Committee of Investigation (Selected from the Stockholders) Appointed by the Direction of the Citizens' Bank of Louisiana . . . , October 18, 1838." New Orleans, 1839.

"Report of the Superintendent." Georgia Railroad and Banking Company Office. Augusta, Ga., n.d.

Rutherfoord, John. *Speech on the Banking Policy of Virginia.* N.p., 1856.

———. *Speech on Banks.* N.p., 1854.

Schwartz, Pedro. "A Central Bank Monopoly in the History of Economic Thought: A Century of Myopia in England." Paper presented at the Institutum Europaeum Conference "European Monetary Union and Currency Competition," Brussels, Belgium, December, 1 and 2, 1980.

Schweikart, Larry. "Reviewing the Economics of Slavery." University of California, Santa Barbara, n.d.

Speech of Honorable James H. Hammond, at Barnwell, October 29, 1858. Charleston, S.C., 1858.

Speech of William Gregg, Member from Edgefield District in the Legislature of South Carolina, December, 1857, on the Bank Question. Columbia, S.C., 1857.

The Story of the South Carolina National Bank. N.p., n.d.

Thomas, David Y. "A History of Banking in Florida." University of Florida, P. K. Yonge Library of Florida History. Gainesville, n.d.

Through the Years in Norfolk, 1636–1936. Virginia Bankers' Association. N.p., 1936.

Timberlake, Richard. "The Significance of Unaccounted Currencies." N.p., n.d.

Transcript of the Record of the Supreme Court of the United States, the State of North Carolina vs. Chas. Dewey. University of North Carolina Library, Chapel Hill, n.d.

White, Lawrence. "Free Banking as an Alternative Monetary System." Pacific Institute for Public Policy Research Conference, n.d.

INDEX

282–84; impact of secession, 286–94;
during Civil War, 294–313; taxation,
305–306; survival through Civil War,
309–10; during Reconstruction,
311–12; accomplishments, 312–13. *See
also* names of specific states
Southern Life Insurance and Trust Company (Fla.), 40, 52, 72, 174
Southern Rail Road Company, 195, 299
Southern Standard, 286
Southwestern Railroad Bank (S.C.),
132*n*55, 310
Stanley, Harvey, 88
State Bank of Arkansas: during Panic of
1837, pp. 62–64, 68; mismanagement
of, 84–85, 164–65, 167–68; responsibilities of directors and officers, 86–87;
charter and capitalization, 159t;
branches, 163; corruption, 163–64;
creation of, 163; New York bond investment, 165–66; liquidation of, 167–69;
antibank sentiment, 205
State Bank of Florida, 173t, 174
State Bank of North Carolina, 55, 127,
128t, 130
State Bank of North Carolina v. *Clark
and McNeil,* 130
State Bank of South Carolina, 55–56, 94
State banks: *See* names of states and
names of banks
States' Rights party, 286
Stephens, Alexander, 117
Strobel, M. D., 222
Stuart, Alexander, 43
Sumner, William Graham, 11
Sunstall, A., 297
Supreme Court, 97, 98, 146
Sutch, Richard, 201, 311
Sylla, Richard, 4, 219, 311
Sylvester, S. J., 165–66

Talley, A., 303
Taney, Roger B., 146–47, 147*n*2
Taylor, John, 13, 251
Temin, Peter, 60–62, 64, 73, 74
Tennessee and Coosa Rail Road Company,
235
Tennessee banks: political economy of,
32; Bank of the State of Tennessee,
53–54, 182, 183t, 186; during 1830s,

53–54; during Panic of 1819, p. 53;
Nashville Bank, 53, 54; corruption in,
54; Farmers and Mechanics Bank, 54;
Fayetteville Bank, 54; private banks,
54; Union Bank of the State of Tennessee, 54, 202; reserve ratios, 66t;
during Panic of 1837, pp. 69, 70, 73,
74, 77–78, 82; reserve ratios, 73, 74;
public confidence, 77–78; Union Bank
of Nashville, 77; wildcat banks, 77;
Bank of Tennessee, 78, 82–84, 88–89,
196, 210, 210*n*38, 276; debt to eastern
banks, 78; small-note issues, 79, 80;
criminal activity in, 82, 84; Tennessee
State Bank, 84; Farmers and Merchants
Bank, 87; violence and, 87; free banks,
169, 170, 272–73, 279–81; aid to education, 182, 186, 243–44; internal improvements, 182, 243–44; regulatory
policy, 182–86; capitalization,
183t–185t; debt collection, 196;
branch banking, 202; Planters Bank,
202; Northern Bank of Tennessee, 210,
303, 310; bankers' careers, 222; railroad
investments, 231, 249; banking priorities, 247; economic growth,
258t–259t, 261, 262, 265t; services to
surrounding states, 263, 284; during
1850s, 267, 272–73, 276–77; Bank of
Middle Tennessee, 272, 280, 297,
308–310; during Panic of 1857, pp.
272, 276, 279–81; Bank of Nashville,
276; free banks, 276, 277; after Panic of
1857, pp. 283–84; early 1860s, 291,
293; during Civil War, 297; survival
through Civil War, 310
Tennessee State Bank, 84
Texas, 8, 257, 263, 284
Thompson, Lewis, 209
Thornton, A. E., 168, 245
Thornton, Abner, 84
Thornton, J. Mills, 2
Timberlake, Richard, 15*n*6
Timberlake, Richard, Jr., 80–81*n*47
Tindal, John, 60
Tocqueville, Alexis de, 6–7, 19
Tombeckbe Bank (Ala.), 51
Toombs, Robert, 117
Touro, Judah, 213–14
Towns, George, 118